D0582118

SHIRT OF LEGENDS

SHIRT OF LEGENDS

THE STORY OF NEWCASTLE UNITED'S NO. 9 HEROES

PAUL JOANNOU

FOREWORD BY

ALAN SHEARER OBE

NEWCASTLE
UNITED

An official publication

MAINSTREAM
PUBLISHING
EDINBURGH AND LONDON

First published in Great Britain in 2004 by
MAINSTREAM PUBLISHING COMPANY (EDINBURGH) LTD
7 Albany Street
Edinburgh EH1 3UG

ISBN 1 84018 962 2

A catalogue record for this book is available from the British Library

Typeset in Copperplate Gothic and Ellington
Printed and bound in Great Britain by
Antony Rowe, Chippenham, Wiltshire

AUTHOR'S NOTES AND ACKNOWLEDGEMENTS

The legend of Newcastle United's No. 9 heroes is one I have been brought up with since a lad. As a youngster growing up in Benwell and Denton Burn, the tales of Hughie Gallacher and Jackie Milburn were folklore on Tyneside, their deeds continually related by grown-ups eager to tell the story. My father knew them both and soon a young Joannou met the great Wor Jackie. Indeed, I was privileged to be at the very heart of his testimonial gathering with my father – sitting next to Hungarian icon Puskas on the team bus from the County Hotel to St. James' Park. He spoke little English, so smiled as I quivered in awe.

Few clubs in Britain possess a shirt so richly dipped in tradition. Its magic has spellbound both myself and thousands of other Geordies for generations. The man who wears the No. 9 shirt inspires us, arousing football passion and fervour so characteristic of the region. Barrie Thomas and Ron McGarry were the first of United's centre-forwards I watched. Thereafter I've roared myself hoarse at the thrilling deeds from the man with the No. 9 on his back. From Davies to Supermac, to Cole and Ferdinand and to perhaps the greatest of them all, Alan Shearer.

Over the years as Newcastle United's official historian I have researched the story of their many renowned predecessors as well as meeting and interviewing several of United's greats. Posthumous thanks to Albert Stubbins, Jackie Milburn and Len White, all true gents of the old school of football. Appreciation also to Alan Shearer, Chris Waddle, Mick Quinn, Ron McGarry, Wyn Davies and, not least, Malcolm Macdonald – Supermac – as a teenager my own hero, whom I can now chat to every match day, still strange to comprehend. Thanks to the many colleagues of those No. 9 heroes spoken to over the years; players including Charlie Crowe, John Anderson, Dave Hilley, Charlie Woods and the great Peter Beardsley. In addition, some sadly no longer with us, notably Ronnie Simpson, Frank Brennan and Bob Stokoe.

The rich source of ex-United players' biographies and autobiographies have been used in research, noted in the bibliography, but especially important are *Come In Number 37* (Rob Lee), *Sir Les* (Les Ferdinand), *Who Ate All The Pies?* (Mick Quinn), *My Life Story* (Peter Beardsley), *Golden Goals* (Jackie Milburn), *The Authorised Biography* (Chris Waddle), *My Story So Far* (Alan Shearer) and *Supermac* (Malcolm Macdonald). Additionally Kevin Keegan's most recent text *My Autobiography* has been invaluable.

Shirt of Legends has been a book planned for several years, since I was involved in setting up the *Number 9 Bar* back in 1980. Many people have assisted along the way. Close friend since childhood and football anorak, now United's Publications Editor, Paul Tully, is thanked for his support, memories and professional advice. Another long-standing friend and United supporter, Bill Swann, has also been of great assistance with his computerised match and player records proving an ideal database. So too has Alan Candlish, whose meticulous day by day record of Newcastle United has been a godsend to filling missing gaps in research. Club directors and officials are also thanked for their support; Russell Cushing, Ken Slater, Trevor Garwood, Tony Toward, Mark Hannen and Steve Spark. Club Photographer Ian Horrocks is acknowledged for his front-cover shot and several of the recent illustrations used. Alan Oliver, through his reports in the *Evening Chronicle*, and the many other journalists over the years of the *Chronicle* and sister paper, *The Journal*, are thanked also. The following individuals have assisted too:

Malcolm Dix, Mike Bolam, John Litster, Lucie Archbold, Steve Wraith, Jim Mitchell, Jerome Borkwood, Gordon Rushworth, Paul Hanson, Steve Preston, M. Jensen and M. Edminson at The Back Page, Ian Christon at The Football League, Simon Inglis, Cyril Dinning, Colin Smith, John Edminson, Tony Stephens at SFX Sports Group Ltd, G. and S. Cosgrove at Imagine and Newcastle upon Tyne Central Library, Local History department.

The enthusiasm of the staff at Mainstream, in particular director Bill Campbell, is acknowledged for producing a first-class publication. Finally, thanks again to Alan Shearer for his Foreword and to John Gibson for his from-the-heart Introduction.

Paul Joannou
Edinburgh, July 2004

FOOTNOTE:
Generally appearances and goals quoted are senior matches, i.e. league, cup and European contests as well as other competitive games. Friendlies are not included.

CONTENTS

FOREWORD

THE No. 9s . . .

Just as the Tyne Bridge, Grey's Monument and the Town Moor are all enduring symbols of Newcastle upon Tyne, so too is the simple phrase 'The No. 9'.

It stands for much more than merely a number on a black and white striped football shirt. It is the symbol of a sportsman who has come to represent the hope and glory of the football fans of Tyneside.

As a young, football-daft lad kicking a ball around with his mates in Gosforth in the late 1970s, I heard the tales and read of the legends – names such as Hughie Gallacher, Albert Stubbins, Jackie Milburn, Len White, Wyn Davies and Malcolm Macdonald.

For any young boy in Newcastle, the impossible dream is to follow in the footsteps of such legends. Only one boy in a generation might ever get that chance . . . and I was that boy.

My dream remained a dream until the famous day in 1996 when, having played for Southampton and Blackburn Rovers as well as England, I finally came home to sign for Newcastle United.

Of course, for a Geordie centre-forward, there could be no other shirt to wear but that magical No. 9; yet I knew that by wearing it I had to live up to the legend that had been born and cultivated over many decades before me. It was my job and my responsibility to maintain the legend.

It is for others to judge whether I have succeeded. But if I can now be said to have done that, and rank alongside those great Newcastle United No. 9s of the past, then it is an honour I accept with both pride and humility.

The story of Newcastle United's No. 9s is a great one, and as the man who has carried a twentieth-century legend into the twenty-first century, I am delighted that the story has now been written.

Alan Shearer OBE
St. James' Park, 2004

INTRODUCTION

A SILVER THREAD THROUGH UNITED'S HISTORY

Geordies are warm-hearted folk who take readily to those who do them proud. They become friends for life, men who are held in the highest of esteem. Legends indeed if they are footballers who transcend their own lifespan and gain a place in Geordie folklore. And if they were privileged enough to wear the No. 9 shirt of Newcastle United, then all is secured.

Fathers will captivate sons with talk of great deeds, just as grandfathers had before them. Thus Hughie Gallacher and Wor Jackie, Supermac and Alan Shearer, walk hand in hand through history. They will never be forgotten and nor should they be, because all of a black and white persuasion owe them a great debt of gratitude.

They are what we all hold dear – dashing heroes scoring splendid goals to slay the greatest of opposition. Men we can see vividly just by closing our eyes.

I grew up on stories of Wee Hughie and on the sight of Wor Jackie running like the wind to unleash thunderbolt shots upon target. I sat transfixed in my Auntie Grace's living room watching a black and white telly as United won the FA Cup three times in five years. She

11

was the only person in our family with a TV set and the wooden chairs were arranged in long lines before the small box so all the family could gather and witness great deeds.

There were many '50s superstars of course but Wor Jackie was my favourite.

It's said you should never meet your boyhood hero because he'll disappoint you. No one is as good as you recall through biased eyes.

But Milburn was when I met him in the press-box at St. James' Park and we became close friends. I wrote a number of books with him and when he died, while I was on holiday abroad, his widow Laura kindly asked me to speak at a memorial service in his native Ashington. I also had the privilege of unveiling a statue to Wor Jackie in Newcastle's Northumberland Street – not many folk receive such an honour.

Supermac – quick and deadly like Milburn – was another idol who became a pal. I was his best man when he married the lovely Carol a few years ago. Malcolm Macdonald walked with a swagger, drank champagne and smoked a big cigar, but when he got on the field he delivered. Oh, how he delivered. He not only scored in every round on the way to the 1974 FA Cup final but did so away from home.

Once he scored all five goals for England at Wembley when Kevin Keegan was by his side and I was sat in the press-box glowing at the achievements of a Magpie leader. All Macdonald's England caps came while he resided on the Tyne. Arsenal was never quite the same and injury sadly finished him before he was out of his 20s.

Alan Shearer is just as deadly and mightily proud to be a Geordie. I've got a terrific working relationship with Alan, who never forgets his roots. Be straight with him and he'll return the favour twofold. Cross him and forget him. Which is the way of most Geordies, is it not?

Captain of England and scorer of 30 international goals, Shearer's personal record is better than any other but it's what lives in people's minds and what exists in their hearts that matters. That is how footballers are judged.

United have had many other great No. 9s of course. Albert Stubbins, a gentle man who also made the St. James' press-box but whose fine goalscoring was blighted by the war years; Len White, the best uncapped English striker of his generation; Wyn Davies, whom I travelled with when United won the Inter Cities Fairs Cup of 1969; Peter Withe, a big man who was to win the European Cup and play for England; Andy Cole, scorer of so many goals in one season, topping

40, that he became a record breaker; and, yes, even the guy who ate all the pies, Mick Quinn, will be remembered! There are many others too; Les Ferdinand, Ron McGarry, Jack Allen. The list is almost endless.

Who was the best? Gallacher, the fiery wee Scot? Wor very own Jackie? Supermac? Shearer? It matters not. Each and every one ought to be cherished for themselves, for their goals and their glory.

Centre-forwards are the silver thread that runs through the tapestry of United's history. From the club's earliest days and the exploits of Peddie, Appleyard and Shepherd, they are privileged men, gifted men, warriors waging war on our behalf.

Above all they are winners, every man jack of them, and deserve our grateful thanks for mighty deeds done and memories secured.

John Gibson
Executive Sports Editor,
Newcastle Evening Chronicle

'If there is one thing more important to a Geordie than a pint of brown ale, it's a Newcastle No. 9. The affinity between the Newcastle United fans on the St. James' Park terraces and the centre-forward is one of the great romances of our time'

Sunday Times

'Whoever wears the famous shirt can become an instant hero. If he's got quality and can score goals, St. James' Park is the best place to be'

Malcolm Macdonald

'I didn't know anything about the history connected with the No. 9 shirt at Newcastle United until I came here, but I soon found out. It's one of those things peculiar to the club, for whoever wears the No. 9 shirt is expected to wear it well'

Robert Lee

'A centre-forward can go through 90 minutes and can only touch the ball twice, yet grab all the headlines and be the hero'

Albert Stubbins

'Fans worship them in a way no player in any other position can hope to be worshipped'

Jackie Milburn

'There's not another club with such a glorious tradition of No. 9s'

Sir Bobby Robson

'I achieved one thing thousands of people have dreamed about and that's pulling on the No. 9 shirt at Newcastle. No one can ever take that away'

Joe Allon

'It's the shirt every Geordie kid would die for and I feel proud and privileged that my name is on the back of it'

Alan Shearer

1. THE LEGEND IS BORN
1892–1925

JOCK PEDDIE, BOB McCOLL,
BILL APPLEYARD, ALBERT SHEPHERD,
BILLY HIBBERT, NEIL HARRIS

Goals are the lifeblood of football. Hitting the back of the net at the top level of the game is a glorious feeling, especially on Tyneside. As Alan Shearer once said: 'To score a goal is great. But to score in front of a big crowd at Newcastle is extra special.' Another No. 9 hero, Malcolm Macdonald, noted: 'Tens of thousands of people dream of the moment. Scoring is all about turning that dream into reality.' From much-remembered blockbuster shots, powered headers and mazy runs, to not-so-often-recalled goalmouth scraps that ended with the ball in the back of the net, centre-forwards are the players who grab most of them. The man in the No. 9 shirt has become the one individual whom supporters consistently treat as a hero – a god-like figure who can do little wrong and who is worshipped by fans from five to fifty years of age through generation after generation.

Football supporters need these hero figures – even now in an age of many varied leisure activities and a high-tech make-believe world. Back in a very different era of cloth caps and pit boots, a larger-than-life character developed and fans adored him. Top players now earn lots of money, have fast cars, are millionaires and are instantly recognised as superstars. To the punter who comes through the turnstile, they are the individuals who can turn a drab weekend into a memorable one – and create a moment to be recalled for a lifetime.

Invariably the weight of that responsibility falls on the shoulders of the centre-forward. Some have revelled in the duty; some have crumpled with the pressure. In the northern outpost of Tyneside, in a working-class environment of Victorian and Edwardian Britain, the Geordie football supporter seemingly had an extra urge to make a hero out of a footballer who pulled on the black and white shirt of Newcastle United. Maybe it was because the ordinary men of the pit, shipyard or factory of the North-east, wanted an outlet for their energies, passions, frustrations and a gallant braveheart, an icon, to look up to. Whatever the reason, a tradition developed to choose a hero-figure, and invariably it was the man who scored the goals and took the glory who captured the attention – the centre-forward.

Although nearly 50 years had still to pass before numbers were introduced and a Newcastle United player actually pulled on what was to be the famous No. 9 black and white shirt, the club's first centre-forward of note was a knightly Geordie called Willie Thompson. Back in 1892 Tyneside was at the height of its industrial might. Shipyards, engineering works and coalfields were a hive of gritty activity all over the region. And in terms of football development the city had seen the demise of pioneer club West End with their great rivals East End moving from Heaton to St. James' Park. Willie Thompson was an East End man and he crossed to the city-centre location during the summer of 1892. By the end of that year the East Enders had changed their name to Newcastle United in a bid to bond the two distinct football communities together.

Thompson was United's spearhead up front. From North Seaton, he sported a magnificent big, bushy moustache in the style of the day. He was a regular scorer during those early footballing afternoons on Tyneside, an age before the Magpies entered the Football League. He took part in East End's – and in essence Newcastle United's – first ever FA Cup proper contest against Nottingham Forest during January 1892. So Thompson was United's first FA Cup centre-forward and the formidable leader was also the club's first Football League centre-forward. As United entered senior action in season 1893–94,

16

Thompson led United's line for their debut in the Football League against Arsenal during September 1893. He didn't get on the scoresheet in a 2–2 draw, but the inaugural league game at St. James' Park – also against Arsenal – resulted in a Thompson hat-trick. In an amazing opening on Tyneside, the Magpies won 6–0 and United's centre-forward couldn't be shackled. Not a big man, Thompson was only 5 ft 7 in. tall, but he was a handful, possessing the pace and shooting ability to cause defenders plenty of problems.

Willie did well during that initial season of league action. He scored ten goals as United began life in the big time. But it could never be said that he was a hero figure to United's small, but growing band of followers. And he was ageing. Thompson was into his 30s and he had recently suffered from what was described as a 'dodgy knee'. As a result, United's directors brought in another centre-forward for the start of the 1895–96 season – and one with a huge reputation. The purchase of Scottish leader 25-year-old James Logan was perhaps the first of a long line of major centre-forward signings at St. James' Park.

Logan arrived with a big claim to fame, as the man who scored a hat-trick in the FA Cup final for Notts County only sixteen months before and still one of only three players to have done so. He was a Scottish international from Troon and after his feat against Bolton in that 1894 final became a noted personality. Having scored over 30 goals for the other Magpies alongside the Trent, Logan arrived on Tyneside from Dundee as a cunning and prolific goalscorer. Stocky at 5 ft 10 in. tall, he replaced the ageing Thompson in United's side and started his days wearing the black and white of United in devastating mood.

On his debut against Loughborough Town he had a proverbial blinder and found the net. He did likewise in his next three games. Logan, in fact, claimed seven goals in his first six matches for United and looked the part. He was an instant hit but against Newton Heath during October Logan was injured and his career at St. James' Park was halted just as it had taken off. Logan picked up a bad knock in the first half. He didn't appear for the second period, United being down to ten men for the rest of the match. The Scot only appeared twice more and had departed before the season was out, to Loughborough – a club obviously impressed with the talents he had shown in his first game for United.

In the close season of 1896, United's directors found a centre-forward replacement in Nottingham Forest's determined goal-poacher Richard Smellie. Another Scot, the man with the unfortunate surname started the way many of United's No. 9 stars did – hitting goals and making headlines. A cool-headed striker, Smellie had been a First Division success with Forest and made an immediate impact a division lower with the Magpies. *Northern Gossip* magazine noted he was 'dashing' and possessed 'coolness which characterises his play'.

On his first outing on Tyneside against Small Heath during September 1896 he claimed a hat-trick, then scored four goals in his next home game against Darwen. Smellie became a rapid favourite with the Geordie crowd, with seven goals in two appearances. United, so it appeared, had found a centre-forward of quality. Richard continued to impress and was top scorer with 15 goals for the season. He was noted in the *Newcastle Daily Journal* as a 'sturdy athlete', who was 'fast' as well as 'a good shooter'. But like Logan, he was to move suddenly and quickly. He left Tyneside in the close season of 1897 when the club had a massive clear-out of players, and didn't appear in the Football League again.

THE GEORDIE'S FIRST NO. 9 HERO

Newcastle were now becoming quite desperate to find a centre-forward who would settle and take root on Tyneside. The club's ambitions were big. They were eager to join the First Division and compete with the best in the football world. United had developed quickly since joining organised competition and during the early part of season 1897–98 were pushing for a promotion place from the Second Division, with veteran Johnny Campbell filling the gap in attack. All they needed was a leader up front. In September 1897, they brought yet another Scot to Tyneside, initially on trial – a 20-year-old, largely unknown player. He was a tough-looking Glaswegian with short-cropped hair. Jock Peddie arrived in the North-east after shining in a friendly match for his club Third Lanark against United. Like Logan and Smellie before, Peddie was an instant hit – but this time the Scot stayed put and gave United great service, becoming in the process the supporters' first No. 9 hero.

At 5 ft 11 in. tall, Jock was mean, keen and a huge character. He scored on his first appearance in front of the United crowd – in a 4–0 victory over Small Heath – and the Tyneside supporters took to him very quickly. It was his arrival that gave the Magpies the impetus and cutting edge to get within touching distance of the First Division.

Once settled, Peddie started to hit the net with ease. He linked with established forwards Willie Wardrope and Johnny Campbell – two more players from north of the border – and United's attacking threat was a potent one. During March and April, he struck a hat-trick against Darwen, scored against Manchester City, hit two against Grimsby Town then claimed three more in a match with Gainsborough. Another goal against Leicester Fosse gave him ten goals in six games. In his first 20 matches for the Black'n'Whites, Peddie had grabbed 14 goals. Jock was the talk of Tyneside and United moved into second place in the race to the top division.

JOCK PEDDIE
FACTS & FIGURES

To Newcastle United: September 1897 from Third Lanark
  £135
From Newcastle United: June 1902 to Manchester United
Born: Glasgow 21 March 1877
Died: Detroit, USA, October 1928
Height: 5 ft 11 in.
Other senior clubs: Plymouth Argyle, Heart of Midlothian
International: Scotland trial
Newcastle United app & goals:
  Football League: 126 app, 73 goals
  FA Cup: 10 app, 5 goals
  Total: 136 app, 78 goals
Strike-rate: League and Cup 57%

Promotion during Victorian times was not guaranteed by finishing first or second in the table. The top two sides had to compete with the bottom two clubs in the First Division – fighting out a series of test matches. Newcastle qualified and faced a mini-league competition with Stoke, Blackburn Rovers and Burnley. But they were rocked by an injury to their star centre-forward. In the opening exchange with Stoke at St. James' Park, Peddie was injured and he missed the following three crucial fixtures. However, United were on a roll and despite the loss of Peddie gained their First Division place with a little help from the game's rulers after a controversial match-fixing row which resulted in the test matches being scrapped and United being voted into the top division.

Peddie was United's top scorer with 18 goals, and many of his strikes came from his terrific shooting. He had power in his boots. *Topical Times* wrote of United's new star: 'Jack was never a hard grafter, but he always justified his choice because of the most colossal power he could put behind a drive.' The sporting magazine added: 'Once he got either foot behind a ball the custodian never had half a chance.' Jock had perhaps the hardest shot in the game at the time. One colleague of the era noted: 'I can picture the expectancy on the faces of spectators whenever Peddie took stance for a shot.' It was usual for Jock to score from 20 or 30 yards and he could hit the ball with seemingly little back-lift or effort. One spectator remembered that his shooting against Loughborough Town once 'sent the net pegs flying at St. James' Park'!

The fans loved the Scot, despite a moody temperament which saw him sulk at times when things didn't go his way on the field. As teammate Colin Veitch said: 'Peddie often irritated the crowd on his moody days.' Yet when Jock was roused into action, the supporters relished it. Veitch recalled in his memoirs that on one occasion when one of Jock's teammates was injured with a heavy challenge against Grimsby, he was so annoyed that he 'rolled up his sleeves to shoulder height and rattled in a hat-trick'. Veitch also confirmed: 'Peddie was the first of Newcastle's centre-forwards of prominence.' United's celebrated England player added he was 'the first of a number of centre-forwards whose popularity with supporters has been a remarkable feature of United's history'. Newcastle's centre-forward tradition was born with the arrival of Jock Peddie.

In the First Division, Peddie continued to score goals and he continued to hog the headlines too, once striking nine goals in seven consecutive matches, and especially after United's first derby encounter with Sunderland which took place at Roker Park in December 1898 – on Christmas Eve. The two local rivals had met before, in the FA Cup and friendlies, but this was the initial Football League contest at a newly opened Roker Park. Sunderland were one of football's elite, while United were the new kids on the block. Few gave the Magpies any hope on Wearside but United had Peddie. And he made the difference.

In front of a capacity 30,000 crowd, which included almost

10,000 Newcastle fans, the game was evenly poised at 1–1 before United's Scottish No. 9 entered the action. Latching onto a huge clearance from Jackson, Peddie stormed through the Sunderland defence with a turn of pace. He saw keeper Ted Doig come out before unleashing a Peddie special. The ball screamed into the net. And he wasn't finished. Jock was the spearhead of another swift counter-attack created by Wardrope and Aitken. Peddie's boot finished off the move and United were ahead 3–1. Although Sunderland pulled a goal back, United held out for a special victory. Peddie was the local hero.

Jock was United's top scorer with 20 goals in that first season in the top division and he remained the Magpies' goalgetter-in-chief, being the highest scorer again in the following two campaigns as the Tynesiders consolidated their position with the elite of football. And the Black'n'Whites did pretty well finishing in fifth and then sixth place as the century turned. While the Scot did the business on the field – indeed tipped for a Scotland cap after trial games – he was a temperamental character and often found himself in trouble off it. Peddie had become embroiled in several disagreements with United's directorate over club discipline. He had been fined, suspended for missing training and, as one entry in the club's official minutes record, for 'turning out in an unfit state'. Jock was often head to head with United's hierarchy and in 1900 was suspended *sine die*, although that draconian sentence was later lifted. He actually refused to play against Wolverhampton Wanderers in 1899!

As a consequence, his days at Gallowgate were numbered. Like Hughie Gallacher, Malcolm Macdonald and Andy Cole in the future, in spite of a first-class return for the side – of 78 goals – he was to be discarded. His sale, eventually to Manchester United, was not a popular move, just like Gallacher, Macdonald and Cole's headlining transfers many years later. Newcastle fans thought much of the Scot. He had almost a cult following on Tyneside and many bemoaned his departure. Before Peddie headed elsewhere, though, United did bring a new centre-forward, Bob McColl, to the North-east, a deal that was the biggest in the country at the time and the two strikers enjoyed a fruitful partnership for a short period.

JOCK PEDDIE No. 9 RATING	
Fan appeal – personality and presence	8
Strike-rate	6
Shooting – power and placement	9
Heading	7
Ball skills	7
Link-play – passing, assists, crossing, team-play	7
Pace	7
Commitment – work-rate, courage	7
Match-winner – power-play, big-match capability	8
Longevity with United	5
Trophy success, international and top football ranking	0
Total No. 9 rating	71

ANOTHER SCOT SETS THE STANDARD

Scotsman Bob McColl was rated as the finest centre-forward in the country, indeed as it was claimed even 'in the world', and his move to St. James' Park in November 1901 was described as the 'capture of the season'. Another from north of the border, McColl was 25 years old and the 'peerless amateur' of Scottish football. An amateur he may have been, but he had recently scored three hat-tricks for the Scots, including a much-recalled treble against the Auld Enemy as Scotland crushed England 4–1 in 1900. Brought up in the Mount Florida area of Glasgow, near Hampden Park, the Queen's Park leader was often a target of the leading English clubs. Derby County tried for his signature, so too did Liverpool. Newcastle United made an attempt but failed, then went back for a second bite.

In the days before a strict maximum-wage rule, turning professional for an amateur was a lucrative move, and after resisting the challenge for a long time McColl took the plunge. United had an edge in the chase for his talents, as winger Willie Stewart had previously been a teammate of McColl at Hampden Park. United offered the shrewd and well-educated McColl what was then a vast £300 signing-on fee plus a weekly wage approaching £5 per week, then big money. Newcastle's director, the eloquent and silver-tongued James Telford – himself a fellow Scot – worked hard to persuade McColl to appear in United's black and white. Known as the Prince of Centre-forwards, McColl

22

decided Tyneside would be the ideal location, close to Glasgow and with a club whose tradition of fielding plenty of Scots in the side meant he would feel at home. Colleague Colin Veitch later wrote of the transfer: 'I doubt if there was a greater sensation. No player of such standing had been connected with Newcastle until the date of McColl's arrival.' It was one of the earliest in a series of sensational, headlining centre-forward transfers in United's history and the first of three big-name No. 9 personalities of the Edwardian era: McColl being followed by Bill Appleyard and Albert Shepherd.

McColl favoured the team game and was not in the Peddie mould of a hell-for-leather, go-for-it centre-forward. He believed in passing the ball, and keeping the ball on the grass for most of the time. He was the strategist at centre-forward. Bob liked to start moves deep and combine with the midfield before gliding into the box to have a go at goal. Not big and muscular, he was only 5 ft 9 in. tall and slightly built, McColl was the elegant artiste in contrast to Peddie before, and Appleyard and Shepherd after. He possessed ball skills, could beat defenders in a dribble, was fast and had a good drive in either foot, being noted at the time as having 'a dangerous shot at goal, no matter the length of range'.

With Peddie still in the line-up, McColl started his career at Gallowgate mainly at inside-forward. He scored on his debut in the centre-forward role against Bolton Wanderers in season 1901–02 and during the following year, when Peddie was out of favour, was United's regular No. 9. McColl claimed only 10 goals in 30 appearances that year as United struggled but nevertheless made his mark and left a deep impression on those around him.

Colin Veitch recorded in his life-story that McColl was instrumental in setting the pattern of United's celebrated football which was to soon dominate the Edwardian era. He said: 'I don't think the majority of Newcastle United followers realise just how much the Newcastle team owes McColl, but I have no hesitation in saying that McColl set the high standard of football which Newcastle United attained shortly afterwards.' The players who remained after McColl returned to Scotland – especially the likes of Veitch, Jackie Rutherford, Alex Gardner and Peter McWilliam – learned from his intelligent play and tactical knowledge. He in effect taught United the team and possession game. Veitch added: 'His was the football example which made that period of prosperity and greatness possible.' McColl set the standard and was responsible for moulding the style of Newcastle's future greatness.

Despite a lack of goals for the Magpies, McColl worked hard on the field without, as one scribe of the day noted, 'expending unnecessary energy'. He had a wonderful sense of positional play, perhaps his greatest asset, and the touch of a master. He was also a gentleman on the field befitting his previous amateur status of the old school. Yet for all his qualities, Bob could never capture the popularity of his predecessor on the field, Jock Peddie. United's faithful wanted the thrill-a-minute style of Peddie. They wanted to roar themselves hoarse as he sped through the middle and unleashed a Peddie blockbuster. McColl was never that sort of player. Contemporary reports noted: 'McColl was not the individual success with United that he had been in Scotland.'

Bob was certainly heavily marked in English football. His reputation was huge and as a consequence was given particular attention, including continual rough treatment from opponents' defenders. One colleague noted that he took a physical battering 'such as no other player until the years of Hughie Gallacher'. While McColl didn't reach iconic status on Tyneside, he did have his days, including one afternoon which robbed local rivals Sunderland of the Football League Championship trophy.

During 1902–03, a season in which United themselves challenged for the championship for a long period, the deciding match of the title chase involved the Magpies. United faced Sunderland on the last day of the season. A victory for the Wearsiders would give them the trophy while Sheffield Wednesday waited anxiously for the result 140 miles south. And at St. James' Park it was a Bob McColl goal which robbed the Reds of the championship. Veitch broke away and the ball ended up with McColl who netted with the ease of the master he was. It was also the first league victory by the Magpies over Sunderland on home soil. Bob's goal sent the silverware to Wednesday's home of Owlerton instead of Roker Park.

BIG BILL ARRIVES IN TOON

During that season United's directors brought their second Edwardian No. 9 hero to Tyneside. With McColl's versatility in mind – he was equally as good at inside-forward – Newcastle purchased 25-year-old Bill Appleyard from Grimsby Town. And what a contrast the former North Sea fisherman was to the stylish McColl. Appleyard was big at 14 stone, was rough, fierce and possessed limited skills. But he was mighty effective at centre-forward. The pair joined forces for a season before McColl joined Glasgow Rangers in September 1904 and just before United were to lift their first trophy. His close friend, director James Telford, was deposed after a boardroom coup and Bob considered he could not continue on Tyneside. McColl totalled 67 games for United and hit 20 goals. Those modest statistics do not though show his true worth to the Magpies. In the following years, the club lifted three Football League Championships and reached five FA Cup finals. The Scot may have not shared in that glory but much of that success was down to the seeds sown by R.S. McColl.

BILL APPLEYARD
FACTS & FIGURES

To Newcastle United: April 1903 from Grimsby Town
£700
From Newcastle United: June 1908 to Oldham Athletic
£350
Born: Caistor 16 November 1878
Died: Newcastle upon Tyne 14 January 1958
Height: 5 ft 10 in.
Other senior clubs: none
International: England reserve
Newcastle United app & goals:
　Football League: 128 app, 71 goals
　FA Cup: 17 app, 16 goals
　Others: 1 app, 1 goal
　Total: 146 app, 88 goals
Strike-rate: League and Cup 60% (overall 60%)

Bill Appleyard made his name with the Mariners during their spell in the First Division during seasons 1901–02 and 1902–03. Although in a side which struggled to survive in the top echelon, Cockles, as he was nicknamed on Humberside, netted 20 goals. He impressed United's officials when the two clubs met in a physical and fiery affair centring on Big Bill. He was purchased for a £700 fee with the aim of taking the weight off United's playmakers, giving them punch through the centre-forward channel. And he certainly did that. He was good in the air and effective on the right, although not so good on the left – his left foot recorded as 'a bit of a swinger'. With almost a shaven head and that bulky frame to carry around, Appleyard was far from a purist, but was an awesome opponent.

He was top scorer in his first season with 16 goals, and for the 1904–05 term Appleyard spearheaded United's trophy challenge, at one point striking seven goals in five games during a crucial stage in the season as spring was in the air. He was the battle-tank with rugged tenacity, surrounded by artistes, the likes of Rutherford, Howie, McWilliam and Veitch. United's side was full of international talent and they provided the opportunities for Bill to create havoc. They complemented each other perfectly. In front of goal, Appleyard was, as one colleague remembered: 'Always on the spot, and his right foot was deadly in its finishing.' He scored 15 goals, and with 4 other colleagues also getting into double figures in the goals chart, United lifted the Football League Championship for the first time. Bill netted one of the goals which clinched the title trophy against Middlesbrough. And that was not all. Appleyard also played his part as United reached their first FA Cup final. United failed in their quest for the double, though, losing 0–2 to Aston Villa in the final.

The Toon Army of Edwardian Tyneside took to Appleyard's robust, almost primitive style at once. He looked a character on the field and quickly became a hero figure in the shape of Peddie before him. His popularity in the coming years prompted Colin Veitch to note that Bill 'stood second to none until the arrival of Hughie Gallacher'. Despite his lack of finer skills, supporters treasured his bustling no-nonsense style.

Appleyard was a regular goalgetter for United, but not as prolific as some like Shepherd, Gallacher, Macdonald or Shearer to follow. In 1905–06, he netted 17 goals while in 1906–07 he was explosive, netting 10 goals in his first 9 games before going on to claim 17 goals in the season once more. With Newcastle United now the country's leading side, Appleyard had his best return for the Magpies the following campaign and was unlucky not to get a call up for England, being reserve against the Scots. He totalled 22 goals in 29 matches in that 1907–08 season, striking the net in 6 successive matches as winter approached. United's No. 9 was extremely effective in yet another FA Cup run which ended at the Crystal Palace national arena. Appleyard claimed eight goals, scoring in every round except the final, when again Newcastle flopped, this time against Wolves. He inflicted damage on Nottingham Forest, West Ham United and Liverpool, and then struck a hat-trick against his old club Grimsby Town – the first by any United player in the competition proper. And semi-final opponents Fulham literally suffered serious damage in the face-to-face meeting with the battling hulk of Big Bill – notably in the shape of goalkeeper Leslie Skene.

Appleyard was deadly as United romped to a 6–0 record semi-final victory. The match perhaps summed up the Newcastle leader's sometimes controversial style of play – clinical and bruising. After 30 minutes of the contest, he put United ahead when Alex Gardner's solo run was stopped with a heavy foul challenge. From the free-kick, Appleyard headed home with a clinical piece of finishing. In the second half, with the Magpies 2–0 in front, the physical side of Bill's game played an important part in the match. He clashed with Fulham's keeper Skene – Bill planting 'a foot between those of his adversary whilst shouldering him at the same time'! Goalkeepers, unprotected in those days, feared the physical players like Appleyard and the Fulham custodian was left a passenger. United struck four more goals as a result and romped into the final with Wolves. United lost again though – this time 1–3 – and Appleyard, like many of his teammates, never performed too well in those finals. One report in *Athletic News* noted: 'We saw little of Appleyard as an effective force. Whatever the tactics the burly fisherboy had invented, he never found the opportunity to show them.'

Now 30 years of age, Big Bill's days at St. James' Park were just about over. One description of the period noted: 'Bill Appleyard could never be called a brilliant footballer, yet his name will live long in the annals of Newcastle United. Whatever his deficiencies were he fitted in well. Bill could hit the ball true and hard, he was always a trier, and his huge bulk assisted him to succeed nine times out of ten.' His record of 88 goals in 146 appearances was excellent. And he lifted two title medals and reached two FA Cup finals.

With Appleyard off to continue his career with Oldham Athletic and United allowing his able deputy Joe McClarence to depart too, United brought in a successor of his at Grimsby Town, a young striker who had impressed many, Bob Blanthorne. From Birkenhead, Blanthorne started his career with Liverpool but had been released and ended up at Blundell Park. He then had a rapid rise to prominence during the 1907–08 season. In his first year as a regular, the lanky, 6 ft 1 in. tall and assertive leader scored 21 goals in 33 matches for Grimsby and was recognised as the best of any new striking talent outside the First Division.

A telling marksman, the Scouser was watched by United's representatives and they compiled rave reports. Blanthorne was also to feature in direct opposition to United as Grimsby went on an FA Cup run and met the Magpies in the quarter-final. Bob was the danger-man, having hit plenty of goals on the cup trail including five in one game against Carlisle United. While Blanthorne played well against United, his side were swamped by a brilliant Magpie display, losing 5–1 at St. James' Park.

At the end of the season Newcastle United paid £350 for his services as a replacement for Appleyard and he was introduced into the action for the opening game of the 1908–09 campaign, a home encounter with Bradford City. Blanthorne, though, had cruel luck. He had played around 71 minutes before a heavy challenge from City's right-back Robert Campbell resulted in the 24-year-old debutant being carried off in agony with a broken leg. Reports from the day noted that a sickening crack could be heard and an appeal was made for a doctor to come to his aid. A certain Dr Appleby volunteered and quickly diagnosed a double fracture of Bob's right leg and set it in splints. He was to be out of the reckoning for almost 12 months. His career and chance to become a United No. 9 hero was over, before it had really started. By the time Bob was fit, Newcastle had a new centre-forward installed, Albert Shepherd. As it happened, Blanthorne was never the same promising player again. The injury took its toll and he never returned to United's first eleven, moving to Hartlepool United during 1910.

The loss of their new striker gave United's directors a major headache. No Appleyard, no Blanthorne and the season well under way. Experiments were tried shuffling players around. England international James Stewart was handed the leader's role, as was Sandy Higgins, another international, this time for Scotland. Both were very good inside-forwards and useful utility players as required, but they were not centre-forwards. Stan Allan was introduced also. A local lad from Wallsend, he was another versatile player and the Tynesider did a good job in the short term, netting goals as a stand-in, before and after Albert Shepherd arrived. The Geordie scored in five consecutive appearances at centre-forward as the Magpies marched for the championship title.

BILL APPLEYARD No. 9 RATING	
Fan appeal – personality and presence	9
Strike-rate	6
Shooting – power and placement	7
Heading	7
Ball skills	6
Link-play – passing, assists, crossing, team-play	8
Pace	7
Commitment – work-rate, courage	7
Match-winner – power-play, big-match capability	7
Longevity with United	5
Trophy success, international and top football ranking	2
Total No. 9 rating	71

It was evident that United needed to find another centre-forward. The local press reported: 'The forward line was not moving quite as smoothly as could have been desired.' United's early season form was still good nevertheless. They were second in the championship race, although United's directors had no intention of staying in the runners-up position. They wanted title silverware again. And to make sure, they made a move for one of the country's best strikers.

ENTER ALBERT SHEPHERD

Newcastle Chairman Joe Bell quizzed the senior members of his side on whom they should go for. Colin Veitch was to quickly reply: 'Albert Shepherd.' Bell noted: 'That's enough for me. Shepherd's my man and Shepherd it will be.' And that conversation reinforced Bell's already-held view that Shepherd would fit the bill. Newcastle United meant business, no matter what the cost – and Shepherd would certainly cost a hefty fee. He was recognised as one of the top two or three strikers in the game. With Bolton Wanderers his record was outstanding. In 123 senior matches before leaving Burnden Park, Albert hit home 90 goals and had reached the England side.

Making a name for himself in season 1904–05 as Bolton won promotion to the First Division, he was then the Football League's chief goalgetter with 26 strikes in his first season in the top flight. The following 2 seasons saw the potent striker claim another 44 goals. He proved he was a regular 20-goal man. Shepherd had already shown Newcastle United's officials what he could do. When facing the Black'n'Whites the previous season, Bolton took care of United by a 0–4 scoreline in Lancashire. And Shepherd scored a tremendous hat-trick. He then went on to net another four goals in his next three games.

Newcastle paid out an £850 fee to bring 23-year-old Shepherd to Tyneside and it was one of the best pieces of business United ever did. In the following seasons, Albert became noted for his rip-roaring dashes through the middle, having a one-way-to-goal approach – much like Malcolm Macdonald in another future era. Shepherd was to claim almost 100 goals in a Toon shirt, and in only 123 matches. He headed United's goal charts for three seasons in a row. Not surprisingly, the crowd took to him almost from his first kick.

ALBERT SHEPHERD
FACTS & FIGURES

To Newcastle United: November 1908 from Bolton
  Wanderers £850
From Newcastle United: July 1914 to Bradford City
  £1,500
Born: Great Lever 10 September 1885
Died: Bolton 8 November 1929
Height: 5 ft 8 in.
Other senior clubs: none
England international: 2 app, 2 goals
Newcastle United app & goals:
  Football League: 104 app, 76 goals
  FA Cup: 19 app, 16 goals
  Total: 123 app, 92 goals
Strike-rate: League and Cup 75%

Shepherd's start in a black and white shirt was extraordinary. At the time, some of United's experienced players and household names were in dispute with the club's directors. Players like Bill McCracken, Alex Gardner, Peter McWilliam, Jimmy Howie and Jackie Rutherford were left out of contention as the 1908–09 season unfolded and for an away fixture against Nottingham Forest, Newcastle's line-up contained several reserve and fringe players. It also included United's big signing, Shepherd, at centre-forward. He made a fine start, scoring in a 4–0 victory, but the win was by no means achieved as easily as the scoreline suggested and it paved the way for one of the most astonishing games seen at St. James' Park – on Albert's first appearance in front of his own supporters.

The success at the City Ground prompted Newcastle's selection committee to ignore calls to reinstate the club's star names. For the massive derby clash with rivals Sunderland, they again gave many of their internationals the day off and tickets in the West Stand, rather than a place in the starting line-up. The consequences were fatal as Sunderland won by the sensational scoreline of 1–9, a result which has gone down in history as the biggest away victory in the top division – and in a derby match too!

In front of a 56,000 crowd, Albert Shepherd had a great opening to his Gallowgate career. The new signing put United on level terms – striking home a rocket penalty just before the break. There was nothing to indicate the avalanche of goals to follow in the second period. On a wet day, the pitch became increasingly greasy and slippery and United found it difficult to play their controlled, passing football. Sunderland, though, adapted better to the worsening conditions. At the end of the second 45 minutes, the Wearsiders had scored another eight goals and United were down to nine men with Whitson and Duncan injured! What could new purchase Shepherd have thought? On every ground in the country the result was met with astonishment. It had been United's blackest day ever. Yet amazingly, out of that adversity came new-found determination, which was to result in brilliant success.

The directors took immediate action. The sidelined stars came back, differences resolved, all forgotten and United – with Shepherd at the forefront – raced to another Football League title with room to spare, totalling a record fifty-three points – seven ahead of Everton. Shepherd claimed fifteen goals in twenty-one appearances, including a four-goal strike at Notts County. During January 1909, he had a purple patch, scoring seven goals in four successive games.

Shepherd was a colourful character, liking a joke, a song and a drink. He mixed his undoubted football talents with moments of pure show-boating. Albert would be often in the news for one reason or another, having the ability to create headlines – some good, some bizarre and some bad. In that match against Notts County in which he bagged four goals, his sensational strike-rate was all based around an agreement he had with his directors. Shepherd was keen to visit family in Bolton after the game and a convenient train departed from Nottingham just after the match. If he missed it, he would not get to his relatives until around midnight. He was determined not to do that, but it meant a very quick exit from the County Ground. Albert had a persuasive tongue and he outlandishly agreed with club officials that if he scored four goals he would be allowed to leave the field and United would have to complete the match with only ten men!

By the break Shepherd was none too pleased. The scoreline was still 0–0. He came out in the second half furious and determined. Grabbing an early goal, he then rapidly fired home three more to give United a 4–0 advantage. Peter McWilliam noted that: 'Every goal was a beauty and well-merited.' Then Albert feigned injury, hobbled off the field, into a taxi and climbed aboard the early Bolton train! That was typical Shepherd.

The following season, 1909–10, Albert had his best year for United, yet it was surrounded by controversy in characteristic Shepherd fashion. The Magpies again challenged for the title trophy and Shepherd fired home 28 league goals including 4s against both Liverpool and Preston North End. In successive games, he bagged six goals in four matches and then a few weeks later struck seven in three outings. United's No. 9 claimed 31 goals all told – the first Newcastle man to hit the 30-goal mark. Albert had formidable shooting power and loved nothing better to scream through the centre-forward channel and fire the ball into the net – usually taking the shortest route to goal. He wasn't a big leader, standing only at 5 ft 8 in., but he was stocky and strong with lightning pace. A touch moody at times, like many great centre-forwards, Shepherd was a brilliant match-winner.

The Black'n'Whites just failed to lift the championship trophy again, but did go all the way in another FA Cup run. Shepherd was on fire. In the opening eight days of 1910, he scored seven goals. With Shepherd as the match-winner their previous three disappointing displays in the final were not repeated – although eventual success had to be achieved in a replay – after Albert had created national headlines over a bribery scandal.

United had a comfortable run to the semi-final in 1910 taking care of Stoke, Fulham, Blackburn Rovers and Leicester Fosse. They then faced giant-killers Swindon Town in the semi-final, but just before that meeting at White Hart Lane a huge sensation blew up involving United's star No. 9. The cup party were stationed at Saltburn on what was then commonly called 'Special Training' in readiness for the important clash. Remarkably, by modern standards, United also had a First Division match against Arsenal the day before the cup meeting with Swindon – on Good Friday. It was taken for granted that United's reserve side would face the Gunners at St. James' Park with the first eleven safely tucked up in a Saltburn hotel. And that's what happened – all that is except top scorer Albert Shepherd. Colin Veitch recorded in his chronicle: 'We were bewildered, stunned, and incredulous! Shepherd was among the certainties for selection in the Cup team.' It was astounding news. Players and reporters, as well as fans, searched for answers, but could get no satisfaction from United's officials.

Shepherd played against Arsenal for United's scratch side in a 1–1 draw. He did travel south but was a spectator at the semi-final meeting with Swindon, United cruising into the final with a 2–0 victory. Slowly the story started to emerge that his omission from the Magpie's FA Cup line-up was because he had been allegedly bribed to let his team down in the semi-final clash. United's directors paid heed to the rumours and pulled Shepherd out of one of the biggest games of the season. None of Albert's teammates could believe that he had been nobbled by bookmakers – although not common practice in those days, such instances certainly did occur. Albert's colleagues were, as one teammate noted, 'incensed' at the unjust treatment of their centre-forward. Veitch recorded: 'We insisted on Shepherd's reinstatement for the final against Barnsley.' There was a real risk of a players' strike before the FA Cup final, or as Veitch tactfully put it 'of some other players being diplomatic absentees'.

With no proof of any bribery taking place, Newcastle's officials had no option but to reinstate Shepherd. He led the line at the Crystal Palace against Barnsley and received some rough treatment from full-backs Ness and Downs in a spirited contest. United's leader sported 'a lump as big as a man's fist on his back that will remind him for some time to come of the kneeing he received'. After a dull 1–1 draw, the rumours were again fuelled that Albert had been 'got at' once more. United's players, including an angry and incensed Shepherd, were determined to rest the scurrilous gossip in the replay.

At Goodison Park the Magpies at last showed their true worth in a final. And Albert Shepherd was the champion of the day, scoring the two goals that brought the FA Cup to Tyneside for the very first time.

There was complete vindication of United's centre-forward. In the first half, he went close on a couple of occasions and had the ball in the net only for the referee to call a halt due to offside. After the interval, though, there was no stopping him. He was on top form. Albert was constantly involved and the press noted: 'Time after time he wanted the ball.' His first strike was classic Shepherd. After 51 minutes, Higgins pushed an 'inch perfect' ball into Shepherd's path. He raced clear of full-back Downs and fired a stinging ground shot past goalkeeper Mearns. The *Daily Mirror*'s reporter was to write that in scoring, Shepherd made one of his 'characteristic dashes'. Soon after, Peter McWilliam surged forward in a brilliant run and released the ball to Wilson, who in turn set up Shepherd. A Barnsley defender lunged in and 'crudely fouled' United's leader. A penalty, the first ever in an FA Cup final! Shepherd coolly stepped up and stroked the ball home to cap a tremendous, match-winning performance.

The following season Albert claimed over 30 goals again – 33 in 38 matches – and once more hit 4 goals in a single match, not once but twice, against Liverpool for a second time and against Nottingham Forest. During a spell of devastating goalscoring, Albert found the net on 18 occasions in 13 matches. It was sparkling form and it earned Shepherd a return to the England side.

Capped with Bolton, for some reason Shepherd was never a favourite of the Football Association's selectors in London. Maybe his moody character and headlining stories counted against him. Rivals for the England shirt during the era were George Hilsdon of Chelsea, Bert Freeman who starred with Everton and Burnley as well as the regular choice, Vivian Woodward of Spurs and Chelsea. In season 1910–11, Albert was the First Division's leading marksman and could not be ignored, especially after his previous season's haul. He made the England side for the clash with Ireland during February and although he did well, scoring in a 2–1 victory at the Baseball Ground, he was afterwards again overlooked to the annoyance of many, not least Albert Shepherd.

The Black'n'Whites once more reached the FA Cup final that season, Shepherd having a penchant for scoring in the run, netting in every round to the Crystal Palace final. He bagged a hat-trick against Bury and scored against Northampton Town, Hull City and Derby County as well as a crucial goal in the semi-final with Chelsea, finishing off a lovely move with Rutherford by firing a shot that sailed past keeper James Molyneux.

Newcastle United were hot favourites to retain the trophy in their meeting with Bradford City, but then were rocked with a huge setback – a serious injury to the crowd's No. 9 favourite just before the final. In a meaningless First Division fixture with Blackburn Rovers at St. James' Park – the match prior to facing the Tykes in London – Shepherd was carried from the field, out of the FA Cup final, and worse, out of football for almost two seasons.

Shepherd himself recorded the fateful moment in his own words: 'I was doing one of my mad rushes, as some people call them, when I collided with the Rovers custodian, and had to be carried from the field.' The pile-up with Rovers' international keeper Jimmy Ashcroft was a nasty one. Albert damaged tendons in his right leg, being 'severely mauled' as it was described and as Colin Veitch recalled: 'It was possible to bend the leg at the knee in the opposite direction to normal.' It was a horrendous injury.

The loss of Shepherd was a massive blow. United lost the FA Cup final – many judges reckoned they would have won had Albert played – and found a replacement extremely difficult to find. That was not surprising as Shepherd had few peers. He was out of action for the whole of season 1911–12 and only played a handful of games in 1912–13 when he found recovery a long, drawn-out affair.

James Stewart and Sandy Higgins were again switched from inside-forward for a spell, but once more United ended up going into the transfer market in a big way. Newcastle's directors in fact sanctioned a British record fee of £1,950 to be paid for Bury's centre-forward Billy Hibbert in October 1911. The Gigg Lane club were then in the top flight and Hibbert was highly rated, having recently won an England cap and registering no fewer than 34 goals on an FA tour to South Africa. With Bury, the 27-year-old's record was first rate: 105 goals in 188 appearances. He had been a regular scorer for five seasons in the centre-forward role. His signature was a prized one, as several clubs wanted to secure his outstanding ability.

Born near Wigan, Hibbert's stay at St. James' Park was a perplexing one. He was a proven No. 9 yet was generally not used in that role – only a third of his 159 games for the Magpies were at centre-forward. Billy, at 5 ft 8 in. tall, was nimble, enthusiastic and a skilful forward, but was often played at inside-forward; in fact he played across the forward line in every position except outside-right. Billy still scored goals, recording 50 for United. But he had more to offer as his record with Bury proved. During his early days at Gallowgate, he netted eight goals in five consecutive games as the attack's spearhead. Had he been given the centre-forward role on a permanent basis, maybe Hibbert could have been another centre-forward legend in a black and white shirt. As it was, United brought in other players to try to fill the gap left by Shepherd's injury; however, they did not grab the opportunity.

Tynesider Jack Peart had been plundering goals in the lower divisions and he returned home to Gallowgate for a £600 fee from Stoke in March 1912. A strong leader with a bustling style, he only briefly stayed in his native North-east but proved his worth elsewhere, appearing for the Football League eleven in a long, much-travelled career. Tom Hall arrived from neighbours Sunderland in May 1913 and had a breathtaking start in Magpie colours, scoring against his old club in a white-hot derby at Roker Park. From Newburn, he was a play-anywhere forward and filled in across the attack in the years up to the First World War.

In May 1914, United tried West Bromwich Albion's leader Bob Pailor for a substantial fee of £1,550. He had an impressive strike-rate with Albion – a goal ratio of success every two games, 47 in 92 outings. He helped the Midlands club to the Second Division title in 1911 and to the FA Cup final a year later. Possessing pace and agility, Bob soon went down with a kidney illness, which had previously left him with only one organ functioning. With war clouds hovering, his career with United was soon to be halted after only five goals in a black and white shirt. Due to a mix of circumstances the signing of Pailor had been an expensive failure.

In between all the new faces arriving at St. James' Park, Albert Shepherd was still desperately attempting to resurrect his career. During the years before the First World War put a stop to football in 1915, United's centre-forward hero made a sustained comeback. In 1913–14, Albert recovered fitness and form to such an extent that he claimed 10 goals in 20 outings. But he wasn't the same player. Sadly the injury robbed Shepherd of his edge. United allowed him to join Bradford City during the close season. Many critics and judges rated Shepherd highly. The great Charlie Buchan reckoned he was the best in the leader's role he had watched until Dixie Dean came on the scene during the 1920s.

ALBERT SHEPHERD No. 9 RATING	
Fan appeal – personality and presence	9
Strike-rate	8
Shooting – power and placement	8
Heading	7
Ball skills	7
Link-play – passing, assists, crossing, team-play	7
Pace	8
Commitment – work-rate, courage	7
Match-winner – power-play, big-match capability	9
Longevity with United	6
Trophy success, international and top football ranking	4
Total No. 9 rating	80

The First World War halted first-class football for four years. By the time Football League and FA Cup action resumed for season 1919–20, Newcastle United needed to rebuild their entire side, like just about every other club in the country, and the position of centre-forward remained a crucial role they had to fill. Shepherd had gone, so too had Hibbert and Pailor. The search was on for another player who could take up the mantle of the crowd's favourite.

UNITED'S FIRST WEMBLEY HERO

Newcastle's directors turned their attention to Scotland where football had, unlike in England, continued almost unaffected by the Great War. As conflict erupted on the Continent, a young Glaswegian began his football career. In 1913, Neil Harris was a noted centre-forward in the making, a Scottish junior international who had made the grade to first-class football by joining Partick Thistle. During the war years, he had developed into a potent striker north of the border and as a guest with Fulham, where he was a success for one season in London, helping the Cottagers to the Victory Cup final in 1919. Harris scored over 100 goals in that period and held the attention of several scouts from south of the border. He was a Thistle favourite, striking 31 goals in season 1919–20 as football got back to normal. Neil 'shone like a beacon' noted the Glasgow club's official history.

United's directors decided to bring Harris to Tyneside and in May

1920 concluded a £3,300 deal to secure the services of the 26 year old. The Scot settled in the North-east quickly and soon had United's fans cheering. He took over from stand-in centre-forward Andy Smailes, who was predominantly an inside-forward, going on to form a good partnership with local lad Smailes, hitting the net on 19 occasions in the new 1920–21 season. During October and November, Harris recorded six goals in five successive matches, including three against local rivals Sunderland as United demolished the Wearsiders 6–1 and 2–0 in the space of a week. His autumn goal spree even took United to the top of the table, and although United slipped afterwards, finishing in fifth spot, the arrival of Harris was hailed a success. One contemporary biography noted: 'He has succeeded in imparting a dash to the United forward line which was lacking.' A replacement for Shepherd had eventually been found.

NEIL HARRIS
FACTS & FIGURES

To Newcastle United: May 1920 from Partick Thistle
  £3,300
From Newcastle United: November 1925 to Notts County
  £3,000
Born: Glasgow 30 October 1894
Died: Swindon 3 December 1941
Height: 5 ft 7 in.
Scotland international: 1 app, 0 goals
Other senior clubs: Oldham Athletic, Third Lanark
Newcastle United app and goals:
  Football League: 174 app, 87 goals
  FA Cup: 20 app, 14 goals
  Total: 194 app, 101 goals
Strike-rate: League and Cup 52%

Another good return of 23 goals was recorded in the following programme as United – and Harris – again had a decent season. Neil wasn't a big striker nor was he a naturally gifted footballer. He stood at only 5 ft 7 in. tall, but possessed a solid frame and the natural aggression of someone born into Glasgow's heart of Tollcross. The Scot was fast, had a fierce shot and the eye for the slightest opening around the box. Neil, with his flowing locks of hair, was described by one writer during the era as being a forward 'possessing the quintessence of dash'.

Season 1922–23 again promised much as Newcastle kept in touch at the top of the First Division, but as in the previous two years could not make a sustained bid for silverware. Harris scored only 14 goals that term and his form deserted him for much of the campaign. In an era when supporters were quick to criticise any player, even their own stars, he received a degree of Geordie stick from the Gallowgate crowd and this continued during the first half of the following season, 1923–24. It appeared that Neil had perhaps lost his touch and his days at St. James' Park were becoming numbered. But the Scot answered the terrace taunts in dramatic style – leading the Magpies on an FA Cup run with a return to tip-top form and ultimately becoming one of the earliest Wembley heroes.

As the new year of 1924 opened the Magpies were just off the chasing pack in the title race, in sixth position. Results had improved from an October slump and up front Harris was supported by two fellow Scotsmen, inside-forwards Tom McDonald and Willie Cowan, while on the flanks Jimmy Low was another from north of the border along with Stan Seymour – although a County Durham lad – a player who had made his name with Greenock Morton. The tartan attack clicked as the FA Cup returned to action and Harris in particular found his shooting boots, striking eight goals in nine matches that catapulted the Magpies to the country's new national stadium at Wembley.

An ever-present in the cup run, he led the line masterfully. Harris grabbed a goal in the opening round against Portsmouth, a well earned 4–2 victory at Fratton Park, and then was a central figure in the four-game marathon with Derby County – hitting a stunning hat-trick in the deciding contest. The Scot was instrumental as the Black'n'Whites defeated Watford and Liverpool then bulged the net when it mattered in the semi-final and final to become Tyneside's FA Cup victor.

Against Derby stalemate had resulted in three thrilling contests and in the fourth meeting – at St. James' Park – the Magpies were on the rack, a goal down and heading out of the tournament. Enter Neil Harris who took on the County defence almost single handed. Inside 24 minutes the Scot ripped home 3 eye-catching and dazzling goals. Firstly, on 20 minutes he took a pass from Tom McDonald in the middle of the park. Neil had the confidence to take on and beat full-back Chandler before setting off on a race for goal. The other full-back, Crilly, came across to try and shepherd Harris away from goal and he seemed as if he was successful until United's centre-forward managed to get in a low, angled drive that flashed across goalkeeper Ben Olney and into the net.

Then 12 minutes later McIntyre, the Derby right-half, handled the ball a few yards outside his own penalty area. The visiting defenders formed a five-man wall but Harris tried his luck, blasting a shot goalwards. It gained a slight deflection off the wall and flew past Olney. Just before half-time Seymour embarked on a brilliant solo run from the halfway line leaving three defenders floundering in his wake. He played the ball to Harris who, with a lack of control, seemed as if he had let the chance slip. But he suddenly shot on the half-turn and fired past Olney for a third time.

Harris also played a key part in the semi-final victory over Manchester City at St Andrews, Birmingham, during March. In front of a 50,039 crowd, United's centre-forward was the focus of a United rally either side of half-time that clinched a place at Wembley. He first had a long drive saved well, then the post came to City's rescue when a Harris header thumped against the woodwork. But a minute before the interval a Hampson free-kick was headed on and came through a cluster of players. Harris was alert to screw the ball to the left of City keeper Jim Mitchell. He 'pivoted on his right heel and swept it into the corner of the net with his left foot'. From a half-hit shot, the ball deceived the stranded goalie and rolled slowly into the net to put United 1–0 ahead. Seven minutes after half-time, the Scot was back to clinch United's place in the final. Newcastle won another free-kick; this time Seymour flighted a deep cross for Harris to beat Mitchell with his head at the far post as he stole in unmarked.

And so to the Empire Stadium at Wembley, north London, which was to rapidly become the new home of football and soon a favourite jaunt for Tyneside's masses. Built a year earlier on the spot of a gigantic steel structure that was planned to rival the Eiffel Tower but which never got past the first stage, Wembley was initially part of the Empire Exhibition. It was the biggest fair the United Kingdom had ever known, sprawling 216 acres over Wembley Park, then a small leafy suburb of the capital. The exhibition, a vast advertisement to a declining British Empire, coincided with the Geordie's first invasion of north London.

By now Harris was at the peak of his form and had not played better at any point during his 11 years in senior football. The season had seen the Magpie's centre-forward grab 22 goals – and there was room for one more from his shooting boots, the most important of his career. In an entertaining final-tie against Aston Villa, Harris banged home the goal that mattered late into the match, the opening strike that broke the stalemate and stopped the final running into extra time. It gave the Magpies the incentive to seal victory.

Harris had a fabulous game beneath the Twin Towers. Had man-of-the-match awards been around back in 1924 then the Scot would certainly have won the accolade. Press comment was universally praising and he gave Villa's respected centre-half, Dr Vic Milne, a torrid afternoon. The *Northern Echo* reporter wrote: 'As a quality specialist, Neil Harris may not be 22-carat, but what he doesn't know about making the opposition take care of him isn't worth talking about.

'He gave Dr Milne a very hot plateful, and Moss and Smart were very careful to get the ball away quickly if they ever thought that Harris was looking into their larder.'

Harris was unorthodox and sometimes erratic, but always dangerous. Another member of the press on that day noted: 'Harris was the stormy petrel of the forward line and was always a thorn in the flesh of the Villa defence.' The *Sports Argus* made the comment: 'Harris was a great forager, and never gave up his attempts to get through on his own.'

It was in the closing seven minutes of the contest that Harris and his colleagues struck to take the FA Cup back to Tyneside. United's centre-forward started a move with Tom McDonald in their own half, inter-passing before feeding Seymour on the flank. The Newcastle winger in turn passed to McDonald again who tried a 12-yard shot, but keeper Tommy Jackson made a good block at full stretch. The ball ran loose and Harris was on the spot. The Scot 'pounced upon it and scored a lovely goal', the ball crashing into the left corner of the net from a thundering shot.

With only minutes left on the referee's watch, Newcastle stormed forward again. Stan Seymour received the ball, cut towards goal and crashed a high drive into the net off the woodwork.

Newcastle had lifted the FA Cup and the first glory day at Wembley was joyfully experienced by players and supporters alike. Harris, meanwhile, capped a marvellous season by being selected by his country for his first international, in the prestige Auld Enemy meeting with England, and at Wembley too. At the time, the England versus Scotland clash was, next to the FA Cup final, the biggest fixture of the season. Harris led the line for the Scots and played well in a 1–1 draw and gave England's pivot – and by coincidence United centre-half Charlie Spencer – a torrid 90 minutes. United's centre-forward was a worry all afternoon and *The Times* noted that 'the occasion proved too big for Spencer'.

NEIL HARRIS	
No. 9 RATING	
Fan appeal – personality and presence	7
Strike-rate	5
Shooting – power and placement	7
Heading	7
Ball-skills	7
Link-play – passing, assists, crossing, team-play	7
Pace	8
Commitment – work-rate, courage	8
Match-winner – power-play, big-match capability	8
Longevity with United	5
Trophy success, international and top football ranking	3
Total No. 9 rating	72

In the aftermath of FA Cup glory, Harris and Newcastle had another satisfactory season in 1924–25. The Magpies finished in sixth place and Neil hit the net on 20 occasions, approaching a century of goals for United in the process. During September, he registered hat-tricks against Blackburn and West Ham United in the space of three home games. By the start of the 1925–26 season, Neil was into his 30s and his pace had begun to wane. Youngsters Jimmy Loughlin and Tom Mordue took over the centre-forward role for a spell as the club's board searched for a replacement. Loughlin, from Darlington, made the headlines in only his second outing for the first eleven, banging home a hat-trick against Leicester City at St. James' Park. But United's board of directors were intent on bringing a star centre-forward to Tyneside. As Harris departed to pull on the other black and white stripes, those of Notts County, in November 1925 for a £3,000 fee, United searched around the football scene for a replacement – with an open cheque-book. They did look at Tranmere's big and bustling leader, Ralph 'Dixie' Dean who actually made a trip to Gallowgate before deciding to remain on Merseyside and soon after sign for Everton. The Magpies also fancied Southampton's Bill Rawlings. But they soon focused their attention on their favourite hunting ground, over the Cheviots and on another Scot – a centre-forward who became, like Dean, one of the game's all-time greats.

No. 9 EXTRAS

EARLY DEATH
Jimmy Logan's time at Loughborough Town – then a Football League outfit – ended in tragedy. Sadly, only two years after his moment of FA Cup glory on the country's biggest stage, he died in 1896 after appearing for his club against Newton Heath. Without any football kit, which had mysteriously failed to turn up, the players had to scrape around for suitable garments and Logan ended up playing in his own clothes in torrential rain – and he had to wear the same clothes afterwards. Logan developed a chill which turned to pneumonia and it claimed his life, a sudden and shock death at the time.

PEDDIE – AFTER TOON
Joining Manchester United just after that club's reformation from Newton Heath in 1902, Jock Peddie actually played in the very first game under the now famous title. He was a success at United's old Bank Street arena in the same moody genius way, scoring more goals, 58 in 121 games over 2 spells. He spent a year with Plymouth Argyle in between and eventually concluded his British career with Hearts in 1907. Afterwards, Peddie headed for North America where he played and coached football. He remained in the States until his death in Detroit in October 1928.

LEGEND ALIVE AND KICKING
While United's tradition of fielding notable centre-forwards was born at the beginning of the twentieth century it became a noteworthy topic among the football world during the 1920s, as recorded by former United skipper Colin Veitch. In a newspaper column, the eminent 'Novocastrian' eulogised over Newcastle's famous centre-forwards. He wrote: 'Have you ever looked at the list?' Veitch added: 'Gaze at it! Peddie, Bob McColl, Appleyard, Shepherd, Hibbert and now Hughie Gallacher – all in the matter of 30 years.'

TOFFEE BOB

After leaving St. James' Park, Bob McColl continued to play for another five years with Rangers and Queen's Park before retiring in 1910. McColl hailed from an educated family and the Scot formed a successful confectionary business with his brother in Glasgow, founding the R.S. McColl confectionary and later newsagents chain, which still has nationwide outlets today carrying his name. He was nicknamed 'Toffee Bob' after a particular brand of his sweets. By the mid-'20s his burgeoning empire had 150 shops in Northern England and Scotland. The business was sold to the Cadbury Group before the Second World War.

REARGUARD EFFORT

Bill Appleyard was a huge figure of a man. Against his former club Grimsby Town in January 1906 he played an important part in the club's 6–0 FA Cup triumph and scored a very unusual goal. A cross was fired into the Mariners' box but most of the players thought the ball had gone out of play. They stopped, expecting a halt in the action. Appleyard half-stopped and casually struck out his sizeable behind as the ball came into the danger area. It struck his backside and bounced into the net with the Grimsby keeper standing watching with a smile! But the referee awarded a goal, to the astonishment of both sets of players, supporters – and Appleyard himself!

A TERROR TO KEEPERS

While Bill Appleyard was not a six-foot-plus centre-forward he was built like the period Dreadnought battleship and was a terror to opposing goalkeepers. They hated the sight of Big Bill and his powerful muscular frame. Then unprotected from almost any sort of charge by forwards, goalkeepers had to put up with the rough stuff and Appleyard, in particular, always tried to put the keeper in the net, as well as the ball. He was involved in frequent goalmouth skirmishes as he barged into the unfortunate keepers time and time again.

BIG BILL – AFTER TOON

Eventually returning to Grimsby Town following a short spell with Oldham, Bill Appleyard retired in 1909 and headed back to Tyneside where he became a popular character, settling in the city's west end and working at the giant Vickers armament factory. He died in Newcastle in January 1958.

SHEPHERD POWER

Albert Shepherd possessed terrific shooting power, having one of the most forceful shots in the business. One old-time United supporter recalled: 'I saw Shepherd score with one shot struck so hard it carried the keeper over the line and into the net!' Shepherd also had the knack of striking not only three goals, but four in a single match for United – he did it on five occasions for the Black'n'Whites and once for the Football League XI against Scotland in 1906.

SHEPHERD – AFTER TOON

Albert retired from the game during the First World War in 1916, and settled in Bolton. He became a well-known landlord at the Crown & Cushion public house, a personality in the town. With the football regime behind him, Shepherd soon put on an enormous amount of weight and became characterised for his substantial frame. He lived life to the full, smoked like a chimney and drank plenty of his own ale. He died in Bolton in 1929.

FOOTBALLING FAMILY

Neil Harris hailed from a notable footballing family. His brother, Josh, appeared for Leeds United as well as Fulham and Bristol City, clocking up over 450 senior matches, while his son, John Harris, became a famous Chelsea player and later a respected Sheffield United manager. He was the Londoners' skipper and totalled 473 games for the Blues over 14 seasons. Another son, Neil junior, also appeared for Swindon Town.

HARRIS – AFTER TOON

Concluding his playing career back in Scotland with Third Lanark, Neil Harris turned to coaching and management initially with Burton Town, then in Ireland with Distillery. In July 1934, he was appointed manager at Swansea Town and just before the Second World War became boss at the County Ground, home of Swindon Town. He died in that town in 1941.

2. THE SCOT WITH THE MAGIC FEET
1925–1930

HUGHIE GALLACHER

When football's authorities decided to implement a significant change to the rules of the game by introducing a revised offside law during the close season of 1925, clubs with goalscoring aces and a potent attack were to reap the benefit. Strikers, and centre-forwards in particular, found a novel freedom as an innovative 3–2–5 outfield formation was unveiled to counter the new rules that saw the demise of the old two-back game.

Newcastle United were at that time on the lookout for a young leader to replace the ageing Neil Harris, and during the opening months of the 1925–26 season their search intensified, as reserve strikers on the books – Willie Scott, Jimmy Loughlin and youngster Albert Pigg – failed to impress in either Football League or North Eastern League action. United's officials had to find a bright centre-forward to take advantage of the new style of football that brought a cascade of goals. Having watched Airdrie's up-and-coming goalscoring sensation, Hughie Gallacher, who had bagged 39 goals for Airdrie in season 1923–24 and was on course to record a 30-plus tally again, United's scouts were soon drooling over the Scot recognised then as

46

'one of the greatest discoveries made in Scotland'. Directors John Graham and Bob McKenzie made frequent visits to assess Gallacher's capability, but they faced a mighty difficult task to persuade the Airdrie club to part with their star player.

At the time, Gallacher's club were second only to Glasgow Rangers north of the border. The Airdrieonians had lifted the Scottish Cup in 1924 and finished runners-up on three occasions in succession from 1923 to 1925. As speculation increased as to Gallacher's possible transfer, the Airdrie fans began demonstrations and were vociferous in making sure club officials knew their opinion. Indeed, there were even threats to burn down the Broomfield Park grandstand should Gallacher be sold. Yet, despite the opposition, in the end there was nothing anyone could do to stop Newcastle's persistence in their bid to land Gallacher's signature. The Geordies were hugely impressed with his talent and were determined not to fail in attracting him to Tyneside.

United were not alone in the scramble to bring Gallacher to England. The Scot's goalscoring talent and football skills were in prime demand with rich English clubs tumbling over one another to watch him. Although only a mere 5 ft 5 in. tall, he was fast, elusive and difficult to knock off the ball . . . and he was slick in the short pass as well as brilliant at making chances for others. Although he was a touch volatile, he had netted 100 goals in his 129 senior games in Scotland. Gallacher had the potential to become a top crowd-puller. Sunderland wanted him, while Everton and two of London's big sides, Arsenal and Chelsea, were linked with the chase too. It was the Magpies, though, who persisted against a dogged resistance by Airdrie not to lose their prized asset. Sent packing by Airdrie directors on several occasions, United would not take no for an answer, and soon Hughie Gallacher was to be a Newcastle player . . . the start of a fabulous five-year reign at Gallowgate.

Long-serving Newcastle United secretary, Frank Watt, said of the Gallacher transfer saga: 'It took weeks, aye months of parleying, repeated confabs, almost innumerable rebuts, and the most painfully fluctuating negotiations before we pulled off the deal.' United were represented at many Airdrie fixtures, and everyone knew it. On the first occasion directors McKenzie and Graham – both well known in Scotland for their raiding – trekked north, they witnessed Gallacher net two beauties. Hughie remembered: 'It was impossible to tell how many times they watched me. It would be idle for me to tell you that I was unaware of their presence.' Gallacher was very ambitious and although he loved playing for Airdrie, wanted a big move south. He never pushed for it, but never hinted that he would reject an approach.

Newcastle United became as equally determined to sign him as Airdrie were to resist all offers. On a visit to Lanarkshire during November 1925, they saw Airdrie's master goal-poacher have another superb game and the Geordie directors decided there and then that they must get their man whatever the cost. The following week United's party travelled north to ambush the Airdrie mid-week board meeting. Secretary Watt accompanied McKenzie and Graham and the trio received a frosty reception at Broomfield Park. But the Tynesiders' delegation stuck with the task and eventually was granted an interview with the Airdrie board. Their tactics were to overwhelm the opposition and lay hard cash on the table – with the hope that a mountain of pound notes would demolish even the stiffest of principles. The tactic worked a treat. As soon as Airdrie's directors mentioned the figure of £6,000, Newcastle jumped in and offered even more! Airdrie's officials were shocked. They readily agreed to the sum.

Hughie Gallacher did not take much persuasion to cross the border. He related in his memoirs: 'England had always seemed to offer the greatest opportunities, and though I was only a lad, I soon decided to accept the move.' At a late hour on the 8 December 1925 a telephone message was received by the remainder of United's eagerly waiting officials back on Tyneside. Gallacher had agreed terms and what was considered a record fee had been established.

That transfer amount was the subject of much speculation. A week before, Sunderland had just paid £6,550 for Bob Kelly to create a national record. On the news of the Gallacher deal, wild rumours spread. A sum of £10,000 was mentioned; the *Newcastle Daily Chronicle* noted that '£7,000 is generally the accepted sum', but in the custom of the day, the actual fee was never released. The club's official comment was: 'The sum paid is the club's business and theirs alone.' In the record books to date the fee is recorded as £6,500. This seems on the low side and it appears that Kelly's record could have been topped, although Newcastle United's official player ledger actually pens the transaction at less, £5,500.

Tyneside's press heralded Gallacher's arrival as the coup of the decade. United were congratulated on signing 'the most famous centre-forward of the day'. They reaped praise in every newspaper. One noted: 'Newcastle United Football Club has affected the smartest stroke of football business that has been transacted in modern times.' The 22-year-old son of a Protestant Irishman from the rugged working heartland of Lanarkshire, in Bellshill, joined a more than competent Newcastle squad. The club wanted the Football League Championship title and Gallacher was going to fill the missing link that would bring the trophy back to Tyneside. He was a vital acquisition and few doubted that the Scot would succeed in English football.

Gallacher arrived in Newcastle to be received by a posse of media. A local journalist pen-named 'Horoward', remarked on his arrival in the city that he is 'a quiet spoken pleasant young fellow'. Another said Gallacher possessed a 'boyish appearance'. Frank Watt noted as he arrived that he was 'just a slip of a lad, but we knew that Hughie had ability'. He definitely did. United's respected administrator was to say at the end of Hughie's time at Gallowgate, five years later, that Hughie was 'the greatest football individualist I have ever known'.

HUGHIE GALLACHER
FACTS & FIGURES

To Newcastle United: December 1925 from Airdrie
  £6,500
From Newcastle United: May 1930 to Chelsea £10,000
Born: Bellshill 2 February 1903
Died: Gateshead 11 June 1957
Height: 5 ft 5 in.
Other senior clubs: Queen of the South, Derby County,
  Notts County, Grimsby Town, Gateshead
Scotland international: 20 app, 24 goals
Newcastle United app & goals:
  Football League: 160 app, 133 goals
  FA Cup: 14 app, 10 goals
  Total: 174 app, 143 goals
Strike-rate: League and Cup 82%

It was the start of 14 seasons in English soccer for Gallacher, a period of much glory, over 300 goals south of the border and numerous sensations. He was a rough, tough little centre-forward. To many who saw his footballing repertoire he was the best centre-forward of all time. Better than Dean, Lawton, Lofthouse, McGrory, or any other exalted striker over the years. Some may have been bigger and more forceful but none had the quite brilliant all-round ability of Gallacher. He was a headline maker and fans either loved or hated him, while the media adored him, always being the subject of a story – for better or for worse. As Gallacher put it: 'I was branded a trouble maker, stormy petrel, problem player . . . these were just a few of the lesser things said of me.' He was also handed plenty of favourable press comment too and became the most talked about player in the game.

Gallacher's debut in the black and white centre-forward shirt was a First Division encounter with Everton at St. James' Park in December. The game turned out to be a thrilling contest between two good sides that ended 3–3 in front of a 36,000 crowd. Gallowgate bubbled over with expectation before kick-off. As the players came out, the Newcastle fans had their first view of Gallacher, a player who was to become a Geordie centre-forward hero like few others since. Hughie said: 'The home fans cheered the first few players tremendously. As I ran out, the deafening cheers turned to a . . . oh! The crowd had just noticed how small I was. Never had I been more aware of my size!'

At 5 ft 5 in. tall, he hardly looked like a footballer who was to take the Magpies to silverware. But Tyneside's initial disappointment was quickly dispelled. Gallacher immediately got into his stride netting two goals and laying on United's other for winger Stan Seymour. Centre-half Charlie Spencer later recalled Hughie's first appearance: 'Gallacher had a big name in Scotland but we were staggered by his size. Then soon after the match began I turned and gave my fellow defenders a thumbs-up signal. We knew a real star had joined us.'

Gallacher's first goal in a Toon shirt came on the half-hour. Willie Gibson sent the ball to the edge of the box. Gallacher had his back to goal, took the pass, pivoted in one movement, then darted between the Everton backs and swept the ball past goalkeeper Harry Hardy as he advanced. It was a classic.

United should have won the fixture with ease, but ahead 3–1, defensive mistakes allowed the Merseysiders to make a comeback. All three Everton goals came from a young future England leader, Dixie Dean, to be Gallacher's great contemporary over the next decade. The *Evening Chronicle* enjoyed Hughie's display. 'Hereward' wrote: 'First impressions of Gallacher were distinctly favourable. No sooner did he touch the ball than one sensed the artistic player. Dwarfed in stature by the Everton backs, he had little or no chance in the air, but on the ground he showed some masterly touches. There were times when he beat three or four men by clear dribbling. Newcastle have found a leader of real quality.'

The crowd were also well pleased with the first showing of the Gallacher talent. He had impressed the Geordie public, and the Scot later noted: 'Just before the match ended I realised I had been taken to the hearts of the big crowd. During a lull in play, a fog-horn voice roared across the ground . . . Howay Wor Hughie!' That roar was to be heard over and over again at Gallowgate during the next five years and Gallacher was to relate. 'Many hundreds of times more was I to hear that inspiring roar from those soccer-mad fans.'

Gallacher shared digs at Whitley Bay with teammates and fellow Scots, Willie Cowan, Roddie MacKenzie and Joe Harris. Tyneside at that time was in severe depression, much like Lanarkshire. Unemployment was high and the General Strike was but a few months away. Yet football – and especially Gallacher's skills – brought smiles to the hard-working folk of the North-east. Hughie, brought up in similar surroundings and around similar people, felt at ease and he quickly settled on Tyneside.

United's new centre-forward was rapidly to exploit the modified offside law as defenders took time to adjust to the untried tactics – just what United's directors had hoped for. A forward's paradise resulted. Newcastle were now ideally placed to monopolise with Gallacher and an avant-garde breed of centre-forward came to the fore to counter the newly introduced third back – or centre-half – game, a player who was prepared to battle with the opposing centre-half and match them with wits, strength and courage.

Respected football correspondent Ivan Sharpe wrote on those new-style centre-forwards of the day: 'He manufactured his own powder and shot, and couldn't be called a model footballer.' They had to improvise, had to possess a universal game to counter man-to-man defending. Sharpe continued, 'and none has reached the all round ability and deadliness of Hughie Gallacher.' Stan Seymour, for long a colleague of the Scot, rated Gallacher as the greatest footballer he ever saw. Seymour said: 'Hughie had everything. He was a little chap yet he had springs in his feet to beat the big men in the air. Hughie had two great feet, he could shoot just as hard with either.'

And United's esteemed manager and director of later years added: 'On the ground he was unbelievable: wonderful control – the ball was seldom more than inches from his feet – which sent him past opponents, a baffling body swerve and a quickness off the mark. He had the cheek to do things with the ball that to others seemed impossible.' Seymour summed up: 'He was a master craftsman in everything he did on the field.' Gallacher was one of a revolutionary mould of centre-forwards who led the way. There were other goalgetters too, lots of them: Middlesbrough's George Camsell, Dixie Dean, as well as Jimmy Trotter of Sheffield Wednesday, Ted Harper at Blackburn, Huddersfield's George Brown, Dave Halliday at Sunderland, Joe Bradford of Birmingham and West Ham's Vic Watson to name only a handful.

In his first 8 games in a Newcastle United shirt Hughie netted an amazing 15 goals. After the opening Everton contest, United's centre-forward scored against Manchester City, then recorded a hat-trick against Liverpool and 4 against Bolton Wanderers, including 3 in the first 25 minutes. Gallacher was immediately hailed the new idol of Tyneside. A group of United fans soon presented him with a medal – a way of showing gratitude in the era – reserved usually for long-serving stalwarts, not individuals who had been at Gallowgate less than two months. The hero worship from the Geordie masses was just beginning to take off. It was to grow into perhaps the most passionate Tyneside has seen, some reckon even more fervent than Jackie Milburn's following 25 years later or Alan Shearer's almost 50 years further on.

Gallacher ended the 1925–26 season with another stunning hat-trick, over FA Cup finalists Manchester City on Tyneside. It was a crucial fixture as City needed a point to stay in the First Division. They missed a penalty, lost 3–2 and were relegated. Wee Hughie, as he was nicknamed, grabbed 25 goals in only 22 appearances for the Magpies. Over the whole season, including his Airdrie games, Gallacher totalled 34 goals. In addition, United's leader had also played twice for Scotland and scored a further three goals since his transfer. An influential player for his country during a period when the Scots dominated the Home International tournament, he registered a hat-trick against the Irish. And at the end of the season, Gallacher helped Scotland defeat England at Old Trafford to cap a marvellous year. It had been quite a campaign for him. But it was nothing compared with what was to follow.

CHAMPIONSHIP SKIPPER

On the eve of the 1926–27 season Newcastle's directors made a bold decision. They stripped full-back and veteran of over 400 games,

Frank Hudspeth, of the captaincy and appointed the young whiplash import, Hughie Gallacher, as the Black'n'Whites new skipper. The decision rose more than a few eyebrows. 'He is too young', some said, 'too inexperienced and temperamental', said others. Gallacher had the perfect answer; his character was one always to make critics eat their words. Hughie recorded in his serialised life story, 'Hughie Gallacher Tells All': 'I knew I had the confidence of a grand bunch of lads.' He went on to skipper United to the league championship title; the last occasion the Magpies have won that major and glittering prize.

The local press also had doubts at the outset of the season about United's potential up front. A question was raised: 'Are United's forwards good enough?' The answer was that they certainly were and United's attack went on to net almost 100 goals between them – the key to Newcastle United's success that year. Gallacher led the line brilliantly. Alongside Hughie were two Scots at inside-forward: Tom McDonald from Inverness, a hard-working midfielder formerly with Rangers, and Bob McKay, another former Ibrox man and future Scottish international. Both complemented Gallacher's style perfectly while wingers Tommy Urwin and Stan Seymour – both capped by England – were at the peak of their careers. The five-man front line only boasted an average height of a mere 5 ft 7 in., yet caused opposing defences havoc. And Gallacher, the leader of the midget pack, always looked for opportunities to play to the gallery. One biography of the day noted: 'Hughie is the tantalising teaser of big blustering centre-halfs, a nightmare to full-backs.' Another contemporary report extensively described his style in the mode of the day: 'He makes a beeline for goal every time, and doesn't waste time with over-elaboration. He merely dribbles within range and lets fly with either foot. His trapping and gliding forward of the ball with the same motion of the foot is something to marvel at, for he plays the ball on the carpet every time, but once he has got it then he can swerve round a player without ever touching the ball with his toes. His body does it all. He feints so naturally with his shoulders that the opponent is simply deluded.'

Gallacher got off to a tremendous start. In the opening match of the 1926–27 season, he smashed Aston Villa's offside-minded defence to pieces, scoring all the goals as Newcastle won 4–0. For the first half of the season, United looked good. They were resolute at the back and a devastating combination up front with Gallacher netting eight goals in five successive matches as Christmas approached. The Magpies were tipped in some quarters for the championship and Gallacher was the main reason. Respected magazine of the era *All Sports* noted: 'Gallacher is making Newcastle United a bigger power.' And following another four-goal strike by the impish leader against Bolton Wanderers it was declared: 'What Newcastle owes to Hughie Gallacher can scarcely be overestimated. He simply covered himself with glory.' The *Newcastle Daily Journal*'s scribe 'Novocastrian' even wondered that perhaps the Scot was superhuman and noted 'whether he did not possess more than the usual complement of feet'! Gallacher was the match-winner. For the next three seasons, he was at the peak of his career and his boundless talent showed whenever he played. He even impressed the often critical sceptics in the deep south, too.

Initial journeys to the capital did not produce anything too spectacular. But a visit to White Hart Lane with Newcastle during November 1926 made both Cockney fans and fickle media take notice. United won 3–1 and Gallacher netted a brilliant hat-trick, had another three efforts go just wide of the woodwork and a further goal disallowed. At this time, Hughie was on a goal feast. He banged home seven in four matches and was on the scoresheet in five consecutive games. Yet he was not only goal-taker, but also provider in chief. He laid on chances for both McDonald and Seymour in particular who bagged goals by the hatful too. Gallacher possessed the natural touch of the traditional Scottish 'tanna' ba'' player, creating openings for forwards good enough to read his play. McDonald and Seymour could, closing in on chances from midfield and the flank. By December, Newcastle were in the top three with the title-chasing pack of Burnley, Tottenham Hotspur, Huddersfield Town and United's North-east rivals, Sunderland.

Hughie Gallacher had been in England for 12 months and had created not only the reputation of being the most feared striker in Division One, but one that also taunted, needled and rattled the opposition defence at times with verbal abuse and niggling kicks and pokes. Much bigger 6 ft-plus defenders did not like his abrasive style one bit. Nothing can be crueller than a venomous insult about one's parentage, lack of courage, immoral way or looks delivered in a rich Lanarkshire accent from a 5 ft 5 in. mischievous and somewhat cheeky wee wisp of a Scot. No one had a tongue quite like Gallacher on the football field. Sunderland and Scotland wing-half Alex Hastings wrote that: 'I never hated anyone so much on the field.' Added to his undoubted football ability and goals threat, as a consequence he was singled out for special attention.

Gallacher was often roughly treated in Scotland, but that was nothing to the punishment that was handed out in the top flight south of the border. Gallacher became a marked man. Opposing centre-halves started not only to resort to foul means to stop his forward runs but to also bait the Scot – knowing his fury was easy to unlock and in so doing potentially getting him into trouble with referees. It was a tactic that worked a treat, time and time again. Gallacher recalled: 'My patience and quick temper were tried to the utmost by players of lesser skill.' The Scot also added. 'I'm not going to get kicked up in the air and reply with a saintly smile.'

Those much bigger defenders crashed into Hughie without thought of possible injury to the centre-forward in virtually every match played – in an era that saw referees allow much of the heavy play go unchecked. The clash of Gallacher versus the centre-half was always a talking point of the game. They kicked and punched him, and used elbows, on and off the ball. Tough men like Sam Cowan of Manchester City, Herbie Roberts of Arsenal, Jack Hill of Burnley – later to be a friend and teammate of Gallacher's at St. James' Park – Bolton's Jimmy Seddon and Sheffield United's Vince Matthews. All were internationals and all powerful giants in comparison to Gallacher. United's leader was fortunate not to suffer serious injury.

Many contemporary players recalled his battle-weary body. Scotland goalkeeper Jack Harkness said: 'I never saw any forward with as many scars and hacks.' Dozens of times he hobbled from the park with legs hacked red and varied in colour from blue to purple. Once he had to be taken to Newcastle Central Station by taxi after a bruising clash with West Ham United because he just could not walk, so harsh was the treatment. United colleague and later brother-in-law George Mathison remembered: 'You had to see his legs to believe the treatment he was given. They were pitted, scarred. You couldn't blame him for losing his cool.'

And lose his cool he did. Hughie once said: 'I am pretty tough, but not tough enough to knit wire netting or bend crowbars, or take deliberate rough usage with a smile.' Tough as he was, such rugged handling affected him, even though he got used to it. Stan Seymour noted that he even saw him at the point of tears in the dressing-room at half-time from sheer frustration. Gallacher found it difficult not to explode and hurl angry comments at his opponents – and the referee. He was the victim of retaliation and constantly had words with officials in charge.

Gallacher had to learn to live with the rough stuff as part of his game. As a consequence, he started to wear a thick pad of cotton wool under his shin pads and also had to hold his frustration, no matter how difficult it was. Hughie took the punishment with remarkable guts and bewildered opponents by coming back again and again for more. One defender of the era remarked: 'That wee fellow was not born. He was quarried.' His temper, though, he could never master. Trainer Andy McCombie once said: 'He could start an argument quicker than anyone else!' Gallacher's teammates even appointed Bob McKay as Hughie's minder on the field. As soon as there was a hint of trouble between players or officials, in stepped McKay to lead Gallacher from a potential flare-up. It worked only in part.

Rugged treatment was the norm on a Saturday afternoon. Against Aston Villa, the post-match comment was: 'The presence of Gallacher on the home side appeared to be regarded as a personal affront by the Villa defenders and their efforts to hold him led to the importation of an element of roughness into their play.' At Tottenham, events boiled over. The bodily attack on Gallacher led to a virtual free-for-all on the pitch. Tottenham's premeditated and unfair tactics towards Newcastle's centre-forward caused a huge rumpus. Finding ordinary methods to no avail, Spurs did not hesitate, as it was reported, to move 'to less reputable tactics'. The match report continued: 'Some of the contestants lost their heads in the second half and so necessitated a general warning from the referee who called all the players together.'

The continual pounding sometimes worked in Gallacher's favour too. Against Manchester City, Hughie went on one of his famed runs, beating three men with consummate ease before Sam Cowan swept in with a reckless tackle that threw Gallacher in the air. Hughie limped away, helped by his colleagues, but he had won a penalty and a resultant goal. Despite some brutal defending, Gallacher would never hide and could never give up the cause; his gritty, battling nature never allowed him to do so. He persisted no matter how many boots were launched at him and it often brought success. In a clash with West Ham United during February 1926, he opened United's account under the greatest of difficulties with tackles flying in from all sides. His second goal was a perfect triumph of mind over matter for he literally had to carry the attendant full-back with him, beating Ted Hufton with a shot that was described as 'amazing in the circumstances'.

While Gallacher never warranted the physical battering he was given for almost ten years, he was no angel. His own style of play quickly goaded the opposition. The Scot would always make sure his opponents knew he was around and a rough tackle on him would be remembered. In that notorious match with Tottenham, centre-half Jack Elkes dished out a few particularly nasty fouls. Gallacher returned the compliment later into the match and Elkes had to retire to the touch-line for extensive treatment. The *Newcastle Daily Journal* went to great length debating this part of Gallacher's game and its consequences. In summing up, it was 'a price which is the unavoidable penalty of greatness'.

On his travels around the country with the Magpies, opposing supporters were quick to barrack and hurl insults at the Scot. They taunted him and admittedly Hughie often played to them, enraging the crowd with a piece of trickery or cheeky showmanship. Despite all the bruises and abuse he received in torrents from away spectators who craved to bait the Scot, Gallacher battled on. He only missed four games of the Magpies' 1926–27 season. As the New Year opened, United hit peak form. They went to the top of the table following an exhilarating run which saw them record six victories in a row. They also started well in the FA Cup, with an 8–1 thrashing of Notts County at St. James' Park – Gallacher scoring a hat-trick within the first 45 minutes, even though handicapped with a temperature of over a hundred degrees just before the kick-off. That game featured one of his finest goals, balancing the ball on his head for a few seconds before allowing it to drop and volleying into the net. The duel of Wee Hughie, at 5 ft 5 in. up against famous Notts County goalkeeper Albert Iremonger, almost 6 ft 6 in. and nearly 14 stone, was a bizarre sight.

The Tynesiders continued in fine form defeating the noted public school and university combination, The Corinthians, in the FA Cup before being surprisingly knocked out by Southampton in the 5th round. But United's league form did not desert the side. Gallacher went on the rampage. Against Everton, a crowd of 45,000 saw United win 7–3, with another 3-goal strike from the Scotsman – the first of 10 goals in a 6-match spell which set the Magpies up nicely for the championship trophy. Included in those goals was another Gallacher classic, this time at Ewood Park against Blackburn Rovers in a 2–1 victory.

Influential winger Stan Seymour reckoned it was the greatest he scored for Newcastle United. The club's future director, manager and chairman later recounted the goal: 'I remember I passed the ball to Hughie and sent him off on a 30-yard dribble down the wing. I tore down the middle. The goalkeeper came out to narrow the angle expecting, like me, that Hughie would send the ball over as I had a clear shot at goal. That was too simple. Hughie pushed the ball gently through the goalkeeper's legs.' It was typical Gallacher. He would never be afraid to try the unexpected and spectacular. Most times it came off; the mark of a genius.

The championship race was now between three clubs: Huddersfield Town – winners of the title for the previous three seasons – Sunderland and United. And it was Gallacher who led the charge on the trophy. Having defeated Everton and Blackburn Rovers, the Magpies then met their North-east foes in a decisive clash during March. A record gate of 67,211 gathered at Gallowgate to watch the top of the table clash and a goal by Gallacher – who else – was enough to seal the points for United. He converted a McDonald- and Lang-inspired attack in the 32nd minute by wheeling round and striking a shot into the bottom corner of the net, off a post. Gallacher went past Albert Shepherd's previous best goalscoring return in a season by passing his 30th of the campaign. But Hughie wasn't finished yet – he kept on scoring.

That win over Sunderland sent Newcastle to two more victories, 6–1 against Arsenal – with a Gallacher hat-trick – and a 3–1 success over Bury, bringing the Black'n'Whites into the vital Easter programme in confident mood and to an equally crucial double with reigning champions, Huddersfield Town, the team of the era.

Another massive crowd packed into United's Barrack Road stadium. A gate of 62,500 saw the battle of Challengers versus Holders and once more Hughie Gallacher was the ace in the pack and the difference between the teams. Just after half-time he found the net following a brilliant neck-twisting effort once Seymour had nodded the ball across goal from a move started by Bob McKay. Wee Hughie was challenged by near-6 ft England stopper Tom Wilson, and to the end of his day the Huddersfield Town centre-half never knew how Gallacher jumped above him. Although the Terriers won the return contest, also by a single goal, Newcastle had a lead in the championship race. They were almost there.

The Black'n'Whites defeated Tottenham 3–2 at Gallowgate and needed a point from a trip to Upton Park and a meeting with West Ham, on 23 April. United gained a 1–1 draw and were hailed as

Football League Champions at St. James' Park 7 days later when United entertained Sheffield Wednesday. United's prolific leader scored both goals in the 2–1 victory to bring his tally to an amazing 39 in 41 games for the season – a new club record and one that stood for 67 years, until another centre-forward sensation, Andy Cole, broke the 40-goal barrier in season 1993–94.

Gallacher received the championship trophy and winner's medal at a later presentation. There were no city-centre parades and no mass celebration. The Football League Championship although a very worthy trophy to land – was then distinctly second in importance to the glamour of the FA Cup . . . and was to be for many decades to follow.

Skipper Gallacher had answered his critics. So too had United's pocket-sized forward-line. Apart from Gallacher, Tom McDonald knocked in 23 goals and Stan Seymour registered 19 – a club record by a winger. Newcastle possessed wonderful team spirit led by the captivating character of Gallacher with all his rough edges. One description noted he 'won fame for his craft, his cunning and his equally amusing and startling personality'. The *Northern Echo*'s correspondent summed up the Scot's contribution: 'In Hughie Gallacher, their centre-forward and captain, they possess a footballer and leader who stands alone in the matter of skill. It was largely due to his brilliancy and the support he derived from his colleagues that Newcastle United gained the League honours.'

Gallacher was a centre-forward who had everything. Distinguished writer for many years, Arthur Appleton, wrote in *Hotbed of Soccer*: 'He stood out as a genius at the game and his superb skill brought moments of joy and unforgettable memories to those who saw him.' He possessed the talent to perform the unexpected and could feint and slip past defenders at ease. He was dangerous from any position near to goal, scoring from seemingly impossible angles, while his shooting was perhaps his greatest natural gift. Hughie had amazing strength in his short, stocky legs and could hit a ball with immense power without much of a back-swing. Another of his greatest gifts was a toughness of spirit and gritty determination. He worked tirelessly for the side, Scotland colleague Bob McPhail writing that he 'seemed to be everywhere, positioning himself for a pass, chasing for the ball, challenging an opponent double his size'. Even his obvious weakness of being so short didn't appear to hinder his play. Seemingly always surrounded by giants, Gallacher was difficult to knock off the ball and could often outjump much bigger defenders, having a prodigious spring in his legs that propelled him upwards.

If Hughie had one weakness, apart from his firebrand temperament, it was perhaps that he tended to elaborate too much with fancy dribbles at times. The *Evening Chronicle*'s correspondent, 'Sentinel', once noted that Gallacher sometimes had a 'tendency with the super-dribbler – that of holding onto the ball just too long, or becoming so involved in his own trickery as to waste the opportunity created'. Gallacher said of his mazy runs that occasionally ended in a cul-de-sac: 'On most occasions there was method in my madness.'

It was, in fact, a marvellous year for the North-east all round. Apart from United's triumph, Sunderland finished in third spot, while Middlesbrough were Second Division champions. Everywhere in the region the talk was of football, and nobody loved it more than Hughie Gallacher. Now idolised on Tyneside, he strutted proudly round the pubs and nightspots of the city and was dubbed the best-dressed young man in the north. Snappily donned out in well-tailored suits and white spats, he often sported a fedora or black bowler and a tightly rolled umbrella. Hughie was a complete '20s dandy. He opened garden parties, graced dances with his presence and adored being recognised and signing autographs. The razzmatazz was made for him. Hughie revelled in showing off and even flashed wads of money – much of it neatly cut worthless paper with a few real notes on top! Gallacher lived life to the full. He often accepted drinks from friends and fans eager to speak to the great man, and also the charms of adoring Geordie women. But despite all the outward signs of a brash, rich and successful sportsman, he always had feelings for the underprivileged. Hughie was a soft-hearted individual and of kind character. Once, when he was waiting for a train at the city's Central Station, he took pity on a poor-looking soul huddled in a corner. Over Gallacher went. He took off his expensive overcoat and gave it to the man: one of the city's down and outs.

Gallacher lived hard, socialising constantly. There were many stories of his habitual drinking and he once ended up in court after a punch-up under the flickering gas lights of one of the Tyne's bridges. But he never forgot his football, the game that had put him where he was. He trained equally hard and never let it be said that his high-jinks around Tyneside affected his game. Even when he had a drink too many he was fit for the Saturday afternoon kick-off. Tales of Gallacher's Friday night sessions were common. Trainer and ex-United international full-back, Andy McCombie, related to future No. 9 hero Albert Stubbins how Gallacher 'would often be canned up on a Friday then on the Saturday score three or even four goals'!

TOON'S WEMBLEY WIZARD

The following 1927–28 season saw Gallacher hit the headlines again when the legend of the Wembley Wizards was created. At the time, the Scottish international side boasted a sensational post-war record. In 21 games since 1919, they had recorded 17 wins, 3 draws and only 4 defeats. The Scots held superior status over Ireland and Wales, and especially over the Auld Enemy, England – then the only match in the international calendar that really mattered.

Gallacher had entered international action in 1924 and had been a regular for the Scots, appearing in ten internationals to season 1927–28. Hughie was his country's spearhead up front. He had registered nine goals and only been on the losing side once, that against England the previous season. By the time the much-awaited annual battle of the Scots against the English was to take place at Wembley in 1928, Gallacher and Co. were ready for a spot of revenge. Indeed, Scotland reached the peak of their dominance on that March afternoon.

While Newcastle's centre-forward didn't get onto the scoresheet, he played a major part in the Scots' celebrated 5–1 victory. The Wembley Wizards were born, giving 'an exhibition of scientific football that was a revelation'. Alongside other Caledonian men of genius, players like Alex James, Jimmy McMullan, Alec Jackson and Alan Morton, Gallacher tore the English apart.

In fact Hughie almost missed that now famous and historic Wembley occasion, as prior to the international he was in the news again – this time for the wrong reasons. Gallacher was handed a controversial and sensational two-month suspension by the football authorities due to continued altercations with defenders, and more importantly, referees. Knowing his temperament was on a short fuse, defenders constantly worked at him, with the result that Hughie often became involved in skirmishes . . . and just as often received a finger-wagging from referees. But Gallacher could never stop the debate. Most players are clever enough to save any remarks to the referee until he is out of earshot, but Gallacher could not do that. He made sure the official knew exactly what he thought of him, eye to eye, and paid the penalty! He later recorded in his memoirs: 'I realise I should have made greater efforts to hold my tongue.'

In refereeing circles, Gallacher quickly built a reputation for himself and was more sinned against than most. Hughie said: 'I was a regular topic among them and some, I'm sure, judged me before I set foot on the pitch.' He constantly complained to officials on the field – whining, arguing and giving his opinion – mostly about the rough treatment he received. But that was not all. Hughie would question most decisions: free-kicks, throw-ins and especially penalty claims. It was one such spot-kick appeal that got him into big trouble on New Year's Eve 1927 during a needle game with Huddersfield Town, the club United had beaten to the title the previous year.

United had comprehensively defeated the Yorkshire side at Leeds Road on the opening day of the season with Gallacher starting the new programme with a hat-trick – and the Magpie striker took some harsh treatment from the Tyke defenders in the return game during December, a tactic designed to stop the little Scot from causing any further damage. Throughout the match he persistently complained to referee Bert Fogg, one of the country's top and most respected officials. Before the game, Mr Fogg had already warned both sets of players that due to the hard, frosty surface he would not tolerate heavy challenges. But as the game got under way, the referee did not act when the tackles began flying in and this incensed Hughie, justly so perhaps, as he was on the receiving end of most of them.

His complaints though were to no avail and then in the closing period of the game Huddersfield went ahead 2–3 with a penalty – a debatable and controversial decision according to the home camp and one that caused Gallacher to blow his top! Moments later the Newcastle leader himself was felled in the box by Levi Redfern. 'Penalty', was the cry, but Fogg would have none of it, despite the waving of a linesman's flag. Gallacher completely lost what was left of his cool and howled repeatedly at the Bolton official in his Lanarkshire dialect, continuing to do so for the few minutes remaining of the match.

As recorded by Hughie in his memoirs, the referee threatened to book him. Gallacher noted that Mr Fogg asked: 'What's your name?' Hughie replied annoyingly: 'If you don't know that, you have no business being on the field.' He added: 'And what's your name?' The referee replied: 'I'm Mr Fogg', inviting the inevitable reply from Hughie who quickly snapped with a cheeky grin: 'Yes, and you've been in one all afternoon!'

As the players trooped off, Gallacher could still be seen making his point and waving his finger at the referee. Stan Seymour later recalled that his colleague was furious, the most irate that he had ever seen him. A friend of Hughie's related what happened in the dressing-room: 'Hughie approached Mr Fogg after the match with intent to apologise. He found the official bending over to go into the bath. Hughie kicked out and pushed him in. He just couldn't resist it!' Gallacher admitted: 'I completely lost my head.'

Bert Fogg was not amused, as could be expected. Gallacher and Fogg had never been on the best of terms and now after this incident the referee reported the Scot to the Football Association in the strongest terms . . . and the FA threw the proverbial book at Hughie. On 20 January, it was announced that Gallacher had been given a two-month suspension. The FA noted in their edict that the lengthy suspension was 'for improper conduct both on the field and at the close of this match, and so having regard to his misconduct in previous matches'. It was a severe penalty that stunned everyone in the game. Normal suspensions were two or three games, or even four matches. Gallacher was out of football for fully two months. He was not even allowed a personal hearing at the Disciplinary Committee meeting. Gallacher asked an open question in the media. In the *Daily Journal*, he noted: 'Why did the FA refuse my request for a personal hearing of the charges made against me? I have not been fairly treated.' He considered strongly that he had been pronounced guilty without trial, an indication of both Football Association and Football League autocratic power at this time.

Gallacher was out of the game and was to miss seven matches for the Black'n'Whites. Additionally, he was not allowed to train and keep fit with his United teammates, nor could he receive any wages. The Scot spent the period back in Bellshill and was offered a contract by a Glasgow newspaper to comment on Scottish Cup ties – and actually made more money than his football earnings would have been!

But for this controversy it would have been another successful year for Gallacher, personally. He had reached a different level of fame as a Wembley Wizard and netted plenty of goals. He scored 11 in his first 11 games for United as the Magpies started like champions. But the side faltered disappointingly after that, although Gallacher continued to find the net, notching 21 in 33 matches. One effort was through the legs of respected England goalkeeper Harry Hibbs, of Birmingham. It was a memory Hughie always cherished. Hibbs later commented on Gallacher's footballing talent, noting that it was 'the best I have ever met'.

Gallacher's enforced absence also gave opportunities to players destined to be in his shadow, notably Jonathan Wilkinson. Auburn haired and nicknamed Monte, the youngster from Esh Winning showed delightful touches when he was given an opportunity. He once netted an unforgettable hat-trick against Aston Villa during one of the most entertaining tussles seen at St. James' Park, a fixture which ended 7–5 in United's favour! He later moved to Everton where he found himself as understudy to the country's other legendary centre-forward, Dixie Dean. Wilkinson did well for the Black'n'Whites striking 11 goals in 27 appearances.

Jimmy Loughlin and Tom Mordue were two other players who could be called upon when Gallacher was on the sidelines. Nicknamed Tucker and from a celebrated local footballing family, Mordue proved a sturdy and aggressive centre-forward at only 5 ft 7 in. tall. Always a favourite, he bubbled with enthusiasm in his handful of outings. Inside-forward Willie Chalmers, like Gallacher also from Bellshill, was a cultured player and he too had the odd game in the leader's role.

A RIFT DEVELOPS

Hughie Gallacher's brush with the game's hierarchy was the beginning of a serious rift between the player and certain members of the Newcastle United board, then led by Alderman James Lunn. At that time, like most sides, the Magpies had not yet been adventurous enough to appoint a full-time team manager, playing affairs being solely the responsibility of the directors, and some members of the club's board were clearly displeased at the Scot's frequent conflicts with referees and ultimately the Football Association and Football League authorities. His seemingly uncontrollable temper was becoming a major cause for concern, even to the point that rumours spread that Newcastle wanted to off-load their No. 9 star.

Speculation was heightened when Arsenal manager, Herbert Chapman, turned up at St. James' Park at the beginning of the 1928–29 season. Gossip circulated rapidly around the streets of Newcastle that Gallacher was heading south to Highbury. But the majority of Newcastle's directors held sway and insisted that 85 goals netted in only two and a half seasons was too valuable to lose. However, Gallacher was stripped of the captaincy before the new season began. Hughie recorded: 'I was not sorry. My impetuous nature was unsuited to the responsibility.' Fellow Scottish international, Joe Harris, was handed the job to start with, a player of a stronger temperament. Gallacher had been reprimanded; he was to stay out of trouble and concentrate on his job in a black and white shirt – to score goals.

Newcastle United had a mediocre season by their standards and as autumn turned to winter the Magpies were struggling at the foot of the First Division table. All was not well in the Geordie camp and Newcastle officials had a clear-out before the year turned. Players went and new faces arrived in a bid to revitalise the side and recapture the 1927 title magic. One notable name to arrive at St. James' Park was one of Gallacher's great rivals at centre-half – captain of Burnley and England – and now of Newcastle – Jack Hill. The pair had clashed many times and the 5 ft 5 in. versus 6 ft 3 in. fascinating duel was one of the most talked about in football at the time.

The changes at Gallowgate brought results and the Tynesiders recovered in the remaining months of the season to finish in tenth position. There was quite a Scots influence at St. James' Park then; in fact it was more like a gathering at Glasgow's Sauchiehall Street than the North-east of England. On one occasion during that 1928–29 season, Newcastle fielded a line-up against Leeds United that contained only one Englishman; ten Scots were in the side, the odd man out being reserve centre-half Ed Wood.

Gallacher was in good company and never once became home sick. Both Tommy Lang and Willie Gibson came from Larkhall, not far from Bellshill, and Willie Chalmers was born a goalkick from Hughie's house in that Lanarkshire town. Glasgow was represented by Bob McKay, Joe Harris and Gallacher's best pal, Jimmy Boyd. Goalkeeper Willie Wilson hailed from near the capital, Edinburgh, Tom McDonald from Inverness and Jimmy Low from Ayrshire. It was home from home.

Hughie had worked hard to control his temper and kept out of trouble for most of the campaign. Despite the mediocre season, he had another profitable goalscoring year being United's top scorer once more, this time with 24 goals. And Gallacher continued to steal the headlines in a blue shirt of Scotland too, recording perhaps his best year for his country. Gallacher scored no fewer than eight goals for the Scots in only three games. Against Wales during October he registered a hat-trick in a 4–2 win at Ibrox in Glasgow. That victory was followed with a crushing 7–3 triumph against Northern Ireland in Belfast and Gallacher received all the praise again. His display against the Irish was even more resounding. A hat-trick in the first quarter of the game and five goals altogether was sensational, as well as a new record – although several sources only acknowledge four of the goals with Alex James claiming one of his efforts. However, the centre-forward had no doubt; Hughie said without question it was his goal, noting: 'Several newspapers mistakenly credited Alex James with one of my scoring efforts.' He combined a treat with Huddersfield Town's Alec Jackson who made five of the Scots' seven goals as well as getting two himself. The referee for that match, incidentally, was none other than Bert Fogg!

The big match of the year, England versus Scotland, was held at Hampden Park and in front of over 110,000 spectators, Scotland won 1–0. Gallacher was very much involved in the goal, albeit a controversial one. Alec Cheyne struck a corner in the dying minutes that swirled in the wind. The ball ended in the back of the England net with defenders claiming that Gallacher had stood on their goalkeeper John Hacking's foot, and stopped the Oldham custodian from clearing the ball. Gallacher was back in the news as usual.

In spite of his good behaviour it was not to last. At the end of that 1928–29 season, the mercurial centre-forward got himself into trouble again. Hughie was caught in a set-to with a referee once more, and again it was the case of back-chat to the official. This time he was lucky. The Football Association only handed out a reprimand and severe warning, but no suspension. Then later, to augment his income, he wrote a series of feature articles for a national newspaper. They were titled 'Inside the Football Game'. And with Hughie Gallacher being involved, they were controversial. The authorities at the Football Association were not amused and censored him again. They fined Gallacher and instructed the Newcastle United player to stop, stating the column was 'causing dissatisfaction in more than one dressing-room'.

Following that incident Gallacher was off on a European tour with the Magpies and into more confrontation – lots of it. Newcastle embarked on a lengthy trek during May 1929 visiting Italy, Czechoslovakia, Hungary and Austria. It was a journey that caused plenty of controversy and Hughie was at the centre of much of it. He described the European adventure that summer as being 'notorious'. Nothing went right. Gallacher and company were 'booed and spat at all over Europe'!

United won their first exhibition game, 1–0 against Ambrosiana Milan – the forerunner of the Inter club. But it was an experience

United's party wanted to quickly forget. In the Milan Arena, the Italians resorted to tactics more at home in the gladiatorial stage of classical Italy! Gallacher in particular received a battering and United's players limped off the field, with Tommy Lang – a player to hardly ever lose his cool – nursing a nasty set of bite marks on his neck, having being sent off, along with his opposing full-back. United mixed it too, with Gallacher trying (and failing) to make himself understood to the Italians, then resorting to the rough tactics himself.

The crowd, who expected a showcase display of top English football, did not like it at all. It was reported in Milan that 'scandalous scenes took place' and that United's players had walked off the field when the Italian national anthem was played, apparently because the crowd intensely booed 'God Save the King'. After the match, a mob gathered around the club's motor-coach. Stones and bottles whizzed at the windows and United's party had to be protected by local Black Shirts – the Fascisti. Skipper Jack Hill, Dave Fairhurst and goalkeeper Micky Burns were all hit. Gallacher noted in his memoirs: 'Frankly I was scared stiff and never more glad to see cops in my life.' There was more trouble at the Magpies' hotel in Milan, United's players having to almost barricade themselves in their bedrooms, and only intervention from a member of the Italian Government who was staying at the same hotel, together with the British Consul, stopped another dust-up developing.

The tour turned sour after that fiery opening. Moving to Austria, Newcastle lost 0–2 to the Wiener Athletic Club in Vienna and then came an embarrassing eight-goal defeat at the hands of the Slovak club in Bratislava. The Magpies were accused of not trying by Czech officials. Newcastle then travelled to Budapest after a 1–1 draw in Prague to meet a Hungarian select combination . . . and more hostility followed, with Hughie Gallacher once again at the centre of all the attention. The match was another rough 90 minutes. Gallacher said of the Continental football he experienced for the first time: 'Their skill was at an absolute minimum and the only way they could stop us was by the crudest tactics imaginable.'

The Black'n'Whites lost 1–4, Gallacher netting with a penalty kick in a match that again saw the crowd demonstrate 'against the conduct of the English team'. United full-back Alf Maitland was sent off and then Gallacher received his marching orders after a punch-up with the home full-back. As the Scot trooped off, hundreds of fans spat and threw coins at him. United's centre-forward was ushered through the seething crowd by armed soldiers. Hungarian officials and players were incensed at the display of their visitors. They even accused United's players, and Gallacher and Maitland in particular, of being drunk and disorderly on the field! A marvellous record exists of the incident, kept by Gallacher's friend and teammate, Maitland. The Hungarian Football Association's official report and letter of strong complaint to the Football Association in London survives and it notes the referee, Gabriel Boronkay's, report on Gallacher's exit, a matter of two minutes after Maitland had received his dismissal:

> In the 28th minute [of the second half] I had to give marching orders to the English [*sic*] player Gallacher because of his rough foul against Borsanyi. I beg to remark that in this moment I was standing quite close to the player and I am convinced that he was tipsy, and as I heard, he drank much cognac between the two half-times.

The Hungarian FA were seething and withheld Newcastle's guaranteed appearance fee, claiming that United did not deserve any payment because the players were intoxicated and not willing or able to play football. The embittered comments of the Hungarians headed for the Football Association in London. Newcastle's party was quick to leave the country.

Back on British soil a full FA inquiry took place to investigate the Budapest incident. Gallacher was at the centre of complaints again. This time the FA allowed Hughie to explain his point of view and in the end the authorities accepted his explanation and officially exonerated him, although the damage to his reputation had already been done. Gallacher explained that he, and some of his colleagues, had been so thirsty that they had washed their mouths out with whisky, hence the alcoholic breath. Alf Maitland backed Hughie, saying: 'It was a boiling hot day so we rinsed our mouths out with a drop of scotch and water.' The United full-back also said that the Hungarians had seen them passing the bottle round and spread the word to the crowd that they were drunk. Maitland added: 'From the kick-off the crowd were howling at us.' Despite the remarkable admission of taking alcohol, the Football Association backed United – perhaps in an era when no matter the validity of the claim, England – in the shape of the FA – was not to be answerable to a small, fledgling organisation in far-away Hungary.

However, the incident and controversial tour in general – from Milan to Budapest – had been an uncomfortable and embarrassing few weeks for Newcastle's directors. Gallacher's track record was again a subject for discussion on the boardroom table and he was singled out for helping fuel the unsporting and derisive behaviour in Europe.

Season 1929–30 was to be Gallacher's last with Newcastle United. Indeed, he almost didn't even see in that new term, as just before the big kick-off Gallacher asked for a transfer, being linked with both Arsenal and Tottenham. Hughie was not pleased when a week earlier Newcastle had signed another Scottish centre-forward, Duncan Hutchison, from Dundee United. He had a huge reputation north of the border having plundered 34 league goals in the previous season. Gallacher saw the purchase as his replacement, especially when it was suggested that the new arrival would be handed the centre-forward's role with Gallacher being pushed to operate at inside-forward.

Fierce debate raged. Gallacher was still King of Tyneside in the eyes of United's supporters and Newcastle's directors were taking a huge risk heading along a path that would see Gallacher move on. Meetings were held between officials and player, disagreements were patched up – temporarily – and Gallacher stayed on Tyneside, extending his contract. However the rift had not been totally healed.

Gallacher started the season in sparkling form, as he tended to do every year. As if to show Newcastle's directors what they would miss if they cashed in and sent him on his way, Hughie hit the net three times on the first Saturday of the season against Manchester United in a 4–1 victory. He went on to score 11 goals in the first 10 games but his goals prowess could not halt the Gallowgate eleven sliding down the table and into 18th position. It was to be a relegation-threatened season for United, and Gallacher, with his 34 goals, saved the Magpies from the drop.

No one appeared more for the Black'n'Whites and no one gave more to the cause than Gallacher in that below-par season. Hughie's commitment was unquestioned, yet his loyalty to the Magpies proceeded to place him into more confrontation – this time with the Scottish Football Association. Gallacher seemingly could not win. Whenever he hit the headlines it upset someone. On this occasion, a club versus country row blew up during April when Gallacher decided he should appear for United in a vital relegation clash with Arsenal, rather than turn out for the Scots against England.

He had impressed again in the blue jersey of his birth that season against both Wales and Northern Ireland, scoring two goals in each victory. One effort at Ninian Park stood out as quite brilliant. It was reported that Gallacher went past no fewer than eight men before scoring! Gallacher was Scotland's most influential player. In the last 5 internationals, he had lashed home 12 goals for his country and had been picked for the prestigious England clash, but Hughie had been asked to sacrifice a cap by United's directors in order to face the Gunners – in days when internationals were played on the same day as the league programme. Gallacher decided his duty lay with his club – and of course Scotland received a hammering, losing 5–2 at Wembley. The Scottish Football Association was far from happy and eventually turned their back on Anglo-Scots players for a period as a result.

United meanwhile drew 1–1 with Arsenal, also in trouble with United at the wrong end of the table. The Londoners had released their Scots gem, Alex James along with England's David Jack. But Gallacher's presence for Newcastle was crucial. He made the goal for inside-forward Joe Devine to earn United an equaliser and a vital point in the battle for safety.

Newcastle's fight to avoid relegation lasted to the very last day of the season and a contest with another side from the capital, West Ham United. Gallacher continued to play his part, being the focal point of everything good in United's play. No one knew it at the time – except perhaps the club's directors – but that critical meeting with the Hammers was to be Hughie Gallacher's last game in a Newcastle shirt.

A crowd of 50,000 saw a single dramatic Joe Devine goal ensure the Magpies' First Division survival. However, before the match another row between Hughie and club officials flared up. Reports circulated that United's centre-forward, who had now netted over 140 goals for the club in five seasons, had been offered to deadly rivals, Sunderland, in a record transfer. Denials were swift and profuse, but the local *Evening Chronicle* newspaper that released the story stood firm by the report. Gallacher was amazed at Newcastle United's attitude. He had actually signed a new contract for the 1930–31 season and noted firmly: 'I do not want to leave.' But within an hour he was apparently being offered to the Roker Park outfit. Newcastle's officials denied the claims but Hughie was adamant and was to record later: 'I learned indirectly that I *had* been offered to the Sunderland club.' He was vexed and added: 'No one has ever shown the door to Hughie Gallacher twice. I am not a pawn to be transferred willy-nilly.' Hughie disliked the transfer system intensely and wrote in a column for the *Evening Chronicle* at the time: 'A professional footballer still has some right to him. For instance, it is for him to decide whether he will go to this or that club; in matters of transfer his is the final word no matter what this or that club or club director may desire to be done.' Hughie wanted to be in control of his own destiny, but was far from being so. Club directors held huge power and footballers were largely the proverbial 'soccer slaves' at the time.

The majority of Newcastle's directors, it appeared, now wanted to cash in on the player despite his goals and unprecedented popularity. Gallacher's apparent inability to keep out of the headlines had now pushed United's officials over the edge, Hughie admitting that he reckoned there were 'personal animosities and prejudices' within the club. Another factor could have been the urgent need for an injection of cash. Most football clubs, like almost every business at the time, suffered from the economic depression which was to soon sweep the world during the '30s.

Another cause for the imminent departure of Gallacher was the relationship between the centre-forward and United's new manager Andy Cunningham. The Magpies had appointed the former Rangers and Scotland ace, initially as a player, in February 1929, destined to become the first man to fill the Gallowgate hot-seat as the year of 1930 opened. A vastly experienced player north of the border, Cunningham had never been on the same wavelength as Gallacher, either as a teammate with Scotland or in United colours. When he became player-manager, there was little rapport between the pair. It was a crucial factor. Gallacher admitted that while he respected his fellow countryman as a player, he was never on the best of terms with the tall Scot. He noted: 'Once Cunningham arrived as boss I knew my days were numbered at Newcastle United.'

Nothing eventually came of the move to Wearside or of an apparent approach at the time by another top club, this time from London. That club turned out to be Chelsea. Hughie made it crystal-clear he did not wish to leave St. James' Park and he was being pushed out of the door. He was proud to be Newcastle United's centre-forward and had a fondness for Tyneside having settled into a relationship with the daughter of a well-known city publican. United fans still worshipped him and as speculation grew as to his transfer, petitions, letters and irate calls flooded the club and local press. They, on no account, wanted Gallacher to be transferred.

The end of season speculation died down for the summer with Gallacher officially a United player again for the forthcoming 1930–31 campaign. Back in favour with Scotland, Hughie travelled with the international party for a prestige meeting with France in Paris. While he was impressing the French public and sightseeing around Notre Dame, the Champs-Elysées and the Eiffel Tower, on Tyneside negotiations were taking place behind his back to make him a Chelsea player. This, after five years as United's top scorer.

A QUICK RETURN FOR HUGHIE

Back on British soil, Gallacher returned to Bellshill for the rest of the summer break. On Empire Day, 24 May, his relaxation was interrupted when an unexpected knock at the door brought him face to face with two well-dressed officials of Chelsea Football Club, Chairman Claude Kirby and scout Jock Fraser, ironically an ex-Magpie player. Gallacher was astonished and completely taken by surprise at the call. He had no intention of discussing the move with Chelsea until the Londoners noted that his club had 'agreed terms with us'. Gallacher was shocked that the Geordies had readily agreed to let him go. Hughie had taken to the North-east and its down-to-earth folk and didn't want to leave the area.

He felt stabbed in the back and said later: 'Why Newcastle United wanted to let me go I never found out. But with such an attitude I was bound to leave the club. Better sooner than later.' The dapper Scot travelled to Glasgow with Chelsea's representatives in a smart suit and bowler hat to meet Newcastle's party in a city-centre hotel. He could have refused to move as he had signed a new contract only a matter of weeks before, but now knowing quite clearly that the United directors wanted rid of him, he decided to obtain the best deal he could from Chelsea. This he did, taking several hours before the transfer was concluded. Hughie's dislike of the transfer system continued and he noted: 'I have been sold like a slave for a bag of gold!'

That bag of gold was, by most accounts, worth £10,000 to United, almost a new record fee, some £890 short of David Jack's transfer when he moved from Bolton Wanderers to Arsenal a year before. Although the exact sum was again a closely guarded secret, some reports had the amount as high as £12,000, a figure never denied by Chelsea or the Magpies.

When the news hit the streets of Tyneside, everyone was amazed – and annoyed. After netting 143 goals in only 174 games for Newcastle United, how the club's most prolific goalscorer was despatched against his will incensed supporters everywhere. The *Daily Journal*'s correspondent wrote: 'Newcastle are bound to miss him, for he is the best centre-forward of the day.' The *North Mail*'s reporter, pen-named 'Man-in-the-Street' wrote: 'Newcastle United's action in transferring Hugh Gallacher is the biggest football sensation for many years.' It was added that it was a 'shock to those Tyneside loyalists who had hoped that managerial shrewdness would safeguard Gallacher's genius to the St. James' Park club'.

Speculation was rife as to the reasons for his departure. It was concluded by many that certain officials were fed up with the stream of headlines involving Gallacher and at his out-on-the-town lifestyle. The level of Hughie's alleged drinking habit was legendary and undoubtedly exaggerated – and had never affected his performances on the field of play . . . the goals still flowed. It was noted that it was even Gallacher's pleasure to take a pint or two before the match on occasion at the Strawberry Inn, adjacent to St. James' Park. Once it was said that United's trainer had to be sent to fetch the centre-forward when he was late for changing – still propped up against the bar! True or not, Hughie's reputation undoubtedly affected his relationship with Newcastle's directors. They had put up with enough and were ready to gain a windfall on selling their prized asset.

In spite of the downside to Gallacher's character, appreciation was plentiful and complimentary to his football ability. The Magpies would miss him. It was noted: 'He is the best in the game today. He has the brains to think a move ahead, the skill to tame the ball, the quick eye to see possibilities and make openings, the craft and cunning and speedy thrust to finish off his manoeuvres, or to turn half-chances into real chances and goals.

'Gallacher's speed of thought and action allows him to take a ball in most awkward positions and send it flashing into the net in the twinkling of an eye. He belongs to the class marked "genius".'

HUGHIE GALLACHER
NO. 9 RATING

Fan appeal – personality and presence	10
Strike-rate	8
Shooting – power and placement	8
Heading	7
Ball skills	9
Link-play – passing, assists, crossing, team-play	9
Pace	8
Commitment – work-rate, courage	8
Match-winner – power-play, big-match capability	10
Longevity with United	5
Trophy success, international and top football ranking	3
Total No. 9 rating	85

Newcastle United had to start life without Gallacher at centre-forward. And they certainly did miss him. His immediate successors, fellow Scots Duncan Hutchison and new leader Duncan Lindsay who was signed from Cowdenbeath, were thrust into the limelight. Both hardly enamoured themselves with Tyneside's public. They had an impossible job trying to replace the country's best striker, and were not up to the role. Newcastle's fans knew that and soon had the chance to see their departed hero back at St. James' Park – and what a reception Wee Hughie received, as if to show club officials that they had made a grave error of judgement.

By one of those strange quirks of football fate, for only the second fixture of the new 1930–31 season and United's opening match at St. James' Park, Chelsea – and Gallacher – were the visitors to Tyneside. There was unprecedented interest in the return of the Scot. Seemingly everyone wanted to see Hughie again. A massive attendance gathered for the late summer afternoon fixture and the largest ever mid-week crowd anywhere converged on St. James' Park. The official gate was 68,386 and it was a new record attendance for the ground, one that still stands, while an estimated 20,000 or even 30,000 according to some reports were locked out around Barrack Road and Strawberry Place. Secretary Frank Watt recalled in his memoirs that '100,000 came to see the match'. Hundreds of spectators sat precariously on the stand roof; others braved tree-top perches and peered out of windows along Leazes Terrace.

Gallacher was greeted with a Geordie roar rarely heard before or since, a 'storm of cheering' never before witnessed for a visiting player. Cloth caps waved and how the Newcastle United fans showed their appreciation to their departed hero. It was an incredible show of emotion. Gallacher admitted in later years that the demonstration of sheer adulation from his Tyneside fans had been the most memorable moment of his life. He said: 'Man, it put the auld lump in the throat.'

Twice before half-time United's former centre-forward – and now Chelsea's – went close for his new club, but Albert McInroy in United's goal saved well. Gallacher was, in fact, a little eager and often caught in the Magpie offside-trap. He – as usual – protested decisions fervently and found himself on the losing side as United stole the points when Jackie Cape nodded home a Wilkinson cross.

As the dust settled following the Scot's departure south and sensational return, Newcastle United had to concentrate on life after Wee Hughie. They needed someone to slip into the centre-forward shirt and grasp the rare opportunity to become a new Geordie idol.

No. 9 EXTRAS

THEY SAID IT
Bob McPhail, Scotland teammate:
'Hughie was a great centre-forward, but a little rascal. He had a vicious tongue . . . I learned swear words from Hughie I had never heard before.'
Jimmy Boyd, Newcastle United colleague:
'There was never anyone like Hughie. He would have run rings round Hidegkuti and Di Stefano.'

A SONG FOR HUGHIE
Such was the adulation for Hughie Gallacher, a song was penned on Tyneside that became hugely popular long after he had departed. Jackie Milburn recalled that even as a small child he used to sing it continually in the school playground. Both Charlie Crowe and Albert Stubbins also recalled the song, to the tune of 'D'you ken John Peel':

D'you ken Hughie Gallacher
The wee Scots lad
The best centre-forward
Newcastle ever had
If he doesn't score a goal
Then we'll put him on the dole
And we'll send him back to Scotland in the morning

GREATS ON GALLACHER
Raich Carter:
'When I saw this stocky little Scot I formed an on-the-spot impression that I have had no cause to revise throughout the passing years. I am sure there has never been better. His basic strong-point was remarkable ball control. Because of it, he had the ability to beat opponents in the minimum of space.'

Tommy Lawton:
'He'd had a fairly traumatic time off the field and in many ways he was a rather misunderstood man, certainly nowhere near as black as people liked to paint him. He was a truly great centre-forward – and when you consider that Hughie was only about 5 ft 5 in. tall, then what he achieved was staggering. Players like Hughie Gallacher appear only once in a generation.'

SUPPORTER'S PLEA
Letters flooded into the local *Daily Journal* and *Evening Chronicle* when rumours spread that Gallacher was to be transferred in 1930. One such letter noted:

> Dear Hughie
> I write on behalf of thousands of your admirers in Newcastle and district. Surely you are not leaving us! Surely the difficulties can be fixed up? You know you have the sympathy and support of the great majority of the spectators at St. James' Park. I appeal to you to remain with us here, I am quite certain the spectators do not want you to go. There is no doubt about their attitude.
> Admirer and well-wisher.

HUGHIE'S INFLUENCE
The legend of Hughie Gallacher was huge in the North-east and influenced many, including future United No. 9 heroes Albert Stubbins

and Jackie Milburn. Stubbins was to say that he was 'brought up and weaned on the legend of Hughie Gallacher'. Milburn's father used to keep telling Jackie that 'you'll never be as good as Hughie Gallacher'. Of course, he would be. And Gallacher was always around when 'Wor Jackie' pulled on the centre-forward's shirt. Milburn recalled that Hughie would 'wait for me outside the main entrance, always at the same time in the same place'. United's former centre-forward hero was quick to pass on tips and comments to the Magpies' star.

THE WHIZZ OF THE BULLET!

Hughie Gallacher always created sensation, controversy and intrigue wherever he went, making headlines from performances such as the day he represented Scotland in 1925 against the Irish League in Belfast, on which he totally destroyed the home side with a devastating display. Gallacher netted five of the Scots' seven goals and not only did he find the net repeatedly but he also made the local fans and supporters feel distinctly second-rate – performing irritating tricks with the ball and teasing the opposition almost to a frenzy. At half-time, a note was passed to Hughie from Irish partisans. It was a death threat. Gallacher would be shot if he did not ease up. Hughie of course ignored the threat and continued his exhibition display. Afterwards he visited friends in the city. He was warned to be careful; Ireland was no place for strangers then. He grinned, until a bullet whizzed past his ear and splattered on a nearby wall as he walked near Queen's Bridge. Gallacher, always a witty character, said afterwards: 'I'll have to extend my stay in Belfast. It seems I still haven't managed to teach the Irish how to shoot straight!'

FORTY AND MORE

Gallacher's League, Cup and international goals tally of 40 or more goals in a season:

46 goals	1924–25 for Airdrie and Scotland
42 goals	1925–26 for Airdrie, Newcastle United and Scotland
40 goals	1926–27 for Newcastle United and Scotland
40 goals	1929–30 for Newcastle United and Scotland

CLUB TOTALS

Gallacher's formidable club-by-club League and Cup appearance and goal record is matched by few:

Queen of the South	9 app	19 goals
Airdrie	129 app	100 goals
Newcastle United	174 app	143 goals
Chelsea	144 app	81 goals
Derby County	55 app	40 goals
Notts County	46 app	32 goals
Grimsby Town	12 app	3 goals
Gateshead	34 app	18 goals
Total	603 app	436 goals

SCOTLAND'S GEM

Gallacher remains one of Scotland's most prolific goalscorers in the blue shirt of his country. Only Kenny Dalglish and Denis Law (with 30 goals each) have scored more goals in full international fixtures, and no player has a better strike-rate:

Full International	20 app	24 goals[*]
Inter-League	2 app	6 goals
Trial XI	1 app	5 goals
Tour XI	6 app	10 goals
Junior International	1 app	1 goal
Total	30 app	46 goals

[*] includes disputed goal v. Northern Ireland

WEE HUGHIE – AFTER TOON

Gallacher spent almost five years with Chelsea and if anything, the headlines created in London even surpassed those on Tyneside – but mainly for his off-the-field activities. He was involved in player-power feuds, rows over money, illegal payments, more suspensions, bankruptcy and brushes with the law. In spite of everything, a constant supply of goals came from Hughie's boot. He moved to Derby County late in 1934 where he nearly lifted another championship medal before heading on to Notts County and Grimsby Town. A nostalgic return to Tyneside occurred just prior to the Second World War when he joined Gateshead's Football League outfit. He retired during the hostilities and remained on Tyneside, still creating news, once being banished from St. James' Park for being too critical in the press!

TRAGIC FINALE

Hughie Gallacher died when aged 54, committing suicide when in a distressed frame of mind prior to appearing at Gateshead Magistrates Court on charges of assaulting the youngest of his three children. He walked to Dead Man's Crossing in Low Fell, not far from his home, and threw himself beneath the York to Edinburgh express train. Hughie Gallacher had departed and created the biggest headline of his eventful life: 'Hughie of the Magic Feet is Dead.'

3. THE No. 9 SHIRT ARRIVES
1930–1947

JACK ALLEN, JACK SMITH, BILLY CAIRNS, ALBERT STUBBINS, CHARLIE WAYMAN

The departure of Hughie Gallacher in 1930 was a huge blow to Newcastle United supporters. Fans around Tyneside were not happy. In the drinking establishments of the region, debate raged as to why Hughie had been sold, boss Andy Cunningham and his superiors in the boardroom taking plenty of criticism. United's management had to fill a huge void in their team plan. Gallacher had averaged almost 30 goals a season for the Magpies and was the club's talisman in almost everything they did. To suddenly lose that outstanding figurehead and regular goals return gave Cunningham a predicament. United's boss hoped that two other Scots would, in part, fill the gap.

Duncan Hutchison was already on the staff, the former Dundee United centre-forward having been purchased during the previous season, and as the Gallacher sale was being concluded United raided Scotland again, bringing Cowdenbeath's star goalgetter Duncan Lindsay to Tyneside for a £2,700 fee. Cunningham rated both players highly and he hoped that between them, his new Scottish strikers would develop, match Gallacher's goal ratio and at least become the focal point of his team plan. It was a hope doomed to failure as both players were far from being a Hughie Gallacher, at the time of course, the best striker in the business. Although they did score goals, Hutchison and Lindsay never remotely answered their manager's call and rarely looked like filling the wee maestro's centre-forward shirt.

Hutchison was a player of charisma and outstanding talent. Stockily built at 5 ft 7 in. tall he had a fast and furious style up front and was a personality who could have become a big name at St. James' Park in the wake of Hughie Gallacher. But Hurricane Hutch, as he had been nicknamed north of the border, never quite made it in England. In the Scottish League, it was different though. Alongside the Tay in Dundee, Hutchison was a popular figure like few before or since. His powerful running and shooting made him a terrace favourite as he plundered over 100 goals for Dundee United prior to his headlining transfer to Tyneside for a substantial £4,050 fee. That transfer to United caused uproar around Tannadice Park with local fans even travelling to Tyneside to present their hero with a lucky horseshoe before his first appearance for the Black'n'Whites.

Duncan Lindsay was in many ways similar to Hutchison. He had been a roaring success in Scottish football, albeit in a lower grade of soccer with Cowdenbeath. Chased by Everton, Hearts, Spurs and Sunderland as well as United, he possessed terrific pace. The tenacious and sturdy leader created plenty of headlines in Scotland and bagged plenty of goals – over 90 in four seasons for the Fife club. But after a bright opening in a Toon shirt, he faded rapidly. Hutchison did likewise.

The two Scots shared the centre-forward role in season 1930–31 as elsewhere Gallacher continued to hit goals for Chelsea. Lindsay was the first of the pair to be given a chance and in his opening eight games recorded a creditable six goals, including an effort in what was a remarkable 7–4 victory at Old Trafford against Manchester United. Hutchison then took over in mid-season and also went through a purple patch as the year turned in January. Hutch netted in five of the seven consecutive games he played, converting seven goals, including a hat-trick in the FA Cup tie with Nottingham Forest. Hutchison hit 14 goals that season all told while Lindsay scored 12. Both were reasonable performances, but neither really grasped the big opportunity available to show they could make the leader's role their own.

Indeed, Cunningham decided that he needed to bring yet another centre-forward to Tyneside halfway through the season when he signed experienced England striker Harry Bedford from Derby County for £4,000. Bedford was over 30 years of age when he arrived at Gallowgate during December and was noted as being a dashing and fearless centre-forward. His record for Derby, Blackpool and Nottingham Forest was first class, and having appeared for England during the mid-'20s, boasted a career total of over 300 goals. Bedford supplemented Cunningham's attacking options and although he was used mainly at inside-forward, scoring 13 goals, the Derbyshire-born striker gave decent short-term service to the Magpies.

While Hutchison, Lindsay and Bedford did find the net for United as the Geordies scored a respectable 83 goals, season 1930–31 was another disappointing year. As Christmas approached, Newcastle were struggling in the relegation mire and they continued to hover in the lower reaches of the division until the end of the programme. United without Gallacher was not quite the same, with the team missing that sparkle of magic the charismatic Scot possessed in abundance.

United's directors soon put the pressure on manager Cunningham. United's performances had to improve. It was clear his replacements for Gallacher were not good enough for the Magpies' centre-forward shirt. As the season came to a close, with United just scraping clear of the dreaded drop into Division Two and finishing in 17th place, the search was on for a new leader of the attack. A tried and tested striker was needed, one who could fill Gallacher's shirt. Both Hutchison and Lindsay were not to remain on Tyneside long. Bury picked up Lindsay during the summer, while Hutchison headed for Derby County before the end of the next campaign.

One of the centre-forwards on Cunningham's wanted list was Sheffield Wednesday's goalgetter-in-chief, Geordie-born Jack Allen. The Tynesider had earned a reputation as being ranked with the best strikers in the business, along with the eminent names of Gallacher and Dean. As Sheffield Wednesday lifted the Football League Championship in both 1928–29 and 1929–30, Allen earned an everlasting place in the Hillsborough club's history as the Owl's top scorer in each title success. He scored 35 goals in the first season then bettered that with 39 a year later. Newcastle United were quick to take notice that one of their own had risen to such prominence – and were alert and ready to act when Allen surprisingly fell out of favour with Wednesday's hierarchy as the '30s opened.

JACK ALLEN
FACTS & FIGURES

To Newcastle United: June 1931 from Sheffield
   Wednesday £3,500
From Newcastle United: November 1934 to Bristol
   Rovers £200
Born: Newcastle upon Tyne 31 January 1903
Died: Burnopfield 19 November 1957
Height: 5 ft 10 in.
Other senior clubs: Leeds United, Brentford, Gateshead
International: none
Newcastle United app & goals:
   Football League: 81 app, 34 goals
   FA Cup: 9 app, 7 goals
   Others: 1 app, 0 goals
   Total: 91 app, 41 goals
Strike-rate: League and Cup 45% (overall 45%)

From Newburn, and converted to the centre-forward role from inside-forward late in his career, Jack immediately took to the pivotal leader's position when given the chance at Hillsborough. He scored in his first game at centre-forward, then struck a hat-trick and then bagged four more in his next match! In his first 14 games as a centre-forward Jack claimed 22 goals. With an overall record of 85 goals in 114 league and cup games at the highest level for Wednesday, Allen was the tried and tested centre-forward United were hunting for.

When the Magpies approached both Sheffield Wednesday and Allen in June 1931, they had little trouble striking a deal. Jack was delighted to be returning to Tyneside, to the club he supported as a lad – a Geordie who returned a hero, very much like Alan Shearer's comeback 65 years later. The 28 year old cost United £3,500 – a modest fee for such an established striker, and one that proved to be a bargain.

Jack's first season back 'hyem' turned out to be quite an eventful homecoming. As the 1931–32 campaign began, United's new centre-forward took time to settle. He had a mixed opening in a Toon shirt, the Magpies starting with three defeats and three victories, while he also missed a penalty against Liverpool. By October though, the experienced Allen and his teammates had moved into a rhythm. Jack was a regular on the scoresheet as United climbed the table to the lofty spot of third place by New Year's Day – the club's highest position for four seasons and the heyday of Gallacher.

Jack scored 12 goals in the league programme as United's forward-line knitted together, the Geordie leader linking well with Tommy Lang and Jimmy Boyd on the wings, and especially the young and emerging Jimmy Richardson at inside-forward. All players claimed goals in a free-scoring forward-line. While league action was much more satisfying than recent seasons, it was in the FA Cup that United – spearheaded by Allen – sent Tyneside into feverish delight.

The FA Cup took centre-stage from January onwards as United embarked on a memorable run to Wembley. Jack didn't grab any goals or headlines as United took care of Blackpool and Southport in hard-fought ties – two games against the Seasiders and three against their neighbours down the west coast at Haig Avenue – and he missed out due to injury in the emphatic deciding contest with Southport, in a 9–0 goal feast at the neutral venue of Hillsborough. But Jack was back in action, and among the goals, in the latter stages of the tournament when it really mattered. He was the danger-man, striking seven goals in the eight games he played, the difference between success and failure.

Against Leicester City in the 5th round, United won 3–1 and Jack grabbed his first FA Cup goal for United. In the quarter-final against Watford, the Black'n'Whites had a field day running out convincing 5–0 winners, and Allen hit a stunning hat-trick. His first came by way of a mighty Fairhurst clearance from defence, Jack latching onto the ball and racing through the Watford defence to fire past Tom Holland. Then after a precision passing movement from box to box without the visitors touching the ball, he banged the ball true and hard with a rising shot that bulged into the St. James' Park netting. His hat-trick was completed with a touch of brilliance as Allen danced past three defenders and interchanged with McMenemy, before tapping the ball home in style. In addition, he made a fifth goal for Jimmy Boyd and rattled the crossbar with another effort. The press recorded that United's centre-forward had 'thrilled the crowd' on that afternoon.

Fate saw United face Chelsea – and Hughie Gallacher – in the semi-final clash at Leeds Road, Huddersfield. Although Newcastle's former idol found the net on that occasion, it was the Magpies' new centre-forward who ended up reaching Wembley after a 2–1 victory and it was Allen who made the headlines. He opened the scoring for United in the 11th minute, firing into the Londoner's goal from 10 yards following a goalmouth scramble, the ball 'rattling into the corner of the net past Millington's right hand'. Jack was a menace to Chelsea all afternoon and, as one reporter at the match noted, had 'been a fighting leader all the way'.

With an aggressive, bustling style Allen was difficult to handle. He battled throughout the contest and worked for fully 90 minutes. Strong with his left foot – some said his right was purely to stand on – Jack was a quick-fire centre-forward; one biography of the day described him as 'leading the line with dash and skill to be always a menace in front of goal'.

United returned to Wembley Stadium for the first time since 1924, during which time the national arena had built up a compelling atmosphere. Players and fans all ultimately wanted to end up at Wembley in the FA Cup final – the biggest match of the season. The stage was set for heroes, and in 1932 Jack Allen became one of those immortal Wembley heroes.

Opponents Arsenal were the dominant club during the '30s and were to finish the 1931–32 season in runners-up position while the Magpies ended some way behind in 11th place. Winning the championship on five occasions and reaching three FA Cup finals in the era, the Gunners boasted an array of talent including Alex James, David Jack, Joe Hulme and Eddie Hapgood. Newcastle could never hope to match the Londoners player for player, but in grit, determination and in Jack Allen they held the aces in a match that has gone down in FA Cup folklore as one of the most talked about of all time.

A gripping contest was played out in front of a 92,298 Wembley crowd on a bright fine day in north London. The Londoners looked the better side early on and took the lead after only 12 minutes of play. A scramble in their own box was cleared by Roberts up field to Hulme. The England winger flashed past Fairhurst and crossed to the far post where Bob John came in from his opposite flank. With both McInroy and Nelson misjudging the ball, then colliding, he had the easiest of tasks of making sure the ball ended in the United net.

Newcastle were not demoralised though. They possessed a side full of courage, resolve and FA Cup spirit and went close on several occasions. In the closing period of the first half, Newcastle pressurised the Gunners' box and then it happened, seven minutes from the break, the goal everyone talked about for years and years – United's equaliser and a Jack Allen strike that has gone down in FA Cup history as 'the over the line goal'. FA Cup final incidents are often contentious in character, but this one has capped them all.

United centre-half Dave Davidson intercepted a Hapgood pass and hit a long raking ball for Jimmy Richardson to chase on the right wing. The Newcastle forward's outstretched leg caught the ball just as it was going to cross the dead-ball line. He whipped in a low cross in front of the Arsenal goalmouth and in flashed Allen to bang the ball into the net with his right foot as the Gunners' defenders hesitated – waiting for the referee's whistle for a goalkick. Arsenal's full-back raised his arms pointing to the line but the only whistle that came was for a goal . . . and the Magpies had equalised.

It wasn't really until after the game was concluded that the arguments started. Press photos from deceiving angles appeared to verify that the ball had crossed the line and gone out of play before Richardson crossed the ball. Film from *British Movietone News* was screened the following week around the country and this also gave support to the claim that the goal should never have stood, by the use of pioneering slow-motion replays. One newspaper report noted: 'By a clever device the film is stopped for several seconds just at the point when Richardson was about to centre the ball. This enables spectators to assume themselves that the ball was well over the white line.' The *Sunday Graphic*'s reporter wrote: 'Every man must have known what was so clear to onlookers – that the ball had crossed the line.' From the Arsenal camp, Charlie Buchan was quoted as saying: 'I could clearly see the white line, with the ball beyond it.' However, respected journalist Ivan Sharpe noted: 'I attached no importance to the photographs, as I know from experience how the touching up process may, quite unintentionally, alter details.' That was a valid point, as photographs were indeed 'touched-up' in order to highlight or even add a ball, in press rooms around the country right up to the 1960s.

United's Jimmy Boyd later recalled: 'I was right behind Jack Allen as the ball came across and I'm convinced that it was a good goal.' United's Scottish international winger added: 'The ball looked over the line from some angles because it was a foot off the ground when Jimmy Richardson reached it.'

The two men at the centre of the storm, referee Percy Harper and goalscorer Jack Allen were adamant. Harper said: 'It was a goal. As God is my judge, the man was in play.' United's Newburn-born centre-forward remarked: 'It was a goal all right, the ball was on the line but not over it.' He added: 'I did not see it go out of play.'

In spite of the furore over United's equaliser, Allen's second goal – and Wembley winner – was unequivocal. After the interval, the Black'n'Whites stepped up a gear to begin to control the game. An almost continuous bombardment of the Arsenal box followed. On 72 minutes, Davidson was again involved as he released the ball to Jimmy Boyd who sent Allen away with a perfect pass. The Magpie leader went past two defenders – Hapgood and Roberts – on a 30-yard goal-bound run and, having a little luck with a rebound to get past the Gunners' centre-half Herbie Roberts, smashed a low shot from the edge of the box that crept into the net off a post as the Gunners' keeper dived late. It was a great winner and capped a wonderful personal afternoon for Allen.

Remarkably, United's goal hero had been a pre-match doubt with a hernia problem and had played the whole game with a very painful abdomen. In addition, he had to leave the field for treatment after being given a 'kick in the knee' from one of his markers. In the wars, Jack battled on nevertheless and afterwards limped from Wembley and ended up in hospital as the team continued their FA Cup celebrations with a break in France and Germany. Allen was described as a 'lively leader' at Wembley and was justly handed the man-of-the-match tag.

After a slow start making an impact in a black and white shirt the name of Jack Allen was now on the lips of every Tynesider. The FA Cup homecoming was as joyous, massive and raucous as any in United's history, as Allen's fellow Geordies shouted: 'Give us Jack Allen. We want Allen . . . We want Allen.' A centre-forward hero is what every Newcastle supporter craves for, but for an individual who is also one of their own, a Geordie hero too – the adulation becomes extraordinary. Jack was the toast of Tyneside.

Much was expected of the FA Cup winners in the following 1932–33 season. Although the Magpies kept in touch with the title race challenges of Arsenal, Aston Villa and Sheffield Wednesday, Newcastle ended in fifth position and Allen had another satisfactory campaign, claiming 19 goals – 38 in 74 appearances since returning to Tyneside from Sheffield Wednesday. Yet there were calls for United to strengthen in attack. Jack was now reaching the veteran stage and by the start of the next programme, he would be into his 30s. His short but sweet period as United's centre-forward hero would soon be over.

Season 1933–34 was a disastrous one for Allen, the club and the supporters. Newcastle United were relegated to the Second Division for the first time in their history – even with a side bristling with top names like Sammy Weaver, Jimmy Richardson, Jimmy Nelson and Jack Allen. Only three goals came from Allen in that catastrophic season and he was on the sidelines for much of the programme, from November onwards. Following a four-goal thrashing at White Hart Lane against Tottenham, Jack's career at Gallowgate quickly ran downhill. Struggling with a knee problem, he eventually had a cartilage operation towards the end of the season. He had returned to the team for a game with Aston Villa, but the knee gave way and Allen ended up in hospital.

Although Jack recovered and took part in the Magpies' pre-season Whites versus Stripes public practice matches, Allen took little part in United's Second Division action, playing only one game before he left to join Bristol Rovers.

JACK ALLEN No. 9 RATING	
Fan appeal – personality and presence	7
Strike-rate	5
Shooting – power and placement	8
Heading	7
Ball skills	7
Link-play – passing, assists, crossing, team-play	8
Pace	8
Commitment – work-rate, courage	8
Match-winner – power-play, big-match capability	8
Longevity with United	4
Trophy success, international and top football ranking	2
Total No. 9 rating	72

United's directors had to act to replace Allen long before his departure. With the side struggling to stay in the First Division, United's beleaguered manager, Andy Cunningham, tried reserve striker John Kelly, a Hetton lad who had arrived from Burnley and then brought in Ronnie Williams during November 1933 to bolster his centre-forward options. An experienced striker with Swansea Town having grabbed 46 goals in 137 league games, Williams was a strong, powerful and bustling leader who eventually pulled on the red shirt of Wales. He took over from Allen in a bid to change the Magpies' fortunes and started with gusto. Scoring on his debut against Aston Villa, Ronnie proceeded to hit eight goals in his first seven matches for the Magpies to the turn of the year. Included was a stunning hat-trick against Everton as United confounded their lowly position by winning 7–3 at Goodison Park on Boxing Day. Williams then scored another against Merseyside's other top side, Liverpool, on New Year's Day, when the Reds were demolished at Gallowgate 9–2. Yet those remarkable high-scoring victories were not built on and United still tumbled into the Second Division.

Williams worked hard and tried to halt the slump, and his 13 goals in 25 appearances was not a bad record, but the Welshman was not the difference between staying in the elite of football and slipping to the also-rans for the first time. During the close season, the club's directors insisted that for the start of a new era in the history of the club, any rebuilding plans crucially needed a new centre-forward as a prime addition. Williams did not figure highly in the future plans.

A NEW KID ON THE BLOCK

Andy Cunningham resigned as manager following United's demotion and as a quick return proved unlikely. A new boss arrived to begin the rebuilding process, Stoke City's Tom Mather. With Ronnie Williams not appearing to be the answer at centre-forward, United took something of a gamble. In the opening weeks of the 1934–35 season, United spent a modest fee of £2,500 on a young fringe striker in Huddersfield Town's squad, Jack Smith, who was far from being a favourite of the crowd at Leeds Road, contemporary reports noting he 'did not get a fair crack of the whip from spectators'. A former England schools international, Smith was 19 years old. It proved an astute piece of business in the transfer market as the Yorkshire lad became an immediate hit. Colin Veitch, then a knowledgeable journalist, wrote of the signing of Smith: 'He gave me the impression of being a go-ahead and fearless leader and it is my belief that Newcastle United have done a good stroke of business.' Another commentator noted: 'When this tall young man has fully developed his physique we shall hear a lot about him. He covers the ground rapidly with his long stride and can shoot.'

A bright prospect in Huddersfield's line-up, then one of the top sides in the country having lifted a treble of league championships, Smith was never a regular, with Dave Mangall hogging the headlines, but had impressed when given a chance in the Terriers' line-up. He claimed 24 goals in only 46 matches and had shown United's watching scouts he possessed talent to develop into a top striker – and this he was quick to do in the black and white centre-forward shirt.

JACK SMITH
FACTS & FIGURES

To Newcastle United: September 1934 from Huddersfield Town £2,500

From Newcastle United: February 1938 to Manchester United £6,500

Born: Batley 17 February 1915

Died: 1975

Height: 5 ft 11 in.

Other senior clubs: Blackburn Rovers, Port Vale

England Schools International

Newcastle United app & goals:

Football League: 104 app, 69 goals

FA Cup: 8 app, 4 goals

Total: 112 app, 73 goals

Strike-rate: League and Cup 65%

With United trying to come to terms with life in Division Two for season 1934–35, Smith's introduction was a shining star in a gloomy air. He quickly showed energetic and goal-hungry ambition as he pulled on the Toon shirt. Smith scored on his debut against Plymouth Argyle and went on an impressive run of scoring soon after, striking eight goals in only five games. Jack looked the part and by the end of the season totalled 16 goals in 28 outings as the Magpies finished just short of the promotion places. The season may have ended in mediocrity and out of the limelight, but the Geordies had found a new centre-forward who could hopefully propel the club back into the elite.

Season 1935–36 reinforced Smith's credentials as a young and emerging goal-poacher. He tallied 26 goals in 36 games – the best return by any United player since the days of Hughie Gallacher. United's manager and directors were satisfied that they had now found a player to develop in the key role. Jack made a big impression, especially after being on the sidelines to start with through injury, when another enterprising and youthful leader, Billy Cairns, took to the stage – a local lad who impressed, grabbing plenty of goals . . . but his time in the centre-forward shirt would have to wait.

Smith was quick off the mark, powerfully built at 5 ft 11 in. tall, good in the air and could use both feet to hit shots with power. In Second Division football, he was a class apart. On his return from injury, Smith plundered 11 goals in only 10 matches up to New Year, including a hat-trick against Bury. He was a free-scoring power who should have propelled the Magpies to a serious promotion challenge. Unfortunately the Tynesiders never quite got there and Jack was soon courted by First Division eyes, especially after he grabbed a double strike in an epic FA Cup meeting with Arsenal during February.

The Gunners had to travel to St. James' Park and a crowd of over 65,000 watched a mouth-watering clash that ended 3–3, United coming back from behind with two goals from Smith. Firstly he converted a telling cross from Tommy Pearson with a 'flashing header' past keeper Wilson, then converted another, jumping among the fists to get to the ball with his head again, as Male and Wilson found themselves second best. In the replay, the reigning league champions went through to the next round and on to win the trophy with a convincing 3–0 victory in front of another 60,000-plus gate at Highbury, but many had noted the name of Smith.

United had a job in holding onto their newly found centre-forward star. He collected another good haul in season 1936–37 with 24 goals in 29 matches and in the short term Jack was happy enough to develop his game in a black and white shirt against the likes of Barnsley and Bury. He registered a four-goal strike against Doncaster Rovers and struck the net on eight occasions in five successive games at one point in the season.

The Magpies did challenge at the top of the table for a period, reaching fourth position, but couldn't maintain a sustained challenge good enough for promotion and slipped down the reckoning. Unsurprisingly, there was soon transfer speculation surrounding Smith. With United's failure to get back into the First Division many considered it was only a matter of time before he would follow the likes of England international Sammy Weaver – who joined Chelsea in a big move – out the door and to a better grade of football.

The following campaign was to be Smith's last for the Magpies. Another disappointing season unfolded; indeed the Magpies were lodged at the bottom of the table instead of the top, and inevitably their prized asset was too good for a relegation scrap to avoid the drop into the Third Division (North). By New Year it was inevitable that Smith would depart south, and after scoring two goals against Manchester United – a club en route for the First Division that year – he joined the Old Trafford set-up during February 1938 for a £6,500 fee.

JACK SMITH
No. 9 RATING

Fan appeal – personality and presence	7
Strike-rate	7
Shooting – power and placement	8
Heading	7
Ball skills	7
Link-play – passing, assists, crossing, team-play	7
Pace	8
Commitment – work-rate, courage	8
Match-winner – power-play, big-match capability	7
Longevity with United	4
Trophy success, international and top football ranking	-1
Total No. 9 rating	69

Newcastle were back to square one, searching for a centre-forward. Fortunately they did have a player already on their payroll who could step into Smith's boots. Billy Hart Cairns was a Geordie born and bred. On the club's staff since joining the Magpies from local side Stargate Rovers in May 1933, Cairns had already shown he could wear the leader's shirt, deputising for Smith successfully on several occasions. He had scored a hat-trick in one of his earliest games at centre-forward – against Swansea Town – and gathered 9 goals in 10 games during season 1935–36, producing an even better return the following year when he claimed 16 goals in 19 appearances including a 4-goal haul against West Ham United. Now 25 years of age the local lad was handed the opportunity to stake a claim. This he grasped and Cairns held the shirt convincingly, up to the outbreak of the Second World War.

Billy was a well-built striker; although not tall – he was 5 ft 9 in. – he was thickset and was not afraid to mix it and battle with the opposition. Cairns possessed a potent threat with his head and could leap and direct powerful headers. As one colleague noted, he 'was as good as Tommy Lawton in the air'. He also had a powerful shot and soon made his mark on the Second Division scene despite being laid low with illness for several periods.

During that relegation struggle in season 1937–38 Billy fought with spirit to help avoid disaster. Goals were difficult to come by for everyone in a black and white shirt, Billy managing only four. But the Magpies steered clear of the drop – by a whisker – and looked forward to a new era as the St. James' Park set-up was overhauled on the arrival of Stan Seymour as director during the summer.

BILLY CAIRNS
FACTS & FIGURES

To Newcastle United: May 1933 from Stargate Rovers £25

From Newcastle United: November 1944 to Gateshead

Born: Newcastle upon Tyne 7 October 1912

Died: Grimsby 9 January 1988

Height: 5 ft 9 in.

Other senior clubs: Grimsby Town

International: none

Newcastle United app & goals:

Football League: 87 app, 51 goals

FA Cup: 3 app, 2 goals

Wartime: 23 app, 14 goals

Total: 113 app, 67 goals

Strike-rate: League and Cup 59% (overall 59%)

The following season saw the Tynesiders fare much better and Cairns showed that he was the answer up front. He claimed 20 goals, including 4 against West Bromwich Albion in an early-season 5–1 rout at St. James' Park and 2 more hat-tricks against Nottingham Forest and Tranmere Rovers. At that point in the calendar, Cairns was on fire, hitting 10 goals in 5 successive games. He was described at the time as being 'a high spirited, hell for leather, shoot on sight centre-forward, determined to score no matter what the risk'.

Billy teamed up with a trio of quality players up front. Former Arsenal and England inside-forward Ray Bowden had much to do with the emergence of Cairns. His creative ability saw many chances engineered while Harry Clifton was a further tip-top player signed, this time from Chesterfield. Billy also had another fellow Geordie for company, a gangling youngster called Albert Stubbins who burst onto the scene and played off Cairns at inside-forward.

In reserve, United's management of Mather and Seymour could rely on Arthur Frost and Scotsman John Park when Cairns was out of action. From Merseyside and a former New Brighton star, Frost scored on his debut in the centre-forward shirt against Sheffield Wednesday while the versatile Park – who found a regular place at inside-forward or outside-right – proved to be a useful player. Willie Scott was another reserve to show promise. A whole-hearted lad from Bucksburn near Aberdeen who had been signed for £3,750 from the Dons, he gave Mather plenty of options as United's fortunes started to improve significantly at St. James' Park. Scott was unlucky, though, to break his leg soon after arriving on Tyneside and was out of action for a long period.

THE No. 9 SHIRT ARRIVES FOR REAL

The threat of war on the Continent increasingly became a reality as preparations for the new 1939–40 season began. Footballers had already started to join the likes of the Territorial Army and there was much concern, gloom and despondency around the country but life, and with it football, continued much as normal. During the build-up to the coming season, the Football Association introduced a well overdue enhancement to the game – the introduction of numbering to players' shirts. For over 50 years, spectators had to watch football without being able to easily recognise the players on the field. No identification or numbering system had been used. A trial was first applied when Arsenal wore numbers on their shirts in season 1928–29, while Chelsea did likewise later that year. Everton and Wolves experimented for the odd game in 1932–33 and that season's FA Cup final saw players wearing 1 to 22 on their backs. But it took another six years before the Football Association and Football League agreed to introduce numbers as compulsory for the 1939–40 season. Even then it was a close vote at the Football League AGM, the innovators just winning the day by 24 votes to 20.

One traditionalist's view in the debate that had raged over the years noted: 'In my view it has definite disadvantages as it tends to stress individuality rather than team spirit.' Simon Inglis in his history of the Football League, *League Football and the Men Who Made It*, wrote: 'Here was the hub of the matter: the deeply rooted reticence of the English to parade an identity. Better to be a face in the crowd, a cog in a wheel, than a star individual.'

Supporters, though, wanted stars and individuals. They wanted to pick their favourites and they wanted to be able to identify who was who. Numbering was here, and here to stay. Fans on Tyneside immediately linked their centre-forward idol to the newly introduced No. 9 shirt. They fitted together perfectly . . . and the centre-forward hero rapidly became the No. 9 hero.

United's first real No. 9 was unveiled on 26 August 1939, in the opening fixture of the new season at Millwall, this after the system was used in pre-season trial games and in the Football League Jubilee Fund match against Gateshead. Billy Cairns pulled on the black and white No. 9 jersey at The Den, the number appearing in red to enable it to be seen over the stripes. Willie Scott was United's first No. 9 to find the net in competitive action. Deputising for Cairns in the home game against Swansea Town, he was on the scoresheet in the 8–1 thrashing of the Swans.

As it happened, just as players received their newly numbered shirts, they were also receiving call-up numbers in the post. Only a week later, Germany's invasion of Poland took place. Everyone knew what that meant. War was declared on 3 September 1939 as Prime Minister Chamberlain's famous reassuring words, 'Peace for our time', fell on stony ground.

The eight-goal rout over the Welsh was United's last in first-class football for seven years. The career of Billy Cairns as United's newly born No. 9 hero was suddenly put on hold. He was unlucky, like hundreds of other footballers. While Cairns continued in wartime football for United – once striking five goals against Halifax Town – his time as United's No. 9 was effectively over. Billy did resurrect his career successfully with firstly Gateshead, then Grimsby Town after the war, playing on until the veteran stage and scoring almost 130 goals for the Mariners.

BILLY CAIRNS No. 9 RATING	
Fan appeal – personality and presence	7
Strike-rate	6
Shooting – power and placement	7
Heading	9
Ball skills	7
Link-play – passing, assists, crossing, team-play	7
Pace	7
Commitment – work-rate, courage	7
Match-winner – power-play, big-match capability	7
Longevity with United	8
Trophy success, international and top football ranking	-1
Total No. 9 rating	71

War saw a Government order quickly decreed to close all places of entertainment and the Football Association cancelled senior competition. As a result, clubs in turn suspended all players' contracts. The authorities thought carefully about how football should continue and a form of localised soccer was considered as the best option. Regional leagues were soon introduced, although some clubs – notably Sunderland – decided to close down for much of the war.

Newcastle United had no such thoughts of wrapping everything in cotton wool and mothballs. With Stan Seymour at the helm, the former star winger decided to use the war years wisely, searching for and grooming a crop of youngsters who would serve a newly built United when war eventually ended. His plan worked a treat. Opportunities for young talent were substantial as experienced players were not always available, many being on service in the armed forces or in essential war occupations around the country. One of those youngsters grabbed the chance to become one of the most cherished No. 9s in United's history.

STUBBINS TAKES THE STAGE

Albert Stubbins was born in Wallsend alongside the Tyne but spent much of his childhood across the Atlantic in New York and Detroit. Returning to the North-east as a 12 year old during the early '30s, Albert had the football bug, playing and watching at every opportunity. He was a Magpie nut and idolised Jimmy Richardson and the rest of United's 1932 FA Cup-winning side. He joined the United staff as an amateur in 1936 turning out for the Whitley & Monkseaton junior club. Stubbins turned professional at Gallowgate in April 1937 when 17 years old. His rise to the first eleven was meteoric, appearing for the A side in the Tyneside League, the Reserves in Central League action and then a first-team opportunity all in the same season, his Football League debut being against Luton Town on the last day of the 1937–38 programme.

An inside-forward then, he was tall, leggy and had something of a fragile-looking physique – even to the point that some of United's directors were convinced he would never make it due to his lack of build, but Stubbins was fast and could glide past opponents with ease. Modelling himself on United's FA Cup star and England inside-forward Jimmy Richardson, his raw talent was evident and playing alongside Billy Cairns in the years leading up to war, Albert learnt and developed. He was highly rated, being quickly tipped for international recognition after a series of silky displays alongside Cairns, one press comment noting 'he has all that suggests he may be an England inside-forward some day'.

Like Cairns, though, Stubbins was unfortunate to see his blossoming craft ruined by the outbreak of the Second World War. Dreams of a career at the top and playing for England were quickly dispelled as Hitler's blitzkrieg rolled across Europe. Stubbins found himself in the midst of a huge worldwide conflict, exchanging a life in the spotlight for a draughtsman's pen in Deptford's shipyard on the Wear, helping produce a steady line of destroyers and cruisers for action against the Kriegsmarine of the Third Reich.

ALBERT STUBBINS
FACTS & FIGURES

To Newcastle United: March 1936 from Whitley & Monkseaton

From Newcastle United: September 1946 to Liverpool £12,500

Born: Wallsend 13 July 1919

Died: North Shields 28 December 2002

Height: 5 ft 11 in.

Other senior clubs: none

England Victory & War international: 2 app, 0 goals

Newcastle United app & goals:

  Football League: 27 app, 5 goals

  FA Cup: 3 app, 1 goal

  Wartime: 188 app, 231 goals

  Total: 218 app, 237 goals

Strike-rate: League and Cup 20% (overall 109%)

Newcastle United and Stubbins were lucky in that Albert had a war occupation that kept him in the region. He remained on United's playing staff throughout the war years and the Wallsend youngster made the most of it, developing into the country's most potent centre-forward. With United for 10 years, 7 of those were destined to be in the unofficial war league and cup tournaments where he blasted an astonishing 231 goals. Conversely his first-class record for the Magpies before and after war was only modest – 30 appearances and 6 goals – yet in war-torn Britain he became a sensation. For the early wartime season of 1939–40, Albert continued at inside-forward but for the following 1940–41 campaign he was occasionally moved into a centre-forward role with Cairns firstly injured and then in the forces. His first game in the No. 9 shirt was during November against York City. He scored in a 3–0 victory and showed glimpses of what goal power was to follow.

Against Sheffield Wednesday Stubbins netted four goals in the No. 9 shirt and in the next fixture scored another three against Middlesbrough, then amazingly within seven days had grabbed yet another hat-trick against the men from Teesside! Stubbins fired no fewer than ten goals in three successive games in the leader's role.

Not surprisingly Albert was switched permanently to centre-forward and in season 1941–42 hit 33 goals. The goals flowed . . . in twos, threes, fours and even fives time and time again. Both Gateshead and Middlesbrough were demolished by the boot of Stubbins, Albert scoring five goals against them in each contest. The new Geordie goal-machine hit purple patches in the weeks and months to follow; 13 goals in 4 matches, 10 in 5, then 15 goals in only 9 fixtures. It was never ending; Stubbins struck 16 goals in 9 consecutive matches, 12 in 8, 14 in 7 and once 10 goals in only 4 outings!

Albert was now rapidly becoming the nation's top striker alongside Tommy Lawton and Jack Dodds of Blackpool, although he was not in the traditional mould of battling, strong target leaders. Albert himself said: 'I was different to most centre-forwards.' Flame haired, the tall and lithe striker possessed a terrific turn of speed and packed a fearsome shot from his size 11 boots – once later in his career striking the ball so hard it broke an unfortunate goalkeeper's arm! A gentleman on the field, he grabbed goals both inside and outside the box and was ready to unleash a shot from anywhere 30 yards from goal. Defenders just couldn't cope when Albert had the ball at his feet and took them head on. Having a body swerve that confounded opponents and balance to run at pace with the ball, United fans roared with encouragement when he went direct for goal – no matter how many defenders were in front of him.

The standard of wartime soccer may have not been as high as normal First or Second Division action, but as Albert said, it was still very competitive: 'Teams were rarely able to pick a settled side due to wartime commitments, but at the same time the guest system enabled many stars to team up alongside each other and play for any club. In fact, sides like Darlington and Gateshead had all-star elevens. I can't say I found a lot of difference between wartime and peacetime football. Everyone still battled to pick up the points.'

Newcastle United also used the guest system to good effect and when Stubbins was otherwise engaged on essential war activities or out injured, the Magpies fielded several dynamic No. 9 strikers from other clubs. Donald Howe of Bolton Wanderers once scored five goals in a match against York City for the Black'n'Whites, while Hugh Billington and Cec McCormack were two more noted centre-forwards to pull on the jersey. Arsenal's Eddie Carr and John Short of Leeds were also prolific scorers at centre-forward for Newcastle – Carr, with 56 goals, proving a particular success – and one of post-war football's great No. 9s, Tyneside-born Stan Mortensen, also appeared up front for the Toon. In addition, several local products developed through the ranks at Gallowgate and proved more than willing centre-forwards in wartime competition. George Moses made a mark in season 1939–40 while Andrew English did likewise the following year.

Goals continued to flood from Stubbins, now a huge favourite with the Tyneside crowd that saw football as a much welcome outlet from the melancholy atmosphere of wartime Britain. In season 1942–43, he grabbed 42 goals in only 29 fixtures, including a remarkable spell during November and December of 13 goals in 6 consecutive matches! The following year his total reached 43 in 32 appearances and in 1944–45 another 43 goals were recorded, in only 31 games. Regular opponent of Stubbins and later skipper at St. James' Park, Joe Harvey, said of the auburn-haired No. 9: 'His goals tally was breathtaking. Albert played practically all his worthwhile soccer during the Second World War, which is a pity, because it means his fabulous scoring feats are generally not shown in the record books.'

Those scoring feats were quite incredible. All told, Albert thumped 29 hat-tricks for the Magpies and he almost achieved an astonishing 5 successive hat-tricks during January and February 1941. Against Sheffield Wednesday, Rochdale and in a double meeting with Middlesbrough, Stubbins found the net with three goals in each contest, and then in the fifth game against York City put the ball in the opposition goal once, then twice. As Albert said: 'The boys kept feeding me the ball and although I hit the woodwork several times, I couldn't get it in the net for the third.' With two minutes remaining, Stubbins crashed a 15-yard shot against the underside of the crossbar. The ball bounced down onto the line and was cleared.

Although Stubbins was a formidable No. 9 and goalscorer supreme, he succeeded without resort to the rough stuff. He was big-hearted and hard-working but Albert was a true gentleman on and off the field. He possessed a placid and controlled temperament in a black and white shirt and rarely lost his cool. Stubbins himself remembered that he only lost control once in his entire career – in a white-hot wartime derby with Sunderland. The usual calm of Stubbins exploded in a set-to with Sunderland's full-back Jimmy Gorman at St. James' Park following a rough challenge on little Ernie Taylor, Stubbins ending up head to head with the Sunderland defender. Words were exchanged and as Albert said: 'I grabbed him by the throat, pushed him down and knelt on top of him.' Punches flew and both players were sent off.

Another colleague of those years, goalkeeper Ray King, noted in his autobiography: 'For such a big man he was amazingly quick, and it was commonplace to see him beat three or four opposing players before hitting a cracking drive.' Defenders hated the sight of Stubbins streaking at them in full flow. He worried them to death. King added that Albert was 'the idol of Tyneside'. With his distinctive flame hair and striking near-6 ft frame, Stubbins was instantly recognisable around Tyneside. He was a celebrity, a status that stayed with him to his last day some 50 years later. Such was his popularity that Stubbins was not only often stopped in the city's streets by well-wishers in 1945 but equally so in 1995.

As peace was restored to the world, football gradually was brought back to normality and Stubbins was recognised as one of the country's top names. Nicknamed 'The Smiling Assassin' by a journalist due to Albert's gentlemanly conduct – the Gorman incident apart – he usually smiled at defenders rather than ending in battle with them. He was also known as the 'fastest man in football' and was selected for the England side in the Victory International against Wales at The Hawthorns. Stubbins, though, was destined to be a shadow to Tommy Lawton in an England shirt.

For season 1945–46 league and cup football was all but restored. The programme was a final transition to full-blooded action and Stubbins was at the height of his goalscoring menace. With gates back to 50,000 once more, Albert continued his bludgeoning of every defence in the country. He netted 40 goals in 33 league and cup matches, starting with a hat-trick over Sheffield United on the first day of the season in an eye-catching performance. Another two five-goal strikes were recorded as well – against Stoke City in a 9–1 victory and against Blackburn, an equally rampant day in an 8–1 triumph.

However, despite his huge popularity and national standing, Albert wanted to play football at the very top. Now 27 years of age, and having lost seven seasons to wartime football, reaching the England side only reinforced his view that in the limited years he had in the game he needed to taste life in Division One and catch up on lost time. Albert said: 'I wanted to pit myself against the best.' And the Geordies were still a Second Division club as football returned in earnest for the 1946–47 season. Stubbins couldn't wait for a new emerging Magpie eleven to develop and gain promotion. He needed to move from Tyneside.

A bombshell hit both the club and supporters in September 1946 when the Tynesider asked for a transfer. United, in the shape of Stan Seymour, pleaded with Albert to stay but reluctantly agreed to his move, understanding the position. There was no shortage of buyers in the queue. Secretary Frank Watt was inundated with offers from clubs, reported as many as 18, with Merseyside rivals Everton and Liverpool ending up as the two front-runners for his prized signature.

ALBERT STUBBINS
No. 9 RATING

Fan appeal – personality and presence	9
Strike-rate	10
Shooting – power and placement	9
Heading	7
Ball skills	8
Link-play – passing, assists, crossing, team-play	8
Pace	8
Commitment – work-rate, courage	8
Match-winner – power-play, big-match capability	8
Longevity with United	10
Trophy success, international and top football ranking	-3
Total No. 9 rating	82

Stubbins talked to both clubs and it was Liverpool who received the nod, Albert noting: 'I did that because I played with many of their players when they were guesting for Newcastle during the war. I struck up friendships with their inside-forwards Willie Fagan and Jack Balmer and as I was a centre-forward I knew that friendship would help on the field.' In addition the Reds assisted Albert to find a columnist role with the *Liverpool Echo*, laying a future for the Geordie in journalism after his football career.

Liverpool paid a near record British fee of £12,500 for his exceptional talent and United were forced to rebuild their post-war side without Albert's formidable goal capability. Stan Seymour turned to one of a group of his up-and-coming locally bred youngsters – County Durham-born Charlie Wayman.

MORE LOCAL NO. 9 TALENT

From Bishop Auckland, Charlie Wayman took over from the versatile George Stobbart – another native talent from Pegswood – who was initially handed the No. 9 shirt following Stubbins' departure at the start of the 1946–47 season. Joining the Magpies in September for £4,650 as Albert Stubbins headed for Anfield, Stobbart was a versatile striker, a 'good all-round leader' and as one colleague said, was 'hard as nails'. Stockily built, he netted twice in his first outing in the No. 9 shirt against Coventry City and was exceptionally quick off the mark, 'faster at times than Jackie Milburn' according to Charlie Crowe. An ankle injury to the solid frame of Stobbart in a fixture with Barnsley at Oakwell was an unlucky break for the former Middlesbrough striker who had scored over 100 goals for the Tees club, but it opened the door for Wayman. Stobbart however proved an able player in the next three and a half seasons to United, although he rarely figured in his favoured No. 9 role.

Like many from the North-east of his generation, Wayman began his teenage life down the pit, at Chilton, and plenty of Newcastle United's stars of the immediate post-war years were to be discovered in this way, grafting a hard slog down the pit-shaft and playing local football.

Charlie was a little terrier at only 5 ft 6 in. tall and hardly looked the picture of a traditional centre-forward. He started his career as one of Stan Seymour's youngsters during the early years of the war at inside-forward or on the wing and had an eye for goal, possessing a finish and a stinging shot with his left foot. Impressing Seymour playing for Chilton Boys and Spennymoor United – scoring 65 goals in one season – and then in a trial, Wayman said of his first meeting with the man known as Mr Newcastle: 'He would not let me go home until I signed a contract.' One biography of the day described him as a 'whole-hearted 90 minutes player', yet when he was handed the centre-forward's shirt there were a few eyebrows raised. Wayman later recorded: 'Everybody at Newcastle laughed when I got my chance.' But Charlie seized the opportunity and certainly made an impact.

CHARLIE WAYMAN
FACTS & FIGURES

To Newcastle United: September 1941 from Spennymoor
  United
From Newcastle United: October 1947 to Southampton
  £10,000
Born: Bishop Auckland 16 May 1921
Height: 5 ft 6 in.
Other senior clubs: Preston North End, Middlesbrough,
  Darlington
International: none
Newcastle United app & goals:
  Football League: 47 app, 32 goals
  FA Cup: 6 app, 4 goals
  Wartime: 71 app, 35 goals
  Total: 124 app, 71 goals
Strike-rate: League and Cup 68% (overall 57%)

Wayman was an instant success in a very different style to some of the big and powerful No. 9 stars of the past. He was a Hughie Gallacher of a player; skilful, impish and knew where the goal was. Charlie commented: 'The things that count are craft, nippiness and positional play, and a determination to challenge in the air.'

In the opening weeks of that first season after the war when football enjoyed a boom around the country – and nowhere more than at St. James' Park where fans flooded through the turnstiles – Wayman showed he packed a punch. He scored no fewer than three hat-tricks in his first three home games at centre-forward: against Newport, Manchester City and Sheffield Wednesday. Charlie was an on the spot hero as Newcastle showed they were going to make a determined bid to get back into the top drawer of football quickly. And what a first outing Wayman experienced in the No. 9 shirt.

In front of a 52,137 crowd at St. James' Park, United entertained Newport County, an ageing side made up largely of pre-war veterans. United's young and forceful eleven tore the Welshmen apart, establishing not only a new club scoring record, but the highest scoreline in the top two divisions – a record that still stands to this day. The Magpies, with

Len Shackleton on his debut in scintillating mood, thrashed Newport 13–0! The irrepressible Shackleton hit a double hat-trick and Wayman crashed home four goals, this after firing a penalty in the opening two minutes against a post and wide – his first ever spot-kick. The diminutive striker then made amends and proceeded to bang home three goals before the interval! Wayman gave Norman Low at centre-half the run-a-round. The son of United's noted half-back, Wilf Low, the Newport defender did not enjoy his day on Tyneside at all. Wayman said: 'He was slow, like many centre-halfs in those days.' Wayman's tenacity, darting runs and pace had Low in all sorts of trouble. It was a fabulous start and he never looked back. Charlie remarked: 'I was a centre-forward ever after.'

Many judges rated the new goalscoring sensation as a great find. He looked an expert opportunist who could delight the crowd with dribbling runs, especially in the box. Colleague and skipper Joe Harvey remembered Charlie as being 'small but brave, quick and a deadly finisher'. *The Journal*'s reporter Ken McKenzie wrote: 'Wayman's quickness to take a chance close to goal did the trick every time.' In that 1946–47 season Wayman totalled 34 goals and he was the country's leading goalscorer while only Hughie Gallacher had scored more in a single season for the Toon. He did much to drive United to challenge for promotion and all was looking good until the Magpies headed off on an FA Cup run in January.

Newcastle were now recognised as a new force, trapped only temporarily out of the elite, and they demolished top First Division side Sheffield United in a run that looked like it would go all the way to Wembley. They faced another Division One outfit in Charlton Athletic in the semi-final at Elland Road and in many quarters United were favourites despite their Second Division status. A forward line of Milburn, Bentley, Wayman, Shackleton and Pearson overflowed with youth, class, attacking ideas and goals. Wayman was by now the fans' idol and dangerman. Yet astonishingly he was dropped for the meeting with the Londoners, George Stobbart being selected in his place. Following a somewhat petty dispute with trainer Norman Smith at Seahouses when the squad was on what was called a 'Special Training' break in readiness for the semi-final, Smith and Wayman had a bitter disagreement and the long-serving trainer reported Charlie to the directors. Wayman recorded: 'Smith was always getting at me. Whatever I did, he would have a go at me.' The story got into the press before the game and the atmosphere in the dressing-room quickly deteriorated. There was trouble in the camp.

It was sensational news, and a decision that shocked everyone, inside and outside the dressing-room. Charlie's colleagues couldn't believe it. Roy Bentley wrote in his autobiography *Going for Goal*: 'We learnt to our dismay that Charlie Wayman was dropped.' He added: 'Many of us thought it was a mistake that contributed towards our defeat.'

United's defeat was heavy. They went down 0–4 and clearly the controversy had affected team morale. They were only a shade of the stylish and attacking eleven that had scored over 80 goals in the season so far. Inquests were held all over the North-east. The local press were critical and had their say while supporters were furious. Newcastle United's management was castigated and accused of a 'lack of acumen for substituting Stobbart for Wayman'. There were many calls for Charlie's reinstatement. One reporter wrote: 'The sooner Wayman returns the better for United.'

Wayman was immediately reinstated, but the pocket-sized striker was not to return for long. The incident soured relationships between player and trainer Smith in particular, to a point where the differences could not be patched up. Wayman was to later record that he never wanted to leave St. James' Park but had no alternative. He said: 'I had to. It could never have been the same again.' And Jackie Milburn spoke of Wayman's frustration after the incident when his teammate couldn't find room to hang up his clothes, Charlie saying: 'Bloody hell! I can't even get a peg in the dressing-room now. I'm off.'

CHARLIE WAYMAN
No. 9 RATING

Fan appeal – personality and presence	7
Strike-rate	6
Shooting – power and placement	8
Heading	7
Ball skills	8
Link-play – passing, assists, crossing, team-play	8
Pace	8
Commitment – work-rate and courage	8
Match-winner – power-play, big-match capability	8
Longevity with United	5
Trophy success, international and top football ranking	-2
Total No. 9 rating	71

Wayman's career with United had promised to develop into something quite special. But now it was all but over. Several clubs clamoured for his services when it was clear United would listen to offers. Wayman had made a big impression on Southampton boss Bill Dodgin – after netting all three against the Saints in a 3–1 United FA Cup victory a few weeks earlier. A fee of £10,000 was agreed and Wayman was off to The Dell and on to a respected career of plenty of goals in the next decade.

United had lost another potent No. 9 and it was their own doing. However, as one door closed another opened for one of Wayman's colleagues. Another local lad was to be handed the No. 9 shirt – and rapidly the unsavoury Wayman business was a thing of the past as United's new choice in the leader's role developed into perhaps the club's biggest ever centre-forward hero.

No. 9 EXTRAS

HURRICANE HUTCH

Duncan Hutchison arrived on Tyneside with a glowing reputation and with the marvellous nickname of Hurricane Hutch. Taken from a dare-devil film star and comic-book character of the era, Hutchison had a rip-roaring style and became a legend to Dundee United supporters. After his stint in England, he returned north of the border to become a Tannadice director in 1953 and was later appointed Chairman. He remained connected with Dundee United for almost 20 years.

CUP CONTROVERSY

Apart from Jack Allen's FA Cup 'over the line goal' at Wembley in 1932, the Geordie striker was also involved in another moment of cup controversy appearing for Sheffield Wednesday in an all Yorkshire semi-final clash with Huddersfield Town in 1930. At Old Trafford, his team lost by the odd goal in three and perhaps the Owls were on the wrong side of some harsh decisions. Huddersfield firstly levelled with what appeared to be a clear 'punched' pass before going ahead and Allen had thought he had netted a very late equaliser when he unleashed a shot in the dying seconds – the ball flying into the net only for the referee to blow for full-time as it was in mid-air and with only 43 minutes played of the second half!

FAMILY AFFAIR
The Allen family made quite an impact on the football scene. Apart from Jack's medal-winning haul for United and Sheffield Wednesday, his brother Ralph was also a celebrated goalscorer, netting over 100 goals, notably for Charlton, Brentford and Northampton. At The Valley, he hit 48 goals in only 54 games and created a Charlton league record during season 1934–35 of 32 goals in the campaign – as the Londoners lifted the Division Three (South) title. Jack's daughter later became High Sheriff of Tyne & Wear, while his two grandsons are barristers in London.

JACK – AFTER TOON
Following a spell with Bristol Rovers, Jack Allen soon wanted a move back to his native North-east and in August 1935 joined Gateshead's Football League outfit at Redheugh Park. He left the first-class scene a year later, appearing for Ashington before settling in the region and becoming a celebrity publican at The Travellers Rest in Burnopfield up to his death.

REYROLLES TO ENGLAND
Welshman Ronnie Williams wasn't a huge hit in the black and white shirt and he had frequent spells in United's reserves. Indeed, during one stint in September 1934 Ronnie played for the club's third eleven against the Reyrolles works side. United's 'A' outfit lost the Tyneside League fixture by 0–3, yet only three days later he was lining up for his country for the first time in a prestige Home International meeting against England! It was quite a transformation. Coming in for the injured Dai Astley of Aston Villa, instead of factory players, he now faced the best England could muster. Played at Ninian Park, Wales lost the match 0–4.

SMITH – AFTER TOON
Jack's move to Old Trafford was not paved in gold as he clocked up a mere 15 senior goals for Manchester United. Although he scored on his debut for the Reds against Barnsley and helped the club to promotion, he struck only six goals in the following season and was soon facing the

prospect of the Second World War like every other footballer of his era. But Jack did well in wartime soccer for the Reds, striking another 160 goals. Smith guested for Burnley during the hostilities and after peace was restored turned out for Blackburn Rovers and Port Vale before moving to non-league football with Macclesfield Town. After football, he entered business in the Manchester area.

BILLY THE KNIFE
Billy Cairns was often under the surgeon's knife during his career, and his overall goals record of almost 250 for United, Gateshead and Grimsby is even more admirable as he twice was in hospital for duodenal ulcer operations as well as having to undergo an appendicitis operation – this in addition to all the normal footballer injuries he had to cope with.

FIRST No. 9
When the No. 9 shirt was introduced in 1939, Billy Cairns was the man to first pull on the famous jersey. It was noted that spectators were none too complimentary, the press noting that 'the numbers gave the crowd a laugh'. A number was sewn over the stripes and was initially very 'indistinct' – a continuing problem over decades for the stripes of Newcastle United. The first centre-forward to wear the No. 9 shirt *against* the Magpies was none other than Hughie Gallacher, who led the Gateshead line in a Jubilee Fund match. He also was the first No. 9 to miss a penalty against United – firing over the bar in front of an 18,092 crowd.

BILLY – AFTER TOON
Billy Cairns guested for several clubs during the Second World War, Liverpool and Sunderland included, and as football got back to normal became a noted goalscorer, firstly for Gateshead where he once netted 42 goals in a single season, then for Grimsby Town. Joining the Mariners in May 1946, Billy enjoyed a long spell at Blundell Park as his career spanned into the veteran stage. He played on until he was over 40 years of age and scored 129 times in 231 senior games for Town, becoming a huge favourite with the other black and whites. On retiring, Cairns was coach to Grimsby for a while and then a popular publican in Cleethorpes to his death.

STUBBINS WITH SUNDERLAND
Albert actually began his football career at Roker Park signing amateur forms for Sunderland in 1935. However being black and white daft,

Stubbins had agreed with Sunderland boss Johnny Cochrane that if Newcastle showed an interest in him, he would be allowed to leave and join the Magpies. United did of course and Cochrane was as good as his word. Stubbins also guested for Sunderland in three games during 1941–42, including an appearance in the War Cup final alongside Raich Carter against Wolves. He scored in the first leg but Sunderland lost 3–6 on aggregate.

SERVING No. 9s

Several of United's centre-forwards joined the forces for the Second World War. Willie Scott, along with colleagues Doug Wright and Dave Hamilton, joined the Tyneside Scottish Black Watch regiment. Scott was one of the 30,000 who did not get away from the Dunkirk beaches in 1940, captured and imprisoned by the Nazis. Charlie Wayman joined the Navy and was an Able Seaman for a period, while George King was with the RAF. Several players remained in the North-east on essential war work; Albert Stubbins was a draughtsman in the Wearside shipyards and Jackie Milburn headed down the pit in a reserved occupation as well as joining the local Air Training Corps squadron.

ALBERT'S FIRST STRIKE

The first of Albert Stubbins' 237 goals in a black and white shirt took place in September 1938 at The Hawthorns against West Bromwich Albion and three days later he scored another, this time at St. James' Park against Burnley. In a deep position, he passed to Billy Cairns and then sprinted through the centre-forward track into space. Cairns hit a return ball perfectly ahead of Albert and as the full-back and goalkeeper raced for the ball, Stubbins slid forward and poked the ball past the two defenders and into the net. Albert said of that significant moment: 'I was so excited I could hardly breathe.'

LIKING THE BORO

The wartime goal-machine of Albert Stubbins was especially in tip-top form when Middlesbrough were the opposition. The Tyneside No. 9 scored no fewer than 42 goals against Boro, including twice netting 5-goal strikes and 6 other hat-tricks!

1939–40	2 goals
1940–41	7 goals
1941–42	7 goals

1942–43	10 goals
1943–44	4 goals
1944–45	10 goals
1945–46	2 goals
Total	42 goals

HAT-TRICK KING

No other player has scored more hat-tricks for Newcastle United in senior games than Albert Stubbins. Hughie Gallacher holds the record in league and cup football with 14 hat-tricks, but Stubbins thumped 29 in wartime soccer!

5-goal strikes	5
4-goal strikes	6
3-goal strikes	18
Total hat-tricks	29

GREATS ON STUBBINS

Jackie Milburn:

'I idolised the man and learned from him the dignity and humility needed to help carry the burden of being a star.'

'He was a gentleman, the epitome of what a professional footballer should be.'

Sir Bobby Robson:

'My boyhood hero. The centre-forward I hero-worshipped as a young lad, a marvellous goalscoring centre-forward.'

MOST MEMORABLE MOMENT

Albert Stubbins never hesitated when he noted that his most memorable moment in a wonderful 16-year career was an April evening in 1937 after a Newcastle Reserves fixture against North Shields Reserves. As he said: 'The day I signed pro for Newcastle United.' He added: 'It tops winning the championship, getting to Wembley and playing for England!'

STUBBINS – AFTER TOON

With Liverpool, Albert Stubbins was just as popular as on Tyneside. He was an influential figure as the Reds lifted the championship in 1947 – scoring the goal against Wolves that clinched the title trophy. The Geordie netted 83 goals in 180 matches, also reaching the FA Cup final in 1950. He left the first-class game in 1953 and joined Ashington before later becoming a Liverpool scout for a period and coaching in the States. He settled on Tyneside, for many years becoming a respected soccer journalist, notably for *The People*.

SGT PEPPER FAME

Albert Stubbins achieved everlasting fame not only for his footballing exploits but also for being one of the 63 characters featured on the sleeve of the seminal Beatles album *Sgt Pepper's Lonely Hearts Club Band* released in 1967. Pictured just to the right of George Harrison, looking over the shoulder of Marlene Dietrich and standing alongside Lewis Carroll, Albert apparently was a favourite of the McCartney family – a testimony to his fame on Merseyside.

COMMONS DEBATE

When Charlie Wayman joined Newcastle United during the early years of the war the transfer was the subject of a debate brought in front of Parliament. Indirectly, Wayman's transfer was brought to the Commons ear when a Wansbeck pitman seeking to leave the mines quoted Wayman's case through MP Alf Robens. It led to a Ministry of Labour ruling on the release of mineworkers from their trade in the immediate post-war years. The Parliamentary secretary to the Ministry of Labour argued that Charlie Wayman was an 'inexperienced' miner who had been released from the Navy, whereas the Wansbeck miner had worked in the industry for many years and was a valuable asset.

CHARLIE – AFTER TOON

On leaving the Magpies Charlie Wayman developed into a most popular striker at all his clubs, notably at The Dell with Southampton and at Deepdale with Preston North End. With the Saints he fired in 77 goals in 107 senior outings then after moving to Preston in September 1950 netted over 100 goals, becoming an influential factor in that club's promotion to Division One and run to Wembley in 1954. Charlie scored in every round of the FA Cup in that year, including the final defeat by West Bromwich Albion. After winding his career down back in the North-east with Middlesbrough and Darlington – scoring over 300 senior career goals – Wayman coached Evenwood Town briefly before working for Scottish & Newcastle Breweries for many years in the region.

4. WOR JACKIE'S REIGN
1947–1957

JACKIE MILBURN, VIC KEEBLE

The man who perhaps created and epitomised United's No. 9 tradition more than any other player had a remarkable introduction to the team he was to serve so well and adore so much. Over 60 years ago, Jackie Milburn sat on top of the St. James' Park steps which fronted the old West Stand waiting for the players to gather for a pre-season trial match. It was a wet and somewhat dismal day. In one hand, he held a pair of borrowed boots wrapped in brown paper, in the other a pie for lunch. An hour or so later, Wor Jackie was racing around the Gallowgate turf making a huge impression on the watching Newcastle United directorate and supremo Stan Seymour in particular. It was the start of a love affair between player, club and supporters still revered to this day.

As a 19 year old, Milburn had written to the club for trials in response to an advert in the *North Mail* during 1943. The teenager was invited to Gallowgate, together with an Ashington friend, for the mid-week run-out, along with a host of other budding footballers at the start of the season. Included was a future colleague, Charlie Crowe, who later won the FA Cup alongside Milburn. The pair met on those famous St. James' Park steps and passed the time together before their big day. Charlie was to say: 'He quickly impressed and was snapped up and walked into the first team.' His performance could have been picked from Roy of the Rovers.

Milburn was selected to appear during the second half of the Probables v. The Rest contest and he did well, scoring two goals. Jack later noted he was fortunate to be surrounded by good players, remembering: 'I was stuck between Bobby Jacques and Charlie Woollett. The service was there. I was lucky.'

Jackie had dazzled with his zest and skill. He was told to come back again for the final public trial at the weekend, The Stripes v. The Blues. Milburn once again made the 15-mile journey from Ashington, had his pre-match meal of a meat pie then proceeded to make the watching Newcastle United directors glow with anticipation at the young, raw player who was running rings around some of their seasoned professionals. Jackie played for the Stripes but at first his side was given a lesson, being 0–3 down at half-time and things did not go Jackie's way. Trainer Joe Richardson, the gritty ex-United full-back, noted at the break: 'You better buck up your ideas son, if you want to come here.' He added: 'Come on lad, snap out of it. Show us what you did last week.' Milburn took note and was a different player. In the second period, the Stripes clicked and Jackie ran riot as he switched to centre-forward netting no fewer than six times as his side rattled in nine goals! The local *Sunday Sun* reporter recorded that Milburn was 'a tall youth who showed great capacity for quick attack and opportunism'. Newcastle's regular No. 9 Albert Stubbins, who played in the first-half but sat out the second period, was mesmerised by what he called 'this electrifying figure'. Milburn was to note: 'From that day on I was in the first team, and I never looked back.'

At that time Stan Seymour ran Newcastle United in all but name. The former Magpie winger was a powerful force and he immediately took a liking to Milburn. He later said of Jackie's dramatic opening: 'Within minutes I knew he had what it takes to make the grade.' He went on to say: 'I decided there and then he was a future star.' Seymour quickly travelled to Ashington to meet the Milburn family and make sure he signed the star in the making. There was little doubt of the outcome as Jackie's father was a United supporter and Seymour was one of his past heroes. Stan recorded: 'I produced the forms and in a flash the eager youngster had appended his signature.' Jackie joined Newcastle United and received a £10 signing-on fee noting: 'I'd never seen so much money in my life.' The date written into the club's official player register was 27 August 1943. Seymour later said that Milburn was his greatest discovery. From that moment, Jackie Milburn rapidly became the Geordies' hero and the club's foremost ambassador for over 30 years. His name became synonymous with Newcastle United and with Tyneside, even to people who only had a passing interest in the game.

JACKIE MILBURN
FACTS & FIGURES

To Newcastle United: August 1943 from Ashington ATC
From Newcastle United: June 1957 to Linfield £5,000
  plus player
Born: Ashington 11 May 1924
Died: Ashington 9 October 1988
Height: 5 ft 11 in.
Other senior clubs: none
England international: 13 app, 10 goals
Newcastle United app & goals:
  Football League: 353 app, 177 goals
  FA Cup: 44 app, 23 goals
  Wartime: 95 app, 38 goals
  Others: 2 app, 1 goal
  Total: 494 app, 239 goals
Strike-rate: League and Cup 50% (overall 48%)

From the working-class coalfield of Northumberland, John Edward Thompson Milburn – surely no other footballer had such an appropriate set of initials as JET – was born in Ashington only a few days after Newcastle United had lifted the FA Cup at Wembley in 1924. Brought up in the traditional workers' terraces, the son of a coal-cutter, his early life revolved around two things – the pit and football. For hours and hours, day after day he practised in the backyard and cobbled streets. From established football stock, his family were all soccer mad and he is a member of what is still perhaps the greatest footballing clan in Britain. The first Jack Milburn played in goal for Shankhouse and Northumberland during the pioneering days of the game. Then there was 'Warhorse' Milburn, a famous local full-back and huge character. He had 13 children and several played football. Tanner Milburn appeared for Ashington during their Football League days and the family grew even further when this particular Milburn had four sons, as well as three daughters. The boys of course took to kicking a ball around the terraced streets of Ashington.

Tanner's brother, Alec, also played for Ashington after turning down a chance with Tottenham and he produced Wor Jackie, while Tanner's offspring turned out in league football too; George, Stan, Jim and Jack. All played for Leeds United except Stan, who appeared for Chesterfield and Leicester City, as well as the Football League side, and all were tough and noted performers. Additionally Jimmy Potts, the Leeds goalkeeper, married into the Milburns. It was quite a family, which became further entangled, as Tanner's daughter, Cissie, gave the football world both Jackie and Bobby Charlton, World Cup winners in 1966.

Milburn left school in 1938 when aged 14. Instead of going down the pit like most of his age group, the young Northumbrian took a job in Dorking as a pantry boy, far flung from his future success. Homesickness soon brought him back north, though, and Jack headed to the local colliery like almost everyone else in Ashington.

He started his football career assisting Hirst East Old Boys and later Ashington YMCA. War in 1939 saw Milburn try to join the Navy but, lacking height, he was rejected. Twelve months later he had shot up to 5 ft 11 in. and worked in the pit's saddlers' shop as an apprentice fitter. His football progress was outstanding. He appeared for the local ATC side, for Welfare Rangers and REC Rovers as well as for the county eleven. But Jackie was never a centre-forward then. He wanted to be a winger and had no thoughts of wearing the No. 9 shirt, even though the Milburn family, and the rest of Ashington, had been brought up on famous tales of United's No. 9, Hughie Gallacher. Jackie's hero was Arsenal's Joe Hulme, fast and dangerous on the touch-line. He later said of those early days: 'I vowed I would never play centre-forward. I played once in that position at school, and I was terrible!' So, despite the tradition which was even then embedded into local society, one of United's most famous No. 9s had no wish to take the centre-forward's role. But football's strange quirks changed that in time.

As a professional footballer, Milburn made an immediate impact. Following on from that dramatic trial for the Magpies, he was thrown into the senior eleven for the wartime contest with Bradford City at Valley Parade. United lost 1–2, but as Jackie recalled it was: 'The most memorable moment of my career, even those Wembley victories can't match it. To pull on the black and white jersey for the first time was something special.' Milburn started at inside-forward in the No. 10 shirt and saw the man who was to be his skipper and friend for many a year, Joe Harvey who was in the Bradford City line-up, score the winning goals. Jackie admitted he was nervous, but in spite of the defeat Seymour told him: 'You'll be in the side again next week.' He was, in fact, in the side for the next 14 years!

That match a week later was to be Jackie's home debut, a return meeting with the Yorkshire club, and it took Milburn a matter of minutes to show the Geordie public what was to follow – the first of nearly 250 goals scored for United – and it was achieved with almost his first kick too, a left-foot drive from 10 yards at the Leazes End, all within 120 seconds of the start. United won 3–2 and the name of Milburn was on the scoresheet.

The Ashington teenager continued at inside-forward – both on the right and left channels – during those latter years of the Second World War, a position that many judges, including ex-England international Charlie Buchan, reckoned was his best. He also played on the flank and showed the swiftness of foot that was to later bag many goals from the centre-forward position. Teammate Ray King noted his speed was exceptional; he quipped: 'He could catch pigeons.' The *Journal's* respected correspondent Ken McKenzie wrote: 'Milburn's speed astonished the crowd.' His pace always troubled opposing full-backs while he could also hit pinpoint crosses . . . and was still a goalscorer from the wing. In season 1945–46, he claimed 16 goals, mainly as he cut in from the right touch-line.

Jackie was still a raw talent and still a part-time professional, like most of his colleagues, but learnt the rudiments of professional football rapidly. Milburn worked in the workshops at one of the local collieries, and combined hard graft at the pit with football's pleasures. Sometimes he worked a double-shift on a Friday evening so he could play for Newcastle United the following day!

As football returned to normal after war, Newcastle United's No. 9 shirt was held by Albert Stubbins and then Charlie Wayman. Milburn continued to learn and impress. In season 1946–47, Jackie remained on the flank, as he did for the start of the following 1947–48 season, alongside such esteemed names of the coming '50s era as Len Shackleton, Roy Bentley and little Ernie Taylor. But following Wayman's controversial departure Newcastle United's management, in the shape of boss George Martin and director Stan Seymour, needed to fill the No. 9 shirt.

At St. James' Park during that period were home-grown young strikers Andy Donaldson from Benwell, and Amble's George King, brother to United keeper Ray King. Both players had much promise. King, a well-built leader, managed only two appearances, but on his debut against Spurs nearly hit the headlines, the press commenting that he 'might even have deserved the heading King of Trumps if he had just been blessed with a bit of luck which would have left him with a hat-trick instead of blanks'. King experienced that the difference between being catapulted into stardom or mediocrity is very slight.

Donaldson, tall and leggy, did have a fine run at centre-forward striking 5 times during August and September 1948 and totalled 9 goals in 31 appearances in a black and white shirt all told. But he was always rated by Seymour to be second choice to Milburn and soon moved to Middlesbrough for a hefty £17,500 in January 1949.

At the time neither player was considered as being ready to be plunged into the first-team limelight and thereafter they were unable to break into the senior eleven with any real conviction. Inside-forward Roy Bentley also showed he could do a job in the No. 9 shirt having swapped roles for a handful of games with Charlie Wayman – netting a hat-trick against Bradford Park Avenue. Yet his time as a centre-forward would be on hold until he pulled on the blue shirt of Chelsea – as well as the white one of England.

The only other real contender for the centre-forward's role was George Stobbart. He was injured, though, and Martin turned to Jackie Milburn, prompted by big centre-half Frank Brennan, who thought Jackie would make a brilliant leader. Trainer Norman Smith did not share the view and even Seymour had doubts, but Martin was adamant Milburn would succeed. Jackie himself was hesitant and it is even recorded in the club's official minutes that he requested a transfer because 'he did not desire to play centre-forward'!

A PERFECT FIT IN THE No. 9 SHIRT

During October 1947 Martin handed the No. 9 shirt to Milburn for the game with Bury and Jackie later recorded that 'for two nights preceding the visit to Gigg Lane, I hardly slept a wink'.

Against Bury, though, he had a touch of luck. The home goalkeeper George Bradshaw broke his leg and had to be replaced by centre-forward Jimmy Constantine. He was no goalkeeper and with Bury down to ten men Milburn had much more room to operate. Jackie rattled in a hat-trick and a new No. 9 hero was born, even though he was a reluctant centre-forward – and furthermore a reluctant hero too. Milburn never considered he had the ability to play the centre-forward's role. But George Martin managed to persuade Jackie to stick it out, maintaining he had all the assets to become a great leader – pace, ability to run with the ball and devastating shooting. Jackie respected Martin highly, he was one of 'the most astute managers I have ever met', he said. Milburn listened, he took in advice and as Jackie admitted later, the switch to centre-forward 'changed my life'.

In Jackie's first three games in the No. 9 shirt he netted six goals! He was an instant success and soon was the talk of the country. Against Luton he crashed home a stunning hat-trick and the *Sunday Sun*'s correspondent wrote: 'Milburn's refreshing pace and enterprise dominated the proceedings . . . Milburn's speed and abandon took him very close to a phenomenal goals glut and encourage high hopes that he will spearhead United to promotion.'

By the end of the 1947–48 season Milburn certainly spearheaded United back into Division One – he was top scorer with 20 goals. One biography of the time described Milburn as: 'Long-legged, fleet-footed and ever willing to have a shot at goal.' He was celebrated also for 'his noted left-hook shot, which he delivers with lightning speed from almost impossible angles'.

During those early months, however, Jack was still a hesitant No. 9 and the club's management acted. Milburn was to have a new partner in attack with the club record £18,500 purchase of Welsh international centre-forward George Lowrie from Coventry City. Lowrie was, at the time, the third most expensive transfer in the game. He had earned much credit since the war ended, scoring 47 times in 1946–47 and in the opening months of 1947–48, as well as grabbing a headlining hat-trick for Wales against England at Wembley. Milburn moved across the forward line as Lowrie was installed at centre-forward. The Welshman almost had a dream start, getting the ball in the net after only 20 seconds against Southampton, but his strike was chalked offside.

The new season brought an opening salvo of three goals from Lowrie but he then turned his knee with no one challenging and was out of action for six months. Lowrie's injury prompted United's directors to push Milburn back to centre-forward and look elsewhere for a player to link alongside Jackie – in almost a double strike role.

Lowrie was eventually replaced by a stocky Chilean, George Robledo who joined the staff from Barnsley for a substantial £23,000 fee along with his brother Ted. Had Lowrie not been injured, Wor Jackie may never have become such a No. 9 hero, nor would Tyneside have bonded so closely to the South American.

As United started life back in the elite of football for season 1948–49, Milburn went off like a bomb. He now had become accustomed to the centre-forward's trade and looked the part. Linking with Ernie Taylor and Bobby Mitchell in particular, Milburn became the country's new rising star. He grabbed 19 goals in that year and in 1949–50 was United's top scorer for the third season in a row, when he hit 21 goals, including a spell of 10 in only 10 appearances. This meant youngsters in reserve, notably Andy Graver and John Duncan, had only a fleeting glimpse of first-team action. Versatile wing-half Frank Houghton deputised in the No. 9 shirt on occasion too – scoring three times.

Milburn was an adaptable leader, not restricted to staying in the centre-forward channel. He roved around the forward line, as Hughie Gallacher observed. The United legend remarked Jackie 'wandered to the right wing, to the left wing' and it 'paid rich dividends'. He was not the robust target centre-forward of tradition. He disliked the ball in the air, while he was not a selfish or ruthless type of striker either. He was of mild nature, Joe Harvey once noting he was 'gentle and generous in victory, always first with the handshake in defeat'. Milburn always considered playing in another colleague on the field, to an extent he was sometimes criticised for not having a crack at goal himself. Indeed Jackie admitted, 'I had a lack of devil.' Had he possessed that ruthless and selfish streak, heaven knows what he might have achieved.

Yet despite his lack of devil, Milburn was a still a radiant player. Jack used his attributes to their full extent – pace, quick thinking, shooting and, as Len Shackleton remarked, a 'never-say-die spirit'. He would chase for the ball, perfecting what was a characteristic Milburn sliding tackle, hooking his leg around the man in possession and pinching the ball. He had the ability to hit the ball with either foot and with tremendous power. Charlie Crowe said: 'He was the most natural striker of the ball I've ever seen.' And he could strike the leather from seemingly impossible angles and with little back-lift. Jackie could turn and fire in a shot in tight positions, on the proverbial sixpence. Goalkeeper Ronnie Simpson recalled: 'How this man could

120

hit a ball! He could thrash it into the net from 30 yards without any apparent effort with either foot.' And as Simpson also remembered, he did it 'all against the book'. Jackie was unorthodox in style, leaning back to crack the ball low into the corner. It was all wrong, but it worked for him.

His other main asset was his pace. Milburn had the stride of a giant. He could run 100 yards in around 10 seconds. When in full flight, Jackie was devastating, racing past defenders head on to goal. He was one of the fastest men in football during what was later known as the 'Golden Age' of the game. The great Shackleton, who had a brief period alongside Milburn in United's ranks, wrote: 'Whenever I think of Jackie Milburn I think of a greyhound going out of a trap.' He possessed tremendous acceleration and not just in a chase. Bobby Charlton recalled: 'His ball control at speed was as good as anyone I've seen. He'd run at defenders to make them commit themselves.' Albert Stubbins was also impressed with this important part of his game, noting: 'Jackie's running power with the ball at his feet was quite astonishing and one of his greatest gifts.'

Jackie also possessed the flair of a supreme match-winner. His electrifying runs had the crowd roaring with delight . . . and he proved to be a big-match player as United's FA Cup exploits were to soon prove. Colleague for a decade, Bob Stokoe, remarked: 'He was the most exciting thing I have seen on a football field.'

All this made him the Geordies' favourite. After the Second World War, people wanted a hero figure and Jackie Milburn fitted the bill perfectly. The crowd took to the local pit-boy who made good. But unlike some centre-forward characters of past and future – notably Hughie Gallacher and Malcolm Macdonald – Jackie's nature was not inclined to seek adulation and attention. He was an extremely modest and even shy man, who liked the quiet life and time at home. He tried to avoid the glory and icon status which was to come his way. That was impossible to achieve yet it never changed him. He was a down to earth Ashington lad from the moment he pulled on the Black'n'White's shirt to the day he died. And he wanted to be just like anyone else. He was always approachable, rarely refusing to have a word. Jack Charlton perhaps summed up his relative in his introduction to Mike Kirkup's biography of Jackie, *Jackie Milburn: In Black and White*. The England centre-half wrote: 'He was everybody's friend! If you ever walked thro' Newcastle with him, you got stopped every two minutes; everybody said Hello to him; everybody called him

Jack.' Charlton added: 'Memories of him playing football were very important to people, but there's got to be more than that for him to make that kind of mark on the area and the society.'

As Jackie Milburn made his imprint on Tyneside and in the First Division, he gained recognition from England's selectors too. He was handed an outing for the Football League against the Irish at Anfield during September 1948, in essence an England trial match. Jackie put on a five-star show netting a hat-trick with Len Shackleton having one of those days only he could produce, laying on a stream of inviting openings for his former teammate. Milburn always recognised the part Shack played in his conversion to a top centre-forward – first during his early days at St. James' Park and later for England. The selectors had to take notice. The following month he made his debut wearing the Three Lions against Northern Ireland at Windsor Park and it was a good start for the Ashington Flyer, as he was sometimes called. Milburn scored in an easy 6–2 romp – a header from a Stanley Matthews' back-post cross. Jackie was in good company; his friend and Tynesider Stan Mortensen netted a hat-trick.

Jack had replaced Tommy Lawton for that game in the England shirt and had answered several critics that judged he was not good enough for the international game. Apart from England's regular No. 9, Lawton, other rivals for the striker's position over the coming years were Mortensen – who switched between inside-forward and centre-forward – Jack Rowley of Manchester United, ex-colleague Roy Bentley of Chelsea, Derby's Jack Lee, Nat Lofthouse of Bolton and West Bromwich Albion's Ronnie Allen. Few of Milburn's rivals possessed his flair, pace and match-winning ability.

In his first five England outings Jackie scored no fewer than six goals. Against Wales at Ninian Park, United's centre-forward rattled in a hat-trick. He had won over most of the national media, some of which had to be convinced that he was a long-term replacement for the ageing Lawton. With two headers and a drilled finish after an amazing 50-yard Shackleton run he had the scribes drooling. One comment noted: 'Jackie never gives in, plays the whole 90 minutes and apart from his ability to split the defence with a dandy dribble and go on to score, he can shoot with deadly aim.' The press also noted: 'Milburn has at last silenced his detractors . . . Jackie Milburn has arrived.'

United's No. 9 was on the plane for the 1950 World Cup in Brazil – the first occasion England had competed in the emerging tournament. As Jackie said: 'To be in Rio, on the fabulous Copacabana Beach, was the realisation of a dream.' The apprentice fitter from the Ashington pit had come a long way indeed. Milburn was sidelined with injury for the opening games and it was just as well – after taking care of Chile, England were humiliated in an infamous 0–1 defeat by the USA. He returned to the side for the following vital fixture against Spain, but England lost by a single goal again, although what appeared to be a perfectly good Milburn effort was controversially disallowed. England were on the next flight home.

JACKIE MILBURN No. 9 RATING	
Fan appeal – personality and presence	10
Strike-rate	5
Shooting – power and placement	9
Heading	5
Ball skills	7
Link-play – passing, assists, crossing, team-play	8
Pace	10
Commitment – work-rate, courage	8
Match-winner – power-play, big-match capability	9
Longevity with United	10
Trophy success, international and top football ranking	5
Total No. 9 rating	86

Despite an excellent record in an England shirt, Milburn never quite fulfilled what he could have achieved for his country. He made 13 appearances scoring 10 goals, but many judges considered he should have won twice that number of caps. Jackie himself admitted that he always felt uneasy when he was in the England camp, it having a somewhat chilled atmosphere compared to the close-knit dressing-room spirit at St. James' Park, while he was also perhaps overawed alongside so many huge stars he did not know well. Tom Finney said: 'He did have an inferiority complex. He never thought he was as good as he was.' Additionally he was often withdrawn from the England squad due to injury or because of a club versus country row, which simmered between the Football Association and the Gallowgate boardroom.

By the time the new 1950–51 season was under way Milburn had become a star attraction around the football community. Defences feared him. Charlie Crowe recalled: 'He was the match-winner – we knew it, but more than that, the opposition knew it.' At 26 years of age he was in his prime and the following two years were to elevate the Northumbrian onto another level. Wor Jackie was to be known in every household in the country as he spearheaded the Magpies to Wembley glory. United's No. 9 hero was to become a national superstar.

THAT SPECIAL WEMBLEY FEELING

Newcastle United had developed into a stylish attack-minded eleven. Goals flowed and Milburn forged a dangerous partnership with Chilean George Robledo, who had also been in Rio for the World Cup with his country. In five seasons together, they notched up almost 200 goals and blended perfectly. Charlie Crowe recalled in *A Man of Two Halves* written by Jack's son: 'Jackie was a better centre-forward when George Robledo came.' Robledo was strong and powerful, worked hard and picked up the pieces after Milburn's thrusts. Jackie would often have a pot at goal from 20 or 30 yards and if it didn't hit the net, the shot frequently resulted in Robledo snapping up a rebound from either the goalkeeper's parry or the woodwork. The pairing was the best in the country. In season 1950–51, as United challenged for both the Football League Championship and FA Cup, 42 goals came by the boot and head of Milburn and Robledo. The following season was even better. They netted 67 and still hold Newcastle United's record goals partnership with that formidable total. Jackie hit 28 – his best ever haul – while Robledo equalled Hughie Gallacher's long-standing record with 39. The Chilean also had the occasional outing in the No. 9 shirt – and grabbed a hat-trick against league champions Tottenham Hotspur in 1951.

Unlike present-day football when the Premiership title and European silverware are paramount, during the '50s it was the FA Cup which was the major prize in the game. Milburn's teammate and friend for all of his adult life, Charlie Crowe, noted: 'The league was mundane, your bread-and-butter stuff. There was no real incentive for us in the league.' And he added with a grin: 'The glamour was at Wembley and the FA Cup.' And how Jackie Milburn loved Wembley Stadium and the FA Cup, as well as all the magic that went with it.

The run to Wembley in 1951 culminated in Milburn's finest hour

– a wonderful double strike in front of the Twin Towers. Jackie scored in every round to that special finale – eight goals in eight games. He netted against Bury and Bolton Wanderers, against Stoke City and Bristol Rovers, then in the semi-final against Wolves.

An early 3rd-round stroll against Bury saw Milburn fire home in a crowded box and the victory took the Magpies to a terrific meeting with Bolton Wanderers. In a game swamped in thrills and in front of a record St. James' Park cup attendance of 67,596, Newcastle won 3–2 thanks to a brace by Milburn within the opening quarter-hour of the second period. Firstly he latched onto a Mitchell header into the box. Facing the wrong way to goal, Jackie 'spun and hit a 15-yard shot into the net'. Then United's No. 9 beat the offside trap, running onto an Ernie Taylor pass and although challenged by Edwards forced the ball home. He also crashed a header against the underside of the bar.

Against Stoke in the 5th round he grabbed a goal after a Taylor pass was deflected into the danger area. Milburn pounced and shot across Herod, the Stoke goalkeeper, from 16 yards into the far corner of the net. The quarter-final against giant-killers Bristol Rovers proved a difficult passage at first. However in a replay at Eastville, Newcastle cruised to a 3–1 victory with a trio of first-half goals, Milburn striking the third. Persistent work by Crowe and Mitchell allowed Robledo to flick the ball into Jackie's path. Quick as a flash he struck a grass-cutter and the ball was in the net.

After a rousing semi-final with Wolves ended goalless, with the Geordie's No. 9 in 'really brilliant form', two goals in the replay – the first by Milburn – in less than a minute sent United to Wembley. Jack was 'impressive' again and on the half-hour he converted with venom and a huge swing of his right leg after the magical little Ernie Taylor evaded two tackles, went past Pritchard in front of the posts and gave Jackie a golden opportunity almost on the penalty spot. Six goals in seven matches – but the pinnacle came against Blackpool at Wembley. Vic Keeble was to say of Milburn's knack of producing the goods: 'He could score astonishing goals. Goals you would remember for ever.' And at Wembley on 28 April 1951 Jackie came up with two of those gems to live for all time.

With the majority of the neutral support with Blackpool, hoping that the nation's favourite Stanley Matthews could be the key figure and take home an FA Cup medal, few outside the North-east gave United much of a chance. But there were a handful of knowledgeable journalists who did not get wrapped up with the Matthews hype. One astute comment noted: 'Newcastle have in Jack Milburn, however, an even greater match-winner on his day. Milburn is my big reason for taking Newcastle to win the Cup.'

In a thrilling contest Blackpool played an offside game against United – and that proved their undoing. In the first-half, the Magpies had been caught nine or ten times and most of the decisions were hairline ones. One of those decisions was ultimately going to be in Newcastle's favour, and so it proved. Five minutes after the break Robledo came out of defence, winning the ball with a strong tackle. He looked up and saw Milburn in space down the centre-forward track. The ball was placed perfectly and Jackie was through on his own. The Blackpool defence stood waiting for an offside decision and were caught square, but the flag stayed down and away Milburn galloped from the halfway line, as one reporter noted in 'a gap as huge as the Sahara Desert'. Jackie kept cool, didn't panic and said it was: 'The longest run I've ever experienced with a football at my feet.' He recorded later: 'I remember running and running until I forced the goalkeeper, George Farm, to commit himself. Then all I had to do was tuck the ball home. I knew from the moment the ball left my foot that I'd scored.' One match commentator wrote: 'Jackie Milburn scorched down the Blackpool middle like a human bullet and then, with almost disdainful ease, slammed the ball into the net.'

If Milburn's first goal was special, his second five minutes later was brilliant in its creation and dazzling in its execution. It remains one of the very best goals scored at Wembley Stadium. Crowe harried Matthews into a mistake and the ball was picked up by Tommy Walker on the right touch-line, deep in his own half. The United winger launched forward 50 yards, went past full-back Garrett and fed Ernie Taylor inside. Newcastle's midfield maestro noted: 'When I got the ball I was wondering whether to try a shot or not, but out of the corner of my eye I saw a black and white shirt streaking along. I knew that only Milburn could move like that, so I decided on a back-heel.' Taylor's delightful and nonchalant pass was met first time and full-on by United's No. 9 from 25 yards. The ball flew into the top corner of the net with Farm at full length groping at thin air. Taylor added: 'My back was to goal when I heard the thud of a shot, and as I spun round I saw the wonderful sight of the ball in the back of the net, and Milburn sitting on the ground grinning.' One reporter described the moment as 'three seconds of sheer football genius'.

Jackie remembered: 'I struck it with all my might and it flew straight as an arrow into the back of the net.' He added modestly: 'It could have gone anywhere!' One journalist in the Wembley press-box wrote: 'Like a shrieking comet it catapulted into the top corner of the net. George Farm, like 100,000 others, stood bewildered.' Another commented: 'It was one of the greatest goals ever seen at Wembley – or anywhere else, come to that.'

Stanley Matthews was generous with his praise after the game. He said: 'It was definitely Milburn's match! His terrific speed made the first. The second was right out of this world! It was the greatest goal I have ever seen, and certainly the finest ever scored at Wembley. A goal that every player dreams about.'

It could have been a Wembley treble for Milburn – in fact Jackie should have gone down in history as the first man to grab a hat-trick in a Wembley final. He had what was a perfectly good goal disallowed for hand ball by referee Bill Ling, after chesting the ball down and sliding it between Farm's legs. Jackie said of the referee: 'He was wrong – I never touched it!' Slow-motion replays much later support Milburn's view. Jack also went close on three other occasions and was unlucky not to hit the net again.

It was a game that elevated Wor Jackie into a national hero. Not surprisingly he made all the news. Milburn afterwards related that that afternoon at Wembley was 'the greatest day in my long love affair with Newcastle United'.

Anything which followed was bound to be an anticlimax, yet many rate the display by Milburn in a thrill-a-minute FA Cup quarter-final with Portsmouth during United's defence of the trophy in 1952 as an even better personal performance. Even the great man himself noted it was 'simply the best match I've ever played in'.

Both United and Portsmouth were in a group along with Arsenal, Tottenham and Manchester United as the glamour clubs of the era. Pompey had twice lifted the Football League Championship in recent years and the FA Cup 6th-round draw had produced a mouth-watering tie at Fratton Park. A pulsating encounter took place in front of a packed and captivated 44,699 crowd that led *The People*'s journalist to call it the 'Cup-tie of the decade'.

In a match which swung from end to end, it was Milburn who took all the compliments with a peerless hat-trick as Newcastle won 4–2. Eminent journalist Ivan Sharpe wrote: 'It was Milburn who carried the Newcastle attack on his shoulders; Milburn who equalised with an injured arm pressed to his side; Milburn who completed the hat-trick with two more individual goals – one of great subtlety and the other of spectacular thrill; and Milburn who just on time raced away again and gave George Robledo the fourth.'

Jackie's three goals were brilliant. The first arrived by way of a long Frank Brennan punt into the Pompey box on 39 minutes. Milburn collected it six yards out and with a characteristic rapid swivel and swing of his right boot the ball crashed into the net with stunning power. Jack's second came in the 62nd minute after Billy Foulkes had collected a loose ball and raced forward through the middle. The Welshman passed square for Milburn who fired in a terrific hooked first-time shot which struck the angle of post and bar and dropped over the goal-line.

Milburn's third goal is rated as one of his best ever. It was Milburn made and Milburn executed nine minutes from the end. Picking up the ball 40 yards out, Jackie had to counter 3 Portsmouth defenders in a veering run. He cut inside from the wing before hammering an unstoppable 30-yard acute-angled shot across and past goalkeeper Butler and into the net. Colleague Ronnie Simpson later remembered: 'It is simply the greatest goal I ever saw in all my life, playing football or watching it.' The legendary United, Celtic and Scotland keeper added: 'I've never seen a ball hit so hard and so accurately from such an impossible position.'

That dazzling victory and personal display at Portsmouth took United and Milburn within reach of a return visit to Wembley Stadium – and a chance of lifting the trophy for what would be the first time in successive years by any club since 1891. Milburn played his part in defeating Blackburn Rovers in the semi-final and the Magpies revisited the lush Wembley turf to defend the trophy.

The 1952 final with Arsenal was a dull affair. And there were no Milburn headlines this time. But United kept hold of the FA Cup with a 1–0 victory thanks to a late goal from Jackie's strike-partner George Robledo. Indeed Milburn had a quiet game by his standards. *The Journal*'s Ken McKenzie wrote: 'Milburn never looked happy and no wonder. He was either not getting the ball at all or getting it to his feet with no backing up to make for inter-passing.' And United's No. 9 struggled with an injury from early into the game. McKenzie added, on seeing Milburn after the match: 'Jackie could scarcely hobble around as a result of damage to upper-leg muscles when he collided with Roper.'

That injury niggled at Milburn for quite a while. He was still

Three of United's earliest centre-forwards to make an impact on and off the field all featured on contemporary cigarette cards of the Edwardian period. Left to right: Jock Peddie, Bob McColl and Bill Appleyard. (© P. Joannou Collection)

Albert Shepherd was an England centre-forward and joined the Magpies at the height of their Edwardian mastery. Shepherd became a huge favourite of Geordie supporters. (© W.H. Swann)

United pictured in 1923 before a fixture with Arsenal. Scottish import
Neil Harris is prominent to the right of goalkeeper Bill Bradley. Left to
right: Curry, Seymour, McDonald, Hampson, Bradley, Harris, Spencer,
Hudspeth, Low, Aitken, McIntosh. (© Newcastle United Archive)

Neil Harris was a crucial factor behind the Magpies' 1924 FA Cup-final
victory, pictured at Wembley against Aston Villa. The Scot netted
United's first goal in the 2–0 triumph. (© Newcastle United Archive)

Hughie Gallacher . . . Wee Hughie: a controversial Scot who became a legendary figure in football and one of United's greatest centre-forward heroes. (© Newcastle United Archive)

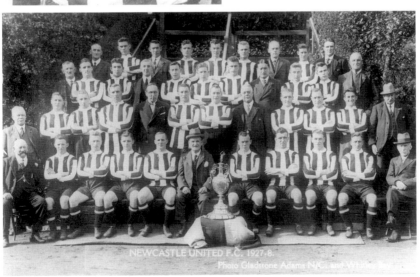

NEWCASTLE UNITED F.C. 1927-8.

Photo Gladstone Adams N/C. and Whitley Bay

Gallacher's brilliant play up-front led Newcastle to the league championship trophy in 1927, scoring what was to be a long-standing record of 39 goals in the season. Skipper Gallacher proudly sits to the right of the famous trophy and next to Chairman John Oliver. (© Newcastle United Archive)

Local lad Jack Allen returned to his native Tyneside after making a big name for himself with Sheffield Wednesday. He was prominent as the Black'n'Whites lifted the FA Cup in 1932, pictured watching the ball hit the Chelsea net in the semi-final clash at Leeds Road, Huddersfield.
(© Newcastle United Archive)

A virtual unknown, Jack Smith burst onto the scene as a raw striker as United battled to get back to the top division. Smith, though, oozed ability and class at centre-forward. (© Newcastle United Archive)

A born-and-bred Geordie, Billy Cairns became the first United centre-forward to actually wear the No. 9 shirt when numbers were introduced during 1939.
(© J. Edminson)

Albert Stubbins rose to prominence during the Second
World War. He is pictured just before the outbreak of the
hostilities in season 1938–39. Back row, left to right:
Smith (trainer), Richardson, Stubbins, Swinburne, Wright,
Ancell, Mather (manager). Front: Birkett, Gordon, Park,
Clifton, Mooney, Denmark. (© Newcastle United Archive)

Inset: One of several local footballers groomed during the
Second World War, Charlie Wayman was an impish No. 9
who became a regular goalscorer during the immediate
post-war era. (© Newcastle United Archive)

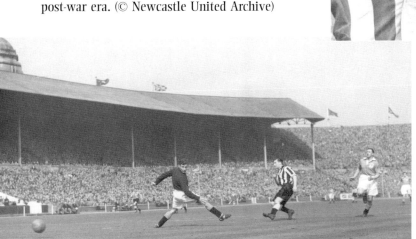

Ashington born and from a famous footballing family, Jackie Milburn
rapidly became a celebrated No. 9 for United. He was nationally known
and made a headline double strike in the 1951 FA Cup final. Wor Jackie
drills the ball past the Blackpool goalkeeper to register the first of two
stunning goals. (© Newcastle United Archive)

Jackie Milburn spent almost 14 years at St. James' Park and scored a record 200 goals. He later returned to the North-east, becoming a sports journalist and much-loved figure. (© C. Crowe)

Vic Keeble took hold of the No. 9 shirt for a period with Milburn
operating alongside. Terrific in the air, he is marvellously captured in
mid flight at White Hart Lane against Tottenham in 1955.
(© Newcastle United Archive)

At Gallowgate for several years
before Milburn departed in
1957, Newcastle needed a
centre-forward replacement and
in stepped Len White, who
took his chance, scoring goals
by the hatful.
(© Newcastle United Archive)

Record signing Barrie Thomas
cost United £45,000 in 1962,
pictured running from the St.
James' Park tunnel wearing the
club's trendy kit at the time.
(© Newcastle United Archive)

Nicknamed Cassius, Ron McGarry was another formidable character in the No 9. shirt. A dressing-room joker, he could pack a punch on the field too. (© Newcastle United Archive)

It took a while for United to land the signature of Welsh international Wyn Davies, but they eventually concluded a deal in 1966, for a record fee of £80,000. (© Newcastle United Archive)

As United entered European action for the first time during 1968, Davies was a menace to Continental defences as the Black'n'Whites lifted silverware. Sporting Lisbon's goalkeeper can get nowhere near the ball in this clash at St. James' Park. (© *Newcastle Chronicle & Journal*)

hampered with it when he flew out with United for a long tour of South Africa and during the following season of 1952–53 he was often absent from the line-up, totalling only 16 appearances and 5 goals. He underwent cartilage surgery during the year, Jackie's first and only major injury. It took him a while to regain form and he was even dropped to the reserves for a short period. Jackie also once turned out for United's third eleven and a crowd of 5,000 turned up at the club's Wallsend pitch to see Wor Jackie in action against Whitley Bay. Newcastle United struggled without Milburn – and without Robledo who returned to Chile – and there was even transfer speculation that Milburn would move too. Not for the first time, headlines had Jackie moving south. As early as 1948, he was on his way to London, while in 1952 it was reported that a huge fee of £30,000 would land him. A year later the Tyneside hero was supposedly off to rivals Sunderland on Wearside. On each occasion, club and player patched up their differences and Jackie stayed put. Other names were tried in the No. 9 shirt, notably Len White and Vic Keeble, as well as Alan Monkhouse and youngsters Alex Tait, Bill Curry and Alex Gaskell.

At the time United's hierarchy, in the shape of a directors' committee – there was no manager as such – began to move Jackie around the forward-line and a whole debate raged as to what was his best position: centre-forward, on the wing or inside-forward. In season 1953–54, he began at outside-right and had what was described as 'the million-dollar look'. He was back at centre-forward for a long spell soon after and back to his best, striking 18 goals in the season. But it was to be Milburn's last as United's regular No. 9. The following year saw the arrival of a new manager, Duggie Livingstone, and Milburn was to be switched around the forward-line. He pulled on the No.s 7, 8 and 10 shirts as first Len White and then Vic Keeble took over the leader's role. Jackie was still a goal threat, though, wherever he played. In that 1954–55 season, he grabbed 21 goals.

VIC KEEBLE, A DIFFERENT STYLE OF No. 9

Of all the centre-forward replacements during Wor Jackie's reign, only Vic Keeble captured the No. 9 shirt for a prolonged period – Len White's day not arriving until after Jack's departure. Alan Monkhouse joined the Gallowgate set-up from Millwall during the 1953–54 season. A strong and effective leader, he wasn't pretty to watch but for a period gave a series of courageous displays and helped United steer clear of relegation. Noted as an 'honest trier' he scored six goals in four games in one run, including a hat-trick against Sheffield United. Alan also took praise during United's 1955 FA Cup campaign, striking two crucial goals in the tie with Nottingham Forest. Before moving to York City, Monkhouse totalled 11 goals in 23 matches, a respectable return.

Alex Gaskell, one of the best young centre-forward talents in the lower divisions, was given an outing during the 1953–54 season. He was purchased from Southport but did not make the breakthrough. Two other youngsters did somewhat better. Bill Curry hailed from Walker and very often looked the part. Operating in the leader's role or at inside-forward, over the following seasons he claimed 40 goals in 88 matches. Curry possessed punch and aggression but National Service restricted his opportunities at St. James' Park. Yet he reached the England Under-23 side before doing well at Derby County, Mansfield Town and Brighton. Alex Tait was also a local lad, from the same heartland of Northumberland as Jackie Milburn. Red haired, skilful and full of dash, much was promised, especially after Tait crashed home a hat-trick in a fiery encounter with Sunderland during December 1956. The teenager kept Milburn out of the side for that game on a foggy and muddy day at St. James' Park and took the acclaim – lots of it! Two close-in goals during the first period were followed by a terrific third. After a Sunderland corner was cleared, United broke away swiftly. Tait chased down the left flank, cut inside and hit a marvellous 20-yard shot into the net. He was dubbed the 'new Milburn', but chose a career in teaching rather than developing into a No. 9 hero.

When Vic Keeble joined Newcastle United while stationed in the Army at Basingstoke during February 1952, he was highly recommended by United's scout and legendary full-back Bill McCracken. As quoted in the press at the time, Keeble was purchased 'as a long-term view because he has the look of a future England player'. From East Anglia, Keeble had a brief spell with Arsenal but made his name with Football League newcomers Colchester United. Well built and 6 ft tall, he rattled in plenty of goals in the lower divisions before scouts took notice.

Keeble still had 12 months to serve in the Army on National Service, so he was only available to United intermittently in the short term. He also had lots to learn. Keeble was a raw youngster and was certainly no real threat to Jackie Milburn's No. 9 shirt at that time.

VIC KEEBLE
FACTS & FIGURES

To Newcastle United: February 1952 from Colchester
   United £15,000
From Newcastle United: October 1957 to West Ham
   United £10,000
Born: Colchester 25 June 1930
Height: 6 ft
Other senior clubs: none
International: none
Newcastle United app & goals:
   Football League: 104 app, 56 goals
   FA Cup: 16 app, 11 goals
   Others: 1 app, 2 goals
   Total: 121 app, 69 goals
Strike-rate: League and Cup 56% (overall 57%)

The styles of Keeble and Milburn were poles apart. Vic was a rough and tenacious centre-forward. He was terrific in the air, big-hearted and far less refined than Milburn. But Keeble was to prove very effective at centre-forward when his chance came. Seasons 1952–53 and 1953–54 brought limited opportunities, as Vic recorded: 'It wasn't easy to get in, and it took me a while to get anything like a regular run.' But in 1954–55 he took an opening when it came his way.

New manager Duggie Livingstone liked Keeble. He preferred to play Milburn on the wing or at inside-forward and selected the persistent, dogged qualities of Keeble in the leader's role. Vic took over the No. 9 shirt as Christmas approached and was very resourceful in his own particular way. Charlie Crowe noted: 'With the ball at his feet, Keeble looked decidedly clumsy, but in the air he was quite majestic.' Jackie Milburn said much the same and recorded: 'He scored so many goals with his nut that I swear he had studs in his forehead.'

Nicknamed by his colleagues, The Camel, because he hunched his shoulders, making him look like he carried a hump on his back, Keeble showed great agility for a man of his build. Like another United No. 9 of the future – Wyn Davies – Vic could leap and power headers with purposeful direction. He was always willing to throw his head at any

131

cross, no matter where the ball was – in the air, or down among the boots. Keeble often scored goals when others shied away. Spectators recalled that he once powered a header into the net from the edge of the box, and jocularly said that he would even take a penalty with his head!

With Keeble installed in the No. 9 shirt and Milburn back to his old position on the wing or at inside-forward, Newcastle embarked on another run to Wembley in season 1954–55. Both players were influential figures, although while Keeble was Livingstone's automatic choice, the manager always thought Milburn's best days were behind him – and that created an almighty storm as United headed for the final.

United's supporters, many in the media and several opponents certainly did not reckon Jack Milburn was in decline. Jackie was still regarded as the match-winner. Nottingham Forest's skipper Tom Wilson, one of United's FA Cup opponents noted: 'Only one man can beat us and he is Milburn.' Wilson's fears were proved correct. Jackie scored what he later considered one of the most satisfying goals of his career. United were a goal down to Forest and heading out of the competition with barely two minutes left when Milburn received the ball well inside his own half. He flew past one defender, then raced to the danger area and as two Forest men converged towards him, banged a shot that roared into the net. Keeble also proved a difficult opponent. He netted five goals during the cup run and in the semi-final replay at Roker Park it was his low bundled-in far-post header that clinched the tie against giant-killers York City and sent United back to Wembley.

During the FA Cup final build-up Livingstone pondered his team line-up. By the time he presented his selection for the big day to the directors for approval at the County Hotel in the city – managers rarely had full control then – a storm was to explode. The manager had left out Jackie Milburn, preferring a forward line of: White, Davies, Keeble, Hannah and Mitchell. When the team-sheet landed on the boardroom table, gasps and growling murmurs ran round the room. Stan Seymour in particular – Milburn's champion, of course – would have none of it. He was enraged. Livingstone's team-sheet was despatched to the rubbish bin in double-quick time and within days the manager had been ostracised, only to survive another few weeks in charge of the first eleven.

Charlie Crowe said: 'It was unthinkable that Newcastle could ever play in an FA Cup final without Jackie Milburn. Even an out-of-form

Jackie was enough to lift the team.' Ronnie Simpson remembered later: 'Newcastle United didn't look the same when Jackie wasn't in the side. I always felt this and I think the crowd felt the same.' The diplomatic quote United's powerful director Stan Seymour gave to the press noted: 'Although Livingstone was normally entrusted with the task of selecting his own team, the directors felt the occasion was so important that we all ought to have a say.' He went on: 'I therefore asked the board, together with the manager, to nominate their teams and, with the exception of Livingstone, we all included Milburn.'

As Newcastle's line-up stepped from the Wembley tunnel alongside the players of Manchester City, Milburn was there, at inside-right. Keeble had the No. 9 shirt, with White demoted from Livingstone's original side, although as fate would have it, he played too when Reg Davies unluckily dropped out due to laryngitis at the last moment. And what a start Milburn had. As if to prove a point, it took Wor Jackie less than a minute to make his manager no doubt feel decidedly uncomfortable and everyone else connected with the Magpies jump for the Wembley rafters.

From the kick-off Milburn forced the pace and won a corner after an exchange with White. The Manchester City defenders, worried by the menace of Keeble in the air, concentrated their defence around United's centre-forward. Milburn was left in space 15 yards out. White's corner was perfect for Jackie to leap and meet with his forehead. The ball rocketed into the top corner with City's goalkeeper, Bert Trautmann, completely beaten. The time was 45 seconds, the fastest ever at Wembley – a record that stood until 1997 when Chelsea's Roberto Di Matteo scored against Middlesbrough 3 seconds quicker.

That opening goal set the Magpies up for another FA Cup triumph, eventually taking care of Manchester City with a 3–1 scoreline. Milburn, soon after his fabulous opening, picked up a stomach muscle injury and could hardly raise a gallop after half-time. Apart from the dramatic timing of the goal, it was also remarkable that Jackie had scored such a picture goal with his head. That was never a strong point in his play. Even Jackie admitted: 'My heading was always something of a joke among the lads.' And it was a point of merriment with supporters at St. James' Park too – fans often gave a mocking cheer when he rose to head a ball! Milburn suffered from fibrositis from an early age – a nasty inflammation of his muscle sheaths around the neck. As a consequence, Jack tended to shy away from too much aerial contact, as he noted 'in case my neck stuck'. Newcastle United tried all sorts to cure their striker of the problem, but it stayed with him for his entire career. Milburn later recorded: 'I hate to think how many goals I might have headed had I been fully fit.' He added: 'I reckon fibrositis cost me more than 50 goals!' Yet Milburn did not do badly. He did learn to deftly flick balls on and he could head a ball well when not challenged, as at Wembley in 1955. Vic Keeble remembered humorously: 'It was the first time Jackie had headed a ball in months and it took him days to get over the shock!'

Jackie Milburn's later days at St. James' Park were in support to Vic Keeble who continued in the No. 9 shirt. In season 1955–56, Milburn scored 21 goals again, even getting back into the England picture, appearing at outside-right against Denmark. Vic Keeble also caught the eye. The ungainly centre-forward had a terrific year and struck 29 into the net. At one stage during the season, he scored 20 goals in 20 games. Keeble claimed four against Huddersfield Town and was a constant danger in a marvellous double meeting with Sunderland over Christmas as United won 6–1 and 3–1 in the space of two days. Vic netted two brilliant headers at Roker – and grabbed another goal at St. James' Park.

Keeble started in the same way for season 1956–57, with Milburn in support again, but then was injured and on the sidelines for a lengthy period. Vic had been purchased to be a long-term successor to Jackie Milburn. However, while he eventually replaced the Ashington idol in the No. 9 shirt for a short spell, he was not to be the next No. 9 hero at St. James' Park. As Milburn's reign came to a close, Keeble was despatched back south to join West Ham United in October 1957 for £10,000. He didn't really want to move and Newcastle directors were in two minds, but as Vic recorded, he was allowed to depart 'because I had a back injury, which I'd picked up playing badminton in the gym'. It was an injury that later forced the striker to retire from the game with a prolapsed disc in 1960 when 29 years of age. Supporters never quite took to Keeble in the centre-forward shirt at St. James' Park, no doubt because his ugly-duckling technique was so in contrast to the flair and dashing style of Milburn. Newcastle supporters unfairly compared the two and as Charlie Crowe remembered, Vic was once misquoted by the press supposedly aiming to 'make Geordie's forget Jackie Milburn'. Of course the Black'n'White Army of the '50s had no wish to forget their local hero, never mind replace him with a southerner. But Keeble registered fine statistics in a black and white shirt; 69 goals in 121 games.

VIC KEEBLE	
No. 9 RATING	
Fan Appeal – personality and presence	6
Strike-rate	6
Shooting – power and placement	7
Heading	9
Ball skills	5
Link-play – passing, assists, crossing, team-play	7
Pace	6
Commitment – work-rate, courage	8
Match-winner – power-play, big-match capability	7
Longevity with United	7
Trophy success, international and top football ranking	2
Total No. 9 rating	70

Wor Jackie's last season at Gallowgate, 1956–57, was much like the previous three. He operated along the forward line claiming 12 strikes. He was now into the veteran stage and his searing pace started to wane. He even received some criticism towards the end of his career; Jack probably knew it was time to call it a day. The last of his record 239 goals for Newcastle United came at Chelsea, in the final game of the season. Milburn was now 33 years of age and on 13 June 1957 he joined Linfield as player-manager, for wages that prompted Jackie to note: 'I was gonna be a millionaire!' His 14-year career with the Magpies was over. The mutual love affair was far from over, though. Like Gallacher before him, Milburn was to become a legend in the years which followed, his popularity seemingly increasing as each decade passed.

Journalist and BBC commentator of old Arthur Appleton, in his book *Hotbed of Soccer*, wrote that Milburn's 'flashing speed, his natural clear-cut style, his ability in sudden penetration, made him the most spectacular and thrill-producing centre-forward of his day'. He was one of few players who could change the course of a game. Jackie Milburn was a real match-winner with his ability to find the net – usually in spectacular, breathtaking style. Jack said later of his career: 'I wouldn't have been half the player without the encouragement of my own local people.' He added: 'They made me the player I was.' It was a unique relationship between footballer and supporter. Milburn's career was one with lots of happy endings. A Geordie pit-lad who became a national hero and Wembley legend. Fiction which became fact.

It was going to be hard for anyone to pull on the No. 9 shirt so famously worn by Jackie Milburn in the last decade, yet several larger than life characters were to follow who roused the crowd – and one arrived in double-quick time who caused some Toon fans to claim he was even better than Wor Jackie!

No. 9 EXTRAS

THE PIT AND THE FOOTBALLER

Jackie Milburn was typical of many north country players immediately after the Second World War, having to combine work at the local coal pit, Hazlerigg Colliery, with playing professional football. Jackie even had the great Len Shackleton as his labourer! Milburn was almost 25 years old when he was able to say goodbye to the dirt and sweat of the mine or the fitting shop. A typical weekend schedule for Jackie was: start at the pit midnight on Friday, finish at 7 a.m. next morning, be at St. James' Park at 12 noon Saturday, kick-off between 2 and 3 p.m.

Once, when he was working at Woodhorn Colliery the manager wouldn't let him off the Saturday shift and as he would miss a Newcastle United game as a consequence, all hell broke loose at the pit! Strike calls were made and threats of a mass walkout took place before he was allowed to pull on the black and white stripes!

SIDELINES

During his career with Newcastle United, Jackie had several sidelines in a bid to boost his maximum footballer's wage of £12 per week in 1947, and £15 per week by the time he left a decade later. He sponsored *Quaker Oats*, endorsed his own brand of football boots, for a time ran a fireplace shop in Ashington and even tried a showbiz agency. Milburn also set up a coach tour business – Milburn's Tours – having a bus named *The Ashington Flyer*. He was also the first Newcastle United player to publish his life story, *Golden Goals*, in 1957. Jackie was also a regular newspaper columnist as a player, which turned into excellent grounding for his post-football career as a sports journalist.

SMOKING JACK

Jackie, like many other footballers of his era, was a heavy smoker. The majority of United's squad enjoyed a cigarette and it was a common sight in the Newcastle United dressing-room to see a procession of players enter the toilets just before kick-off – and at half-time – for a smoke. Milburn even had a quick drag to settle nerves in the Wembley dressing-room prior to his FA Cup final crowning glory in 1951 and said: 'I found four other fellows puffing away like mad!' Club officials did not mind; they even provided complimentary Player's cigarettes! While Jack liked to smoke, he was almost a tee-totaller – his favourite drink being a cup of hot water!

ON YOUR MARKS

Milburn was an exceptional sprinter and he earned an odd few extra quid during the '40s in the somewhat dubious goings on of professional sprinting – full of assumed names, handicaps, betting and mischief. Jackie took part in the prestigious Powderhall meeting in Edinburgh and the local blue-ribbon Morpeth Olympics. As John Gibson related in his biography of Milburn, *Wor Jackie*, he could have become a top champion earning lots of money, but Jack – thankfully – decided to concentrate on football instead.

SUPERSTITIOUS JACK

Jackie was a touch superstitious, like many players. During his early days, he would continue his pre-match habit of eating a meat pie, and for many years he grasped a white handkerchief tightly during a match, while he liked to run out onto the pitch fourth in line. Many of United's FA Cup-winning side had superstitions during the club's three runs to Wembley Stadium. Jackie Milburn carried around a lucky ebony elephant charm in the pocket of his shorts as well as wearing the same tie from the 3rd round onwards.

FA CUP MONEY

Milburn, together with colleagues Bobby Mitchell and Bobby Cowell, won the FA Cup three times yet never lifted a fortune for their success. After his career, Jackie was quick to remind people that he was paid the princely sum of £73 16s 0d for his treble medal haul.

Charlie Crowe once noted: 'In 1951 the bandsmen of the Coldstream Guards got more money for playing at Wembley in the Cup final than we did!'

BEST GOALS

Jackie rated four goals as his best ever:

December 1947 v. Tottenham Hotspur (St. James' Park) – a rocket shot from outside the box which screamed into the corner of the net. Spurs' keeper Ted Ditchburn noted later that it was the hardest shot he had ever faced.

April 1951 v. Blackpool (Wembley) – his dash from the halfway line before slotting the ball past George Farm to give United the lead. Jackie said: 'This was a goal for the connoisseur, the one every centre-forward dreams of scoring.'

April 1951 v. Blackpool (Wembley) – the second astonishing strike after Ernie Taylor's delightful back-heel, Milburn's shot crashing home into the top corner of the net. Stanley Matthews said: 'The ball flashed like a rocket past Farm.'

March 1952 v. Portsmouth (Fratton Park) – a 40-yard run past defenders before hitting an acute 25-yard shot past Butler. Ronnie Simpson called it: 'An incredible goal, I've never seen a ball hit so hard.' Bobby Mitchell said: 'Jackie hit what I class as the best goal I've seen in football.'

BOB'S XMAS DEBUT

Bob Stokoe made his first-team debut for the Magpies on Christmas Day 1950 in a Tyne–Tees derby with Middlesbrough. Usually a wing-half or centre-half, Bob appeared in the No. 9 shirt in emergency with both Milburn and Robledo unavailable. He played well and found the net with an equalising strike in a 1–2 defeat at Ayresome Park.

TEN-SECOND STRIKE

Against Cardiff City during November 1947 Jackie Milburn was quick off the mark – scoring after only ten seconds from the kick-off. Stobbart and Milburn interchanged and Jackie fired the ball against centre-half Fred Stansfield, chased the rebound and hit the net from 15 yards with a powerful shot. Remarkably Cardiff equalised Milburn's opener inside two minutes! Jackie's strike is the quickest by a United player in league and cup football, equalled only by another No. 9 – Alan Shearer in 2003. Another centre-forward hero – Malcolm

Macdonald – scored one of the fastest goals on record anywhere, in a friendly during 1972 – in only five seconds!

FA CUP GREAT

The FA Cup's centenary celebrations in 1981 immortalised the all-time greats of 100 finals – a best eleven was selected and Wor Jackie was named in the No. 9 shirt:

Trautmann (Man City)

Spencer (Aston Villa), Hapgood (Arsenal)

Blanchflower (Tottenham), Wright (Wolves), Moore (West Ham),

Carter (Sunderland), Charlton (Manchester United),

Matthews (Blackpool), Milburn (Newcastle United), Finney (Preston)

MILBURN SHORTS

- During season 1944–45 Jackie appeared in the red and white of Sunderland as a wartime guest. He played twice against Gateshead, but kept his goals for when he pulled on the black and white shirt of Newcastle. Milburn failed to score on both occasions for the Wearsiders.
- Jackie was a gentlemanly player on the park and was never cautioned by a referee in his 14-year career in England. Top official of the era, Arthur Ellis, said: 'If there were 22 players on the field like Jackie you wouldn't need a referee!'
- In the summer of 1980 at a lavish ceremony, Milburn became a Freeman of the City of Newcastle upon Tyne – an award given to only those very special people who have served the city so well. He was the first ex-footballer to be honoured.
- Celebrated television programme *This Is Your Life* featured Jackie Milburn in December 1981 with Eamonn Andrews surprising the North-east legend with his version of Jackie's life-story.
- A crowd of 45,404 packed St. James' Park for a belated testimonial in May 1967, some 10 years after his final match for the Magpies. Despite the time gap, no one forgot Wor Jackie.

TYNESIDE STANDSTILL

Not long after retiring, Jackie Milburn died in October 1988. His funeral procession made its way from Bothal Terrace in Ashington through Newcastle, past St. James' Park to St Nicholas's Cathedral. Tyneside came to a standstill on that day with the route lined by over

30,000 mourners. His ashes were sprinkled on the St. James' Park pitch. Lasting tributes were made in the city to his name: Newcastle United's main stand is called the Milburn Stand, and there is a Milburn Drive in the city's west end, while a bronze statue of the No. 9 legend is located on St. James' Boulevard.

STARS ON MILBURN
Sir Tom Finney:
  'He was the fastest thing in football, and won world-wide admiration.'
Sir Bobby Robson:
  'An absolute legend. A wonderful fellow. Quick as lightning with a wicked shot.'
Nat Lofthouse:
  'What a wonderful guy Wor Jackie was. They will never forget him on Tyneside – or anywhere else.'
Frank Brennan:
  'Jackie was not only a brilliant footballer, he was a kind-hearted, loveable bloke.'
Bobby Mitchell:
  'He was perhaps unique – not only as a player, but as a person.'

SIX FOR JACKIE
On tour in North America during the close season of 1949 Milburn struck the back of the net six times as United defeated Alberta All Stars by the wide margin of 16–2, Newcastle's biggest scoreline in all games. Jackie scored 31 goals in the 10-match schedule of the exhibition tour – an average of a hat-trick every game!

WOR JACKIE – AFTER TOON
Following a spell at Linfield in which Milburn sampled European Cup football and scored over 100 goals, Jackie tried senior management with Ipswich Town in January 1963. He succeeded Alf Ramsey at Portman Road but Milburn had a rough passage, inheriting an ageing squad. He had to rebuild and Ipswich were relegated. Milburn was not cut out for the managerial jungle and he returned north to cover local football from the press-box. Based in Newcastle, he was the *News of the World*'s reporter at both St. James' Park and Roker Park until his retirement in 1988.

KEEBLE – AFTER TOON

On joining West Ham United, Vic proceeded to become an important part in the Hammers' return to the First Division in 1958. He totalled 49 goals in 80 senior games before having to retire due to a back injury. He afterwards became a journalist for a period living in Essex, before concentrating on a long stint in charge of administration for Chelmsford City. His son, Chris, joined the Ipswich Town staff in 1995 and was later with Colchester United.

5. WHITE-HOT LEN
1957—1966

LEN WHITE, BARRIE THOMAS,
RON McGARRY

When the doyen of Tyneside, Jackie Milburn, departed for Ulster in the summer of 1957 a huge chasm was left at St. James' Park, one as big as the mouth of the River Tyne. Wor Jackie had been a living legend at Gallowgate for 14 years and personified everything Newcastle United stood for. St. James' Park was a different place without Milburn. The question asked by every Geordie supporter was: 'How could United replace Jackie Milburn?'

Milburn had moved aside from the centre-forward role two and a half years earlier allowing Vic Keeble to claim the No. 9 shirt. But Keeble himself was to head south from Tyneside to become a Hammer at Upton Park and Milburn was, of course, the fans' idol. United needed not only to find a centre-forward replacement but also someone who could take on the mantle of the Geordies' champion. It was an unenviable task for someone and no player immediately came to mind who could become a goalscoring hero. On the staff at the time were youngsters Bill Curry and Alex Tait who had both already made an impression. They were at an age when a breakthrough – especially in Curry's case – should have been made.

Also in contention was Alan Monkhouse, but he soon moved on.

United turned to a stocky utility forward who had been signed from the Third Division outback almost five years earlier in 1953 – Len White. Originally purchased by Stan Seymour as something of an afterthought following a move for White's England B colleague Jack Grainger, Len arrived at St. James' Park as a deputy for outside-right Tommy Walker and someone who could fill-in across the forward line.

Len White was a player who transformed an average career into a startling one over the space of a close season, and he did such a formidable job in the United No. 9 shirt that he was rated by many who saw him play to be just as good as Wor Jackie. To reach that pinnacle of respect White had to be something special and he proved to be a great No. 9 in his own right.

White was born in 1930 in the small Yorkshire town of Skellow, not far from Doncaster. He was brought up in a working-class community just like Milburn, and like most youngsters of his time in Yorkshire, started down the coal pit, a similar upbringing for many footballers of the era. White started playing amateur football in his teens and his first club of note was the colliery side at Whitwick. He soon had Football League clubs taking notice of his potential. Leicester City offered the youngster a chance but he didn't make an impression at Filbert Street and soon returned to the Yorkshire coalfield and Upton Colliery FC.

White continued to stand out at that level, as a winger with acceleration, grit and determination. He often hit the net too, showing tremendous pace and power in his shooting – qualities to be an asset when he moved into the centre-forward's role some time later. Rotherham United were the club to give White another crack at becoming a professional footballer and he joined the Millmoor staff in May 1948. Close to home, Rotherham suited White perfectly.

Len remained a miner and combined hard work in the pit with more hard work on the training ground in his spare time. Without really claiming a regular position in the Millers' line-up, Len helped his club to promotion from the Third Division as champions in 1951 during his first season in the big-time.

White was an emerging player. He claimed 13 outings in Second Division action during the following season and 20 matches during 1952–53. It was in that season that fate brought him to the attention of Newcastle United, when Rotherham were drawn to play the Magpies in an FA Cup tie during January 1953.

Rotherham were FA Cup giant-killers that year and created club history when they reached the 5th round of the competition. Scouts flocked to watch them and several of the Millers players made an impact. White's team provided United with a problem or two and the Black'n'Whites – trophy holders that year – were dumped out of the cup after a famous tussle at St. James' Park. The Magpies lost 1–3 in front of a 54,356 crowd, a headlining reverse after United had taken the lead through Vic Keeble.

Following the shock defeat, Seymour took out his cheque book in search of new talent. Rotherham's Jack Grainger – a talented goalscoring outside-right – looked the part, netting twice and making another against the Magpies, but the Tykes, managed at the time by ex-Magpie Andy Smailes, would not part with their star winger. Seymour also knew of the promising talent of White, United having watched the player impress against both Barnsley and Fulham. With Aston Villa and Portsmouth also eyeing the Yorkshireman, he made a bid for White and succeeded in return for a fee of £12,500.

LEN WHITE
FACTS & FIGURES

To Newcastle United: February 1953 from Rotherham
   United £12,500
From Newcastle United: February 1962 to Huddersfield
   Town, cash/exchange deal
Born: Skellow 23 March 1930
Died: Huddersfield 17 June 1994
Height: 5 ft 7 in.
Other senior clubs: Stockport County
International: none
Newcastle United app and goals:
   Football League: 244 app, 142 goals
   FA Cup: 22 app, 11 goals
   FL Cup: 3 app, 0 goals
   Others: 1 app, 0 goals
   Total: 270 app, 153 goals
Strike-rate: League and Cup 57% (overall 57%)

Competition was extremely fierce at Gallowgate then. United were recently twice FA Cup victors, and White had to battle for a place on the right side of the forward line with the experienced Walker, as well as Billy Foulkes, Tommy Mulgrew, Reg Davies and of course Jackie Milburn, who operated in several positions up front at the time. With such an array of talent, Len remembered: 'I had to be patient.' He added: 'It was a great Newcastle team in my early days, and the likes of Milburn and Mitchell were impossible to push out of the side.'

White, still locked in an important post-war reserved occupation down the pit, continued as a part-time professional during his opening months on Tyneside, finding a job at Burradon Colliery initially. He noted that his formative period at St. James' Park saw him able to train only 'on Tuesday and Thursday evenings for a long while'. That hindered his progress at Gallowgate and White said: 'Not until I went full-time did I really begin to settle in at St. James' Park.'

He made his Toon debut against Liverpool in 1952–53 but rarely got a regular start during that season, and the following campaign was also on the fringe, totalling 13 games out of a possible 47. He was used mainly at outside-right, but Len was also handed the No. 9 shirt for the first time too. He led the line against Wolves and again with Arsenal in opposition during April 1954. Len recalled that playing in Jackie's No. 9 shirt 'was something of a fright'. Indeed his outing against the Gunners was a total surprise.

Not in the party for the First Division clash – one of the fixtures of the year – White was actually tucking into a good lunch and a couple of pints when Monkhouse sustained an ankle injury at St. James' Park only hours before the kick-off. Officials frantically went in search of Len and found him in The Windmill pub. Despite his hearty meal and refreshment, White pulled on the centre-forward shirt, played well and scored in United's 5–2 victory! Len grabbed the fourth goal, banging in a rebound from a Hannah 25-yarder. *The Journal* made the comment that White is a 'good player who needs only consistent opportunity'.

During the 1954–55 season White became more of a regular in the side. Wearing the No. 7 jersey, again he had the odd outing at centre-forward, but it was as a winger that he started to make an impression and give glimpses of what was to follow – scoring four times against Aston Villa, all in the first half. He possessed good close control which, added to his pace, could cause problems on the flank. Part of a free-scoring forward line of White, Milburn, Keeble, Hannah and Mitchell, United embarked on an FA Cup run during the season and Len played his part all the way to the final at Wembley.

He firstly grabbed a close-in equaliser in the quarter-final against Huddersfield Town to keep United in the hunt for the trophy, then in the semi-final meeting with giant-killers York City – when future Magpie striker Arthur Bottom made a big impression on United's directors – White grabbed the all-important first strike in the replay at Roker Park. With barely four minutes on the referee's watch, White started and finished a defence-splitting move that saw Milburn skip down the right touch-line and send a dangerous ball into the box. White, who had continued his run from deep, met the pass and found the net from six yards.

Boss Duggie Livingstone had a shock for Len, though. He was not in the manager's starting eleven for the final. It was a huge blow for the Yorkshireman. After playing in seven matches in the cup run, he was only named as a reserve. However, Len was in good company, as Livingstone had also left Jackie Milburn out of his final team! As it happened, both White and Milburn played, Len coming into the side on the eve of the final when Reg Davies was unfortunate enough to drop out due to a throat infection, and as mentioned in the previous chapter, it was White who put over the ball from a corner kick which Milburn headed into the roof of the net after only 45 seconds. Ironically, within a minute of the start of the showpiece occasion against Manchester City the pair combined to score the fastest goal in a Wembley final at that time.

White placed the ball for a corner kick and hit the cross for Wor Jackie to rise and plant a header into the roof of the net. Yet as Len recorded, it was something of a fluke as the cross was for Vic Keeble! He noted: 'I aimed it for the far post, but miscued. It fell short. But a flying figure in black and white got to it and as the City defenders hesitated, Jackie Milburn's header rocketed into the net!'

White had a good match at Wembley although he picked up an ankle injury. He had a hand in United's second goal too scored by Bobby Mitchell, sweeping the ball from wing to wing for Mitch to cut in and score.

The gritty Tyke remained a fixture in United's side for 1955–56 and 1956–57 swapping forward roles with Milburn, Keeble and with Alan Monkhouse when he entered the action. White and Milburn – at centre-forward – often interchanged during play. Len said: 'The great thing was that Jackie, also a right-winger turned centre-forward, could easily switch with me, depending how a game was going.' And the flexible approach gave United an added option in attack.

In the opening weeks of the 1957–58 season as United tried to get used to life without Milburn and on Keeble's departure to West Ham, White was handed the No. 9 shirt as something of a gamble. Newcastle United's directors had mixed views as to whether he could take over from Milburn and Keeble – both players having registered a formidable goal record for the club. In fact, Stan Seymour was quoted in the press as noting: 'We must sign forward strength.' The Magpies made a headline and shock move in that season for one of the country's top strikers, Sunderland's Charlie Fleming – a No. 9 with a Gatling-gun boot – before Len fully established himself. That deal with their neighbours never materialised but they did splash out on York City's Arthur Bottom who had scored 105 goals in 158 appearances in double-quick time. Strong as the proverbial ox, he appeared alongside White at inside-forward on occasion. Bottom joined the promising talent of Tait and Curry in a fight for the No. 9 shirt with Len.

WHITE ANSWERS THE CALL

White had scored fewer than 40 goals in a little over four seasons for the Black'n'Whites up to taking hold of the centre-forward shirt – hardly a goalgetter's pedigree – but the Yorkshireman answered Seymour's call for power up front from within the dressing-room. In the four seasons to follow, he clocked up over a century of goals.

The turning point in White's career – and United's search for a man to replace Milburn – took place as winter approached. White firstly showed his doubters that perhaps he could end the search at Kenilworth Road against Luton Town in November 1957. It was a contest that saw Len strike two goals in a 3–0 victory. The match report of the day noted: 'It was a great triumph for White, to get two goals on his emergency centre-forward comeback.' The emergency No. 9 tag was to turn to a permanent one in rapid fashion.

Against West Bromwich Albion in a 3–0 victory he scored two more as well as striking the woodwork three times in the opening half! It was the start of a run that saw the new No. 9 hit 17 goals in only 14 games.

Len really buzzed against the Baggies. After his unlucky first half, he hit the net, first chasing a through-pass from the England starlet Eastham. He neatly tricked Sanders, the advancing keeper, before shooting home from 15 yards. Then Eastham pulled a ball back inside to White. He missed it completely with his right foot but recovered quickly enough to lash it in at the far post with his left.

From that scintillating display against the Midland side in December 1957, to an injury almost three and a half years later against Tottenham in March 1961, White banged home 105 goals in 131 appearances – an 80 per cent strike-rate, almost a goal a game.

White's style of play in the centre-forward channel thrilled spectators. One goal against Manchester City highlighted his modus operandi: 'Len White accelerated into a through-the-centre dribble, beating four defenders, then struck the ball past goalkeeper Trautmann.' It was typical White. Another watching scribe noted: 'A solo dribble by Len White from 15 yards inside his own half ended with a great 12-yard shot into the net.' The reporter wrote that it was a goal that 'Jackie Milburn, even the late Hughie Gallacher, could have envied'.

Although White was, as colleague Charlie Crowe remembered, a 'quiet, unassuming man who never sought the limelight' he burst into action when he wore the Black'n'White's famous No. 9 jersey. Not a conventional type of centre-forward, he often played in a deep role. White would pick the ball up and weave in and out of challenges with a testing change of pace before getting into range – and bang – the ball flew towards the goal. It was a style of play that had the terraces roaring with excitement in the mould of Milburn before him and Macdonald after. He roamed to the flanks too, cutting inside before firing towards the goal. Although not tall, at only 5 ft 7 in., he was sturdy, could resist defenders and leap high for the ball in the air. Crowe added: 'He just bubbled and buzzed all over the front line and popped up where he was least expected.' The fans loved him – a new No. 9 hero was created.

White ended the 1957–58 season with 25 goals in 32 games, including a spell when he hammered 12 goals in only 10 fixtures. For the next campaign, he had a new manager to impress. Former Manchester United star Charlie Mitten breezed into St. James' Park with a fresh approach during the summer of 1958. Mitten was to quickly put together a famed trio in black and white shirts – White was soon to link with schemers George Eastham and Welsh maestro Ivor Allchurch.

The new boss splashed out a club record fee of £28,000 to bring the highly rated Allchurch to Gallowgate and alongside Eastham – a marvellously gifted inside-forward – White found he had the sort of service all centre-forwards dream about. The Welshman, with his graceful distribution of the ball around the park, became the focus of everything good about United's play. Allchurch, nicknamed The Golden Boy of Wales, was hugely popular, prompting and probing from midfield.

Despite White's goals and the undoubted talent of Allchurch and Eastham, Mitten's Newcastle United were frustratingly unpredictable in the three seasons to the beginning of the '60s. They could be scintillating on occasion and defeated Everton 8–2 and Manchester United 7–3. Yet the Magpies quickly reverted to woeful displays too, losing heavily to Tottenham, Blackburn and Manchester City. But Mitten did produce a mini-revival. He guided the Black'n'Whites from a relegation-threatened side to mid-table although still some way from recapturing the glory days of the earlier '50s when United challenged for trophies.

In those entertaining victories over Everton and Manchester United, White capitalised on the service provided by Allchurch and Eastham. United's centre-forward scored a hat-trick in each game. Against Manchester United, the Geordies were lively with punch and precision in attack, and as one report noted 'they had, in Len White, a leader who could burst into the game to score a brilliant goal'.

White did exactly that on three occasions, first with a gem of a strike. He ran out to the wing and beat three men before playing a pass to Eastham. United's inside-forward controlled the ball as he turned across field with White behind him. He then slipped a short pass that the No. 9 took in his stride and flicked the ball over goalkeeper Gaskell's head and into the net from a sharp angle.

Bob Stokoe was the creator of the second, spotting an opening that Len took on the edge of the penalty area. His finishing was perfection as he blasted in a superb drive to make it 3–1 at the interval. White claimed his hat-trick after Jackie Bell crashed a screamer of a shot against an upright, United's centre-forward reacting faster than Gaskell as he nodded in the rebound.

It was the same story against Everton. White registered United's third goal in a devastating opening spell, mopping up a rebound close-in after George Luke's header had been pushed out to him. White then scored what was described as 'a glorious goal'. He took a pass from Luke in his stride and after linking to Eastham 'slammed the return into the net'. Len claimed United's seventh goal of the day after more good Eastham approach play with another stinging shot past Albert Dunlop.

In season 1958–59 White scored 25 goals again and the following campaign was much the same story. He netted 29 goals this time and only United's inconsistency stopped the Yorkshireman from being part of a really good United side and capturing the glamour and spotlight much of his football deserved. As good as United's attack was, the defence continued to leak goals, spoiling all the good work that White did up front.

Len had become fully established in the centre-forward shirt and only occasionally moved to the wing to allow the odd tactical change and an outing for the likes of Curry and Tait, as well as opportunities for youngsters Terry Marshall, Carl Wilson, Jimmy Gibson, Malcolm Scott, Billy Wright and Bob Gilfillan in the No. 9 shirt when he was out injured.

Curry was the pick of a group of emerging players. Already fully established as a forward of quality, Bill had become United's first ever Young England player after Under-23 level internationals were introduced in 1954. With 11 goals in 23 matches during 1957–58 and 9 in as many outings the following season in the centre-forward shirt, Curry should have been a real contender for a regular slot up front, perhaps alongside White. But the Walker striker left his native North-east in July 1959 to continue his career elsewhere.

Teenager Jimmy Gibson and winger turned occasional centre-forward Terry Marshall were both given fleeting opportunities. The tall Gibson had arrived on Tyneside on the recommendation of Jackie Milburn at Linfield and the Ulster youngster found the net in only his second outing in Milburn's famous No. 9 shirt against Nottingham Forest. But the full-blooded and tearaway leader drifted to non-league football. So did Marshall.

Centre-half Malcolm Scott was switched to the centre-forward role against Leeds United during September 1959 and the well-built Tynesider found the net twice in a 3–2 victory when up against future World Cup winner Jack Charlton. The watching media were impressed, one reporter noting he 'proved well worthy of a prolonged run as leader of the attack'.

Like Scott, Billy Wright showed up well when out of position in senior action. The former Blackpool outside-left pulled on the No. 9 shirt against Everton during August 1958 and also hit the target. Scotsman Bob Gilfillan arrived from Cowdenbeath following an eye-catching spell at Central Park in Fife. A diminutive striker at 5 ft 9 in. tall, he was only rarely handed the No. 9 shirt, soon moving back north of the Cheviots. Carl Wilson, the son of '30s centre-half Joe

Wilson, had black and white in his blood. He was a one match stand-in for White as an 18 year old. But Carl had no fairy-tale story as the Magpies lost 0–3 against Blackpool.

White's goal power at the time was one of the best in the top division and the rip-roaring manner in which he grabbed dozens of his goals impressed many. Len often picked up the ball in midfield then strode forward with verve into the danger area to cause mayhem. Charlie Crowe reckoned his ability to move through the gears was significant. He noted his 'great change of pace and ability to step up a gear was special'. And another colleague Bob Stokoe said: 'He seemed to score nothing but spectacular goals.' Many came from 25 or 30 yards – and most after a run past two or three defenders showing craft, great balance and confidence to have a go.

He was, as George Eastham recorded, a 'tenacious centre-forward' too. With close-cropped hair, his tough miner's upbringing showed on the pitch. He took a battering at times but could give as good as he got. Teammate Charlie Woods, later chief scout under Sir Bobby Robson at St. James' Park, recalled: 'He was quite small and stocky – but he had a great leap, great pace, and great skill. Predominantly right-footed, but he could use his left, he was an all-round outstanding player. In my career, he was the best centre-forward I ever played with.

'Jackie Milburn would go past opponents with sheer pace, but Lennie did it with pace and skill. He was a master at running at opponents, dribbling past them twisting and turning. His control was superb. He also had a very powerful spring and was a truly fine header of the ball. As a person, he would take no nonsense. Once we were travelling home from a match upstairs on the bus – Lennie lived in Fenham and my digs were close by in Two Ball Lonnen – and a chap on the bus started having a go at him. Lennie dealt with it in his own way . . . let's just say he won the argument!'

Some older supporters even likened Len's technique to that of the legendary Hughie Gallacher – small, stocky and difficult to knock off the ball. And like Gallacher, he was formidable in the air for such a small centre-forward, standing at only 5 ft 7 in. tall. He would have little trouble in leaping to bullet a header towards the goal. Crowe considered he 'was the best in the business from 1957 to 1961'. United's correspondent for *The Journal*, Ken McKenzie who watched the Magpies for over 40 years, wrote of White: 'At his peak and playing in the No. 9 shirt, he can fairly be nominated as the finest centre-forward and goalgetter in Magpie history.' Better than Gallacher and Milburn, McKenzie reckoned. Many supporters agreed.

White's predecessor as the crowd's favourite, Jackie Milburn, respected White immensely, but was honestly critical – rare for Jackie, who only occasionally said a bad word against anyone. Milburn noted: 'He had pace, good close control and was an effortless finisher, but he was short, and that doesn't help.

'Had he been two inches taller my guess is he'd have become England's centre-forward.' Jackie continued: 'If I had to criticise him it would be to say he had a tendency to withdraw into his shell if things didn't go right.'

LEN WHITE
No. 9 RATING

Fan appeal – personality and presence	9
Strike-rate	6
Shooting – power and placement	9
Heading	7
Ball skills	8
Link-play – passing, assists, crossing, team-play	8
Pace	9
Commitment – work-rate and courage	8
Match-winner – power-play, big-match capability	8
Longevity with United	9
Trophy success, international and top football ranking	2
Total No. 9 rating	83

The call hailing 'White for England' was loud and vociferous from the North-east. At the height of his goalscoring, Len was selected for the Football League representative side to face the Irish at Anfield. At the time, Inter-League games were important matches in the calendar, and in some quarters recognised as almost full international trials. In November 1958, White pulled on the shirt of England's league eleven and led the line with dynamism. Alongside the likes of Johnny Haynes, the Irish were outclassed and fell 5–2 with Len crashing home a stunning hat-trick – in the space of seven short minutes.

The calls became louder for an England place for United's centre-forward. White himself noted: 'I felt I had a chance after scoring those three goals.' At the time the England leader's spot was up for grabs.

Sadly Manchester United's Tommy Taylor was the choice until his untimely death in the Munich Air Disaster. Several players vied with White for the role. Favourite was the rugged Derek Kevan of West Bromwich Albion who had appeared in the 1958 World Cup in Sweden, while the veteran Nat Lofthouse was even recalled. Ashington's Manchester United starlet, Bobby Charlton, eventually received the nod at centre-forward while youngsters Brian Clough and Joe Baker were to challenge too as the '60s unfolded.

The men with power at the Football Association, manager Walter Winterbottom and his superiors, never looked to the far north. The top brass at Lancaster Gate ignored Len. Many northern critics noted that White was perhaps a victim of the perceived cold shoulder of the North-east at the time. Vic Keeble remembered: 'I swear that if he had been playing in the south, he would have been an England regular.' White later said: 'Even one cap would have done me. It would have meant so much.' He added: 'It was a disappointment but that's the way it was.' The pride of Tyneside remained on the fringe – the best uncapped centre-forward in the club's history.

At the start of the 1960–61 season boss Mitten knew he required to strengthen his side. Even in attack the former Manchester United star considered he needed fresh blood and pondered switching the White goal-machine back to the wing. Mitten made a serious bid to land Motherwell's exciting centre-forward Ian St John, a long-time target of United. In his authorised biography *Bogotá Bandit* by Richard Adamson, Charlie said: 'I thought, boy, can this lad play.' United came close to bringing St John to Gallowgate and had agreed terms with the player before the deal was wrecked by Bill Shankly and Second Division Liverpool. Mitten related that Shankly had been apparently tipped off by one of his own Newcastle directors – Stan Seymour – after a boardroom row about the transfer. St John even later related that he was heading for Tyneside and said: 'I didn't want to go to Liverpool, because Newcastle were the big club.'

Mitten also tried to land another player who would become, like St John, a huge star in the '60s. United's manager was keen on signing Jimmy Greaves and the future England goalscoring sensation admitted in his autobiography that there had been an illicit approach offering 'two grand in cash and a car salesman's job'. Nothing came of the move, nor of a bid to woo Denis Law, then with Huddersfield Town. Looking back now, the thought of White alongside any of those icons of the '60s fills the imagination agog with tantalising thrill.

However, Mitten's search for quality talent did not end there. In defence, he wanted Leeds United's centre-half Jack Charlton, a blood relation to Jackie Milburn, but again Newcastle's boss was thwarted.

Players of that quality didn't arrive on Tyneside and in fact Mitten lost one of his star men when George Eastham began a controversial, much headlining dispute with the club – and the Football Association as well as the Football League – that ultimately ended in the High Court. Worse news was to follow too. Ivor Allchurch the man who made United tick wasn't happy either; like Eastham, he asked for a transfer. The Welshman wanted to move back to South Wales and had also run into trouble with his boss. Mitten intended to try the elegant playmaker in the No. 9 role – being determined to move White to the flank – but Allchurch would have none of it. He was adamant he was no centre-forward and actually refused to appear wearing the shirt on three occasions. Something of a rift between player and manager was evident.

With White still in the No. 9 shirt, Len continued where he had left off in the previous season – with goals and more goals, despite his manager's tactical intentions to move the Yorkshireman from the role he was suited to best. As if to prove a point, he became the Magpies' top scorer for the fifth season in a row with 29 goals from 38 games.

Newcastle started that 1960–61 campaign in fine mood. The Black'n'Whites defeated Preston North End 3–2 on the opening day of the season with a White treble – a hat-trick of 'brilliant goal-poaching'. United then battered Fulham four days later by seven goals. But after that the defence caved in time and time again regardless of White finding the net on a regular basis. They lost four goals in a quick return meeting with the Cottagers, then six to West Bromwich Albion, five each to Arsenal, Everton, West Ham United and Burnley, as well as four to Chelsea, Tottenham and Wolves. By the turn of the year Newcastle United had slipped to 19th in the table and faced a mighty relegation battle.

With Eastham permanently sidelined, effectively on strike, White became United's only real hope of avoiding the drop into the Second Division. Allchurch – who never let his simmering dispute affect his play – helped too. But more often than not Allchurch was left to battle away deep and as the press commented, White was frequently 'stranded and helpless in the centre'. Yet he was still a danger. White led the attack with menace. Up front United scored a credible 86 goals in First Division action – only 7 clubs netting more. Yet Len's thrust in the box was too often wasted. The problem was that the Magpies conceded 109 goals – the worst defensive display in the club's history.

154

WHITE HART LANE BLOW

After New Year the Black'n'Whites struggled, winning only once in eight league matches. Newcastle badly needed a victory and turned up at White Hart Lane during March for one of the fixtures of the season down and almost out. Spurs were riding high. They were destined to lift the championship and cup Double that year and possessed a talented side led by Danny Blanchflower and packed with stars like Cliff Jones, Dave Mackay, Bobby Smith and John White.

United astonishingly won 2–1 – coming from a goal down – to cause the shock of the season. But ironically it was a victory that probably sent United tumbling into the Second Division – as they also lost Len White for the rest of the campaign with a bad injury. With only two minutes left in the game, White went for a short corner and Tottenham's Scottish international hard man Dave Mackay jumped at United's No. 9 with a reckless tackle from behind that crunched White's ankles. Len crumpled in a heap with his ligaments horribly damaged. A colleague noted the tackle 'as a shocker' and one reporter at the match penned: 'Mackay appeared to be in mid air before making contact.' White battled on but was helped off at the final whistle and had to have his boot cut off in the dressing-room.

Len remembered the incident: 'Everyone was delighted my ankle wasn't broken but, in hindsight, it would have been better if it had been, because the torn ligaments were a mess.' White was to also note that his ankle 'never felt the same again'. Sadly, the injury wrecked Len's career and robbed United of one of their finest centre-forwards. Although in time he recovered, the striker was never the same glittering player again.

After collecting two precious points in London, Newcastle – without White's influence – dramatically slumped. They quickly faced a humiliating 1–6 defeat to Chelsea on Tyneside with Scotsman John McGuigan taking over the No. 9 shirt. A versatile forward who had been signed from Southend United in June 1958, McGuigan tried his best in the remaining games of the season but was never a cut and thrust centre-forward in the mould of White. He showed, as the local press noted, 'steady industry' but missed several chances that White would have gobbled up. He also possessed 'calm efficiency' but little punch in the box where it mattered.

By the end of the season Mitten's side tumbled from football's elite with Preston and not surprisingly United's boss was soon out of a job as the Magpies began life in Division Two. Before he was sent on his way, though, Mitten brought in a new centre-forward during the summer months of 1961, Leicester City's Welsh international leader Ken Leek. A £25,000 purchase, Leek was one of several new Mitten signings and he was a proven striker having netted 25 goals for Leicester in 1960–61 before a controversial bust-up on the eve of that season's FA Cup final. He claimed seven goals in nine FA Cup matches in City's run to Wembley, but was then dropped for the big occasion.

Tall and quick, Leek began his career in a black and white shirt with headlines – a hat-trick in a 6–0 pre-season friendly romp against Danish side Aarhus. He looked to be a class act and showed he was an able player – scoring five goals in two games over the space of a week – in convincing wins over Bury, by 7–2, and Brighton, by 5–0.

The Welshman was good in the air and a threat on the ground prompting rave reports including the comment that he 'was wonderful to watch'. But Ken was often played out of position at inside-forward – Mitten strangely choosing others in the pivotal role at centre-forward. Leek found it hard to settle and soon moved on after only 14 appearances and 6 goals, to Birmingham City for a similar fee, where he continued to score goals for both club and country.

McGuigan and emerging youngster Ken Hale were given outings in the No. 9 role as United struggled to come to terms with life a division lower. Hale, from Blyth, began brightly and it was noted he was 'leading the attack with magnificent quickness and positional intelligence'. Ken was a stocky forward with good control and vision, but he wasn't an out and out leader of the attack. Later, he was prominent with Coventry City and Oxford United.

Len White returned too. After a five-month lay-off, the experienced No. 9 was recalled, although back in his original position on the wing. However, Len was brought back too soon and as George Taylor wrote in the press at the time: 'He should still have been on the touch-line convalescing.' Others noted that White 'was only a shadow' of the player who delighted everyone. Len did show flashes of his old brilliance. Against Luton Town he took a pass from Alf McMichael then 'swerved speedily through the defence and rammed the ball home'. He was dropped to the reserves but on his recall grabbed a hat-trick against Bristol Rovers and supporters sensed a comeback. One of his goals was a gem – typical White: 'Down to the byline went the little man, cork-screwing his way past two men. He looked up for help and found none. Deciding to go it alone, he cut deep into the middle and, while harried by two more defenders, suddenly pivoted on his left foot before hammering in a right-foot shot which rattled the underside of the bar before entering the net.' The press highlighted the 'return to favour of the dazzle, thunder, and flash of little Len White'.

But White's long stay at St. James' Park was coming to a close. His trainer throughout the '50s, Norman Smith, was put in charge as a short-term measure on Mitten's departure until a new manager was appointed in the close season of 1962 – one of Len's former skippers, Joe Harvey. Smith, the portly but highly experienced ex-Huddersfield Town wing-half started a process – completed by Harvey – that swept the St. James' Park corridors and dressing-room clean. One of the casualties was Len White, Smith holding no sentimental empathy for a player he had worked closely with for almost a decade.

White, at almost 32 years of age, was part of an exchange deal with Huddersfield Town put together by Smith which brought forward Jimmy Kerray to St. James' Park during February 1962. White never really wanted to leave Tyneside after serving the club with distinction for nine years, although he knew it was time for a change having already written out a transfer request. He later commented: 'I don't mind admitting I shed a few tears when Newcastle let me go.' White played through the glory years at Gallowgate, and some bad years too. He ironically earned his reputation as United slid towards the Second Division. Appearing in every forward position for the Magpies, White will be remembered as a No. 9 first and foremost, a rip-roaring one who became a hero figure to a generation. Testament to his eminence is that only two players have scored more goals for Newcastle United – Jackie Milburn and Alan Shearer. White bagged 153 for the Black'n'Whites in league and cup football – and without the benefit of penalties season after season. Many who saw him play still consider Len to be the best No. 9 ever in a Magpie shirt – he was simply White-hot!

United enthusiast Alan Candlish was one. He said: 'At his peak, he was probably Newcastle's greatest centre-forward in my lifetime.' One goal stands out in Alan's memory, a cracker against Wolves: 'The little No. 9 won the game with the only goal of the match and what a gem it was as he ran, twisting and turning his way from the halfway line to the edge of the penalty area, before letting fly with a rocket of a shot. He hit the ball so hard it came back from the back stanchion of the goal and rebounded out of the penalty area. Even Stan Cullis, the respected Wolves manager, described it as the greatest goal he had ever seen.' That was Len White – an effervescent striker who thrilled the crowd with his particular brand of centre-forward play.

THOMAS AND McGARRY

When Joe Harvey's inspirational style of management arrived in the summer of 1962 he was content to give his forward options a chance as he took control. With White, McGuigan and Leek gone, his options were limited. He could choose from Ken Hale and Jimmy Kerray – both inside-forwards – or youngster George Watkin, who was soon to be given his debut in the No. 9 role against Bury but was unlucky to come across a determined ex-Magpie in Bob Stokoe at centre-half. Harvey relied on Norman Smith's record signing of the previous January when the club spent a fee of £45,000 to bring Barrie Thomas to Tyneside.

BARRIE THOMAS
FACTS & FIGURES

To Newcastle United: January 1962 from Scunthorpe
   United £45,000
From Newcastle United: November 1964 to Scunthorpe
   United £20,000
Born: Measham 19 May 1937
Height: 5 ft 10 in.
International: None
Other senior clubs: Leicester City, Mansfield Town,
   Barnsley
Newcastle United app & goals:
   Football League: 73 app, 48 goals
   FA Cup: 2 app, 1 goal
   FL Cup: 3 app, 1 goal
   Total: 78 app, 50 goals
Strike-rate: League and Cup 64%

A free-scoring centre-forward for a more than decent Scunthorpe United eleven in Division Two, he had scored a club record 31 goals at the Old Showground in only two-thirds of the 1961–62 season before United splashed out. Thomas was another centre-forward brought up in the coalfields of Britain. Having scored 70 goals for the Irons – eventually to be recognised as one of Scunthorpe's finest goalscorers – Thomas showed he could thrill the crowd with bags of enthusiasm and running power, if not with finesse. As he said himself: 'There is nothing I like better than slamming the ball past the goalkeeper.' Barrie liked the trimmings and attention of being a star. He drove a flash Jaguar and when he joined the bigger stage at St. James' Park, relished becoming United's centre-forward.

A former England youth player, like Len White he had been jettisoned by Leicester City following a teenage debut for the Foxes, but resurrected his career with, at first Mansfield Town, then Scunthorpe. Thomas stood 5 ft 10 in. tall and was lithe and extremely fast. Installed in the No. 9 shirt, he was Harvey's centre-forward choice as the United boss attempted to put together a side to regain the club's First Division status. Thomas was dynamite at times, hitting the net on 41 occasions for both Scunthorpe and the Magpies during that 1961–62 season. Colleague Dave Hilley remembered: 'Barrie was full of energy and had a terrific shot. He would do anything to score a goal – even once barging me out of the way to get his foot to the ball and hit the net before I could!'

Although he was sometimes erratic in front of goal, his goal ratio for the Black'n'Whites is first class, once netting in six consecutive matches for the Magpies. Thomas scored 50 goals in only 78 appearances for United, including a characteristic hat-trick in a Tyne–Tees derby against Middlesbrough. His first in the convincing 6–1 victory was 'opportunism ten yards out', the second a 'rocketing header' and the third another from close in, 'almost off the goal-line'. He was described as a centre-forward who 'had a fleeting stamp of near England class'. It was form that certainly reached the attention of his country's boss, Walter Winterbottom, and earned Barrie a call-up to the full England training squad at Lilleshall in preparation for the 1962 World Cup in Chile. While Thomas was down the pecking order for ultimate selection with players like Ray Crawford, Bobby Smith, Gerry Hitchens, Alan Peacock and Johnny Byrne ahead of him in the England reckoning, he was considered good enough for contention. The only thing that stopped Thomas really making a huge name for himself was a series of niggling injuries. Thomas appeared to be constantly dogged by knocks of one description or another at St. James' Park.

BARRIE THOMAS No. 9 RATING	
Fan appeal – personality and presence	7
Strike-rate	6
Shooting – power and placement	8
Heading	8
Ball-skills	7
Link-play – passing, assists, crossing, team-play	6
Pace	8
Commitment – work-rate, courage	8
Match-winner – power-play, big-match capability	7
Longevity with United	4
Trophy success, international and top football ranking	-1
Total No. 9 rating	68

He had some of the worst injury luck imaginable – frustrating both for the player and his manager, who could never get a promotion momentum going in either 1962–63 or 1963–64. Thomas would be in the side for a run, then out. He would return, perhaps too early, and was out again. A fully fit Thomas was something United's attack badly needed. He was always eager to get to the ball in the box – perhaps too keen at times, often going in pursuit of lost causes. *Northern Football* magazine noted: 'He may not be one of the world's best footballers, but he plays his heart out.'

In season 1963–64 Thomas grabbed 21 goals in his busy style, described as a 'speedy live-wire' with a hound-doggish attitude of 'chasing loose balls'. It was also noted that he always 'kept going, fighting tigerishly for every ball'. He blasted a hat-trick against Plymouth Argyle and after a two-goal strike against Grimsby Town it was noted: 'What more magnificent sight is there than Barrie Thomas in full flight, scorching through the centre with the ball habitually ten yards ahead of him.' Yet, Thomas was in and out of the side again. He missed 15 games in that league campaign as United tried to push into the top 2 places.

The following year saw United's manager make a determined effort for promotion and during the early part of the 1964–65 season, as Thomas missed a hatful of opportunities, Harvey decided to make a change in his centre-forward strategy. Thomas infuriated

A No. 9 of power and charisma, Macdonald rapidly became the new centre-forward hero – here scoring in the semi-final against Burnley. (© Newcastle United Archive)

To be hailed as Supermac, Malcolm Macdonald burst onto the football scene in eye-catching fashion during 1971. (© *Newcastle Chronicle & Journal*)

The departure of Supermac to Arsenal in 1976 led to a whole line of centre-forwards in the No. 9 shirt over a short period. Few were a success, but Chris Waddle was, and earned glowing praise as well as an England place. (© www.sporting-heroes.net)

Small and tricky, Micky Burns operated in the No. 9 shirt in a different style to many – and was a success. (© Newcastle United Archive)

The arrival of international striker Mirandinha from Brazil in 1987 caused plenty of headlines: he was the first Brazilian to appear in top-flight English football. (© Newcastle United Archive)

The Magpies needed a striker by the time Micky Quinn arrived in Toon during 1989. The chirpy Scouser made an immediate impact by hitting four goals on his debut against Leeds United. (© www.sporting-heroes.net)

As the Geordies began their much-publicised resurgence under Kevin Keegan during season 1992–93, unsung hero David Kelly led the line with endeavour and plenty of goals. (© Newcastle United FC)

The first of Kevin Keegan's aristocrats in the No. 9 shirt was Andy Cole, United's record purchase at £1.75 million. That fee, though, was soon to be dwarfed. (© *Newcastle Chronicle & Journal*)

Andy Cole was an instant sensation, rewriting the record books by striking 41 goals as United entered Premiership action in 1993–94. (© Newcastle United FC)

When Keegan sold Andy Cole to rivals Manchester United, the Newcastle manager had to find a replacement. He went for one of the best in the business, Les Ferdinand. (© Newcastle United FC)

Big and powerful, Les Ferdinand became immensely popular in the No. 9 shirt. Sir Les was the focal point of United's entertaining charge on the Premiership title. (© Newcastle United FC))

What the Shirt of Legends means to the ranks of the Toon Army – tradition, passion and pride. (© Newcastle United FC)

Only one centre-forward was perhaps better than Les Ferdinand – and he was a Geordie, Alan Shearer. When Sir John Hall (left) and Kevin Keegan (right) had the opportunity to bring Shearer back home to join Ferdinand, the United duo didn't hesitate – at a new world-record fee of £15 million. (© Newcastle United FC)

Shearer reached two FA Cup finals with the Magpies, guiding the side through both semi-finals at Old Trafford with glory goals. Against Sheffield United in 1998, United's No. 9 rams the ball into the net for the deciding goal of the contest. (© Newcastle United FC)

A year later against Tottenham Hotspur, Shearer netted twice, including a brilliant effort from the edge of the box. The 30,000 from Tyneside at Old Trafford were ecstatic. (© Newcastle United FC)

While Shearer took over the No. 9 shirt from Les Ferdinand, the pairing did play together for one season and the £21 million strike force hit 49 goals, the best in the country. New manager Kenny Dalglish broke the radiant partnership by selling Sir Les to Tottenham. (© Newcastle United FC)

Captain Courageous: Alan Shearer leads by example in the No. 9 shirt and, like every Geordie, gives his all to the United cause – even when it hurts. (© Newcastle United FC)

Alan Shearer in typical raised-arm pose as another goal hits the net.
Shearer will call it a day during 2005 and the Shirt of Legends will be
passed on . . . another No. 9 hero will start to make folklore.
(© Newcastle United FC)

many and had several critics. Apart from being frequently on the sidelines and while he always scored goals, he also missed countless chances too. After a display against Luton Town, one critic noted: 'Thomas was a complete ham in this game – until he struck two into the net within the space of four minutes.' And as Dave Hilley said: 'He was a difficult forward to link with, not really being a team-player.' Needing more consistency in his line-up, he sold Thomas back to Scunthorpe United in November 1964 for less than half the money United had paid for him. Harvey relied on a versatile forward he had brought to Tyneside from Bolton Wanderers for £17,500 in December 1962, Ron McGarry.

McGarry had played successfully alongside Thomas for several months. Signed as an inside-forward who could switch to the leader's role too, McGarry had begun his sporting career as a tough rugby league player in Whitehaven. Switching codes in 1960 at Workington – then managed by Joe Harvey – he found a place at Burnden Park alongside another player with future Magpie connections, Wyn Davies. Ron was thickset at 5 ft 9 in. tall and possessed battling qualities brought from the scrum and pack. Harvey knew the player well and knew he could do a job as United entered combat in a bid to get out of Division Two. United's boss called him 'a Robledo type of player'. Harvey added: 'He might not have been a great footballer but he had a heart as big as they come.'

McGarry was never quite as good as United's Chilean star and may not have been the classiest of forwards, but he was effective and somewhat underrated, described as an 'honest-to-goodness workhorse' up front. McGarry packed the 'shot of a mule' and he wasn't afraid to graft. He was also a tremendous asset to dressing-room spirit. Witty and full of wisecracks, Ron was a real character with bags of tricks that livened up even the dullest of days. Colleague Bobby Moncur described Ron as a 'king of clowns . . . a joker supreme'. Dave Hilley said he was 'the life and soul of the dressing-room'. He was a touch brash and had a mouth to go with it, once saying: 'I may well frighten the opposition to death by talking.' But he was likeable and easy-going and the fans savoured his lively character on and off the field.

RON McGARRY
FACTS & FIGURES

To Newcastle United: December 1962 from Bolton
  Wanderers £17,500
From Newcastle United: March 1967 to Barrow £3,500
Born: Whitehaven 5 December 1937
Height: 5 ft 9 in.
International: None
Other senior clubs: Workington
Newcastle United app & goals:
  Football League: 121 app, 41 goals
  FA Cup: 6 app, 3 goals
  FL Cup: 5 app, 2 goals
  Total: 132 app, 46 goals
Strike-rate: League and Cup 35%

His rapport with United's supporters was quick to take off. Ron knew how to become a personality player. Early into his days at Gallowgate he made all the headlines in a dog-fight with Swansea defender Mike Johnson at the Vetch Field. Johnson had been 'chopping' Ron down all through the match and just after a Kerray chance was skied, the confrontation erupted into a boxing match in the penalty area. Fists flew – no handbags in this clash – and the referee had little alternative but to send the pair off. As McGarry left the field, teammate Gordon Hughes said: 'Hard luck, Ron.' McGarry responded as quick as you like: 'Think nothing of it . . . I'd have taken him in the fifth anyway!' He was dubbed Cassius after boxing sensation Cassius Clay. McGarry was built like a boxer and the whole of Tyneside caught on to the nickname. That was reinforced at St. James' Park when Ron had another few rounds with Coventry's Ronnie Farmer, being sent off again for 'an upper-cut that would have been absolutely splendid in the St. James' Hall'.

McGarry also now had a catchphrase of 'I'm the Greatest', again pinched from legend Cassius Clay. And it stuck. He loved to play to the crowd. In front against Cardiff City, Ron was confident enough to start a routine of performing ball-juggling tricks. Legend has it that he turned to the St. James' Park crowd with raised arms and shouted to the Popular Terrace: 'Who's the greatest?' The roar came back: 'McGarry!'

Joe Harvey additionally had another option up his sleeve on the departure of Thomas. Also in his plans was locally born Bobby Cummings who had returned to St. James' Park for a second spell following a productive stay with Aberdeen. From Ashington, the curly-haired Cummings had an early period at Gallowgate as a budding star, but only managed 34 Central League outings over 3 seasons. He was a totally different type of centre-forward to McGarry. Cummings was slightly built, possessed what was described as 'delicate ingenuity' and was a cooler character than McGarry; a thoughtful, unselfish player, he was always looking for openings and able to bring colleagues into the game. He could graft too, and noted as a 'determined little fighter', Cummings proved to be a more than useful contrast to McGarry. Harvey used both players in the No. 9 shirt – and at inside-forward too – with clever selection during the 1964–65 season.

It was soon evident that the Magpies were going to be one of the favourites for promotion. United's former FA Cup-winning skipper had assembled together a solid if not flamboyant side, marshalled by an exquisite half-back line of ex-England player Stan Anderson, centre-half John McGrath and the balding but experienced head of Jim Iley. Added to that backbone were Scottish playmaker Dave Hilley as well as a batch of rising stars: Alan Suddick, David Craig, Frank Clark, Bob Moncur and Bryan Robson.

McGarry's powerful displays were influential too – he ended up top scorer with 16 goals as United headed towards the Second Division Championship and a place back in the top flight. Cummings supported him, hitting eight into the net. By the time rivals Northampton Town left Tyneside during December after a top-of-the-table fixture, Tyneside supporters were confident a resolute push for promotion was assured. United demolished their rivals 5–0 and McGarry was the star of the show. Described as 'rampaging', United's centre-forward struck a hat-trick. His first was a rocket from close-in, his second a gem – one of the best goals Cassius scored. He nipped round one defender, then went past 2 more before striking a drive from nearly 30 yards that flew past ex-United keeper Bryan Harvey and into the net off the post. His hat-trick was claimed with a scooped shot from a David Craig cross.

Ron was dubbed by many as being a curious player, with one commentator writing: 'He seems so awkward, and yet capable at times, of flashes of the highest skill.' Jackie Milburn, then just starting off reporting from the press-box on United's matches made the comment:

'He isn't the lame duck some people thought.' Good at holding off challenges and linking up, his manager noted: 'McGarry's the heavy man in our forward line and he suffers for it. But you never hear him complain.' Ron took the weight off United's attack and took punishment up front, but he knew how to handle himself too, dishing out a fair share of retribution both fair and foul as Messrs Johnson and Farmer found out.

As the Black'n'Whites headed for the promotion run-in McGarry was on the sidelines, having picked up a muscle injury that needed hospital treatment. In stepped Bobby Cummings to the No. 9 role for the final ten games of the season – and the likeable Northumbrian was proficient in everything he did. He netted in crucial victories over Portsmouth and Norwich City then soon after took part in the biggest game of the season – the promotion clincher against third-placed Bolton Wanderers.

A Good Friday crowd of nearly 60,000 crushed into St. James' Park and Cummings played a major part in United's 2–0 triumph. Apart from a good all-round display, he had a hand in the winning goal for Jim Iley in the 57th minute. Iley recorded: 'Bobby Cummings laid the ball off and then got out of the way because he knew I was going to have a smack at it.' Iley did that all right – the ball flew past England goalkeeper Eddie Hopkinson and into the net. Newcastle United were back in the First Division. And McGarry saw it all from the terraces, discharging himself from the club's Jesmond hospital. He wasn't going to miss the big day.

RON McGARRY
No. 9 RATING

Fan appeal – personality and presence	8
Strike-rate	4
Shooting – power and placement	8
Heading	7
Ball-skills	6
Link-play – passing, assists, crossing, team-play	7
Pace	7
Commitment – work-rate, courage	8
Match-winner – power-play, big-match capability	7
Longevity with United	4
Trophy success, international and top football ranking	-1
Total No. 9 rating	65

It was not lost on Newcastle's management that for a new era in the First Division more quality talent was needed – especially up front where finer skills were in short supply. Long-serving director Stan Seymour was quick to point out: 'We must improve our attack.' *The Journal* was also to declare: 'A big, strong centre-forward of class is the number one objective.' Even the players under the spotlight knew their limitations. Almost as soon as promotion was achieved McGarry asked for a transfer. He honestly told the media: 'I don't think I'll be a success in the First Division. I've played in it before and I know.' He added: 'It's brute strength and ignorance that has got my goals this season.'

Yet finding a top-class centre-forward was not easy. It took the club almost one and a half years before a new No. 9 arrived on Tyneside. In that period, the Magpies struggled for their First Division life as goals were hard to come by. For season 1965–66, both McGarry and Cummings started United going but they managed a mere six goals in the programme. Harvey did bring Albert Bennett back to his native North-east from Rotherham United, but he was not an out and out centre-forward, although he occasionally wore the No. 9 shirt. Also to arrive from the manager's former club of Workington was 22-year-old Kit Napier. It was hoped that the tall and leggy Napier could develop into a No. 9 of quality. His first appearance prompted some to note that he has 'skill, positional sense, flicks, back passes and distribution of considerable accuracy'. But Napier didn't have punch and penetration where it matters – in front of goal. He quickly moved on to have a fine career in the lower divisions. Reserve striker Peter Noble was handed a few outings, but like Bennett he needed a centre-forward to feed off and soon moved south as well, and to a career of note with Burnley.

Cummings and McGarry moved too. Both had served the club well. Cummings claimed 14 goals in 45 matches before heading down the A1 to assist Darlington and Hartlepool with distinction, while McGarry crossed the Pennines for Barrow. As jovial as ever, he noted on his departure: 'I always wanted to be a Barrow Boy!' Ron hit almost 50 goals for the Magpies and will be a player always remembered.

The centre-forward position was becoming a real problem for the Magpies. Harvey even tried centre-halves Bill Thompson and Ollie Burton, such was his dire need. Newcastle searched the country and were linked with all of the emerging star No. 9s: Tony Hateley, Ron Davies, John Ritchie as well as another Davies, Bolton's Wyn Davies. But Harvey couldn't land any of them. However, Joe was a dogged character. He knew he simply had to bring one of them to St. James' Park, or United would tumble back into the Second Division. Eventually his determination paid off. Newcastle United were soon to have a new No. 9 hero.

No. 9 EXTRAS

LEN'S FAVOURITE
Len White confirmed that his favourite match in the black and white shirt for Newcastle was the terrific 7–3 victory over Manchester United during the New Year holiday period of season 1959–60. He said: 'It was the best of so many memorable games – and I got a hat-trick.' A crowd of 57,200 at St. James' Park were given plenty of festive cheer. United led 3–1 at half-time then demolished the Reds in the second period with another four goals. Apart from White's treble, Newcastle's goals were scored by Ivor Allchurch, George Eastham, Gordon Hughes and Jackie Bell. Albert Quixall (2) and Alex Dawson replied for the Old Trafford club.

THE FAMILY WHITE
Len White hailed from a noted family of Yorkshire footballers. He was the youngest of six brothers who loved the game, while his father was a distinguished amateur. Albert appeared for Aldershot in the war years; Jack was a seasoned campaigner over six years with Bristol City (skippering them in 232 appearances) while he also totalled 200 games for Aldershot; another brother, Fred, was at one time on Bradford Park Avenue's books.

FRIENDLY ROUT
Centre-forwards Len White and Bill Curry each scored five goals in friendly routs against Brazilians Bela Vista (1958–59) and the British Olympic XI (1956–57). In the exhibition game with Bela Vista, White's strike partner Arthur Bottom netted five goals as well in a 12–1 slaughter of the tourists. Curry scored all United's goals in a 5–0 victory over the Olympic amateurs.

WOR JACKIE'S INFLUENCE

Jackie Milburn assisted Lennie White enormously during their time at St. James' Park, Len recording that he was 'always a great help to me, passing on advice and little tips'. And Milburn made sure he knew what the No. 9 shirt meant at Gallowgate, White recalling that his famous Tyneside colleague said that 'it was something special, and over the years I learned what he meant'. Milburn once noted that White was the 'best Newcastle United player never to be capped for England'.

A DOG'S LIFE

Manager Charlie Mitten was famed for his love of dogs – especially greyhounds – and once at St. James' Park, Len White was said to have been thrown off the treatment table to allow his manager's prized canine friend a spot of treatment on its hind leg by United's physio, before running at Brough Park. White was not alone; Johnny Haynes had to wait his turn at Craven Cottage, while it was often the same story at Old Trafford!

ALLCHURCH TRIBUTE

Ivor Allchurch was a highly respected player during the '50s era, for many years the most capped individual ever for Wales and winning the MBE for his services to the game. For almost four seasons, he played alongside Len White and said of his centre-forward colleague: 'Out of all the players I've played against and alongside, perhaps the best of all, for his true approach and professionalism, would be for me Len White.' A valued tribute indeed.

WHITE – AFTER TOON

At Leeds Road with Huddersfield Town, Len White continued to score regularly, hitting 39 goals. He then crossed the Pennines turning out for Stockport County, even though he was very much a veteran. Approaching 36 years of age, injury started to curtail his appearances and in the summer of 1966 Len joined Altrincham, ending his days in the senior game with almost 300 goals to his name. But he was far from finished playing football. In fact, after a spell in Ireland with Sligo Rovers, White played on in local football around his Huddersfield home until into his 50th year, whilst working for a tractor manufacturer in Yorkshire.

TEENAGE SENSATION

Barrie Thomas was a precocious teenage star who joined Leicester City – then in the top division – during July 1954. He was quickly to gain a debut in the Football League and as a 17 year old netted a fabulous hat-trick for City against Bolton Wanderers at Filbert Street – in only his fifth outing. Yet in spite of his headlining start, Barrie was soon discarded by the Foxes and had to resurrect his career elsewhere.

THOMAS – AFTER TOON

Returning to the Old Showground in Scunthorpe after his period on Tyneside, Barrie continued bagging goals, including a five-goal strike in a single outing against Luton Town in 1965. He joined Barnsley in November 1966 and again proved a dangerous striker in the lower divisions. A cruciate ligament injury forced him to quit the scene in the summer of 1968, the Magpies playing a testimonial for Thomas. His overall career total of more than 250 goals remains evidence of an admirable career in football. He later managed his home-town club, Measham Swifts, and ran a haulage business, until past crippling football injuries forced his retirement.

SOLDIER'S LOT

For three years Ron McGarry was a Guardsman in the British Army, although in characteristic McGarry style he made sure he wasn't called up to do much soldiering. Ron found himself in charge of the sports stores and playing fields. He played football too, scoring plenty of goals for 27 Company – on one occasion netting 18 in one match!

CALLING CARD

At the peak of his popularity on Tyneside, Ron McGarry came up with the novel idea of printing calling cards to hand out to opposing players! Sitting at home watching the popular television western series of the time, *Have Gun Will Travel*, he remembered: 'It just came to me. I jumped up on my feet. That's it. That's for McGarry.' He continued: 'Paladin's a hired gun, I'm a hired forward. He's fast on the draw, I'm fast on the draw. He hits the target. I hit the target.' Ron's cards spelt in big bold lettering: *Have Goals Will Travel. R. McGarry (Newcastle United)*. And he dished them out all over the place!

CASSIUS – AFTER TOON

Ron McGarry headed for Australia after his spell with Barrow, joining the Bolgownie club as player-coach in 1968. He soon returned to England and the North-east, being appointed Gateshead player-manager in 1972 before appearing in minor football in the region. Cassius loved Tyneside and settled in the area, having various occupations from newsagent to bookmaker. Over the years he has lost none of his haughty character.

6. THE MIGHTY WYN
1966–1971

WYN DAVIES

When Newcastle United lifted the Second Division Championship in 1965 and returned to football's elite the game was quickly changing – just as society was going through a revolution that saw pre-war ideals and propriety disappear for good. Money started to play a much larger part in who would be football's winners and losers as the old style of the '50s and remnants of autocratic boardrooms rapidly disappeared.

Newcastle United had to think differently at board level. They had to act and spend big to consolidate their First Division place and attempt to compete with the best in the country at the time – then Liverpool, Manchester United, Everton and Tottenham Hotspur. Manager Joe Harvey knew he needed a big-name signing in attack. In 1965–66, and for the beginning of the 1966–67 campaign, the Magpies struggled to score goals. Harvey knew only too well of the exploits of his former colleagues, Wor Jackie and Len White, in the No. 9 shirt. He was determined to bring another No. 9 hero to St. James' Park.

McGarry and Cummings failed to step up the grade for season 1965–66 and the manager's other options in the centre-forward role were extremely limited. He became desperate and tried central defenders Thompson and Burton up front when forwards Willie Penman, Peter Noble and Kit Napier found the No. 9 shirt too hot to handle. In that season, United scraped away from an immediate return into Division Two by a whisker. Scoring only 50 goals they steered clear of relegation in a fight with no fewer than nine other clubs by defeating Leeds United on the last day of the season. United's attack was clearly not good enough. New blood was needed and the Magpies had to join a buoyant marketplace.

Seemingly every major club in the country wanted a centre-forward. Harvey was locked into a transfer market that was very competitive, and at a time when fees spiralled. Newcastle United's record purchase was the modest £45,000 spent on Barrie Thomas, while the country's biggest transfer was recorded when Denis Law moved to Manchester United for £116,000. Any decent goalscorer could command a fee approaching six figures.

The man Harvey wanted was one of a group of talented strikers who were the talk of the transfer market. There was Aston Villa's Tony Hateley and Celtic's Yogi Hughes as well as Neil Martin of Hibernian. Mick Jones of Sheffield United, John Ritchie at Stoke and Norwich City's Ron Davies were also much sought after. Newcastle United were linked with them all. But Harvey went for another striker in demand, Bolton Wanderers' centre-forward Wyn Davies, a 6 ft 1 in. flame-haired Welshman.

Harvey had been impressed with the ability of the Welsh leader to cause havoc in opponents' defences. Indeed, Newcastle's promotion dream less than a year before had almost been shattered by Davies in the epic Good Friday clash with Bolton at St. James' Park. That promotion decider started badly for the Magpies with Davies almost hitting a hat-trick in the first half. He caused all sorts of problems in the air until a clash with John McGrath left him a passenger and the game turned United's way. Bob Moncur later noted: 'I'm sure his form that day did a lot towards bringing him to Tyneside.'

In October 1965 the Geordies made an approach for the Welshman who was eager to leave Burnden Park for the First Division having lodged four transfer requests. United were not alone in a chase for his signature. Sheffield Wednesday wanted him. Both Arsenal and Sunderland were linked with a bid too, but Harvey got there first. Having settled a fee of around £70,000 with Bolton, all that was needed was for Davies to agree to United's financial package. Yet that was far from easy.

Newcastle had not perhaps moved fully from the days when players were forced to accept whatever a club offered – the maximum wage having been abolished only four years before when the top weekly payment of £20 disappeared for good. England schemer Johnny Haynes soon became the first £100 per week footballer and very quickly, in 1963, the retain and transfer system was demolished after Newcastle United ended up in the High Court as a culmination of the George Eastham saga. Players now had previously unheard-of-power. It was a fundamental change to football and it took the Magpies – along with many other top clubs – some time to modernise their wage structure. United's players at the time didn't earn anything like £100 per week – Ollie Burton received a basic £35 per week when he signed a new deal in 1963 while Ivor Allchurch had been Newcastle's highest earner at £60 per week. On United's promotion, the club's First Division stars took home less than £50 for a week's work. If players were good enough they could now call the tune in financial negotiations. And Davies did exactly that.

Directors Stan Seymour and Fenton Braithwaite conducted the face-to-face negotiations along with Harvey and Wyn Davies . . . and the two sides were miles apart. Davies later wrote: 'It has since been reported that Newcastle offered me £45 a week basic wage and a £2,000 signing-on fee and that I asked for £70 a week plus £7,000.' Although the exact details were never confirmed, the gap was too wide to bridge and the deal collapsed, with Davies branded in some places as being greedy. He said: 'I came in for a lot of criticism on the sports pages for asking for too much money but I still thought my terms were reasonable enough with so big a transfer fee involved.'

Newcastle's delegation headed back to Tyneside disappointed and no doubt somewhat disillusioned with the significance that players' wage demands now had in football. Chairman Lord Westwood was to say: 'Now, when you have negotiated with the clubs you are not nearly halfway there and have to start the battle with the player.' He added: 'I do think something will have to be done by the League to put some limit on this business. It is getting out of hand.' That was a somewhat antiquated view which Newcastle United had to put to one side, no matter how difficult. Times had completely changed and the Magpies had to live with a new way in football. Davies didn't find the big move elsewhere and remained at Bolton. Newcastle meanwhile continued to struggle for goals.

By the start of the 1966–67 season Joe Harvey was still searching for his centre-forward – and was becoming frantic. It was much the same story as the new season opened. The Toon found goals increasingly difficult to score and as winter approached they were once more destined for another uncomfortable relegation battle. Ron McGarry carried the weight manfully but scored only 5 goals in 15 matches at centre-forward before his departure. Boss Harvey and his directors faced the wrath of supporters as the club struggled. Following a poor showing at Gallowgate as West Bromwich Albion won 1–3 the frustrated crowd turned. Chants of 'Resign, Resign' and a chorus of 'We've the worst board in the land' echoed round St. James' Park. Hundreds of annoyed fans waited outside the main entrance singing to the tune of The Beatles' popular song, 'We are all in the sinking submarine'!

The demonstration pushed United into action, in spite of an unwillingness to move with the times and pay the price for big-name players – as had occurred elsewhere. Tony Hateley (£100,000) moved to Chelsea, Martin (£50,000) to Sunderland, Ron Davies (£50,000) to Southampton and soon after Jones (£100,000) joined Leeds, while Ritchie (£70,000) signed for Sheffield Wednesday. With that background, United's board sanctioned another bid on improved terms for Wyn Davies.

Exactly a year after their first bid to land Bolton's 24-year-old Welsh centre-forward, United made a fresh approach. Joe Harvey was determined this time he would get his man. Having scored 12 goals in the first 12 games of the new season – and 74 in 170 outings for the Burnden Park club – the Welshman showed he could be the answer to United's dire need.

A fee was soon once again agreed with Wanderers, reported at £80,000 and even £90,000, although Davies later maintained the fee was only £70,000. United's party met the player just outside Bolton and this time, as Wyn confirmed, United were ready to pay the rate for the job, saying that 'the terms were a lot better'. Although negotiations were at times difficult, Davies being cautious and reticent, a deal was done as Wyn was by now more willing to move from Bolton following a series of rows. At the end of negotiations, Joe Harvey suffered an agonising few minutes as Davies kept United waiting while he discussed the move with his mother on the phone. The conversation was conducted in Welsh so United's delegation of Harvey and director Wilf Taylor couldn't understand the content! It was a tense moment. Wyn said: 'At first, I was reluctant to move so far from Wales . . . it would be like being in Scotland.' He added later, though: 'But as it turned out, it was the best move I ever made.'

United had landed their new centre-forward – but only just. Also in the hunt were Manchester City. Their boss, Joe Mercer, made a last-minute attempt to get in on the act, but was too late. It was just as well, as with Manchester being so close to Bolton – and to Wyn's home in North Wales – Maine Road would have been the ideal choice for Davies rather than some 150 miles to the North-east. Davies later said of City's bid: 'In all probability I would have turned Newcastle down for a second time.'

From a working-class family in a Welsh-speaking community of Caernarfon, Davies never planned to become a footballer, although he was hooked on the game, worshipping Wales legend John Charles. He lived in a council house in the shadow of Mount Snowdon, worked at a slate quarry in his teens and had to be pushed by his family in a bid to become a professional. As an inside-forward with local clubs Deiniolen, Llanberis and Caernarfon Town, Davies attracted scouts from Aston Villa and Manchester United who both invited the leggy and sturdy Welsh youngster for trials. But it was North Wales club Wrexham, then in Division Three, that secured his services during December 1959 as an amateur. He signed as a professional for a modest £500 fee the following April, some dubbing him as the new John Charles, although he didn't move into the regular centre-forward's role until making a switch to First Division Bolton Wanderers during March 1962, having totalled 26 goals in 67 games for the Red Dragons.

The ability of Wyn to get to balls in the air took the eye and he made rapid progress at first the Racecourse Ground then Burnden Park. Appearing for the Welsh youth and Under-23 sides, Davies was on his way to becoming a star. His record at Bolton was top class. Wyn scored plenty of goals and developed into a feared centre-forward and soon a full international one too. He was always something of a menace in aerial play, but also with ability on the ground to hold the ball and bring colleagues into the game. United boss Joe Harvey was to use that traditional target No. 9 role as a platform to develop his Magpie eleven. Wyn Davies was to be the central figure in that side.

On the day Davies turned up at St. James' Park there were hundreds of press, television crew, radio teams and supporters waiting for the first glimpse of United's record-breaking signing. He arrived sporting a crew cut, donning a fur coat and carrying his boots. Quite a reception greeted him; it was an extraordinary mass of people wanting interviews, autographs and just a glimpse of the new Tyneside personality. Wyn Davies was United's first superstar of the modern game, although Davies himself was a reluctant one, never keen to take the limelight.

WYN DAVIES
FACTS & FIGURES

To Newcastle United: October 1966 from Bolton
  Wanderers £80,000
From Newcastle United: August 1971 to Manchester City
  £52,500
Born: Caernarfon 20 March 1942
Height: 6 ft 1 in.
Other senior clubs: Wrexham, Manchester United,
  Blackpool, Crystal Palace, Stockport County, Crewe
  Alexandra
Welsh International: 34 app, 6 goals
Newcastle United app & goals:
  Football League: 181 app, 40 goals
  FA Cup: 8 app, 3 goals
  FL Cup: 3 app, 0 goals
  Europe: 24 app, 10 goals
  Total: 216 app, 53 goals
Strike-rate: League and Cup 25%

Following in the footsteps of previous Bolton centre-forwards to have moved to Tyneside, Albert Shepherd and more recently Ron McGarry, Davies was plunged into the public eye like never before. The level of media attention was unprecedented and was new to both the player and football in the region. Never before had such a spotlight been pointed at one footballer. The likes of Gallacher and Milburn didn't have to cope with the media pack – television and radio as well as conventional press hacks. Football in the '60s and '70s witnessed an enormous growth in media coverage of the game, especially on television which became a mesmerising and indispensable part of the public's newly developing way of life. Newcastle United's No. 9 hero now had to live with that huge glare of attention too.

As if to feed the media even more, Wyn's first appearance in a black and white shirt only 24 hours after arriving in the region was in a hostile derby encounter with Sunderland at St. James' Park. With United struggling near the bottom of the table – having just lost by six goals at Blackpool – the Wearsiders held the upper hand that season, but the arrival of Davies caught everyone's imagination on Tyneside. There was huge expectation that Harvey's record No. 9 acquisition would make a difference.

At the end of October, a captivated crowd of 57,643 gave Davies a rousing Geordie welcome as he ran onto the pitch from the West Stand tunnel wearing the black and white stripes. The Welshman did make a difference as a leader of United's attack, but it was going to take time for the new centre-forward to make a telling change. Sunderland cruised to a 0–3 victory, but Davies received much praise on his debut. He created two great chances with powerful headers as he rose majestically to outjump the Sunderland defence while another soaring leap saw the ball in the net only for the referee to call for a marginal offside decision. It was noted that Wyn 'rose like a bird to beat Jimmy Montgomery with a magnificent header'.

At the time Davies joined Newcastle United, football was not only changing in terms of management, professionalism and finance, but also moves occurred to alter strategy on the pitch. Alf Ramsey's successful tactical change that saw England win the World Cup in 1966 by eradicating the old style of play with inside-forwards and wing-halves, transformed the face of football. Davies joined United just as everyone – players and supporters – was getting accustomed to new formations. Gone for good was the 'WM' or 3–2–5 style of play and the wing-half and inside-forward were destined to history. In came 4–4–2 and 4–4–3 formations with double centre-halves, midfield players and strikers. Wingers disappeared – only to later return as wide midfielders – while the overlapping full-back, and later wing-back, arrived on the scene too. Thankfully the tradition of the centre-forward remained, most clubs developing attacking options with a No. 9 spearhead and a goalscoring partner alongside.

Now that Harvey had his own No. 9 spearhead, United's boss had to blend a side to get the best out of Davies. The Welshman needed a supply of crosses to utilise his power in the air and also a partner who could capitalise on the centre-forward's knock-downs, lay-offs and space creation in the box. At first, though, United had difficulty in combining an effective eleven.

It took a few weeks for Davies to settle and even longer to find, as it was recorded, 'strong running wingers to provide the chances'. Newcastle's desperate drive to steer clear of relegation became a struggle and the local press felt for Davies. It was noted: 'Poor Wyn Davies. The big-buy leader with that lean, hungry look will surely go leaner and hungrier still until his mates realise he's not a miracle worker who can turn hopeful lobs into helpful goals.'

For the rest of the 1966–67 season the service Davies was given was nothing short of dreadful. As a consequence, he rarely found the net and Newcastle found themselves stuck in the bottom places of the table scoring even fewer goals than before. Wyn's first strike came against Sheffield Wednesday in a most welcome 3–1 victory during November – with what was to become a typical Davies header, leaping at almost 45 degrees above Wednesday's centre-half Sam Ellis to nod home Suddick's corner. After that, slowly but surely, United started to improve. Wyn's teammates began to provide a better supply-line and while Davies only grabbed six goals in the First Division programme, it was enough to pull the Magpies away from the trapdoor – but only just, as they finished in 20th position with 4 points to spare following a late flurry of victories at the end of April – Wyn inspiring United to maximum returns against West Ham United and Southampton.

Davies displayed 'energy and work-rate' in a 1–0 win over the Hammers – thanks to a 15-yard back-pass by a harassed West Ham defender, Jack Burkett. Then in a relegation four-pointer with the Saints he battled on with a cut temple and managed to score with a 'characteristic nod' from a Clark free-kick as United triumphed 3–1.

The highlight of the season was a Davies hat-trick in a thrilling FA Cup tie against Coventry City at Highfield Road. The 4–3 United success was a match reminiscent of the glory days of the '50s, described as a 'throbbing, bubbling cardiac-inducing epic'. Davies showed his true class and what United could expect if they could build a team around him. He played havoc with the Coventry defence and gave City's respected stopper, George Curtis, 'the run-around'.

Wyn's hat-trick was an accomplished treble. In the first minute, he held off Curtis then accelerated past him before scoring with a 'tremendous right-foot shot' from the edge of the box. Then after good work from Robson and Hilley, the ball was pulled back and Davies thumped it into the net for his second. The same duo combined again and the Welshman 'hurtled skywards' to ram home a dangerous cross . . . and United's No. 9 had another header in the net only to be rather harshly judged for pushing.

As the season came to an end, critics and fans judged Davies with mixed opinion. There were doubts as to whether he was the right man. Some said he had 'been a disappointment'. Even colleague Bob Moncur acknowledged Davies received 'almost as much criticism as praise'. One view in the press noted: 'Davies is an enigma. He wins the high balls; his presence is a smouldering constant threat to the opposition. But he's still not getting the goals he should.' Davies was at times unlucky in front of goal however, on many occasions each season striking the woodwork – efforts that so easily could have improved his strike-rate by quite a margin.

There was even transfer speculation that he would move on while a debate raged that United had actually purchased the wrong Davies – and should have brought Wyn's Welsh international colleague and namesake, Ron Davies, to Tyneside instead. Ron had moved to Southampton and developed into a threatening striker, eventually hitting 153 goals for the Saints. Comparisons were often given column space while there was speculation that Harvey was to splash out again and even bring the other Davies to St. James' Park as a twin strike-force. Wyn Davies was never a goal-poacher in the mould of Jimmy Greaves and would never be as prolific as Ron Davies. He once said: 'I've never looked upon myself as a goalscoring machine,' and added: 'I like to take part in the build-up. If my teammates are cracking them in and I don't get one I'm happy.'

At 6 ft 1 in. and 12 st., Davies was powerfully built and was never afraid to put himself around – a bit like Vic Keeble in style. While Wyn wasn't a genius on the deck, he could hold the ball and control the forward line. He didn't possess the speed or ferocious shooting of Milburn or White before him, nor the brilliant ball control of Gallacher or Stubbins, but like Keeble, Davies was formidable in the air. Having the ability to seemingly hang in the heavens and soar above his rivals like a bird of prey, his aerial menace was rarely matched by any defender. United fundamentally had to utilise the Davies factor much better in the new season. Despite some criticism, Wyn was soon to make a big impression – not only in the North-east, but also on the Continent. Very shortly, Wyn of Newcastle was to become a cult figure on Tyneside and lift a European trophy, something Ron of Southampton never got near to.

KING OF THE CASTLE

Season 1967–68 was to prove to be a turning point in both United's fortunes and those of Wyn Davies. The Magpies brought in new talent to supply Davies. Raiding wide men Jim Scott, Tommy Robson – and later Jackie Sinclair – made a difference and up front Wyn forged a rich partnership, firstly with Albert Bennett, then with Bryan Robson. In defence, Bob Moncur developed into a skipper in the mould of Harvey and Scoular before him, and into an accomplished international defender. Harvey had almost overnight blended a team that transformed United's fortunes – and in the process the Black'n'Whites reaped the benefit of a Davies-led attack.

In the opening game of the new season against Southampton the Geordies roared to a 3–0 victory. United's style and tactics were typical of the Davies era at St. James' Park. Former United and England star Ivor Broadis wrote in *The Journal* that Davies 'was the architect of the success'. All three goals involved the Welsh international. Newcastle's opener came from ex-Hibs winger Scott after Davies had been the focus of attention, creating space in the box by taking Gabriel out of position in a jump for a cross. Bennett volleyed home the second as Wyn was first to another flighted ball, nodding perfectly back to his strike partner and the third was another tactical success, as Wyn again created space by going for a high ball. He flicked it into the path of Tommy Robson who headed into the net. Davies hadn't scored but he created all three goals with his brand of centre-forward play in and around the box. It was distinctive of Newcastle United's approach over the next three years – a ball to Davies who would create havoc or space and leave pickings for others. It worked a treat and Davies in no time at all became King of Newcastle.

There were no relegation worries for United now. Indeed, following a 5–1 mid-week demolition of Chelsea at the end of August, Newcastle – and Davies – were even respected by their sternest critics. United's display against the fashionable Londoners was terrific, and Wyn received much praise. It was highlighted that Davies had emerged as a First Division centre-forward who was 'both skilled and indomitable' and one who showed immense 'character'. Chelsea had no answer to headers that kept 'dropping into open spaces' and it was reported that he 'created such apprehension that they mounted a guard of three over him'. Of course that fell perfectly into United's tactical plan. With three men marking Davies, other Magpie strikers could capitalise.

United's centre-forward claimed two goals in that 5–1 victory – a far-post header in 'wonderful style' and a powerful shot 'on the turn'. Wyn could have easily had a hat-trick in a magnificent performance – the evening United's centre-forward was at last accepted by United's faithful after ten months in a Magpie shirt. Bonetti made a fabulous tip-over to stop another Davies goal and then Wyn crashed a further effort against the post. The press noted United's display was 'completely unrecognisable as the team that struggled so desperately last season'.

Newcastle continued to grow in confidence and understanding as the season developed. In attack, Davies was supported by a rejuvenated Albert Bennett, a leggy, curly-haired lad from County Durham. The former England Under-23 striker recaptured his confidence and Bennett linked with Davies almost to perfection, picking up the many loose balls from Wyn's aerial assault. He scored ten goals as United even reached the dizzy heights of fifth spot and chased a European place. Fate though wrecked Albert's promising liaison with Davies. A bad knee injury against Coventry City put him on the sidelines when the pairing had netted 21 goals. That unlucky mishap for Bennett was, as often happens in football, a fortunate opening for Bryan Robson, who answered Harvey's call for someone to step into the partnership.

Robson had been at St. James' Park for some time. Nicknamed Pop, the Sunderland born, 5 ft 8 in. tall striker joined United's junior set-up in 1962. He had operated across the forward line without making a huge impression but Robson flourished with Davies alongside. In the seasons to follow, the pair scored almost 100 times, with Pop taking the major share of 66 goals. He was elevated to his country's Under-23 line-up and Football League eleven. Many considered he was good enough to reach the full England side too.

Now nicknamed Wyn the Leap and often wearing distinctive white boots, Davies' characteristic manner was making an impression around the country. With flame hair, and shirt frequently outside his shorts, Davies was a player who stood out. While he was an airborne master, he was underrated with the ball at his feet and possessed a stinging shot at times. He could also expertly kill the ball dead on his chest and breast it strongly to a colleague – to the roar of the fans – a much admired feature of his repertoire. Jimmy Greaves once made the comment of Davies' particular technique: 'Wyn was a whole-hearted competitor whose aggressive, driving style of play made him a handful for any defence.' One of his biggest foes, Sunderland's skipper Charlie

Hurley rated Davies highly. 'We had some great battles. He was one of the most difficult centre-forwards to play against,' said Hurley.

As United pushed for a European spot, they relied on Davies and a formidable home record. While the Magpies stuttered hideously on occasion on their travels, at Gallowgate they were awesome and Davies continued to develop a bond with the Geordie crowd, his popularity now growing into a cult following. United's fans appreciated his intrepid and fervent approach. He was often in trouble with referees, either for disputing decisions or for head-to-head confrontations with defenders. Wyn was tough and relished the old-fashioned duel with his centre-half. He always gave as good as he got; consequently there were often fireworks on the pitch, and that just made the union between player and supporter even stronger. He was the Toon's talisman, just as Milburn had been in the past, and Macdonald and Shearer were to be in the future. Yet Wyn shunned the spotlight as much as he could, as Bryan Robson noted: 'He was a loner when he arrived and he stayed that way.' Jackie Milburn summed up the Welshman as being 'the only man to wear the famous No. 9 black and white shirt who kept himself to himself'.

Davies found goals a little easier to come by now he had support. He was United's top scorer in the season with 12 goals, which included spectacular headers against Arsenal, West Ham United and against Sheffield Wednesday, on a day United won 4–0 and 'when all the sceptics were silenced'. There was a revenge victory over Sunderland as well in front of 59,579, Wyn sticking out a long leg to give United a 2–1 triumph. With European qualification on the horizon however, United slumped as the season's finale drew to a close. Thoughts of applying for passports were disappointingly forgotten – initially, at any rate.

Newcastle finished the season in tenth place, an unsatisfactory position after being in reach of the leaders at one point. Yet the somewhat strange rules of European qualification that existed at the time saw the Magpies scrape into the Inter Cities Fairs Cup by the back door. It was a significant moment in the Black'n'Whites' colourful story. European football had arrived in the North-east for the very first time. What a huge impact it was to make – and Davies was to create quite an impression on the Continent too.

The Inter Cities Fairs Cup competition – soon to be re-named the UEFA Cup – had at the time unique and somewhat bizarre entry conditions that only allowed one competing club from each European city. That worked in United's favour at the end of the 1967–68 season as the Magpies slid down the table seemingly out of European contention. Although finishing below Everton, Spurs and Arsenal, because of the one-club-one-city rule, United leap-frogged over those sides to qualify for a UEFA tournament and bring European football to the Gallowgate arena.

Season 1968–69 became a milestone campaign in the eventful history of Newcastle United as the Black'n'Whites shocked everyone, including themselves, by not only performing well in European action, but concluded a memorable season by lifting the trophy at the first attempt. At the forefront of United's remarkable achievement was Wyn Davies, who led United's attack with gusto and courage. He caused Continental defenders all sorts of problems with his own particular brand of British centre-forward play – one totally alien to the European style.

EURO DANGER-MAN

Action on the Continent took centre stage and overshadowed the domestic programme, the Black'n'Whites cruising to a mid-table position and exiting – as usual at the time – from both FA Cup and League Cup competitions. Davies again had what could be considered only an average time in front of goal – managing 11 strikes in First Division fixtures. Not spectacular figures on the face of it. But the Welshman's worth was much, much more than the bare statistics show. He was never a 20-goal-a-season striker and needed support from others. His partner, Bryan Robson, grabbed 30 goals over the programme – the first United striker to do so since the '50s – and in the Inter Cities Fairs Cup, the Davies–Robson combination was a significant threat.

The big Continental defenders from Spain, Portugal, Holland and Hungary had no answer to Davies. He was the danger-man and many noted that United would never have been so successful in Europe without him. Club Chairman Lord Westwood made the comment: 'I can say that without Wyn Davies, United would never have won the Inter Cities Fairs Cup.' His towering leaps and physical play had accomplished defenders in all sorts of trouble time and time again.

Wyn's experience playing for Wales against Continental opposition served him well. By now Davies was a regular with the Welsh, appearing on 34 occasions all told for his country. Wyn was to say: 'The Continentals couldn't cope with the high ball in the air.' Bryan

Robson recalled a clash between the No. 9 and Real Zaragoza's experienced centre-half Santamaria: 'Wyn climbed above him – I still remember the look of astonishment on the Spaniard's face.' Davies teased and tortured the Europeans into tantrums. He and Pop Robson were there to capitalise on the mayhem.

Over the next three years of United's opening salvo in Europe, Davies did not miss a game, playing in all 24 contests. He ended up as the club's top scorer in Euro action too, with ten strikes in those games, while in domestic football he largely allowed others to find the net, notably Pop Robson. It never worried him though. He said once: 'It matters little who knocks them in.' His contribution to Joe Harvey's team-plan was worth more than goals. In courage and determination, he showed guts that earned him much respect. In United's opening European foray, Wyn picked up a broken nose, a fractured cheekbone, a badly gashed shin and a stack of bruises. Yet he flinched from no one and played on and on through the pain barrier as European defenders resorted to any foul tactic in an attempt to stop him. His manager said Davies was 'one of the most courageous players I have known'.

From the opening European adventure against seasoned campaigners Feyenoord, United's master-plan was to pump the long, high ball up for Davies to knock it down for Robson. Alternatively, it was a run down the wing followed by a telling cross for Davies to capitalise on. It wasn't exactly scientific football, perhaps not great stuff to watch and the media gave United stick. But it worked wonderfully well. Full-back Frank Clark commented in his book *Kicking With Both Feet*: 'We had a secret weapon. In fact, it was so secret we weren't aware of it ourselves until the tournament got under way.' Clark added: 'It was none other than the direct, journeyman approach to the game which had been so roundly slated by the press. It was completely new to our more sophisticated opponents and took them by surprise.' Frank went on to applaud his centre-forward colleague: 'The focal point of the team was Wyn Davies. He was big, brave and very good at getting on the end of long balls hit from the wings.'

United shocked the Dutch, and the rest of Europe, by giving Feyenoord a 4–0 hiding in the club's European debut on a September evening in 1968. Davies won everything in the air and as Frank Clark said: 'Feyenoord didn't know what to do about him.' He had a hand in the first goal, was responsible for the second after crashing a 25-yarder against the bar and scored the fourth himself – a fierce downward header from a Jim Scott free-kick.

United were off and running. They faced two more experienced Continental sides in Sporting Lisbon and Real Zaragoza in the following rounds. Both games were close and Davies made significant contributions. Against the Portuguese his expertise in the air created the all-important breakthrough in a tense second-leg when all was level at 1–1. A training ground routine was executed magnificently as a Gibb free-kick was met by Davies. A perfect head-down enabled Pop Robson to leap and volley a spectacular winner. Real Zaragoza's defence couldn't cope with Wyn's bustling approach in either leg and Davies got on the end of another Gibb free-kick, this time hitting the net himself with a stooping header to register one of two vital away goals in La Romareda stadium.

United's No. 9 hero scored two against Vitoria Setubal as United recorded a 6–4 aggregate victory, a triumph that took the Geordies into the semi-final to confound all the critics. And a Battle of Britain encounter took place against Glasgow Rangers, another side with plenty of European pedigree. Yet it was the novices of Tyneside who defied the odds by taking a 0–0 draw at Ibrox then a 2–0 victory at St. James' Park. The killer second goal was all about United's 'Davies Plan'. An Ollie Burton long free-kick was met with a characteristic Wyn leap. He climbed above his marker, Ron McKinnon, and headed the ball down perfectly for Jackie Sinclair to volley past Gerhardt Neef and into the net from ten yards. Newcastle United were in the final.

For the fifth occasion in six ties the Tynesiders met a highly experienced European side, Hungarians Ujpesti Dozsa, a club recognised as one of Europe's best at the time. But Newcastle's European spirit couldn't be broken; neither could the power of Wyn Davies who had a hand in goals in both legs. In front of a near 60,000 crowd at Gallowgate, Davies latched onto a free-kick, chested the ball down in the box and fired goalwards. The ball was parried by goalkeeper Szentmihalyi and Bob Moncur crashed in the rebound to break the deadlock and set United on their way to a 3–0 advantage. And in the second leg in Budapest, although going in at the break worried and 0–2 behind, United dramatically hit another three goals to lift the glittering Fairs Cup. Davies secured the remarkable conquest by again flicking the ball into the path of a fellow striker – this time young substitute Alan Foggon – who sprinted through the defence to hit United's third goal in a 3–2 triumph. The Welsh flier had valiantly played the game with a broken right cheekbone and was quickly off for surgery on his return to England. Following the success Davies said: 'It's nice to know all the physical buffeting is over and the cup is on the sideboard. I've been in hospital twice as a result of Fairs Cup injuries but I'm happy at the eventual outcome.'

More European action followed and by now United had earned respect. Nicknamed The Mighty Wyn, United's No. 9 again spearheaded the Black'n'Whites to a Fairs Cup run that almost reached the semi-finals. A short trip north of the Cheviots for the opening round to face Dundee United at Tannadice saw Davies rip the Scots apart. He ravished Dundee with two goals inside three minutes as centre-backs Gillespie and Smith chased big Wyn's shadow all evening. Two thudding headers ended in the Dundee net while United's leader also struck the woodwork on two more occasions with wonderful efforts from his auburn head.

The Magpies met sterner opponents in FC Porto and fellow English club, Southampton, but won through to the quarter-finals to face Belgian aristocrats, RSC Anderlecht. There was a real chance of United going all the way in their defence of the trophy and against the Belgians a terrific tie unfolded.

Newcastle had to claw back a two-goal deficit at Gallowgate and a vociferous 59,309 crowd were ecstatic as the Magpies headed for the semi-final by striking three goals. As usual, Wyn played a big part creating space for forward colleagues Robson and Dyson. Davies leaped for a Clark free-kick and the ball ended in the net for the opening goal as Robson's follow-up header was helped over the line by Foggon. But in the dying minutes Anderlecht were handed a chance and the unmarked Nordahl rifled the ball past Willie McFaul to send the Belgians through to the last four on away goals.

United's centre-forward was the focus of plenty of attention as 1970–71's European adventure unfolded. The Magpies faced one of Europe's giants, Internazionale of Milan. Packed with famous names from the summer's World Cup in which Italy reached the final – Boninsegna, Mazzola, Burgnich and Facchetti included – the Italian superstars simply could not cope with the threat of Davies and resorted to all sorts of foul means to try to stop the Welshman. Bob Moncur recalled that the match was 'the most violent in which I've played'.

Wyn's terrific header through a row of bodies a minute before half-time in the giant San Siro stadium gave United a crucial away goal as the Geordies headed back from Milan with a much applauded 1–1 draw. Davies was a handful for Italian defenders Facchetti and

Guibertoni all evening and the press noted: 'In seven days Inter must find an answer to the airborne menace of Davies.' Their answer was to substitute boxing and wrestling for football in the second leg at St. James' Park – and that didn't work either as Wyn stood up to every foul move that headed his way.

A crowd of 56,495 were inside Gallowgate to witness one of the most remarkable matches in United's annals. Wearing an unusual change kit of all red, United stormed forward against their illustrious but callous opponents and had Inter on the rack. Soon the pokes, kicks and elbows flew in Wyn's direction. He was often dumped on the deck by the Italians and the crowd howled in derision time and time again. The main culprit was Giacinto Facchetti, a seasoned international defender and recognised as one of the best players in the world at the time. But he couldn't cope with United's Welshman. Davies had him rattled.

Moncur put United ahead after 29 minutes with a glancing header as the Italians' defence all focused on Davies at a corner, but the flashpoint of the match occurred two minutes later as United's centre-forward challenged Inter keeper Lido Vieri at the Gallowgate End of the ground. Wyn feigned a shoulder charge, but didn't touch the goalkeeper – yet Vieri elbowed Wyn in retaliation and then fell to the ground as if poleaxed. The referee, the experienced Joseph Minnoy, awarded an indirect free-kick to United and in true Latin fashion all hell was let loose for fully four minutes as the excitable Italians argued and jostled both United's players – and Davies in particular – as well as the referee. The mayhem erupted further when Vieri lost his head completely and flattened the poor referee with a lovely left hook! He was not surprisingly sent off and three policemen had to enter the field to calm the situation down.

From that moment Davies was even more of a target. Bob Moncur remembered: 'Wyn was kneed in the small of the back then punched in the face, drawing blood.' Press comment noted: 'The big Welshman was first kicked by one Italian and then punched by another.' The provocation of United's centre-forward was unprecedented and even boss Joe Harvey considered taking his star No. 9 off for his own protection. But Davies would have none of it. He battled on manfully and incensed the temperamental visitors even further by diving forward to head home United's second goal despite a blatant bodycheck after Keith Dyson had thumped the crossbar in the 70th minute – the goal that sealed the tie. Wyn Davies was quite magnificent in both games. Considering the circumstances, perhaps it was his finest performance for the Magpies.

It appeared that Davies would again be the key to another United European trail as he destroyed unknown Hungarians Pecsi Dozsa at St. James' Park in the 2nd round. Two goals from his famous head gave United a comfortable lead on an evening he could have scored many more. The Hungarians, like Facchetti and company, couldn't get anywhere near Davies in the box and were vulnerable to every cross aimed at the Welshman. But in the second leg United let themselves down badly, going out of the tournament in a penalty shoot-out.

STRATEGIC CHANGE
That exit in the town of Pecs on the other side of the Iron Curtain marked the end of United's European adventure . . . and with it perhaps the end of the Davies era at St. James' Park. Manager Joe Harvey had to think of a change in strategy. He had fallen out with Davies' partner in attack, Bryan Robson – Pop moving to West Ham United in a controversial record move during February 1971 – while United had failed to make an impact on domestic competition. Harvey decided it was time for a change.

WYN DAVIES
No. 9 RATING

Fan appeal – personality and presence	9
Strike-rate	3
Shooting – power and placement	7
Heading	10
Ball skills	7
Link-play – passing, assists, crossing, team-play	8
Pace	7
Commitment – work-rate, courage	9
Match-winner – power-play, big-match capability	8
Longevity with United	5
Trophy success, international and top football ranking	3
Total No. 9 rating	76

With Robson's departure south, two players entered the action as United's boss experimented. John Tudor arrived on the scene in a move from Sheffield United and he was pushed up front, with Davies employed in a deeper position as the Magpies utilised a different tactical plan – without a constant high ball. Davies, as it was noted, 'roamed a lot more than usual' and it worked in part as Wyn showed he was not just a target man and could play with the ball at his feet. But United missed the goal power of Robson who continued to hit the net for the Hammers instead of the Magpies. It was noted: 'The plain fact is that Newcastle's striking power is almost nil.'

Tudor struggled to impress – although he would in time – and Harvey pushed young local product Keith Dyson into the attack too. An England Under-23 player, he scored three goals in his first two games as Wyn's deputy in a very different style. Dyson could hold the ball and shield it expertly, possessing good touch and placement of his shot.

Davies scored only six times that season – including those double strikes over Pecsi Dozsa and Internazionale. A total of two goals in domestic football was clearly not good enough. In a First Division match against Everton during March, Davies picked up injuries to his thigh and knee and was sidelined – a rare occurrence, as the Welshman had seldom missed a game over the previous four and a half seasons. When he did, outings were handed to Jim Scott and Bryan Robson in the No. 9 shirt. On this occasion, Dyson stepped into the role and it proved to be the beginning of the end of the Mighty Wyn's reign on Tyneside.

During the Welshman's five weeks in the treatment room, manager Joe Harvey was planning a major change in his team formation. After almost five years of the tactical plan of hoisting the ball for Wyn to cause turmoil, Harvey decided to scrap the ploy totally. He was determined to find a new centre-forward who could become as popular as Davies, but who could also give the Magpies a new dimension. Within six months United's somewhat dour brand of European fighters were to be transformed into a flamboyant array of skilful entertainers. And Wyn Davies was not to be part of the makeover.

Davies made his final bow in a black and white shirt for the last games of the 1970–71 season, against West Bromwich Albion and Coventry City. But he wasn't handed the No. 9 shirt; Davies was given an unaccustomed role down the right-flank, with Tudor and Dyson up front as a twin attack. However, Davies impressed in his new position – in fact he laid on two goals for David Young and Tudor in a 3–0 victory over Albion at St. James' Park when Toon supporters saw the unusual sight of their No. 9 hero galloping down the touch-line with the ball at his feet as if he'd been a winger all his career.

While the season was drifting to its conclusion, Harvey had already decided who he was going to bring to St. James' Park as Wyn's replacement – a young, raw and audacious Cockney called Malcolm Macdonald. Wyn had no wish to depart from Tyneside. He had settled well to the Geordie way of life. Davies hoped he could have been a part of United's new plan. He was to say: 'I feel Malcolm and I could have played very well together, with his pace and my flick-ons.' But it never happened. The closest they came to a partnership was to appear together on United's close-season-team group photo. Just as the season was about to get under way in August 1971, Wyn was despatched to Maine Road, joining Joe Mercer, the manager who had just lost the race to sign him five years earlier.

Wyn Davies may not have been a prolific goalscorer in the true tradition of United's No. 9 heroes, and he received as much criticism as praise, but the big Welshman was an exceptional personality with a whole-hearted attitude. Joe Harvey was to say of his centre-forward that he was 'neither quick nor a prolific scorer. But my goodness he was brave'. And his skipper Bob Moncur wrote: 'It is not only a matter of what he can do with that head of his but what influence he has on the other team. Often he destroys them almost before a ball is kicked.' In an era of T Rex, Led Zeppelin, flared trousers and mini-skirts, Wyn Davies became a cult-figure on Tyneside and made a deep impression on supporters who watched him week in, week out.

Davies later said that those days on Tyneside were 'the best years of my life'. His soaring leaps and knock-downs would have been missed had his replacement in the No. 9 shirt not been so instantly a success in a breathtaking and thrilling fashion. A new legend was soon to be unveiled.

No. 9 EXTRAS

KIDNAP PLOT

Wyn Davies arrived on Tyneside in October 1966 just as the local university rag-week was in full swing and some students latched onto the bright idea that they would kidnap United's new superstar! A well publicised campaign of 'find Wyn Davies' was launched while United took the threat seriously, Davies being whisked away to a secret location until his big debut against Sunderland – to Dave Hilley's home in Heaton. The cloak and dagger stuff worked and Wyn ran out against the Wearsiders without a hiccup.

WELSH TRICK

Davies had a trick up his sleeve when he got into tight situations on the field or with the media – he would start to speak in his native Welsh tongue, and no one could understand a word he said! As a teenager the only language he could speak was Welsh and he confirmed as he joined United that 'it's only in the last three years or so that I have really mastered English'!

HIGHFIELD HIGH

Despite all the great European exploits Wyn Davies reckoned his best game in a black and white shirt for the Magpies was the thrilling 4–3 FA Cup triumph over Coventry City in January 1967. Davies recalled in an interview: 'I got a hat-trick. I remember hitting one from outside the box that flew into the far corner.' Two more headers at Highfield Road had Coventry reeling. It was his only treble for the Geordies.

FULL MARKS

During the '60s and '70s the local morning daily, *The Journal*, published merit-marks for United's players after each performance. One point indicated a nightmare, while ten was superlative. It was rare for any player to obtain full marks, but Wyn Davies did so, getting a '10 out of 10' for his magnificent 'storming display' against Chelsea during August 1967. United won 5–1 and Davies scored twice.

TOP-DRAWER SAVE

England World Cup-winning goalkeeper Gordon Banks rated a save made from a Wyn Davies effort against Stoke City in January 1968 to be one of his best ever – even topping his much celebrated stop from Pele in Mexico during 1970, Gordon confirming: 'My own opinion is that I had a better one from a Wyn Davies header.' In a game at the Victoria Ground a Jim Iley-driven free-kick was met full on by Wyn, but incredibly Banks finger-tipped the ball over the woodwork. It was a breathtaking stop which even had Davies applauding in appreciation. Banks later said: 'Davies ran on to it and didn't half get some force into his header. Somehow I managed to get the ball over the bar to safety.'

GEORDIE MELODY

The Leazes End choir sang their hearts out during the Davies era at St. James' Park; three songs in particular championed their No. 9 hero. One taken from a famous Christmas tune, another from Manfred Mann's number one hit in January 1968, 'The Mighty Quinn':

> Come on without. Come on within
> You've not seen nothing like the Mighty Wyn

and a festive classic:

> No-el, No-el . . . No-el, No-el
> Davies is King of New-cass-el

as well as pure football invenion:

> Aye – Aye – Aye – Aye
> Marshall is better than Yash-in
> And Davies is better than Eu-se-bio
> And Sunderland are in for a thrash-in'

DAVIES – AFTER TOON

Wyn played for several clubs after his five-year stint at Gallowgate. At Maine Road, Davies looked certain to win a championship medal in season 1971–72, but City missed out by just one point. He moved the short distance to join Manchester United for the following season and when in his 30s started to drift around the lower leagues, as well as having a stint in South Africa. He retired from the senior circuit in the summer of 1978 after almost 700 outings and over 200 goals to his name. Afterwards Wyn played non-league football for a while, settled in Bolton and worked for many years at Warburton's Bakery, as he always said: 'Making dough!'

7. SUPERMAC
1971–1976

MALCOLM MACDONALD

Malcolm Macdonald's first association with Newcastle United made a deep and lasting impression. As a six-year-old wide-eyed youngster, he was taken to Craven Cottage, a few yards from his family home, to watch his local favourites Fulham entertain the Magpies. United were one of the teams of the era, recently three times FA Cup victors and they faced Fulham as holders of the trophy in the 4th round of the 1955–56 competition. What an introduction for the fresh-faced young lad in short pants.

The match was a classic, won 5–4 by Newcastle but not until the Londoners had come back from a three-goal deficit to lead 3–4 and the Geordies had themselves fought back to level the contest and then clinch a dramatic late victory. Malcolm was too young to take in much of what happened on that afternoon, but he remembers: 'As a kid I never forgot the black and white stripes.' Little did Macdonald imagine that some 15 years later as a 21-year-old budding football star, he would become the Magpies' record signing and destined to become one of the club's biggest No. 9 heroes.

Malcolm Macdonald was brought up in the shadow of Craven Cottage in a sporting-mad family. His father was a Yorkshireman who appeared for Hull City as an amateur, once played alongside Geordie hero Stan Mortensen for the RAF and even had a spell living in the North-east, in Blyth, for a period turning out for Blyth Spartans. Malcolm soon caught the football bug with favourites like Bryan Douglas and Johnny Haynes. He quickly stood out playing for Sloane Grammar School in Chelsea and from an early age set his mind on becoming a professional footballer. He trained with both Fulham and QPR and was rejected by Chelsea for being too small. The teenager was given a chance with non-league Barnet, but when the family moved to Sussex, Macdonald started playing for Forest Row, Knowle Juniors in Sevenoaks then at a higher grade, in the Southern League with Tonbridge. It was there he first met up with Harry Haslam who became Malcolm's mentor as he moved to Fulham and on to Luton Town.

After a brief period wearing the Crystal Palace youth shirt, he was offered terms at Selhurst Park, but with his boyhood favourites Fulham also interested in giving him a break in the professional game, Macdonald ended up at Craven Cottage, joining the Second Division club in August 1968.

With Fulham, 18-year-old Malcolm was signed as a full-back but made his mark as a striker when the side went through an injury crisis up front. Boss Bobby Robson was on the first step of his long managerial career and was persuaded by Harry Haslam, who had joined Fulham as scout, to give Macdonald a go in attack – the young Cockney was a hit scoring five goals in eight senior matches. Robson wrote in his book *Time on the Grass*: 'I saw at once he had the potential to be an outstanding goalscorer. He was very quick and had a thunderbolt of a shot in his left foot.' Robson added that even then Macdonald was a 'brash, cocky lad'. Malcolm had broken through but just as things looked to be going well for the newcomer the future England and Newcastle manager was sacked and Johnny Haynes took over control at the Cottage. Haynes had no time for Macdonald – his former boyhood hero didn't rate Malcolm either as a full-back or a striker.

Harry Haslam also left Fulham at that time, moving to Luton and he saw in Macdonald a star of the future. He recommended his protégé to Hatters' boss Alec Stock and Luton paid the paltry fee of £17,500 to take him to Kenilworth Road in July 1969. His record for Fulham was 13 appearances and 5 goals. Those modest statistics were soon to explode into impressive ones.

Macdonald's footballing career took off after he joined Luton Town and became a regular centre-forward. He blossomed rapidly in seasons 1969–70 and 1970–71 as Luton climbed from Division Three to within reach of a promotion place to the First Division. And on the way the goals flowed. Macdonald scored 28 in league and cup action during 1969–70 and then hit the 30 mark the following season. Included was a notable FA Cup performance against First Division Nottingham Forest. Malcolm struck four goals in two games, including a hat-trick. It showed he could worry top flight defences as well. Macdonald was a rough diamond and caught the attention of several First Division managers with his brand of raucous centre-forward play. Many a time he powered his way through packed defences showing a blistering turn of speed, ending with a whiplash shot and the ball bulging the net. He possessed a sometimes outrageous self-confidence, boasting frequently how he would rattle goals past one team or another, caring little for the diplomatic approach.

Joe Harvey had been captivated by the raw power and ostentatious personality of Macdonald. He watched the new talent on several occasions and joined the chase for the Cockney striker towards the end of the 1970–71 season. He was not alone. Other First Division clubs were interested, notably Chelsea and Manchester United. A total of 58 goals in 2 seasons was an impressive haul, yet Macdonald's rough edges and limited pure football skill made some waver.

Harvey was determined and while some other managers hesitated, Joe pulled out all the stops to bring him to Tyneside. He knew that goals made football tick – and Macdonald could score them. United's boss was finally convinced as he watched that goalscoring ability along with director Stan Seymour at Kenilworth Road. Macdonald fired a hat-trick on the very last day of the season against Cardiff City. Stock and Harvey had just about agreed a fee, but the hat-trick gave Luton an opportunity to play hard-ball and push up the price. Macdonald's three goals cost United another £30,000 – £10,000 a goal! Harvey said: 'I had bought a 21 year old of pace and power whose confidence was boundless.' Joe added: 'What a sight he is in full flight.'

The fee agreed was a staggering £180,000 – the third highest fee ever paid in the country after the transfer of Martin Peters and Ralph Coates, and the costliest purchase for a striker. It was also a cool £80,000 more than United's previous record laid out for Jimmy Smith. The transfer market had escalated rapidly, and would do so even more in the coming years. The first £150,000 deal had been recorded when Allan Clarke moved to Leicester City in June 1968 and by 1970 only a dozen or so six-figure deals had been completed. That was all to change. In March 1970, Peters cost £200,000 when he joined Spurs and fees spiralled, quickly doubling and even trebling in size.

On the eve of the 1971 FA Cup final a deal was concluded. Macdonald travelled to meet Joe Harvey at the Great Northern Hotel near King's Cross. The pair hit it off straight away. Malcolm took only half an hour to decide to move so far north, remembering that Harvey 'talked me into joining Newcastle'. Joe sold him the No. 9 role as Mac recalled: 'He talked about the traditions of the club, the great supporters and the importance of the centre-forward role, his need of a goalscorer – and how I could become a huge star.'

Soon he was receiving the same motivation from the legendary Jackie Milburn: 'Jackie made a big impression on me and I listened carefully to his advice. He always told me the crowd wanted me to give them enough excitement and incident in 90 minutes so they could go to work happy. He added that I had the ability to make their dreams come true. Jack said the relationship with their No. 9 centre-forward was something very special.' And Milburn was right of course.

Some judges considered Harvey took a huge gamble with Macdonald. Labelled the most exciting new talent to hit the scene in years he was, though, untried at the top level. A few considered it was a deal doomed to failure and that United had paid far too much for the player. Macdonald did not have the skills for top-level football, they said. But those doubts were quickly to be washed away in a glut of goals. Macdonald made his critics eat their words in no uncertain terms by sticking the ball in the net. The sceptics soon became fewer and fewer.

The man United supporters were to very shortly call Supermac cruised into the St. James' Park car park in a chauffeur-driven, gleaming black Rolls Royce. Malcolm Macdonald made a dazzling and eye-catching impact on his first day on Tyneside. His manager said: 'I just know this fellow can be another Jackie Milburn to the supporters.' Harvey added: 'You're going to love this man.'

Malcolm was supremely confident in his own ability as always. He said on that first day on Tyneside: 'My goals got me on the verge of an England Under-23 cap last season and with United I think I can go even further.' Immediately Macdonald gave himself a target of 30 goals for the new 1971–72 season – a brazen statement from someone who had not played in the First Division before. As Malcolm confirmed in his autobiography, *Supermac*: 'The press put me down as a cocky bastard from the start.'

Macdonald was brash and somewhat arrogant. He had bow legs, wasn't a giant at 5 ft 11 in., but possessed a powerful frame – strong legs and shoulders – and sported a good head of hair and formidable sideburns in the style of the day. On the field, he knew where the goal was, had a one-track mind for scoring and a toothless grin every time the ball ended in the net – the legacy of a clash on the field. Jackie Milburn was to say after witnessing Macdonald in full flow: 'I've never known any player who retained his appetite for goals the way Macdonald did.' And even if he missed chances – which he did of course – he never let a skied shot undermine his self-assurance, Mac would always have the confidence to try again. Malcolm was to say: 'My philosophy on football was . . . never be afraid to miss . . . the title of a book I later did.' Macdonald was to become a huge personality, developing into a devastating goalscorer and showbiz headliner. The Geordie crowd, as Joe Harvey predicted, just loved him.

MALCOLM MACDONALD
FACTS & FIGURES

To Newcastle United: May 1971 £180,000 from Luton Town

From Newcastle United: August 1976 £333,333 to Arsenal

Born: Fulham 7 January 1950

Height: 5 ft 11 in.

Other senior clubs: Crystal Palace, Fulham, Djurgardens

England international: 14 app, 6 goals

Newcastle United app & goals:

Football League: 187 app, 95 goals

FA Cup: 23 app, 14 goals

FL Cup: 18 app, 12 goals

Others: 30 app, 17 goals

Total: 258 app, 138 goals

Strike-rate: League and Cup 53% (overall 53%)

With Macdonald the centre of attraction United started preparations for the 1971–72 season deep in France, on the Massif Central and a friendly encounter with St-Etienne. Although United fell 1–2, Macdonald started in the way he was to continue, with a stunning goal. A knee-high cross from Frank Clark was pounced on by United's new No. 9 and he smacked a volley into the net.

Serious action began in familiar surroundings for Macdonald – with two fixtures in the capital against Crystal Palace and Tottenham Hotspur. It took a while for the Magpies new style of football to begin to knit together – and with it the Macdonald power to be unleashed. Newcastle lost at Selhurst Park and picked up a point at White Hart Lane. Press comment was mixed on the unveiling of Macdonald. One scribe wrote: 'He obviously felt the extra pace of the First Division a little and didn't show the real power of his shooting.' Another remarked: 'There were glimpses of the hell-for-leather approach of Malcolm Macdonald.'

Within three days that hell-for-leather approach was no longer a glimpse as Macdonald showed Tyneside and the First Division all the rip-roaring vitality that made him such a hit in the '70s. Newcastle entertained Liverpool for the opening match on Tyneside, a top-drawer fixture at the best of times. Newcastle fans were expectant. They had a new centre-forward and most had never seen him before. A crowd of almost 40,000 saw a truly remarkable home debut for Macdonald as United won a thrilling game 3–2 – and Macdonald scored a hat-trick!

Former United player Ivor Broadis wrote in *The Journal*: 'Supermac has arrived. Newcastle supporters old enough to remember Gallacher and the younger element still warmed by Milburn acclaimed Tyneside's hero of the '70s.' Broadis continued: 'Three times his explosive left foot blasted Liverpool and three times he steadied a rocking Newcastle boat.'

Malcolm's opening strike, an equaliser, came from the penalty spot – a rocket into the roof of the net after David Young had been felled. His second put United in front, and was a gem. He made something out of nothing as he dragged a short pass away from a defender to make a position. Then, wallop, a stinging cross-shot high past Ray Clemence from the edge of the box. The third was the end to a sweet United move involving Frank Clark, Terry Hibbitt and John Tudor. Macdonald received the ball and another cross-shot ended in the net, this time low into the corner.

And that was not all. Macdonald cleared off the line in defence and was carried off concussed – legs bent and groggy – after going for a fourth goal, Clemence thumping into him in a reckless way in a chase for the ball. All that could be heard around the Gallowgate arena was a new roar of 'Supermac, Supermac.' It was Roy of the Rovers stuff. A new hero had arrived – and his boss Joe Harvey missed it all, away scouting for new players!

Malcolm later confirmed those goals, were 'the most important of my career'. He said: 'It told the Geordie people they had a centre-forward on their hands and it started the tremendous relationship with the crowd that has never died.' Macdonald revelled in the big-match atmosphere he now was a part of. He said: 'The noise and intensity made me feel a way I never had felt before. I said to myself I want more of that!' He added: 'I loved it, and it was a huge inducement to score more goals.'

Joe Harvey continued rebuilding his Magpie side around Macdonald. He brought in Leeds United midfielder Terry Hibbitt, who was soon to bond with Supermac to perfection, and within a few weeks Blackpool's effervescent Tony Green joined Hibbitt in midfield, as did Tommy Cassidy and later Terry McDermott. Jimmy Smith began to emerge too and all were to stroke the ball around in a pleasing way. By the end of the season the Black'n'Whites had blended together and a fresh, entertaining line-up had taken shape. Macdonald had been a huge success. He netted 26 goals – just short of his bold target. On Tyneside, no one could say anything against him – Macdonald was the new icon.

After a season of watching Macdonald develop at the highest level praise was lavish. Jackie Milburn noted: 'He had explosive pace and power, a murderous left foot and was aggressive in the air.' Wor Jackie added: 'Malcolm is the most exciting personality there has been on Tyneside for years because he has thrown the coaching manual out of the window.' Many away from the North-east also rated him highly too. Master manager Jock Stein was to say: 'This boy is the kind of player that pulls in the fans. He is strong, eager, always on the look out for goals. His type gives the game excitement.' The Football League's own mouthpiece, *League Football* included a feature on his rapid impact on the scene. It noted he was 'built like a middleweight boxer, possessing the speed of a human Concorde and packed with an explosive blistering shot'.

Supermac himself admitted he learned much in that first season. He was unrefined, inexperienced and was the first to admit he was limited technically, but Macdonald's strengths of power, pace and goalscoring overcame his weaknesses. And in time he would improve his ball control, link-play and positional sense as well as heading and ability with his right-foot. He still had critics, some out of the North-east delighting in knocking his arrogant style, no matter what he did. They were quick to stress he didn't work hard enough, didn't chase back and missed as many chances as he scored.

However, despite some flak Mac was rapidly elevated into the England reckoning. Called up to the senior squad by Sir Alf Ramsey, Malcolm appeared for the Football League and the Under-23 line-up, scoring against Wales. He was on the road to becoming a full international, making his debut against Wales at Ninian Park at the end of that first season in the big-time.

Season 1972–73 was another successful year for Macdonald in spite of a cartilage operation when he was out for six weeks following an injury against Leeds United in mid-September. He had just scored a glorious winner at St. James' Park – acclaimed as one of the goals of the season – but five minutes later was led away in the arms of the two trainers after a 'horrendous' twist of his leg. A partnership developed that campaign with John Tudor, who had started to show his worth, the pair scoring 37 goals.

Tudor, deputised for Mac in the No. 9 shirt, and was an ideal contrast to Macdonald. Fair haired, an honest worker up front, Tudor was unselfish – a text-book player who knew where to run and knew how to make space. He gelled with Supermac and Tudor became a popular player with United's Black & White Army. The duo forged a dangerous combination. Over four seasons, they averaged almost 40 goals.

A perfect hat-trick against Coventry City showed Macdonald's game was improving. He was now becoming a danger with his 'other' right boot and a winner in the air. His first was a right-foot blaster off the crossbar, the next a scintillating effort with his left from an acute angle, and to round off a treble for the connoisseur, a diving header that left the keeper stranded. He also scored a hat-trick for the Young England side, three against Wales at Swansea and pushed further his claims for a regular England place. Brian Clough championed Mac. He said: 'They need him. He's got all the assets.'

Another knee injury saw Macdonald again on the sidelines during the early part of the 1973–74 season – missing two months following more cartilage trouble after a League Cup tie with Birmingham City.

The pack was shuffled and Ulsterman Tommy Cassidy even had a spell in the No. 9 shirt. The midfielder moved up front for three games, scoring against Ipswich Town. The skilful Irish international had another outing later in the season and again did well.

Youngster George Hope was another player given a three-match run in the No. 9 shirt. The local lad from Haydon Bridge in the Tyne Valley scored the winning goal on his home debut against Manchester United during November 1973. In the 70th minute, he climbed well to hit a great header past Alex Stepney from Hibbitt's accurate cross. It was a goal all young centre-forwards dream about but Hope was unfortunately injured stepping off a train and his chance of impressing further was lost.

Another junior development, Keith Robson was handed a role up front as well. Strongly built and good with his left foot, Robson – like Hope – was never able to break the Macdonald and Tudor partnership, but did well elsewhere, notably at Upton Park with West Ham United. Also to impress from within United's ranks was young Tynesider Paul Cannell. He made his debut in attack and developed over the coming seasons, netting twice as Supermac's deputy in a League Cup tie against Southport – his first outing wearing the No. 9 shirt.

FA CUP FEVER

In spite of injury Malcolm still totalled 25 goals in the season and came back in time to lead the Magpies on their first determined FA Cup run for many a year. And what a run it was. He scored in every round on a dramatic road to Wembley as he 'teased, tormented and finally tortured the opposition'.

United began their FA Cup campaign against non-leaguers Hendon. Having lost embarrassingly to Hereford United only two years before, the Geordies again stuttered to begin with. At St. James' Park, Hendon earned a deserved 1–1 draw but in the replay at Vicarage Road, United destroyed the minnows by winning 4–0, Supermac playing his part; scoring once and securing a penalty. It was a similar story in the 4th round when lowly Scunthorpe United again battled for a 1–1 draw on Tyneside only to receive the Macdonald hammer in the replay, two spectacular second-half goals settling the tie. Mac firstly brought down Frank Clark's pass then bulldozed a passage past two defenders before striking a shot past keeper Geoff Barnard. Then a Barrowclough cross was met perfectly by Macdonald's head to give United the edge in a comfortable 3–0 victory.

Newcastle's FA Cup trail turned into a serious bid for the trophy after a magnificent display at The Hawthorns against West Bromwich Albion in the 5th round. The Magpies put on a five-star show and Supermac was at the heart of the action in a game that Malcolm considers 'was the best team performance I've ever played in for anyone – United, Arsenal and England'. One broadsheet press comment noted: 'Macdonald had a great afternoon, scoring the vital first goal and being critically involved in the second; his speed and opportunism tore the heart out of the Albion defence.' His opening header broke the deadlock while Malcolm also had a characteristic breakaway goal at pace through the middle cancelled out – a part of his play all defences feared. On this occasion, centre-half John Wile pulled him back and the referee blew up instead of playing the advantage. Mac was strong enough to keep going and find the net. It was a ploy United always looked for and one that sent United through, first the quarter-final, and then the semi-final, in breathtaking style.

Nottingham Forest faced Joe Harvey's cavaliers in the 6th round and a controversial tie it turned out to be. At Gallowgate, United found themselves 1–3 behind in a pulsating match and once Pat Howard was sent off, the Magpies were tumbling out of the competition – only for a mini pitch invasion to halt the game, allow United to regroup and counter Forest to win in a gripping and sensational fashion by 4–3! However, Forest appealed to the Football Association and the result was controversially annulled, a replay being ordered at neutral Goodison Park.

United had to start again. Ninety minutes of stalemate followed, as did extra time and another replay was needed – again, bizarrely, at Goodison Park. This time Supermac was the difference as he latched onto a Jimmy Smith-headed pass bang through the centre of the field. Mac was off in distinctive mode – head down, arms and legs in full flow like an Olympic sprinter chasing the ball, with defender Dave Serella in his wake desperately trying to catch him by fair or foul means. As he reached the penalty area, Macdonald fired a low drive and the ball flew past Jim Barron to send United into the semi-final – for a second time!

Newcastle were one step from Wembley. FA Cup fever hit Tyneside like never before and Supermac was the focus of attention. He was United's danger-man, the one all the opposition feared, and in the semi-final at Hillsborough it was United's No. 9 hero who stole all the headlines. Macdonald produced *the* enduring images of his era –

breaking through solo fashion to score two glory goals which swept Newcastle United to Wembley.

A crowd of 55,000 were at a sunny Hillsborough to witness the clash against Burnley – then a respected First Division eleven. They held the advantage for much of the game until two scintillating breakaway goals within the space of ten minutes of the second half heralded the Geordie roar of 'Supermac . . . Supermac' around Hillsborough. Ivor Broadis writing in *The Journal* noted: 'Never mind Mac the Knife – he was bludgeon, rapier and broadsword all wrapped up into one glorious package.'

In the 67th minute a long ball out of defence sent Macdonald chasing through the centre-forward track from the halfway line with his marker Colin Waldron struggling to keep pace. Waldron desperately tried to haul Mac to the ground, but the United leader's strength and determination kept him going. As he saw the eyes of Alan Stevenson, Mac fired a shot which hit the keeper, only to pick up the rebound, coolly move inside and find the net right-footed. He wheeled away, both arms aloft in glorious celebration. Colleague Tommy Cassidy remembered: 'There was hardly another centre-forward in the league that could have scored that goal.' And much credit was given to referee Gordon Hill who played an advantage when a clear foul was being committed by Waldron.

Ten minutes later he was back with almost a carbon-copy goal. As Burnley pressed hard for an equaliser, Tudor cleared his lines on the edge of United's box. The ball dropped for Terry Hibbitt who instinctively hit a superb half-volleyed 50-yard pass beyond the Burnley central defence for Macdonald to gallop clear from the halfway line. No one could catch him. As Stevenson advanced, Mac drilled the ball low and hard past him. United were at Wembley and the headlines belonged to Supermac.

While Macdonald rightly took the acclaim, much praise was also given to his partner, midfielder Terry Hibbitt. Macdonald's second killer goal at Hillsborough was characteristic of the relationship that had developed on the field between United's centre-forward and the likeable but petulant Yorkshireman. Hibbitt possessed a sweet left foot and time and time again he hit the ball from the left of midfield perfectly for Macdonald to run on to – a simple tactic but one that was hard to stop. Macdonald remembered: 'It was a totally natural bond. We rarely needed to work on tactics.' It was a formidable double act that worked a treat.

Newcastle – and boss Joe Harvey – returned to Wembley for the first time since 1955 with much expectation, even though they faced Liverpool, the unrivalled team of the era. In Macdonald, though, they had a match-winner even Bill Shankly and Liverpool feared. Sadly it turned out to be a bad day for Newcastle United at Wembley and a bad day for Supermac, as United hardly got out of second gear and lost by three goals. Mike Langley in the Wembley press gallery wrote stingingly: 'Supermac fired only two shots, the first not until the 77th minute. Both skewed yards wide.' He continued: 'Macdonald needs the ball on a platter. He didn't get it. Hibbitt, his usual butler, seemed to have awarded himself a half-day off.' The more sympathetic regional press noted that Mac 'was hardly served at any time with a ball of any accuracy, timing or weighting'.

It was a super-flop final for the Magpies. Macdonald reckoned that a tactical change for the game with Liverpool was partly to blame: 'I believe we beat ourselves. We elected to put an extra man in midfield and had winger Stewart Barrowclough on the bench. All through the run we had Barrowclough and it worked well. At Wembley, there was no width on the day.' He summed up his Wembley nightmare: 'It was the worst game I had ever had personally and the worst team performance I'd been part of.'

Despite the Wembley let-down Malcolm Macdonald was now labelled as the most exciting striker in the country. Former United No. 9 Albert Stubbins said: 'He's the old-fashioned centre-forward who goes straight for goal.' Stubbins went on: 'He is a devastating all-round striker, making up for a lack of pure skills with pace and the ability to hit the ball with awesome power.' His strike partner John Tudor once recorded: 'He's got a tremendous finish, he just swings his foot at the ball and sometimes you don't give him a dog's chance, and yet it flashes in. He does everything wrong. He swings his foot like a sledgehammer, but when the ball meets it – pick that one out.' England colleague Kevin Keegan remarked: 'He's got a style of his own, different from anyone else.' Burnley manager Jimmy Adamson said: 'You could have ten poor players in your team and Macdonald, and you'd still win matches.'

Supermac possessed a one-track mind and was in some quarters criticised for it. As with many centre-forwards, he was selfish and did not work back too often. Like some of the finest goal-poachers, he stood around up front waiting for the chance to find the net. When the chance came – he went for goal. That caused some conflict, even within the St. James' Park camp, with coach Keith Burkinshaw always attempting to make Malcolm track back and forage for the ball. That was something Macdonald would rarely do. He once agreed with Jackie Milburn that it was imperative that a centre-forward always had to have enough energy to latch onto an opportunity even in the last moments of a match. Malcolm said: 'As a consequence I always kept some strength for that last minute so I never worked back as some would have liked.' Macdonald also recorded: 'The more goals I scored the more single-minded and arrogant I became.'

Everyone knew he was quick and powerful, especially on the left. But Malcolm also had a first-class record with his head around the six-yard box while his right foot was deceivingly good too and was not, as many said, just for standing on. As an added bonus, Macdonald possessed a dangerous long throw – once causing Notts County goalkeeper Eric McManus to fumble the ball into his net in an important League Cup quarter-final during December 1975.

KING OF TYNESIDE

Supermac was King of Tyneside and United supporters hailed their No. 9 hero wherever he went. While Mac was all raw power on the pitch as a player, he was a stylish and articulate individual off it and was never short of a word – often talking long and sensibly on football. He had the superstar image and liked the high life of Newcastle. He ran a trendy fashion boutique, frequented nightclubs and restaurants and was often seen with a bottle of champagne and a big fat cigar. But as friend and local journalist John Gibson wrote: 'The trappings of fame rested easily on his broad shoulders.' It was just what the Geordie fans wanted from their swaggering idol. The hero worship never bothered Macdonald, he said: 'It's part of the game. I had to be prepared to accept it, although the intensity in the North-east is immense and unlike anywhere else.'

By the time the 1974–75 season was under way and Supermac continued banging in the goals, he was now touted strongly for a regular place in the England line-up. Although the Londoner had made his debut two years before, he was far from being an automatic choice. By then Don Revie had taken over from Sir Alf Ramsey and while the former Leeds boss was a reluctant Macdonald fan, the media pressure to give United's No. 9 a run in the Three Lions shirt was immense, one comment noting: 'Macdonald shows all the fire, all the pace, and all the eagerness that stamps him very much England class.' There were a lot of good England strikers around, but few – if any – had the same goalscoring appetite as Supermac. Mick Channon and Martin Chivers were two first-rate strikers with all-round ability, while the veteran Geoff Hurst was still in contention. Joe Royle, Allan Clarke, Frank Worthington and Ipswich Town's David Johnson all came into the reckoning too. But Macdonald was given his chance.

In a prestige friendly – the 100th international match at Wembley – against old rivals and World Champions West Germany, Supermac received his big opportunity and did well. England won 2–0 and in what the press noted as 'one of their finest performances for years', Malcolm was instrumental in attack and worried the great Franz Beckenbauer all evening. He went close on three occasions before converting Alan Ball's cross with a 'power header on the far post'. The Wembley arena echoed to the now familiar thundering roar of 'Supermac . . . Supermac'.

Macdonald looked like cementing a place in England's attack, reinforced following an extra special performance at Wembley a few weeks later – one that saw United's centre-forward write himself into the history books. In England's next fixture, a European Championship qualifier against Cyprus, Macdonald set a Wembley record by striking all five goals in his country's 5–0 victory and equalling the scoring feat by any England player. Only a linesman's flag stopped Mac from becoming his country's greatest scorer out on his own as he found the net for a sixth. It was a brilliant performance of opportunism in the danger area. All five of Mac's goals were scored from in and around the six-yard box. Wembley's giant scoreboard at the end of the game shone brightly – Supermac 5 Cyprus 0!

Yet that performance, noted by Macdonald as a 'boyhood dream come true' and hailed in the media, was seemingly not to boss Don Revie's liking. Quite amazingly Revie never congratulated his centre-forward for the five-goal feat. Macdonald noted: 'He was a strange bird. He admitted to me I was not his choice and if I didn't score I would be dropped. And after the five goals he actually ignored me. Revie never said a word. No congratulations. Nothing!'

The England boss never made Macdonald feel comfortable in the England camp, although he was not alone; other players received a frosty reception too during Revie's dismal period in charge. That was in complete contrast to Ramsey, who did rate Newcastle's centre-forward. Malcolm revealed in his autobiography *Supermac* that the England boss was on the same wavelength as Joe Harvey who always said to him: 'You are only there for exactly what you do here. Don't listen to the clever dicks. You keep doing for England exactly what you do for us. Don't change!' Macdonald received the same message from Ramsey. But it was not like that with Revie.

The former Leeds supremo did not continue with Macdonald in the England side to the disgust of many. He did get the odd outing, mainly as substitute, but was never given the lengthy run he deserved. Kevin Keegan wrote of Supermac as a front partner in his book *Against The World*, an insight into the England set-up at the time: 'I was never sure what to do. If he got the ball on his left foot within 40 yards of goal, then he was determined to shoot. But my game springs to life much closer in.' England's top player at the time went on: 'With Supermac, that wasn't on. It was almost impossible to build a tactical relationship with him.' Despite Macdonald's success, seemingly his style of play wasn't suited to international football; Revie – and Ron Greenwood afterwards – ignored Tyneside's No. 9.

In domestic action wearing a black and white shirt though, no one could stop Supermac. In season 1974–75, he netted 27 goals – 33 including his England haul. At one stage, Macdonald netted eight goals in five consecutive matches. He was top scorer in the country and by far the goalscoring sensation of '70s football. There were players who consistently scored plenty of goals, strikers like Everton's Bob Latchford, Martin Chivers at Tottenham and John Richards at Wolves as well as England colleague Mick Channon, but none had the charisma, showbiz appeal and ability to stir the crowd as Supermac. He averaged almost 25 goals a season for the Magpies. He was invaluable and as the Geordies unveiled a new manager in the summer of 1975 no one could have even dreamt that United's boss could ever consider parting with the Toon's No. 9 hero. Yet that is what happened almost from the start.

AT ODDS WITH LEE

Despite Macdonald's goals, United failed to make a sustained impact on becoming trophy challengers and Joe Harvey's long reign as Newcastle manager came to a sour end at the close of the 1974–75 season. Exits in both the League Cup and FA Cup to lowly opposition in Chester and Walsall, as well as a mid-table league placing, saw Harvey move upstairs and a young, bright new face, Gordon Lee, arrived at St. James' Park. There had been mutual respect between Supermac and Joe Harvey that worked a treat – unfortunately, from the off United's star player was at odds with Lee.

A former Aston Villa full-back who had learnt the manager's trade in the lower divisions with Port Vale and Blackburn, Lee was of the new breed of boss. He was athletic, expected lots of hard work and team effort. He wasn't used to working with star players and he had no time for egos and hero figures – or flamboyant talent that fans adore. He once famously remarked: 'People keep on about stars and flair. As far as I'm concerned, you find stars in the sky and flair is something at the bottom of trousers.' A collision course with Supermac – and others like Terry Hibbitt – was inevitable.

Malcolm Macdonald was guesting in South Africa with the Lusitano club in Johannesburg when the appointment of United's new boss broke . . . and he immediately got himself into hot water. Like most supporters, Macdonald was expecting a big-name manager: Brian Clough, Bobby Robson or perhaps Jack Charlton, not an unknown figure. In a phone call to the local media, Mac instinctively retorted when told of the appointment: 'Gordon who?' And the comment was splashed all over the press. When the pair eventually met, the relationship was distinctly cool, especially after Lee's opening words were to accuse Macdonald's close colleague Terry Hibbitt of being a troublemaker. Malcolm commented later: 'He seemed to go out of his way to make enemies of people. He seemed hell-bent on creating a divided dressing-room.' Malcolm added: 'I wasn't on the same wavelength as him but, most importantly, he wasn't on the same wavelength as Newcastle United.'

Despite these personality clashes, Gordon Lee did make a difference to the club's ability to compete with the likes of Liverpool for trophies. His hard graft and team ethics saw the Black'n'Whites make a bid for double Wembley glory – and push for European football. What was missing from the manager's ideology was that major clubs like Newcastle United also needed star quality – and heroes. Lee never saw this as an important ingredient in his master-planning. It was soon clear that Supermac – one of the biggest stars and biggest heroes in United's history – was not part of Lee's long-term planning. Colleague Micky Burns, an expensive signing from Blackpool, recorded: 'After three months with Gordon Lee in charge, it was obvious Malcolm was going to go.'

Macdonald was still scoring goals. He started with a bang as if to show the new boss he was the best striker in the business, hitting two fine efforts at Ipswich in what was called a 'wonder performance'. He grabbed 24 goals but wasn't, for once, the Magpies' top scorer.

Macdonald had a new partner for season 1975–76, Lee bringing ex-Manchester United striker Alan Gowling to St. James' Park to replace the injured John Tudor. Gowling was an immediate success, striking 30 goals in his gangling, awkward looking style. Rescued from the depths of Division Four with Huddersfield Town, Gowling was full of running and endeavour. The pair complemented each other well. Macdonald had the glamour and Gowling the toil. Alan fed off Supermac and had the best season of his career. He noted in his biography *Football Inside Out* that Macdonald 'always takes a lot of stick from defenders and that has often given me extra time and space to exploit it'. Macdonald though was never too happy playing with Gowling. He noted that his ungainly style 'confused me' and he was forced into playing a deeper game, as he admitted, 'to get out of Alan Gowling's way'!

With Macdonald and Gowling up front, fed by Joe Harvey's expensive signings of Tommy Craig and Micky Burns, as well as Lee's hard-working aide, Geoff Nulty, United reached the final of the Football League Cup for the very first time – and at one stage looked like they would end up at the Twin Towers in the FA Cup as well. Along the way, Supermac produced several moments of magic for his manager to savour.

Macdonald was noted as 'the outstanding performer of the night' as he hammered home a sizzler in a 3–1 victory over high-riding QPR and was then involved in that bizarre goal direct from a throw-in against Notts County at St. James' Park in the quarter-final. The County keeper, pressurised by Gowling and Nulty, flapped at the ball and fumbled it into the net for the only goal of the game. Mac said afterwards: 'That is certainly the strangest goal I have been involved in.'

In the two-legged semi-final against Tottenham Hotspur, Macdonald was a constant threat and laid on the opening goal for Gowling in the deciding contest at St. James' Park as United won 3–1. That victory took United to a Wembley meeting with Manchester City. Although United's squad had been decimated by an unlucky influenza bug, they performed with credit but lost 1–2 to a much fitter City eleven. Supermac set up the equalising goal for Gowling in the 35th minute. United's No. 9 said after the game: 'I would love to see what would have happened if both sides were 100 per cent fit. My legs were like jelly in the second half and there were at least three others who felt exactly the same.'

In the FA Cup Macdonald ravaged one of his favourite opponents, Coventry City, in a 4th-round replay at Gallowgate. He scored twice as United won 5–0 and earned a standing ovation after a brilliant all-round performance. *The Journal*'s correspondent noted: 'All night he tormented and terrorised the City back four.' Even Gordon Lee admitted: 'It is the best I have seen him play.' And against Bolton Wanderers he did the same in an epic three-match tie which included a Macdonald wonder goal – another everlasting moment of the Supermac reign on Tyneside that was coming to a close.

A marvellous end to end 3–3 draw was played out at Burnden Park, Macdonald striking two goals of real quality. His first was pure Supermac. Tommy Cassidy placed an astute and precision ball over the top and Mac was off. His pace and control took him clear of Jones and Ritson and then round goalkeeper Barry Siddall to score. The second, just before the interval, was one of his best ever. Receiving the ball with his back to goal from a throw-in just outside the Bolton box, he swung to strike a right-foot volley over his left shoulder from 25 yards; Siddall didn't have a chance as the ball looped into the top corner of the net.

Newcastle eventually won the tie at neutral Elland Road and faced Derby County in the quarter-final – but the timing was all wrong for United. The 6th-round tie was scheduled straight after the League Cup final and United were still flu-ridden. They fell 2–4 at the Baseball Ground to the reigning league champions.

MALCOLM MACDONALD
No. 9 RATING

Fan appeal – personality and presence	10
Strike-rate	5
Shooting – power and placement	9
Heading	8
Ball skills	7
Link-play – passing, assists, crossing, team-play	8
Pace	10
Commitment – work-rate, courage	8
Match-winner – power-play, big-match capability	9
Longevity with United	5
Trophy success, international and top football ranking	2
Total No. 9 rating	81

As the season drew to a close speculation was widespread that Macdonald's rift with his manager was irreconcilable. Supermac was to head south in spite of his massive popular support and in the last competitive game of the season he signed off in spectacular style – as if to show Gordon Lee what he would be missing. It was a 'Super Show from Mac' as Tottenham were demolished 3–0 at White Hart Lane. One match report noted: 'If Newcastle manager Gordon Lee, watching this comprehensive victory stone-faced, needed any assurance that Malcolm Macdonald must be an integral part of his next season's plans, then it surely came in the second-half display of brilliance.' Malcolm first struck the bar for Burns to score, then scored an awesome volley which almost ripped the net off.

Lee though was unmoved and other clubs started to hover like vultures. Derby County, Liverpool, QPR as well as Belgian giants Anderlecht were linked with Supermac. So too were Arsenal. The departure of the Toon's No. 9 hero was not an amiable parting. Macdonald was bitter and United supporters were astonished that the club were selling their biggest asset. They were irate. Some purchased a wreath, draped in black and white and delivered it to Gallowgate with a bereavement card noting . . . 'In memory of dear departed Supermac'!

Macdonald took time to explain his situation in detail through both the local and national media. On conclusion of the transfer saga, he wrote in the *Sunday Mirror*: 'A lot of people think that I forced Newcastle into letting me go. That's not true.

'With a thriving business in the city, a lovely plot of land where I intended buying a new home and some of the greatest supporters in soccer, I felt that I would finish my playing career in Geordieland. My first four years with Newcastle were a real honeymoon. I loved every minute of every day. But after Gordon Lee arrived the honeymoon for me was well and truly over.' Supermac continued: 'I'm afraid I would never be able to understand Gordon Lee and his tactics.'

He later recalled: 'I never wanted to leave. I loved it on Tyneside – they were the best days of my life.' On departure Malcolm noted: 'The Newcastle people treated me like a king and they will always have a special corner in my memories.'

Controversy raged and claim and counter-claim were plastered all over the press. It was clear that the dressing-room was divided over Supermac. There were two camps. Alan Gowling wrote in his biography: 'There were some players who felt Malcolm was being pushed out, others who claimed that it was time for him to go.' Gowling added that there was much discussion around 'how much he meant to Newcastle United' and 'how much he contributed to the team effort', as well as 'about Mal's popularity with the supporters who loved the excitement that Malcolm brought to their lives'. Critically, some players followed the Lee line and believed it was time to challenge the 'star image'.

Apart from the split with his manager, Macdonald also confirmed that it was evident that United's directors also wanted to cash in on his talent. Supermac's market value had exploded with transfer fees continuing to grow enormously, United's bank balance had the potential to be significantly increased. In addition, some considered Mac had a suspect knee and that now was a good time to sell.

Perhaps Macdonald had also outgrown Newcastle United at that time. The club was still struggling to be run as a professional outfit compared to others and as Macdonald confirmed by the time he had experienced life at Highbury, it was like 'chalk and cheese'.

His sale was a controversial talking point, not only for the rest of 1976, but for years after the event. Supporters on Tyneside still debate the transfer with passion to this day – shades of Hughie Gallacher's similar exit to London almost 50 years before.

As preparations for the new season began, Macdonald became a firm target of the Gunners. He didn't take part in the traditional photo-call for the Magpies new 1976–77 team group, and instead was talking to Arsenal boss Terry Neill. After somewhat frustrating discussions that saw negotiations move from £275,000 to £300,000, United eventually accepted a new record fee of £333,333.34p – one of the most unusual amounts ever settled – down to the last penny, to ensure the amount was over a third of a million pounds as had been agreed between Lord Westwood and Sir Denis Hill-Wood.

Macdonald left Tyneside in the style he arrived – in a private executive jet. His United career had been the stuff of legends. To United fans he was the greatest thing on two legs – Geordie folklore. He scored 138 goals, many in 'Roy of the Rovers' fashion that had supporters roaring in support. The '70s belonged to Supermac. No one could touch him in the goalscoring stakes.

Maybe Jackie Milburn summed up Macdonald's departure perfectly. He wrote at the time: 'When Supermac left something died on Tyneside.' He was right. It took a decade and more to replace the player who had become one of the club's greatest No. 9 heroes.

No. 9 EXTRAS

SUPERMAC, SUPERSTAR

The famous Geordie nickname of 'Supermac' was the result of a spontaneous reaction of the Gallowgate crowd during Macdonald's home debut at St. James' Park in 1971. United's Black'n'White Army of the time took the words from the hit musical tune 'Jesus Christ Superstar' and came up with:

Supermac, Superstar, How many goals have you scored so far?

The rousing chant of 'Supermac . . . Supermac' was also born and was roared on every ground United played. Macdonald said: 'Supermac came alive once I ran out at St. James' Park. Newcastle and their magnificent supporters made me what I am.'

SUPER-WAGES

When Supermac joined United he received unheard-of wages for a Newcastle United player. Macdonald was on a weekly wage of £70 plus appearance money, bonus and £9,000 as a slice of the £180,000 transfer fee. By the time Gordon Lee had sold Mac to Arsenal, his wages had risen to £300 per week and a bonus of £2,000 for 35 appearances or more, plus another £2,000 for 25 goals or more.

FIVE-SECOND STRIKE

One of the quickest goals anywhere on record was banged into the net by Malcolm Macdonald during a pre-season friendly with St Johnstone in July 1972. At Muirton Park in Perth, John Tudor kicked the game off on the centre-spot as usual and as Macdonald recorded: 'He rolled the ball to me and I whacked it into the back of the net. Quite honestly, I don't think anyone will score a goal faster than that.' He went on to note: 'I saw the St Johnstone keeper standing on the six-yard line and when John Tudor rolled the ball, he was still there so I took a huge whack and the ball sailed over his head into the net.' It was timed at between four and five seconds!

SPRINT KING

Macdonald's pace up front was exceptional. Supermac took part in various invitation celebrity sprints including the television *Superstars* series and also a PFA Footballers event in which the explosive Macdonald showed he was good enough to run in the Olympics! Over a distance of 100m he could clock 10.4 seconds. Malcolm once noted: 'If I hadn't have been a professional footballer I'd have been representing England at athletics.' He added: 'I was a natural sprinter, but I had to work at it – and I worked on it an awful lot in training.'

SUPER-GOAL

Malcolm Macdonald rated a very special strike against Leicester City in First Division action during August 1975 as his greatest goal. With United defending the Gallowgate End box from a corner and Macdonald guarding a post, the ball broke from defence and Irving Nattrass made a surging run up the right flank. Macdonald raced from his own goalmouth through the middle of the park in support of his full-back. City were caught by the counter-attack. Nattrass saw Macdonald and squared the ball to him. Supermac picked it up 35 yards out, and just as everyone expected him to take the ball on a few strides, he let fly first time. The ball travelled straight as an arrow, rising into the top corner of the Leazes goal. Macdonald said: 'As I hit it, I knew instinctively that there was nothing on this earth that could stop it going into the net.' He added: 'Throughout my entire career I only hit one perfect shot and that was it.'

INJURY PLAGUE

Following his knee injuries at St. James' Park, Macdonald was plagued by further problems to his knees at Highbury. All told he had several operations and collapsed in agony in a comeback match at the Elfsborg Stadium in Sweden as his left knee went again. Injury wrecked his career in August 1979 after 469 senior appearances and 251 goals in England. He said: 'My knee was in a terrible mess.' Later in life Macdonald endured crippling pain from his football injuries which led in part to a period of alcohol addiction. He needed more surgery on his knee to ease the discomfort.

SUPERMAC – AFTER TOON

At Highbury, Macdonald continued to score goals – netting 29 in his first season in a Gunners shirt and 26 the following year. He reached Wembley again, although the intensity of fame was never quite as it was on Tyneside. Injury however struck him down in the 1978–79 season. Macdonald spent two months with Swedish club Djurgardens but couldn't fully recover and Supermac's career was over at the age of 29. Afterwards Macdonald had a period in charge of Fulham and Huddersfield Town before leaving the game and running a series of pubs in the south and in Northumberland. He later moved to Milan for a period and then returned to his adopted city of Newcastle, becoming a popular radio broadcaster, journalist and celebrity speaker – following the fortunes of the Magpies closely.

8. FROM BLACKPOOL TO RIO
1976–1993

MICKY BURNS, PETER WITHE,
IMRE VARADI, CHRIS WADDLE,
PAUL GODDARD, MIRANDINHA,
MICK QUINN, DAVID KELLY

The next era in the colourful history of Newcastle United was one of very mixed emotions; the highs of exhilarating free-flowing football to the depths of despondency as the Magpies went to rock bottom – with no fewer than nine managers. In the process, the Shirt of Legends was passed from player to player with alarmingly regularity. More than 40 centre-forwards pulled on the No. 9 shirt including many one-off or short-term appearances, while several players of mediocre pedigree were on display. However the increasingly frustrated Black'n'White Army of the late '70s and '80s did also see short bursts of quality on stage from the likes of Peter Withe, Imre Varadi and Chris Waddle, who developed into one of modern football's biggest names. There was Scouser Mick Quinn and David Kelly, and of course the very first Brazilian to compete in the Football League, Mirandinha.

Manager Gordon Lee's plan to fill the void left by Supermac was to look to his squad. He had no intention of plunging into the transfer market and buying big – and certainly had no inclination of replacing one superstar with another. Newcastle supporters brought up on big-name players had a long wait until the No. 9 shirt was filled by another soccer celebrity.

Lee considered he could change the Magpie's team formation successfully by switching midfielder-cum-winger Micky Burns into a centre-forward with more traditional front runners Alan Gowling and the fast-developing Paul Cannell in support. Burns now had a somewhat free and roving role across the front line in the No. 9 shirt and for a season it worked well.

Micky Burns had arrived at St. James' Park two years before in June 1974 from Blackpool for £170,000 – United's second highest fee paid – and had been a late developer to the professional game. Qualifying as a teacher and holding a degree in economics, Burns was a part-timer during his early days. He appeared in the 1967 FA Amateur Cup final for Skelmersdale United and took the full-time plunge with Blackpool during 1969. The Lancashire lad flourished at Bloomfield Road, becoming a noted forward in Division Two netting 62 goals in 203 matches for the Seasiders.

On joining the Magpies though, Burns took time to settle and was inconsistent under Harvey's Gallowgate regime. However Gordon Lee got the best out of Micky and his intelligent and thoughtful football brought dividends. A versatile player with good ball control, Burns could play a traditional wing game, operate in midfield or act as a front runner, especially just behind the centre-forward. Only 5 ft 7 in. tall, he was full of trickery and often went on runs past several opponents. He supported Macdonald and Gowling successfully, then took on the goalscoring role on Supermac's departure.

Thirty years of age and with an eye for goal, Burns was almost an ever-present in season 1976–77, in a very different style of No. 9 to the past. Micky's deft touch on the ball was a delight and it was noted that the 'little man with the twinkling feet was always a danger to defenders'. He often fell deep and played in the 'hole' between midfield and attack. Micky was suited to that pattern, collecting 17 goals in the season while Cannell hit 13 and Gowling 12. There were even calls for him to be called up into the England squad.

Geordie Paul Cannell deputised for Burns in the centre-forward shirt occasionally and played the traditional leader's role, even though he wore the No. 8 jersey. On Macdonald's departure, Paul was given a regular slot in the side and grasped his chance. Boss Gordon Lee had been prepared to offload the youngster to Blackburn Rovers, but

Cannell bounced back, at one stage in the season the press even claiming that the Tynesider was 'becoming Newcastle United's new Malcolm Macdonald'.

Dark haired, full of running, good in the air and with a competitive edge, Cannell grew in confidence as he gained experience playing regular first-team football. He noted to the media: 'For a long time I haven't been rated, but I think I have now proved I have something to offer.' He did, netting on three consecutive Saturdays against Liverpool, Manchester United and Leeds. Paul grabbed the headlines with a brilliant diving header against the Merseysiders to ensure United claimed full points, while at Leeds, his solo goal from a halfway-line run was also exceptional. Cannell scored some important goals in that season and all told netted 20 goals in 70 games for the club before moving to Washington Diplomats in the USA.

With United's attack of Burns, Gowling and Cannell blending well, Newcastle finished the season in fifth position, the club's highest spot for all of 26 years – and this despite the controversial departure of manager Gordon Lee in February 1977. Selling himself to Everton, he left Tyneside shocked and bemused. The Magpies' board turned to Lee's assistant, Richard Dinnis, to fill the breach – and that caused even more hullabaloo.

With little football pedigree Dinnis was always a stop-gap and not a long-term choice of the directors. But he held sway in the dressing-room and the club's playing staff made their strong feelings known to the board that they wanted Dinnis as permanent boss. Unfortunately that caused conflict and a players' revolt was played out in the media. Micky Burns was one of the protagonists of an unsavoury affair that was to send United into disarray.

The players got their manager – for the time being – and repaid the club by qualifying for Europe again. On the face of it, the previous summer's trade of Supermac appeared to have been vindicated and Lee's abdication overcome. Everything at Gallowgate looked rosy. However, as season 1977–78 began the Magpies fell apart dramatically as the club tumbled from being one of the country's top sides to Second Division mediocrity. It was inconceivable that such a slide would have occurred with Supermac wearing the Magpies' No. 9 shirt.

Following a fine opening win against Leeds, when Micky Burns started where he had left off, in dazzling form scoring twice in a 3–2 victory, United then lost ten fixtures in a row – a club record. Not surprisingly they were rock bottom of the First Division and following the Black'n'White's exit from the UEFA Cup at the hands of eventual finalists Bastia, Dinnis was sacked. That was no surprise, the remnants of the previous internal rift still being evident. United needed a strong character to lead the Magpies, to hopefully steer clear of relegation and to install some discipline in a dressing-room which had now become a nest of rebellion.

Former Wolves boss and past England wing-half Bill McGarry was handed the somewhat unenviable job. A tough nut both as a player and manager, McGarry had a huge task – a near impossible one. He had to make changes, and over the next 12 months an extensive remodelling of the Magpies took place. But McGarry couldn't save the club from relegation as they slumped alarmingly.

Burns continued to play well in the turmoil. He scored 16 goals and remained in the centre-forward role until the new boss reverted to a more conventional tactical line-up midway through the season. Both Gowling and Cannell departed as McGarry started to clear out the bad feeling within the inner sanctum. Micky was given a more familiar attacking midfield role before also being discarded and sold to Cardiff City with 51 Magpie goals to his name in 191 senior outings. In came two new strikers from Scotland, Clydebank's Mike Larnach and Mark McGhee of Morton. Both were relative unknowns and both were young, green and not up to a relegation dog-fight.

A fee of £100,000 was spent on Larnach, while another £150,000 was splashed out on McGhee. Larnach had a competent start, even if United fell by two goals as Liverpool gave the Magpies a drubbing. The Scot showed glimpses of promise, but he lacked fire-power in front of goal. Mark McGhee showed flashes of exceptional ball skills, able to adroitly hold the ball, turn and slip past defenders in mazy runs. But he had much to learn and like Larnach was ineffective. McGhee, though, did eventually become a quality striker, a Scottish international who would return to St. James' Park for a second spell, this time as a highly respected player.

The centre-forward position was now a problem with no one player scoring from the pivotal position from mid-January onwards. With both Larnach and McGhee promising players for another day, McGarry tried other options. Junior product Kenny Mitchell was given a handful of opportunities in attack – scoring against Wolves – while tall and gangling South African striker Andy Parkinson was afforded a brief opportunity. Both options were unsuccessful, although the blond-haired Mitchell did develop into a solid if not brilliant player, a versatile and gritty character who later switched to central defence and made 73 appearances for the Magpies. McGarry even had midfielders Graham Oates and Geoff Nulty in the No. 9 shirt for odd outings. It was the start of a steady flow of players to pull on the famous jersey in the coming years.

With United's relegation assured the manager was planning for the following campaign before the abysmal 1977–78 programme was complete. Priority was to secure a worthy No. 9 in the black and white shirt. During the close season, McGarry needed to lift supporters and make a big signing – and bring a centre-forward to St. James' Park who would give a boost to flagging morale. United's boss may not have been a huge success during his period in charge of the Magpies, but he did land the surprise transfer of Peter Withe from league champions Nottingham Forest. It was a master signing.

WITHE GIVES UNITED HOPE

McGarry had limited funds to play with but he was convinced a new and quality centre-forward would pay dividends. He splashed out a club record fee of £200,000 for Withe in August 1978 after the Liverpudlian had played a prominent role in Forest's Championship and League Cup Double victory, scoring 19 goals that season. A dispute with his manager Brian Clough followed and the tall and well-built striker was persuaded to drop a division in a bid to revitalise the Magpies. Withe gave United's supporters hope of quickly rekindling the big-time at St. James' Park as he became a popular character in the No. 9 shirt – albeit for a short period.

Withe took over the centre-forward position from Kenny Mitchell and stand-in Jim Pearson for the match against Luton Town one week into the new season. As United won by a single goal, Peter made an impact straight away, one commentator noting 'he had a remarkable debut, which made him an instant hero'. A chirpy Merseysider, Withe had been much travelled before teaming up with Clough at the City Ground. Very much a journeyman footballer, even trying the game in both South Africa and the USA to earn a wage, his career was transformed by the charismatic but volatile manager. He was strong and brave, a 6 ft 2 in. upright-looking striker with aggression to his game who played the target centre-forward role well. Good on the deck, his heading ability was also eye-catching.

McGarry had to find his big centre-forward an effective partner up front and halfway through the season he went to the other extreme in the transfer market by bringing local non-league star Alan Shoulder to Gallowgate from Blyth Spartans. Prominent in Spartans' noted FA Cup run of the time, the mining deputy exchanged life down the pit for the glamour of one of the country's biggest clubs. It was reminiscent of the days of Milburn and Wayman and the traditional call at the pithead for a footballer to magically appear from the earth.

The little and large partnership of Withe and Shoulder was an immediate success. From similar working-class backgrounds – Withe started as an electrician in the Mersey docks – they complemented each other well. Withe was all left foot, Shoulder stronger on his right. Both showed a bellicose streak as well as a never-say-die spirit. Peter held and laid the ball off and was a menace in the box while Shoulder often picked up the pieces – shades of the Wyn Davies and Pop Robson partnership nearly a decade before. Shoulder said: 'He was one of the best target men you could have ever had in your team.' Withe hit 16 goals and Shoulder 11 as the Magpies finished the season five places off a promotion spot.

McGarry's newly developed Magpie side did make a sustained push for promotion the following season. Withe, complete with characteristic sweat-bands around his wrists, led the charge. He scored 11 goals – and Shoulder an impressive 21 – as United again missed getting back into the First Division. They were favourites for promotion until the spring, being in the top three but then slipped back to ninth place. Nevertheless the Gallowgate masses took to Withe's whole-hearted displays.

He endeared himself even more to United's crowd with a sterling performance in a Tyne–Wear derby contest on New Year's Day 1980. United won 3–1 on that cold Hogmanay afternoon and Peter's display was first class. He was described in the press as the 'latest in a long line of Newcastle's belligerent number nines'.

United's failure to get back into the big-time resulted in a double blow. Not only had they to start all over again for the following season, but they were going to have to do it without Peter Withe. Everyone knew he was too good for Second Division football and it was essential that the Black'n'Whites achieved success if they were to keep their star centre-forward.

In the close season of 1980 he moved to Aston Villa for a £500,000 fee. No one could blame him – and he went on to trophy-winning success at Villa Park as well as international football. Withe said: 'It was only ambition that led me to leave.' He continued: 'I knew that if United weren't promoted, and therefore weren't matching my ambitions, I would be leaving.' He totalled 27 goals in 83 games for the Geordies, while his younger brother Chris went on to play for the club too.

As McGarry's period in charge came to an end and new boss, the up and coming Arthur Cox, looked at his options, a whole line of players were to briefly don United's No. 9 shirt. Ex-Wolves forward Billy Rafferty and fellow Scot John Connolly filled in before 27-year-old Ray Clarke – a £180,000 signing from Brighton in July 1980 – pulled on the jersey. But the former England youth player's time as United's centre-forward was to be dogged by injury.

Clarke was in and out of the side. When fit, he showed a precise touch on the ball and was good at lay-offs and flicks, but rarely looked like the threatening goal-poacher he was when he lifted championship and cup medals in Holland with Ajax. Ray noted to supporters when he arrived: 'I'll be judged on how many goals I score.' Clarke managed only 3 in 18 matches and was soon transfer listed. A knee injury eventually forced Clarke to quit the football scene only a year after joining the club.

Billy Rafferty, usually the strike partner, was a tall and at times dangerous player. He could play centre-forward and switched to the role once Clarke was on the sidelines, but never scored enough goals – only eight in his St. James' Park career. Cox then tried expensive purchase Bobby Shinton – although not a centre-forward – as well as ex-North Shields midfielder Peter Cartwright and another young talent who had been plucked from the local non-league circuit, Chris Waddle. A former Tow Law Town winger who possessed exceptional ability on the ball, United took a chance with his raw skills as he joined the Gallowgate staff in the summer of 1980 for all of £1,000. He was handed the No. 9 shirt for a match against Shrewsbury Town and then at Chelsea. Up against the Londoner's giant stopper Micky Droy, the youngster from Gateshead didn't have a good afternoon as United were thrashed by six goals. Waddle hardly touched the ball at Stamford Bridge and was despatched to learn his trade in the reserves. He would, however, be back in the first eleven and in the centre-forward shirt, developing into an unconventional No. 9 of pure quality.

Manager Arthur Cox searched high and low for a centre-forward, trying – but failing – to land Manchester United's Andy Ritchie. Then in December 1980 he came up with an exiled local lad, 22-year-old Mick Harford, who had made an impression in Division Four with Lincoln City. He was a tall and agile leader who hailed from Wearside and was to carry the tag of being one of United's biggest signings – as well as the most expensive export from the lower division – at £216,000. There were high hopes he could be moulded into the goalscoring machine United desperately needed.

Harford, though, failed to capture the increasingly frustrated Geordie fans' imagination. John Wardle, writing in the local press, was soon to remark: 'The former Lincoln striker was struggling to make any real impact.' To be fair, Harford was at that time an inexperienced striker and had joined a Magpie eleven in the throes of rebuilding. He was given little support or service, so perhaps it wasn't a surprise that he lacked confidence and netted only 4 goals in 19 outings. He moved on in the summer of 1981, to Bristol City for a £160,000 fee after only eight months on the staff. However, Harford was to prove he had what it took to develop into a top-class striker. Later joining Luton Town and Chelsea, he became an England centre-forward in season 1987–88.

VARADI AND WADDLE CREATE AN IMPACT

The summer months of 1981 saw Arthur Cox contemplate his rebuilding plans. It was all change in the No. 9 shirt again. The former Chesterfield chief and Sunderland assistant boss dipped into the transfer market once more and this time succeeded in finding an effervescent centre-forward who was a hit in terms of both goals and crowd rapport.

Imre Varadi was born in London of a Hungarian father and Italian mother and was on show to kick off the opening day of the 1981–82 season at St. James' Park against Watford. A £125,000 purchase from Everton, Varadi was a product of the Harry Haslam stable and followed in the footsteps of Haslam's most famous discovery, Supermac. He had shaped his career without too many highlights at Letchworth Town and Sheffield United before joining the Goodison set-up in 1979 under controversial ex-Magpie boss Gordon Lee. He was young at 22 years of age, dark and swarthy, not tall at 5 ft 9 in. but quicksilver fast. Varadi had shown Cox in limited appearances for Everton that he possessed talent to develop – and once scored the winner in an FA Cup derby with Liverpool. Indeed other clubs were also interested and United almost missed out on his signature when Benfica took him to captivating Lisbon just before he landed on Tyneside. After one trial game, the deal fell through when Benfica's manager departed – and Cox stepped in and took a chance.

By now Arthur Cox knew what the centre-forward shirt meant to the club and he, in turn, sold the legend to Varadi. United's new signing later confirmed: 'In truth, I was probably naïve and didn't fully understand what the No. 9 truly meant to the Geordies – but I soon found out.'

Known as Ray, the newcomer was an instant hit and as the Cockney said, it was, 'The start of two of the best years of my football life'. In his first full season as a regular first-teamer, he was an ever-present. Varadi netted 20 goals as the manager's rebuilding plans started to take shape and show promise. He grabbed a hat-trick at Cardiff City, then a brace in his next league match with Derby County. Ray liked nothing better than to sprint down the middle in pursuit of a through pass. It was just what the Black'n'White Army wanted – a centre-forward who knew where the goal was.

At Ninian Park, Varadi's opening strike arrived as he took a right-wing cross from Trewick and expertly turned quickly, giving himself space to rifle a shot past goalkeeper Ron Healey from ten yards. Then Waddle dribbled his way to the byline and crossed for Varadi to nod in from five yards. It was three for United's new No. 9 as Newcastle carved the Cardiff defence wide open to give Waddle a shooting chance from the edge of the area. He only half hit his shot but the alert Varadi raced in like a flash to turn the ball past Healey.

Derby's defence fared little better against the pace of United's opportunist centre-forward. Shinton knocked in a long cross and the ball seemed to be running out of play but Varadi didn't give up the cause and made contact, his effort creeping into the far corner of the net leaving goalkeeper Steve Cherry stranded. Imre found the net again as Cherry's wayward clearance forced Ramage to play it back to his keeper, only to set it up beautifully for the attentive Varadi. The striker confidently took the ball round the keeper before slotting it home.

He had his critics, often being handed unfavourable comments in the media for his somewhat erratic finishing – and he did miss plenty of opportunities – but he frequently earned the same goalscoring chance by express pace, while he was often snapping at defenders' heels at every opportunity. Varadi was honest and workmanlike, packed a good shot and his fizz-bang-wallop type of football clicked with the punters. Geordie supporters had long been waiting for someone to put up on a pedestal and Varadi fitted the bill – although like Withe, it was only to be a short-term pact.

Varadi and his colleagues needed a touch of experience to help the side develop into real promotion contenders. In the summer of 1982, United brought in a new partner for their No. 9 and in the process completed one of the most significant deals in the history of the club. During August, Cox played a trump hand by signing England skipper Kevin Keegan in a sensational deal.

Ray found himself in a totally different St. James' Park – now the focus of the nation as Keegan captivated the region. Keegan's influence was massive on and off the field and as a result Newcastle pushed strongly for a promotion place in season 1982–83. In the process, Keegan made sure the Magpies started to play neat, fast, attacking football with the ball passed around the field – a level way above normal Second Division standards.

Varadi hardly missed a match again – Waddle and on-loan Howard Gayle deputising at centre-forward – while the Cockney found the net regularly alongside Keegan, grabbing another 22 goals. But as United started to change their tactics, he found gelling with Keegan more difficult. Although as a pairing they were a danger, Keegan hitting 21 goals too, Varadi's finer skills were at times questionable, not possessing the same control and vision of his partner. Some moves tended to break down as Keegan attempted to play accurate one-twos. That style sometimes did not suit Varadi and his greyhound-like sprints. The local press debated the inter-play and lack of assistance for Keegan: 'Can United ever give the striker the sort of support he needs?'

As a consequence Varadi was to become a sacrificial pawn as Cox generated cash in order to purchase another more subtle and skilled partner for the former England star. Although Varadi had closed the previous campaign with 11 goals in his last 10 matches and netted a total of 42 goals in 90 appearances – a fine record for any striker – manager Arthur Cox dropped a bombshell just as the 1983–84 season was about to get under way. He sold his talented poacher to Sheffield Wednesday for £150,000.

When Ray departed it was no secret that the choice was not his. He loved the club and the area and many fans did not agree with United's decision to sell him – of course at the time not knowing what Cox had planned as a replacement deal. United's centre-forward received more than a thousand letters voicing appreciation, a mark of his popularity. Varadi said later: 'I never wanted to leave Tyneside, but I was forced out.' He added: 'I would have stayed at Newcastle for the rest of my life, but I wasn't given the chance.' Instead, Ray continued plundering goals at Hillsborough and later prominently with West Bromwich Albion, Manchester City and Leeds.

Despite the flak he received, Cox engineered a master plan that was to work to perfection and ultimately achieve promotion – and in the process deliver to the fans a new centre-forward from within. Supporter anger over the sale of Varadi was quickly forgotten. The money received from Sheffield Wednesday was rapidly spent bringing home to Tyneside the highly skilled and talented Geordie, Peter Beardsley, exiled in North America with Vancouver Whitecaps. Beardsley instantly clicked with Keegan – a rapport that was to last for many years to come.

United's attacking formation changed shape. Keegan and Beardsley were small, compact ball-playing strikers and the Magpies didn't have any recognised centre-forward in the traditional sense. After the experienced and versatile forward David Mills filled the gap for a short period, Cox turned again to Chris Waddle and handed the Tynesider the No. 9 shirt . . . and a totally different style of centre-forward evolved.

CHRIS WADDLE
FACTS & FIGURES

To Newcastle United: July 1980 from Tow Law Town
 £1,000

From Newcastle United: July 1985 to Tottenham Hotspur
 £590,000

Born: Gateshead 14 December 1960

Height: 6 ft.

Other senior clubs: Olympique Marseille, Sheffield Wednesday, Falkirk, Bradford City, Sunderland, Burnley, Torquay United

England international: 62 app, 6 goals

Newcastle United app & goals:
  Football League: 170 app, 46 goals
  FA Cup: 12 app, 4 goals
  FL Cup: 9 app, 2 goals
  Total: 191 app, 52 goals
Strike-rate: League and Cup 27%

Waddle had developed his game considerably since his arrival at St. James' Park back in 1980. Twice rejected by Sunderland as a kid,

Coventry City signed him as a schoolboy but he didn't progress and even Newcastle were reluctant to give him a chance to start with. On trial at Gallowgate as a teenager, Waddle admitted: 'It wasn't a memorable experience. Tommy Cassidy clipped me on the ankle and I remember going home and saying there was no way I was going back.' But he did, exchanging life at a sausage seasoning factory as boss Bill McGarry was persuaded to add him to the staff as a callow but promising youngster.

Although Chris had an awkward, lumbering style he possessed natural ability to play on either wing and slowly he learnt his trade as a professional footballer. Waddle was star-struck at first and found it difficult to come to terms with the huge leap from non-league football to the senior game, especially when Kevin Keegan arrived in town. But Chris showed flashes of real potential as he began hogging the left touch-line, once even being compared to the great Bobby Mitchell, and supporters took notice as he scored twice in an FA Cup match against Sheffield Wednesday, one goal being a strike that Chris rated very highly. He smacked the ball on the edge of the box as it bounced up; keeper Bob Bolder had no chance as it flew into the net. Full-back colleague John Anderson said: 'During his early days Chris was a far better player than people gave him credit for, although he never looked like a footballer. But he grew in confidence in his own ability the more experienced he got and became a brilliant player, one of the very best. And then he received deserved recognition.'

Cox and Keegan nurtured the Geordie and even at times bullied him in an attempt to bring Chris out of his shell. It slowly worked. He gradually built up his stamina and learnt to cope with the limelight. Although at first an out and out winger, he had the eye for a goal and frequently netted in United's Central League eleven. Waddle recalled: 'Arthur Cox reckoned he could solve a problem with me at centre-forward.' Knowing the reputation the shirt held, United's boss asked a young Waddle: 'Can you handle it?' Chris saw it as a huge opportunity. He remembered: 'Being a local lad I knew the tradition of the No. 9 shirt. At certain clubs, certain shirts are special. At Newcastle United, it's the No. 9 shirt. I said – yes.' Chris noted: 'I was shy, but it could bring me out of my shell. It worked. It did. Wearing the No. 9 shirt gave me inspiration. It gave me a lot more confidence.'

For the 1983–84 season Waddle was given a free role, roving across the front line. Added to Beardsley and Keegan, Newcastle found they had a trio with unlimited vision and skill. The result was glitzy football of the highest order – and with it, plenty of spectacular goals.

Waddle flourished. In a 4–2 victory over Portsmouth, he scored twice, first converting Terry McDermott's through pass, Chris reaching the ball just ahead of goalkeeper Alan Knight. Despite the keeper bearing down on him the Tynesider kept his head and neatly flicked the ball from the edge of the penalty area to drop over the keeper and into the net. Before the break, he grabbed another, the best goal of the game. Beardsley found Waddle wide on the right and Chris cut inside to go past two defenders before unleashing a daisy cutter of a shot that whistled past Knight into the far corner of the net.

Then as promotion rivals Manchester City were comprehensively demolished 5–0, Waddle put on a five-star show along with Beardsley and Keegan. He roamed both wings, often cutting inside, and had the beating of any defender at will. Beardsley was to say of his teammate: 'Defenders didn't have an answer to him. Chris would step over the ball one way, then the other, and although the ball hadn't moved he would have sent the defender the wrong way every time.' He added: 'Waddle was a scorer of great goals rather than a great goalscorer and developed into a fantastic player.'

Waddle loved to run at defenders and although he frequently went past opponents in mazy runs full of body swerves and dummies, he was aware that he had to do something with the ball afterwards. His left foot possessed a wicked bend on the ball and he often hit a tantalising, swinging cross into the box. And Chris was still learning. His armoury of that educated left foot would become even more fearsome in years to come.

Up to the festive and New Year period Waddler, as he was nicknamed, really came into his own. His previous shyness and inferiority all disappeared. In seven games, the loping, 6 ft tall, 23 year old scored 7 goals as United consolidated their position as promotion challengers alongside Chelsea, Sheffield Wednesday and Manchester City.

A winning goal against Barnsley prompted a delighted Cox to note: 'It was a goal fit to grace a Cup Final. It was absolute class.' Waddle started a move and hit a ball to Terry McDermott. The former England midfielder's drive was blocked and Waddle picked up the loose ball on the edge of the box. He curled a sublime shot with the outside of his foot for the ball to loop over the keeper into the far corner of the net.

By the finale to the season, as the spring sunshine glowed brightly, the Waddle, Beardsley and Keegan front trio were unstoppable, a scintillating combination matched by very few attack formations in the club's history. Against Carlisle United they linked impeccably as United won 5–1. They fused and sparked again when Derby County arrived at Gallowgate for what was the telling promotion fixture. Newcastle won 4–0 with Waddle creating the opening goal for Keegan, going past two defenders in a left-wing run before crossing superbly. Then he scored following quick one-touch inter-passing, running into the box before striking a low shot into the corner. And to round off the season the front three all scored again in the final match of the programme, as Brighton were swamped 3–1 in a promotion party. Chris netted with a rare header from a Keegan cross.

Waddle had come of age and became a huge success in the No. 9 shirt. He scored 18 goals in the successful campaign alongside Keegan (28 goals) and Beardsley (20 goals). The transformation from part-timer on the wilds of Ironworks Road in Tow Law to accomplished professional footballer was complete. Yet Waddler was not content. He had the ability to reach another level and in the coming years would go all the way . . . to a world stage.

BIG JACK'S CHANGES

Newcastle United, or so it appeared, were about to recapture some degree of their past status. However a double blow hit the Magpies. Firstly Kevin Keegan retired – that was expected – then boss Arthur Cox resigned only weeks before their rebirth in the top echelon of football. As is Newcastle United's way, it was a huge shock, especially as he departed to lowly Derby County after a contract dispute.

Newcastle needed a new boss, and quickly. Into the breach stepped a long-standing Geordie hero, Jack Charlton, who had proved himself a dedicated manager with Sheffield Wednesday and Middlesbrough. At first, Big Jack left the side alone, seemingly content with the stylish football created by Waddle and Beardsley. Indeed, the Magpies were top of the table by September as Aston Villa were comprehensively beaten 3–0 at St. James' Park. Chris Waddle was on fire, answering questions raised as to whether he was good enough for the First Division. Against Villa he netted twice and made one for Beardsley. His manager noted: 'He saves his energy during a match, then explodes. When he does, he's terrific.'

Waddle struck for the first time three minutes into the second half. Latching onto a deflected Beardsley pass and taking advantage of John Ryan's dummy run to make space, he hit a glorious right-foot shot past goalkeeper Mervyn Day. Then another testing Waddle shot fell for Peter Beardsley to score. Near the end Waddle ran onto Ryan's through-ball and eased off defender Evans before again sweeping the ball majestically past Day. Waddle showed he could perform at the top level and noted afterwards: 'I've scored better ones, but they haven't given me greater pleasure.'

He bagged 16 goals that season and was a new star of the game. Tony Hardisty writing in the *Sunday Express* noted Chris as a 'tall and graceful front-runner with a sweet and silky body-swerve and explosive shooting', who had now 'finally found the stage his skill and persistence deserve'. John Gibson wrote in the *Evening Chronicle*: 'Waddle became the talk of the Tyne and blossomed from a kid of genuine promise to a master craftsman.'

At nearly 24 years old, Waddle had developed into a top First Division footballer. With a distinctive mullet haircut, he possessed deceptive pace and match-winning ability. The Tynesider took over the Keegan mantle as Chris noted: 'Once he had gone, someone had to become the new hero for the fans and we all know how the Geordie fans love a scoring centre-forward.' Able to go past defenders with twists and turns at will, he produced an explosive shot and ability to get fans on the edge of their seats. In addition, he developed into a dead-ball expert too, whether from corners or free-kicks, having the gift to curl the ball viciously. The Black'n'White Army expected things to happen when Waddler got the ball. Such was his progress, Chris was soon championed for a place in the full England squad, having already tasted the Under-21 set-up.

That cause was reinforced as England boss Bobby Robson witnessed Waddle have a field day at Loftus Road, a game that Chris reckoned was his best in the United No. 9 shirt. Against QPR on their much maligned artificial surface, he dazed the Rangers defence rattling in a magnificent first-half hat-trick as United roared to a 4–0 lead. He also made two other goals for McDonald and Wharton in what was a truly breathtaking 5–5 draw. Waddler's third goal just before the break was 'a real stunner'. He picked up a loose ball on the edge of the penalty area and curled an inch-perfect shot past the groping fingers of Peter Hucker into the top corner of the net. Peter Beardsley was to say of his teammate on that day in West London: 'He did things that afternoon any player in the world would have been proud of.' Robson was soon to include Waddle in his England squad. He made his debut for his country against the Republic of Ireland at Wembley.

Charlton, though, never saw Waddle as a centre-forward in the traditional sense and as United stuttered after a bright opening to the season, he was determined to revert to a style of play he enjoyed much success with at Sheffield Wednesday and Middlesbrough – with a solid, non-flamboyant strategy. And it meant a change in centre-forward. First he tried on-loan striker Ian Baird from Southampton, but his battling and fiery technique was not a success.

During February 1985, the former England World Cup winner signed not one centre-forward, but two – both beanpole strikers in Tony Cunningham and George Reilly. Initially Charlton made a bid to land Reilly, Watford's noted leader, but Graham Taylor would not deal and therefore attention was switched to Manchester City's Cunningham. A £75,000 deal was finalised, then Reilly also became available, so Jack purchased him as well, at a fee of £200,000.

Reilly was born in Bellshill, the same Scottish town as Hughie Gallacher, but that's as far as the comparison went. Reilly was almost a foot taller than his legendary predecessor at 6 ft 4 in., while the Watford striker could not be said to be a highly skilled footballer. An ex-bricklayer, he was an awkward customer for defenders with a powerful physique at 14 stone and had learnt the game the hard way in the lower divisions with Northampton and Cambridge.

The spirited Cunningham, also tall and leggy at 6 ft 2 in., had an occasional outing in the No. 9 shirt during his stay at Gallowgate, and although his record of 6 goals in 51 games was far from brilliant, his never-say-die attitude was appreciated by the crowd which always backed a player who gave commitment. The Jamaican afterwards admitted he enjoyed his stay on Tyneside, making the comment: 'The pinnacle of my career has to be wearing the No. 9 for Newcastle, probably the most famous shirt in British football.' But the manager's plan was not to pay dividends. Cunningham said: 'Jack liked the tall guys up front and liked to play long balls all the time, but it didn't really work for us because big George Reilly and I were too similar in style.'

Although Waddle initially kept hold of the No. 9 shirt, his role changed to a more conventional wide midfielder, while his skilled partner Peter Beardsley was also told to play deeper and wide, a policy that did not go down well with either player – or spectators. Before the switch, Waddle had netted 15 goals as a striker. A new formation saw the pair hit only a handful. To many it was a waste of talent that should have been used where it could really hurt the opposition. Peter

Beardsley commented on the switch in his book *My Life Story*: 'It was not good news for Chris Waddle and myself. If you've got a couple of big guys up front it's obvious that the manager is going to try and play to their strengths in the air.' He added: 'That was not the way I liked to play my football and I know Chris felt the same.'

Charlton, though, wrote in his autobiography: 'Waddle and Beardsley were playing up front and they kept telling me they needed a big guy to take some weight off them.' And to give credit to United's boss, his switch in tactics ensured Newcastle stayed in the First Division, always the first priority in that opening season back in the limelight.

By March, George Reilly had taken over the treasured No. 9 shirt with Cunningham as his twin strike partner in attack. The media penned: 'Jack's beanstalks certainly provided a new type of show at St. James' Park.' It was also noted: 'We will just have to wait and see if Reilly and Cunningham take the weight off the gifted Waddle and Beardsley – or whether they just get in the way.'

Reilly received the crowd's backing, yet probably not for his goalscoring exploits or rip-roaring play. He earned a popular following for donning a head-band as a result of a wound suffered against West Bromwich Albion during September 1985 – his 28th birthday. Reilly took a stray elbow in the face from Michael Forsyth in only the second minute of the game. He had stitches inserted at half-time and had the ever witty Geordie crowd chanting 'Rambo . . . Rambo' in the second half. It was as though he had walked out of the set of the cult Hollywood film. He was given the nickname of Sylvester Stallone's character hero and it stuck.

Charlton's lanky strike force of Cunningham and Reilly managed only four goals that season as United finished mid-table. The Toon's sparkling football of 1983–84 had been replaced by mediocre fare lacking a scientific touch. Newcastle supporters were not impressed and expected a huge improvement for the new season with the boss encouraged to spend money and purchase quality.

Instead of attracting top names to Tyneside the Magpies found that they had lost one of their star assets when Chris Waddle left to head south, joining Tottenham Hotspur in a record £590,000 deal during July 1985 – short of United's valuation of £750,000, but a fee that had been settled by tribunal. Waddle – and for that matter Beardsley too – had not been happy with Charlton's tactical switch.

Speculation of a move simmered for several weeks before the end of the 1984–85 season and Waddle took some jeers from the crowd as he ditched his home club. With the passing of time though, most supporters later understood his position. He wanted a club that could further his career. At the time, the Black'n'Whites could not guarantee that. Away from Tyneside, Chris was to mature into one of England's foremost players of the era. He totalled 52 goals in 191 games for the Magpies.

Losing Waddle was a blow. United's following were not happy and with few signs of fresh blood arriving at Gallowgate, at the pre-season friendly with Sheffield United they expressed angry frustration – a noisy blast towards Charlton. That prompted Big Jack to pack his bags and head fishing – or as it was, shooting grouse. Newcastle United were in another mess within only 12 months of their previous turmoil.

CHRIS WADDLE
No. 9 RATING

Fan appeal – personality and presence	8
Strike-rate	3
Shooting – power and placement	8
Heading	6
Ball-skills	9
Link-play – passing, assists, crossing, team-play	9
Pace	8
Commitment – work-rate, courage	7
Match-winner – power-play, big-match capability	8
Longevity with United	5
Trophy success, international and top football ranking	2
Total No. 9 rating	73

The Board appointed from within this time, ex-goalkeeper and first-team coach Willie McFaul moving into what was now becoming a very hot seat in the manager's office. A favourite of the terraces as a player, McFaul had little time for Reilly or Cunningham as a centre-forward option. Brought up at St. James' Park with the likes of Davies and Macdonald, the former Magpie keeper knew the importance of the club's No. 9 shirt and its ability to catalyse supporters. At the top of the Irishman's shopping list was a new leader up front – but his first attempt at filling the breach was doomed to failure.

George Reilly departed to West Bromwich Albion in December 1985 after only 33 appearances and 10 goals in the centre-forward shirt, noting at the time he was 'astounded that Newcastle were ready to sell'. As a replacement, McFaul brought in the robustly built Billy Whitehurst, ex-Hull City, as the Toon's new No. 9 talisman. Whitehurst joined the Magpies in the same month for a £232,500 fee. Well built at 6 ft 1 in. tall and muscular, Billy was another whole-hearted striker who had netted over 50 goals for the Tigers. Another former bricklayer too, Whitehurst was predictably, though, the same type of player as both Cunningham and Reilly; hard-working, committed and who would run through a brick wall for the side. McFaul said of his new signing: 'He's a big strong lad with a very big heart.' But importantly, he was limited in football ability and not able to hit the net repeatedly at the top level.

It took a while for Whitehurst to get off the mark – eventually hitting the target against Ipswich Town in his ninth match. A physical player, he never shirked a confrontation or a tackle, once sending Paul Bracewell flying with one challenge that sidelined the future Magpie star for many months. He managed seven goals in total for the season, hardly in the legend class, while the following campaign saw the Yorkshireman fail to strike the target. As United's fans became irritated at United's lack of progress, they turned on Whitehurst. He was barracked for a period and made an indiscreet gesture to the crowd. Billy later recalled: 'I gave the "V" sign and that was it. All hell let loose.' His days were over in a black and white shirt after only 7 goals in 31 matches and in October 1986 he joined Oxford United.

McFaul tried junior goalscoring marvel Joe Allon at this troubled time. From Washington, he was to be given piecemeal opportunities over the coming seasons. With long blond hair, Allon was a Magpie fan to the core and had plundered almost 120 goals for United's reserve and junior line-ups and even eclipsed Paul Gascoigne as the Magpies lifted the FA Youth Cup in 1985. An England youth international, he made his debut as an 18 year old against Stoke City and was unlucky not to earn an extended chance in the side to prove himself. Full of running, aggression and eager to sniff out a chance, Joe scored his first goal against Coventry City, the highlight of his career. He made United's opener for Peter Beardsley in the 3–2 victory, when as Paul Tully wrote: 'He curled an extravagant shot around Ogrizovic from near the touch-line and his crazy celebrations were repeated all around the ground as the Tyneside fans saluted one of their own.'

Allon scored only two goals in ten appearances before moving on to Swansea City, although he later made a big-time comeback with Chelsea. Allon was immensely proud of pulling on the United centre-forward shirt. He said afterwards: 'When I look back I achieved one thing thousands of people have dreamed about, and that's pulling on the No. 9 shirt at Newcastle. No one can ever take that away.'

With Peter Beardsley soon to follow Waddle out of the St. James' Park door, McFaul had to think again. He was encouraged by the media and fans to only buy players with a high degree of skill and quality credentials, rather than technically limited, although honest, journeymen like Reilly, Cunningham and Whitehurst. McFaul recognised this, his second centre-forward proving to be a player of exceptional talent, although his time in a black and white shirt was short and sweet.

Paul Goddard could not be described as a leader of the traditional style. He was not big, not powerful and didn't have exceptional pace. But the ex-QPR forward had a football brain and the know-how around the box as well as exceptional ball control and vision. Newcastle United paid West Ham United £415,000 during November 1986. It was a new club record fee and the Magpies needed his talent. They had slipped to the bottom of the table and were in desperate need of someone to give them a lift. The centre-forward position was again a problem. For almost three months, United scraped around for a leader up front to make an impact.

After midfielder Andy Thomas and Tony Cunningham pulled on the jersey as stand-ins, Goddard was installed in the No. 9 shirt for much of the 1986–87 season alongside Beardsley and the Magpies' new Geordie hope, the teenage sensation Paul Gascoigne. McFaul dispensed with the big, brutish striker tactics and got back to pure football.

Goddard's deft touches, ability to lead the attack and clinical finishing proved crucial in United's fight to avoid the drop and in the process Goddard became a most popular player in the No. 9 shirt. Capped by England when at Upton Park, Paul gradually steered United to safety. He had a slow start finding the net, scoring only once in his opening 12 league games, but then hit a purple patch. When Newcastle needed it most, he found his touch with seven goals, one in each of seven consecutive games that earned five victories and two draws – 17 precious points. Goddard later confirmed: 'It was a wonderful time for me.'

THE BOY FROM BRAZIL

With 13 goals in 29 outings, Goddard was a success and for the start of the new 1987–88 season McFaul gave Sarge, as he was nicknamed, a new partner up front . . . and he was something a bit special – the very first Brazilian to play in the Football League. A star who had graced the Maracana of Rio, Mirandinha joined the Black'n'Whites from Palmeiras for another club record fee of £575,000 in August 1987. It was a deal that caught the imagination of the football world and of Tyneside – and that's exactly what boss Willie McFaul wanted. United were back in the limelight.

Born on the edge of the Amazon rainforest, Mirandinha had just made a big impression in the celebrated yellow jersey of his country by striking the winning goal at Wembley against England. As a centre-forward in Brazil, he had reputedly scored almost 300 goals. He was hardly a giant, slightly built at 5 ft 8 in., nimble and extremely fast with a shoot-on-sight football philosophy.

Newcastle United and McFaul needed a big deal at the time. Heavily criticised for the departure of both Waddle and Beardsley, they required a larger than life character with magnetism to lift the spirit. McFaul had originally gone for Wimbledon's John Fashanu, but at over £1 million, United baulked. The Brazilian option was cheaper. Newcastle's boss watched Mirandinha play well at Hampden Park against the Scots then dazzle against the formidable pairing of Tony Adams and Terry Butcher at Wembley. It was enough to convince McFaul that Mirandinha was good enough.

As could be expected, the purchase of Mirandinha caught the public's imagination and on Tyneside sales of yellow and green Brazil shirts, as well as sombreros, hit the roof. On his arrival in the North-east after a 7,000-mile and 26-hour journey from South America, he noted through an interpreter: 'I am coming to Britain to prove I am one of the best players in the world.'

It was a bold move by United's boss. There were many sceptics, including some high-profile doubters like Tommy Docherty who said: 'Newcastle have made a big mistake. Mirandinha is never going to fit in at St. James' Park or take Peter Beardsley's place.'

McFaul spoke about the transfer and was to honestly admit: 'Some may see it as my biggest gamble.' It certainly was – and in the end it was not to pay off. It was also to cost the Ulsterman his job.

The arrival of the 28-year-old South American was one of the first of what was to become a long line of foreign imports to St. James'

Park. Only Chilean pair George Robledo and his brother Ted had made any real impact on Tyneside up to then. It was hoped that Mirandinha would have the influence that Argentinians Ossie Ardiles and Ricky Villa created at Tottenham a few years before.

Involved in the transfer was Malcolm Macdonald, one of Mira's agents at the British end of the deal. Supermac rated the little Brazilian highly and said at the time: 'I know the lad has phenomenal skill. He is just the right player to create the type of excitement they like on Tyneside.' Mac went on: 'He is lightning fast. He packs a good shot in both feet and for a small man he is good in the air.'

From a large family and born into poverty, he was christened Francisco Ernandi Lima da Silva. He lived in a shanty town and worked down a salt mine as a kid, but he was to move apace from rags to riches. The striker picked the name of Mirandinha – as is the custom in Brazil – from a popular footballer. He started playing amateur football for his local side Fortaleza and soon made an impression moving step by step to bigger clubs including Botafogo, Crezero, Santos and Sao Paulo giant Palmeiras. Football earned him a small fortune and it was noted that by the time he arrived in England he owned several properties back in Brazil including a 200-acre pig farm.

Manager Willie McFaul gave the boy from Brazil the No. 10 shirt – Pele's number of course – for the new 1987–88 season with Goddard retaining the centre-forward jersey, although Mirandinha would regularly wear the celebrated No. 9 in time. The grand unveiling of Mirandinha to the English football public took place on a Tuesday evening at Carrow Road during September 1987 and he actually wore the No. 9 shirt as Goddard was sidelined. A couple of thousand Geordies made the long trip to East Anglia clad in sombreros, Brazilian shirts and waving colourful yellow and green flags. An unspectacular 1–1 draw resulted with Mira, as he was to be nicknamed, having a quiet debut in the English game, although he did impress at times. It was noted: 'The first Brazilian to play in the Football League gave glimpses of his exciting talent. United's record signing demonstrated his pace, skill and willingness to shoot on sight – just the qualities United expected.'

His first appearance at St. James' Park was supposed to be a Samba Spectacular but the occasion was noted as a 'depressing anticlimax' as Wimbledon secured a 1–2 victory. As the Gallowgate End terrace waved their Brazil flags and danced the samba, on the field United put in a laboured performance. Mirandinha did show he was 'quick and incisive' and as one match report noted 'showed flashes of Brazilian brilliance which suggested he will be a fine addition'.

The little South American had to adapt quickly to his new surroundings. It was a vast culture shock for him – exchanging a way of life of the sun-drenched Copacabana to the chilly and rainy north of England. Mirandinha again showed flashes of Brazilian magic as he combined with Goddard and the fast-emerging Gascoigne, who befriended the new import straight away. In Mel Stein's biography of Gascoigne, *Gazza*, he noted that the pair became 'soul mates' and the boisterous Geordie 'assumed the unlikely role of teaching Mira English'.

Two goals from the Brazilian at Old Trafford against Manchester United in a 2–2 draw made headlines as Mira hit the net for the first time. A crowd of 45,137 witnessed the occasion and his electric pace worried Paul McGrath and Kevin Moran all afternoon. It was noted that Mira 'silenced the baying hordes of Old Trafford fans with a magical two-goal burst'. After seven minutes, Newcastle scored with their first attack. A free-kick was awarded just outside the Reds' box and up stepped Mira to crack a shot straight for goal. It took a deflection off Moran and whipped into the net. His second arrived from a corner and the Brazilian was on the end of a Hodges flick, hurling himself forward to head home from close range. It was almost a stunning hat-trick from Mirandinha as he waltzed around Duxbury to curl a brilliant shot from a narrow angle against the crossbar.

But Newcastle United and Mirandinha had a less than satisfying start to the season and were struggling for points. By December though, the Magpies regained form and Mira netted in four games in a row as the Geordies climbed to mid-table. The combination of Goddard and Mirandinha started to click and was at times a delight to watch. They liked the ball on the ground, to their feet or into spaces to run on to.

At times, however, Mirandinha also looked a mediocre player. A slight and dusky figure, he didn't possess the glittering array of skills associated with most Brazilians and his first touch wasn't always the best. But his pace over ten yards and blistering shot could be match-winning. He would shoot from anywhere: 40 yards out, or at seemingly impossible wide angles. In addition, he could lose a defender with a single turn or swerve. He may not have been in the class of Pele, Jairzinho or Zico, but he could still cause problems for any defence.

Mirandinha was also somewhat difficult to play alongside, having a selfish streak that saw him head for goal when a pass was a far better option – and it sometimes produced fireworks. Paul Gascoigne often became frustrated with his colleague; Stein, Gazza's agent for many years, wrote he was regarded by the rest of the team 'to be less than a team player'. Stein noted: 'Paul and he nearly came to blows in dressing-room post-mortems, but the little Brazilian just nodded as if he understood and continued exactly the same way.'

John Hendrie also echoed Gazza's feelings. The Scot said: 'He was so greedy with the ball that you needed two balls on the pitch – one for him and one for the rest of the team.' His first season was a hit and miss affair. Scoring 12 times, Mirandinha both thrilled and frustrated in equal measure. But considering the vast change in environment for the Brazilian, everyone was satisfied with the result as he bedded in.

Goddard scored ten times that season as United finished in eighth spot and again looked the part, one of McFaul's few automatic choices on the team-sheet. He missed only five games, Andy Thomas and Michael O'Neill, a bright youngster from Northern Ireland who had made a big impression with 13 goals, deputising in the No. 9 shirt while the up-and-coming Ashington youngster, Tony Lormor, made his debut at centre-forward for the last game of the season against West Ham United.

Although Goddard was established on the field, off it his wife was homesick and failed to settle in the area. As a result, the Newcastle striker was destined to move south at the end of the season. Goddard said later: 'It was a pity I had to leave Newcastle the way I did.' He departed to join Arthur Cox at Derby County for a £425,000 fee, having netted 23 goals in 72 appearances for United. McFaul commented afterwards: 'My biggest mistake was allowing Paul Goddard to leave.' United missed his intelligent play around the box.

The summer of 1988 was not a good close season for the Black'n'Whites. Not only did Goddard cross the Tyne Bridge south, but Newcastle also lost Paul Gascoigne to Tottenham; the third Geordie superstar in the making to desert the camp in only three years. Newcastle supporters were in uproar and the seeds were sown of what was to follow – a long and controversial battle for control of the club. It was even more important now that Mirandinha made his mark. McFaul handed the sable Brazilian the No. 9 shirt and he was the manager's big hope now that the player had experienced 12 months of life in the region.

Off the field Mirandinha was a delightful personality. No one quite knew if he could speak English on his arrival, but by the time he left he could understand and communicate well, albeit in the Geordie version. He was a godsend to the media, the focus of much attention, and comically he would often play his trump card to journalists when not wanting to answer questions. He would say in broken English, Manuel style: 'I do not understand.' He organised Brazilian theme parties at his Tyneside pad and enjoyed life in Toon. But he did find it difficult coming to terms with the English winter, wearing black tights and gloves to fend off the cold at times. Colleague John Hendrie wrote in his book *Don't Call Me Happy*: 'As soon as the bad weather came you would never see him at the training ground.' Mira would prefer to be in front of a raging fire at home.

In a bid to arrest the flak McFaul went on a £3 million spending spree for the start of the 1988–89 season. However, from the outset it was evident that McFaul's remodelled and expensive line-up was finding it difficult to blend together. He had three players of a similar style going forward: Mirandinha, along with two Scots, John Robertson and John Hendrie. Newcastle started badly again but unlike the previous campaign did not recover.

Mirandinha once more showed flashes of genius, but United needed more than a fleeting glimpse of his ability. At Anfield against the league champions, United surprisingly won 2–1 as he scored from the penalty spot and was a danger to the Reds all game. He gave Nicol, Venison and Gillespie a torrid time, scoring the winner at the Kop end after John Hendrie had been felled just inside the box. The Tynesiders needed that sort of display from their No. 9 week in, week out.

With Newcastle drifting towards the Second Division the long-serving McFaul was sacked in October, being replaced by Jim Smith, successful boss of QPR. Smith, known as the Bald Eagle, had to motivate the players he inherited to stop the slide. That was a difficult job and he was forced to start a rebuilding process in parallel with a fight to avoid the drop – all in six months. It was a task doomed to failure.

Smith needed his Brazilian star to play an important role and early into the Bald Eagle's days on Tyneside he was to write that Mira 'became a hero in the tradition – though not in the same esteem – of Jackie Milburn and Malcolm Macdonald'. Smith later recorded in his autobiography, *Bald Eagle*, that he was 'the one with extra-special talent, the little bit of magic that could have got us out of the hole we were in'. United's new boss had to spur on his star centre-forward and that was a huge challenge. In the end, Smith admitted: 'It was one task I could not handle. I tried everything I could think of.'

Mirandinha soon clashed with his new boss and the relationship deteriorated rapidly. Smith was to say: 'He did not have the stomach for the scrap.' Mirandinha's form was inconsistent and it infuriated his manager. When things went wrong, he tended to drop deep and invariably lose the ball in dangerous positions. He was in and out of the side, injured or not, Smith once noting that 'for an injured man he could get off the park pretty quickly'. Mirandinha never relished the physical side of the First Division. Smith wrote in his programme notes: 'More than once I questioned his commitment to the cause. I always felt that he was more interested in the welfare of Mirandinha than in the well-being of the club that was paying his wage.' Transfer requests followed and he was frequently after more money, seemingly always having to bail his family out back in Brazil. Middlesbrough were willing to take him to Ayresome Park, but that deal fell through.

Several players pulled on the No. 9 shirt as Smith tried to fashion a winning combination. Expensive McFaul purchase John Robertson and fellow Scot Darren Jackson – both to feature for their country in the coming years – were given brief run-outs as was Michael O'Neill, Liam O'Brien, Gary Brazil and Rob McDonald who was purchased mid-season from Dutch football with a reputation of playing alongside Ruud Gullit at PSV. Ian Bogie, who looked to be another home-grown midfield gem, was handed the shirt for the FA Cup meeting with Watford. Danish striker Frank Pingel was also given a chance up front. All of them failed to grasp the opportunity. Smith even turned to centre-half Andy Thorn in desperation. He appeared in attack on five occasions. It was left to Mira to give the Magpies a glimmer of hope.

During March, he hit a patch of goalscoring form as United defeated Everton and Norwich City. The South American rose to the occasion and found the net in both games. It was just what United needed if they were to escape the drop, but it was only a brief flurry. The Magpies then met fellow strugglers Sheffield Wednesday at Easter and lost 1–3. Mirandinha had several great chances to win the game for United, but as Smith said, annoyingly he 'fluffed them'. United's boss noted: 'He seemed to lose interest at a time when we needed players to roll up their sleeves and battle.' After that, United didn't win another match, Mira never scored again and the Black'n'Whites were relegated.

Most judges considered that Mirandinha may have succeeded in a good side that was full of confidence and with quality players around him. His pace and shooting ability would have been capitalised on. Colleague John Anderson confirmed: 'He was unlucky to be at Gallowgate at a time of upheaval, change and relegation. That didn't help. He would have been a much better player in a better side and at a different time.' Supporters had a good rapport with Mira, but they always thought that, for a Brazilian, he should have displayed so much more. But the South American was not cut out for an English relegation dog-fight and in the end he was something of a Brazilian misfit.

Mirandinha's short period at Gallowgate was all but over. His two years on Tyneside were a bamboozling combination of magic and brooding, of erratic radiance. Mirandinha found the net on 24 occasions for United in 69 matches before returning on loan to Palmeiras in July 1989. He eventually made the deal permanent, United taking a considerable loss of over £400,000 on the transfer. Jim Smith was not one to be diplomatic with his words. On his departure, United's boss said that as far as he was concerned 'he can rot in Brazil'. Mira afterwards travelled far and wide playing the game, but never touched the heights other Brazilian celebrities did.

THE MIGHTY QUINN

Priority for Jim Smith, like many of his predecessors at Gallowgate, was to find a worthy No. 9 to lead Newcastle United's bid to regain their First Division status. While many of Smith's imports as he wheeled and dealed through a whole squad of players failed to impress, his purchase of Portsmouth's Mick Quinn during June 1989 was a huge success.

A characteristic Scouser, witty and cheery, Quinn had scraped a living in football for the first few years of his career at Tranmere, Derby, Wigan, Stockport County and Oldham. Moving to Portsmouth in 1986, he established himself as a noted centre-forward and tasted top flight action in season 1987–88. Although Quinn had over 150 goals to his name, Smith still had some reservations. He did want Everton's Wayne Clarke at first, but then switched his attention to Quinn. Smith was to record in his book *Bald Eagle* that his 'reputation as a Scouse scallywag who liked a bet made me apprehensive'. Smith, however, completed the deal and Quinn joined United for a fee of £680,000, an amount set by a Football League tribunal with United claiming the figure was too high – even though Pompey's asking price of £800,000 had been slashed. But 27-year-old Quinn was to repay the Magpies quickly with a goalscoring spree to match anything seen for years at St. James' Park.

MICK QUINN
FACTS & FIGURES

To Newcastle United: June 1989 from Portsmouth
£680,000

From Newcastle United: November 1992 to Coventry
City £250,000

Born: Liverpool 2 May 1962

Height: 5 ft 10 in.

Other senior clubs: Tranmere Rovers, Derby County,
Wigan Athletic, Stockport County, Oldham Athletic,
Watford, Plymouth Argyle, PAOK Salonika

International: none

Newcastle United app & goals:
Football League: 117 app, 59 goals
FA Cup: 7 app, 4 goals
FL Cup: 9 app, 0 goals
Others: 7 app, 8 goals
Total: 140 app, 71 goals

Strike-rate: League and Cup 47% (overall 51%)

Micky Quinn possessed a poacher's instinct when in the box. He was a natural goalscorer and wanted a bigger stage, even though United were in the Second Division. He knew the Magpies had massive potential. And he knew what to say when he arrived in Newcastle, noting: 'There was only one place I was going to come and that was Tyneside. You just have to look at the place and the way they revere their centre-forwards. I feel honoured to be wearing the No. 9 shirt.' Despite the well rehearsed introduction, Newcastle supporters were not immediately taken with Quinn's purchase. Mick had to work to convince the Black'n'White Army. He wrote in his book *Who Ate All The Pies?* that when he arrived they soon asked: 'Who the f**k is Mick Quinn?' Geordie fans quickly found out as Quinny started rattling the ball into the net.

Smith also brought back to Tyneside Mark McGhee, who had left over ten years before, his chance of a vocation at the top in ruins. But McGhee resurrected his career under Alex Ferguson's guidance at Aberdeen before moving to Hamburg and Celtic. He returned to St. James' Park as a 32-year-old international, an experienced trophy-winning striker. His close control on the ball and unselfish play blended with Quinn's goal intuition. McGhee partnered Quinn in a twin strike-force and the pairing was a tremendous success, netting 61 league and cup goals as the Magpies pushed strongly for promotion at the first attempt.

The opening day of the season saw United's new centre-forward face another big-spending club in Leeds United at St. James' Park. As the Gallowgate arena was bathed in sunshine and United won 5–2, Mick Quinn wrote himself into Geordie folklore, becoming an instant No. 9 hero. In a most remarkable debut, Quinn scored four goals in front of a 24,396 crowd, a stunning performance. Quinn's first hit the net after 18 minutes with a right-foot penalty, then he headed home Kevin Brock's cross ball just after half-time. The centre-forward was on the mark again when he converted a dangerous centre by Gallacher and his last was the best of the lot – showing composure as he raced from the halfway line to a Dillon through pass to slot the ball into the net for a fourth time past Mervyn Day. Quinn remembered the joy of grabbing a hat-trick: 'I went nuts and ran towards the Gallowgate, arms outstretched.' Only the great Len Shackleton has produced a better first outing in the club's black and white stripes when he converted six goals against Newport County back in 1946.

Mick continued to have an extraordinary start in the Novocastrian's shirt. He struck nine goals in his first five games, the best on record from the start of a season. After his Leeds opening salvo, Quinn scored against Leicester City, Oldham, Bournemouth and Oxford United. Then soon after he fired home another hat-trick, at Brighton. Quinny was on a roll and admitted that that season at St. James' Park provided his 'happiest days in football'. It almost brought international recognition too with Jack Charlton keen for him to appear for his Irish side, but disappointingly for Mick his ancestral links were too distant even for the Republic.

Quinn had a terrific season as he plundered Second Division defences. Aided by McGhee who created many of his goals, Mick almost powered United to promotion – the Magpies failing at the last hurdle, in the play-offs, to Sunderland of all clubs – and the prolific partnership also led United on an FA Cup run, ended only by Manchester United in the 5th round.

The Merseysider scored 36 senior goals all told and picked up the coveted Adidas European Golden Boot award. Only the likes of Hughie Gallacher, George Robledo and Andy Cole have scored more in a season for the Black'n'Whites. Mick became at the time only the fifth player in the club's history to top 30 goals. Apart from Quinn and McGhee up front, young Scot John Gallacher performed well in his first season and he pulled on the centre-forward shirt when Quinn was sidelined.

As United tried again to reach the First Division in season 1990–91, the warfare behind the scenes for control of the Magpies reached melting point and Jim Smith was caught in the middle of a hornets' nest of football politics and corporate dealing. His line-up never lived up to being one of the bookie's favourites for success; indeed United slipped the opposite way in the Second Division table as injuries and the warring factions took their toll.

Quinn did his job, claiming 20 goals and hardly missing a game – Wayne Fereday and Archie Gourlay deputising for an odd outing. He was highly rated by many and as a consequence United had to fend off a £1.2 million bid from First Division Wimbledon. His manager described Quinn as 'an ugly-duckling player' and noted that 'he looks awkward and unathletic'. However, Quinn had the knack of scoring goals. At 5 ft 10 in. tall, though not the picture of a well-primed athlete, Quinn knew the centre-forward's business and was king of the six-yard box. He was single-minded about goalscoring, quick to get himself into the right positions in the danger area and conjure goals out of nothing. With back to goal, he could control the ball, shield it and turn in one movement while he needed little back-lift in firing towards the target.

The Merseysider could strike them with his right or left foot, his head, or any other part of his anatomy. Teammate John Anderson said: 'Mick was the most natural goalscorer I ever played with. He hit the ball in any fashion, a toe-poke, with his backside, shoulder – anything to find the net.' Many of his strikes were well placed close to the post rather than power-packed, and he rarely scored the spectacular effort, although one dipping volley against Derby's Peter Shilton from the edge of the box was a bit special. Most, though, were close-in conversions. In the dressing-room, too, he was important. His bubbly personality and impish sense of humour rubbed off on his colleagues.

His partner Mark McGhee didn't have such a good time this time round. The Scot soon moved to wind down his career in Sweden. Smith tested new faces. He brought in 6 ft 1 in. Australian

245

international Dave Mitchell on a loan deal from Chelsea, while Tommy Gaynor (Nottingham Forest) and Paul Moran (Tottenham) were tried up front as well, also on loan. All failed to impress alongside Quinn.

By the time winter turned to spring, manager Smith had taken enough. As the pressure mounted on and off the field, he resigned during March. United turned to Swindon Town's auspicious young boss, 38-year-old former World Cup winner Ossie Ardiles, as the club's fifth manager in only seven years. With refreshing ideas, Ardiles started almost from scratch, dispensing with many of Smith's ageing squad and introducing a batch of young Magpies from the junior set-up to regular action; rising stars like Lee Clark, Steve Watson and Steve Howey. Wearsider Howey, after brief substitute appearances, in fact began his career up front, wearing the centre-forward shirt against Charlton.

Ardiles though saw Mick Quinn as his key man. The former Argentinian midfielder described Mick as his most influential figure. He said: 'I have never known a player with more hunger for scoring goals' – and Ardiles had played with the best in the world. Quinn signed a new three-year contract and was happy with life on Tyneside. He enjoyed being recognised as one of the club's No. 9 heroes and now understood what football – and the Shirt of Legends – meant in the region. Quinn admitted that on joining United that he was 'aware of it – but as an outsider looking in'. Mick said: 'Everyone told me about it – and I quickly found out what it meant.' He noted: 'Geordieland is like a nation within a nation, and it needs its own idols. If you wear the black and white shirt for Newcastle then you are treated like a movie star.' He went on to add: 'Every kid wants your autograph, punters in every pub want to buy you a drink and women throw themselves at you. If you wear the sacred No. 9 shirt you can times that by three.' Mick enjoyed the nightspots of a vibrant city like several of his predecessors. He also enjoyed time at Gosforth Park, having a love of horse racing too.

With a youthful new-look side, the 1991–92 season started as ever with much optimism. However the campaign was to be nothing short of a disaster. Ossie's kids found the going tough and by the time the table took shape the Magpies were in touch with the bottom of the division instead of the top. Disaster struck when Mick Quinn was badly injured during October 1991 scoring a goal at his old stamping ground of Fratton Park.

In a 1–3 defeat Quinn slid in to net United's goal but also crashed against a post damaging his knee. Skipper Kevin Scott said: 'It's hard to imagine a bigger blow to us in our current position.' He was to be in plaster for six weeks and out of action for over four months with a torn cruciate ligament.

Without Quinn's prowess in front of goal United had a major problem. Steve Howey was given an extended run of ten games but only managed a single goal. He noted at the time: 'I could save United money in the transfer market.' The tall and well-built Howey did, but not as a centre-forward. He developed instead into an England centre-half. Nigel Walker and David Roche also filled the gap briefly.

Gavin Peacock, who had been signed from Bournemouth, was an emerging talent but not a centre-forward. Other options included Andy Hunt, a young striker plucked from the non-league scene. Hunt, though, was somewhat overawed at the prospect, noting he had enough to worry about trying to establish himself as a top footballer without taking on the mantle of the centre-forward shirt. He chose to wear the No. 10 jersey and went on to secure a decent career, if not at Gallowgate, then south with West Bromwich Albion and Charlton. Also given an opportunity was former England B centre-forward Justin Fashanu who arrived on trial. He played only once, against Peterborough United, before moving on in a much travelled career and to a sad death.

United needed a replacement for Quinn. Ardiles looked at the marketplace to see who was available. He didn't have a bag of gold with the club's finances in a perilous state so was restricted in whom he could buy. His choice though was a good one, spending £250,000 in December 1991 on Leicester City's David Kelly, just fending off an approach by Sunderland.

At 26 years of age and from Birmingham, Kelly had been around the circuit with Walsall – where he scored plenty of goals in the lower divisions – West Ham United and latterly at Filbert Street. He wasn't of the spectacular breed or, like Quinn, a poacher. Kelly was a player's player: honest, workmanlike and with good if not brilliant all-round ability, but most importantly he could find the back of the net.

Kelly gave a boost to the side although it wasn't to help Ardiles much as points were still hard to secure. United continued to slide and the Argentinian was sacked ten weeks later after less than a year in charge. Kelly, however, was to prove a great servant to Ossie's successor as the Black'n'Whites started a rapid transformation, heading on an expressway that led to a mega-club footing and new-found status.

THE PIED PIPER RETURNS

By this time Sir John Hall's takeover of the Geordies was almost complete and his plans to regenerate Newcastle United into one of Europe's nouveaux riches was already on the boardroom table. Ardiles had left United in a hazardous league position – facing the Third Division for the very first time in a century of football. Sir John quickly acted – and in stepped 'The Messiah', a dramatic return to football for Kevin Keegan as manager of Newcastle United.

In the three months that remained of the 1991–92 season Keegan needed allies on the pitch if he was to avoid a catastrophic drop into Division Three. In David Kelly – and Gavin Peacock – he had two players who gave their all to United's cause at this critical time.

Kelly was a hard-working centre-forward, nicknamed Ned; he was mobile and made lots of runs down the channels to give United options. He could get behind defenders and netted 11 goals in United's relegation fight. Supporters appreciated his efforts and Kelly was to hold a special place in their roll of honour.

Keegan's charisma and Pied Piper-like leadership revitalised the club. Fans and players responded, but it was still an uphill fight to gather enough points to scrape into the safety zone – and it was David Kelly who gave United a lifeline by securing six points at a vital stage. After he had netted twice on Keegan's theatrical comeback against Bristol City, Kelly's contribution proved crucial. Firstly, in the season's Tyne–Wear derby confrontation at Gallowgate during March, Kelly converted a cross with a delicately headed strike at the Leazes End of the ground. It was a precious goal.

Even more important was his late winner against Portsmouth. With only two matches remaining United faced the FA Cup semi-finalists at St. James' Park. The equation was simple enough. The Magpies had to win. In a nail-biting contest, Keegan's men were up for the fight but couldn't convert the chance to hit the net and the game looked to be heading for what would have been a disastrous 0–0 stalemate. But the gods were with Newcastle United.

In the 85th minute Micky Quinn – back after his injury and on as substitute – flicked the ball into the path of David Kelly who hit a fabulous angled half-volley from just inside the box past goalkeeper Alan Knight. It was one of the most important goals any United No. 9

had scored in one hundred years of football. Mick Quinn was to say: 'It was such a big game and such a big, big goal.'

Gavin Peacock wrote in his book *Never Walk Alone*: 'The place just erupted like you've never heard before. The relief flooded all over everybody. You could feel it – relief from the whole of Newcastle that we'd got three points that in effect saved us.'

In the final do-or-die confrontation of the season against Leicester at Filbert Street, Kelly further played his part against his former club as Gavin Peacock struck a fine opener then harried City's Steve Walsh into a dramatic injury-time winner for United. The Magpies were safe and Keegan was ready to launch the new Newcastle United.

With the Hall regime now in full control and an enormous transformation under way, Keegan swung into action for the start of the 1992–93 programme. David Kelly and Gavin Peacock were the former England skipper's first choice strike-force with fit again Mick Quinn frustratingly left more often than not on the bench. David Kelly's hard-working effort was preferred . . . and Quinny was not happy. United's former prolific No. 9 had to watch Keegan's eleven take the division by storm, winning their opening 11 fixtures and galloping to the top of the table – in the process capturing the imagination of the football world as the sleeping giant awoke.

As a consequence there was friction between Quinn and Keegan – ironically, as Keegan had been Quinn's own hero as a lad on Merseyside having posters of his idol on his bedroom wall. Quinn thought he should be part of the parade, noting: 'With my goalscoring record at the club, I believed, I should have been in the starting eleven.'

Now into his 30s, United's boss was already looking to the future and Quinn was not in his longer-term plans. He needed to make room for younger talent. Quinn spilled his heart to the tabloid press and Keegan didn't like it. He was placed on the transfer list and his days became numbered on Tyneside – being sent into 'football purgatory' as Mick described it.

Quinn said of his departure: 'It was one of those things that happen in every football club. I thought I was good enough to play in the 1992–93 championship side, but Kevin wanted a certain type of player.' Keegan wanted athletic, mobile forwards and Quinn was not that sort of striker. Mick Quinn was to leave as United's roller-coaster gained momentum. He joined Coventry City during November 1992 with 71 goals to his name. He said afterwards: 'I loved my time at St. James' Park and I am proud to have worn the No. 9 shirt.'

MICK QUINN No. 9 RATING	
Fan appeal – personality and presence	8
Strike-rate	5
Shooting – power and placement	8
Heading	7
Ball-skills	7
Link-play – passing, assists, crossing, team-play	8
Pace	7
Commitment – work-rate, courage	7
Match-winner – power-play, big-match capability	7
Longevity with United	3
Trophy success, international and top football ranking	-1
Total No. 9 rating	66

Kelly meanwhile led the attack with gusto. Capped by the Republic of Ireland – qualifying thanks to his father – he had the best season of his career. David was United's top scorer with 28 goals as the resurgent Geordies ran away with the First Division title – newly renamed on the introduction of the Premier League.

As the Magpies' rebirth gathered momentum, ambitions were high. Keegan looked to strengthen his squad, even making an audacious attempt to bring Southampton's emerging England Under-21 centre-forward, Geordie Alan Shearer, back home. A £3 million bid was tabled – and rejected. That deal was to be put on ice; however Keegan was not to rest on his laurels. United's magnetic boss eyed another young striker – former Arsenal kid and Bristol City leader, Andy Cole. Keegan shattered United's transfer record by paying a staggering £1.75 million for the 21 year old in March 1993.

Lithe and fast, Cole had barely a year of regular first-team football behind him but he was to learn and grow in stature rapidly. Cole replaced the injured Peacock with eight weeks of the season to go. The outcome was not in doubt and Cole just made the Black'n'Whites an even more potent force. Linking with Kelly, the pairing was unstoppable.

Andy's first appearance was at Swindon, coming off the bench for a brief taste of life in a black and white shirt. He made his St. James' Park entry against Notts County and showed the brilliance and deadly goal-poaching sense that was to soon be unleashed on the Premier League as United's new No. 9 hero, but for the present, Cole played alongside Kelly in the No. 8 shirt. The new partnership claimed three of the four goals that destroyed County with Kelly adding two more to his growing tally while Cole opened his account in the seventieth minute. Receiving a ball from his strike partner in the box, he swivelled and struck the ball in one poetic movement with tremendous power past keeper Steve Cherry and into the Gallowgate End net. His manager noted afterwards: 'It was a real striker's goal. He will get a few more of them.' Keegan was right. Cole certainly did.

Andy then netted his first hat-trick for the Magpies as Barnsley felt the full force of Keegan's entertaining machine. Kelly led the line brilliantly as the Tykes were mauled 6–0 on an evening that United's new striker indicated he was going to become something special. Cole's first saw him cut inside two defenders before whipping home a drive past keeper Whitehead. He then slipped past a defender in the box, fed Kelly on the wing, ran into the danger area and converted an inviting cross. His last was another mark of the master goal-taker. Rob Lee pulled the ball back for Cole to control and crack the ball into the net in blazing style.

The promotion climax was played out on a Tuesday evening against unfashionable Grimsby Town, at the Mariners' Blundell Park arena in Cleethorpes and fittingly it was Kelly and Cole who grabbed the goals that sent United into the Promised Land of the Premiership. After the break, Rob Lee powered past three defenders before slipping the ball into Cole's path. As Doug Wetherall wrote in *The Mail*: 'Grimsby's Gary Croft had no chance of catching the speedy record signing. Keeper Wilmot was beaten low to his left.'

Kelly grabbed the second which sealed promotion to send the thousands of travelling Geordies in every corner of the old stadium into delirium. Wetherall noted: 'Cole's pass put him through and it seemed he had gone too wide to his left in eluding Wilmot but he overcame the tight angle with a left foot shot just inside the near post.'

It was gala time at the promotion encore as United welcomed Leicester City to Tyneside on the last day of the season. The championship trophy was presented and Newcastle went out in style by winning 7–1 – and the attack duo each struck a hat-trick. In front of a live television audience, the Magpies were 6–0 ahead at half-time. It was brilliant stuff with Kelly bagging his three goals by the interval, including two picture-book headers following perfect crosses from

Clark and Robinson. Remarkably, that joyous afternoon marked the end of David Kelly's stay on Tyneside.

Keegan was already planning a makeover in the summer. Cole had made his mark scoring 12 goals in only 11 starts. He was ready to take over the No. 9 shirt alongside a new partner. Kelly was sold to Wolves for a £750,000 fee after 39 goals for the club in 83 games. He did a fantastic job for United, somewhat the unsung hero, first seeing off relegation then lifting the First Division Championship trophy. But now the No. 9 shirt had been passed on and belonged to a rising star, Andy Cole.

No. 9 EXTRAS

DEBUT DELIGHT

Micky Burns made a dazzling debut for the Black'n'Whites in a pre-season Texaco Cup contest with Middlesbrough during August 1974. Having already set up goals for Macdonald and Cassidy, he netted with an eye-catching solo goal. Jackie Milburn writing in the *News of the World* commented: 'The close-season buy simply tore Middlesbrough apart.' United's legendary centre-forward described his goal: 'In the 86th minute he brought the house down with a brilliant piece of magic. Almost standing still, he cheekily evaded four tackles, walked past the keeper and tucked the ball away. Sheer brilliance.'

HERE AND THERE

Newcastle's Leazes End choir of the era sang loud and clear a Micky Burns bestseller:

> Micky Burns, Micky Burns
> He's here – He's there
> He's every f**kin where
> Micky Burns, Micky Burns

TROPHY SUCCESS

Peter Withe went on to trophy success at the highest level after leaving Tyneside. With Aston Villa he first was an influential player with 20 goals in their 1980–81 Football League Championship success then led Villa's attack to the European Cup in 1982. Peter scored the winner in the final, a 1–0 victory over Bayern Munich in Rotterdam. The Villains also lifted the Super Cup by toppling Barcelona over two legs. He scored 90 goals in 232 matches for Villa and Withe also went on to appear on 11 occasions for England.

THE NUMBER 9 BAR

During June 1980, the Newcastle Supporters Association opened the *Number 9 Bar* close to St. James' Park at Gallowgate as a tribute to the club's centre-forward legends. It was opened by Jackie Milburn and was packed with No. 9 memorabilia. The bar later moved to *The Magpie*, opposite the stadium and then to *The Willows* in Walker. Malcolm Macdonald and Mirandinha re-opened the lounge. A roll of honour gallery of United's centre-forwards decorated the walls – now housed in the Milburn Stand of St. James' Park.

WADDLER – AFTER TOON

At White Hart Lane with Spurs, Chris Waddle played alongside fellow Geordie Paul Gascoigne and became a regular for his country, reaching the FA Cup final before a record sale to Marseille in July 1989. The fee of £4.25 million was at the time the fourth highest transfer ever paid, behind Maradona, Gullit and Lajos Detari. After much success in France, he returned to Britain, joining Sheffield Wednesday in 1992, and then wound down his career with a series of clubs including Sunderland. Recently Chris has been a regular expert summariser for BBC *Five Live*. Earlier in his career he also entered the music scene, appearing on the BBC's *Top of the Pops* with Glenn Hoddle singing 'Diamond Lights' in 1987. When in France, Chris cut another record, this time with Basil Boli, entitled 'We've Got a Feeling'.

LE DRIBBLEUR FOU

In France for three years, Waddle became an idol at the Velodrome as Marseille became a leading club in Europe. Alongside the likes of Papin and Tigana, Chris lifted three French titles and reached the final of the European Cup in 1991. In Provence, he developed his game enormously to become a world star and for his showmanship was given the nickname of *Le Dribbleur Fou*, which roughly translates to The Dribbling Jester.

MOST-CAPPED GEORDIE

With 62 caps for England, Chris Waddle is one of Tyneside's most-capped players. He played in both the 1986 and 1990 World Cup finals, missing a crucial penalty kick in the semi-final shoot-out with West Germany which may have taken Bobby Robson's national side into the final against Argentina. Alan Shearer (63 caps) is the most capped Geordie followed by Waddle, Peter Beardsley (59 caps) and Paul Gascoigne (57 caps).

GEORDIE SAMBA

When Mirandinha set foot on Tyneside the Toon's Gallowgate Enders were quick to put together a Brazilian samba for their new hero to the tune of the Conga:

> We've got Miran-din-ha,
> He's not from Ar-gen-tina,
> He's from Bra-zil,
> He's f**kin Brill.

KEEN TO IMPRESS

Mirandinha was a player with a one-track mind for scoring goals. He would shoot from anywhere and was ever so keen to impress on his arrival. On his debut at Norwich, colleague David McCreery remembered: 'The thing that sticks in my mind is Mira trying to score with a free-kick from the halfway line – and that was just about his first touch of the ball!' United's Northern Ireland international went on: 'He just grabbed the ball, put it down and gave it a wallop. The ball went nowhere near the Norwich goalkeeper – in fact the effort was embarrassing, but it was an immediate indication of the way Mira approached his job.'

DIRTY DOZEN

Mick Quinn's early career was often littered with controversy, being one of the so-called 'Dirty Dozen' at Portsmouth. Mick himself described them as 'a bunch of reprobates who, because of their attitude or unruly behaviour didn't fit in at other clubs'. Quinn was a bit of a lad; pubbing, clubbing, gambling and womanising. In 1987, when he was Pompey's top scorer, he served a 21-day sentence in Winchester Prison for drink-driving and driving without a licence or insurance and when at Stockport County he moonlighted by playing for the Liverpool History Dept football eleven, under the pseudonym of *Kevin Dalglish* – after certain heroes of his: Keegan and Dalglish of Liverpool!

MICK'S SING-A-LONG
Mick Quinn had several songs penned for him during his time at Gallowgate. There was a rewording of a Wyn Davies classic:

> Come on within, Come on without
> You've not seen nothing like the Mighty Quinn

And a Geordie chorus of;

> Micky Quinn, Micky Quinn, Micky Quinn

But the best, a witty few lines as recollected by Quinn himself was;

> He's fat, he's round, a number nine we've found
> Micky Quinn, Micky Quinn

No. 9 FANZINE
The fanzine explosion of the early 1990s saw the launch of several titles on Tyneside. Included was *The Mighty Quinn* named of course after Mick Quinn's Toon exploits. His subsequent departure led to the editorial team asking supporters to submit suggestions for a new magazine. The results were unanimous . . . *The Number Nine* was born. It was the natural choice and the fanzine trebled its circulation as a result.

QUINNY – AFTER TOON
Mick Quinn remained with Coventry City until season 1994–95 when he went on loan to Watford, Plymouth and back to Portsmouth. He then tried life in Greece, joining the PAOK Salonika club in 1995, while he also had a brief spell in Hong Kong. He retired and entered the world of horse racing, firstly at Mick Channon's training complex then operating his own stable. Quinn has also become a pundit on Talksport radio, speaking knowledgeably on both sports.

HAT-TRICK TIME
David Kelly scored a remarkable hat-trick on the first of his 26 appearances for the Republic of Ireland. Against Israel in Dublin

during November 1987, he rattled three goals into the net as the Irish won 5–0. And hat-tricks were the talking point of an astonishing game at Filbert Street in December 1990 as Leicester defeated the Magpies by 4–5. Kelly struck three goals for City, and Micky Quinn fired home a treble for the Magpies. Kelly of course then went on to hit the net with another three goals, this time *against* Leicester and *for* the Black'n'Whites less than three years later.

9. KEV'S ARISTOCRATS
1993–1997

ANDY COLE, LES FERDINAND,
ALAN SHEARER

In a rapidly changing football world, Kevin Keegan recognised that Newcastle United needed big-name stars, players who could stir the emotions and get supporters on the edge of their seats. The Magpies had a long tradition of being lavish spenders in the transfer market and if they were to be a success in the new Premier League he would have to buy big and buy well.

With finances completely remodelled and the club now extremely prosperous, money was to be available in seemingly unlimited amounts. As a result, over the next five years a whole line of fabulous footballers arrived on Tyneside and supporters thrived on the many hero-figures to pull on the black and white shirt.

Kevin Keegan had been – and was still – one of those heroes and he knew at first hand what could be achieved with the full backing of the soccer-mad Toon Army. Keegan was also fully aware that Newcastle United's centre-forward heritage could work to his team's advantage. If he could find a top quality No. 9, the fans would back United even more. United's boss was not only to sign just one No. 9 hero – he brought three of them to St. James' Park in the coming years as the

Premier League became arguably the best competition in the world. All three were to be aristocrats of the new super-league – Andy Cole, Les Ferdinand as well as the biggest of them all, Alan Shearer.

The first of Kev's aristocrats to make an impact was Andy Cole who had already shown in his first few weeks in a Magpie shirt a preview of what was to follow. The Nottingham-born striker's rise to prominence was rapid and nothing short of sensational.

Following trials with Nottingham Forest, Andy joined Arsenal's youth set-up in October 1985 having appeared for local Trent junior sides Parkhead and Emkals. Born into an expatriate Caribbean family, Andy was a confident teenager, an England schools and youth international, and at Highbury he spent two years at the Football Association's Lilleshall School of Excellence which took the very best of the country's budding football stars, putting them in a meaningful structure to encourage the cream of the country's youthful talent to progress. That was a good grounding for the rising footballer; however back in the marble halls of Highbury, Cole found it difficult to gain first-team recognition. Boss at the time, George Graham, knew about his scoring exploits at youth and reserve level – Andy having reached the FA Youth Cup final with the Londoners – but Kevin Campbell, Paul Merson and Ian Wright were all ahead of him in the pecking order. As a consequence, Cole only received two call-ups to senior action, including the Charity Shield showpiece at Wembley against Tottenham in 1991. He recorded in his autobiography *Andy Cole*: 'I felt I was being held back.'

The youngster moved on in search of regular action, first to Fulham on loan for three months during season 1991–92, then to Bristol City also on loan, signing permanently at Ashton Gate in the close season for a £500,000 fee. A taste of regular action was what the young striker needed. In Fulham's colours, he hit the net on 3 occasions and when at City, scored 8 goals in 12 matches to help steer the Robins clear of relegation. Then, in his first full season of 1992–93, Andy continued to make an impression in City's red shirt by striking 16 goals.

Cole was a hit in Division One and reached the England Under-21 set-up. United's boss had already taken note of Cole's name, Andy having caught the Keegan eye in City's fight to avoid the drop. And Kevin Keegan was further impressed with Cole's display against United in January 1993 at Ashton Gate. During the action, Cole's electric pace saw him skate round Steve Howey in the narrowest of spaces to get into the six-yard box. Keegan noted: 'He was not rewarded with a goal on that occasion, but I had never seen skill like it at that level.' Newcastle's chief saw Cole's pace, direct approach and finesse on the ball as real potential for the future. He was a live wire. Andy showed he had quick feet and a goal-poacher's brain.

United watched him again and were ready to break the million pound barrier and smash the club's transfer record by a colossal margin. Newcastle made a move to land Cole's signature that same month, but finalising the deal was not easy. Indeed, negotiations dragged on until just before the transfer deadline in March, the Magpies having several bids turned down, but an increased sum of £1.75 million was a huge amount which Bristol City could not refuse, and Cole finally became a United player.

At the time the Black'n'Whites were top of the table and certainties for promotion. Keegan said then: 'We should buy from a position of strength with an eye on what we need to meet the challenge of the Premier League.' Along with Rob Lee's acquisition, the purchase of Cole was the manager's first step in putting together his team of Entertainers. A high-profile press conference was organised to announce the record arrival of Cole – the first of several glitzy gatherings to become the norm at St. James' Park over the coming years. Lee wrote in his book *Come In No. 37*: 'As far as the lads were concerned Andy was just some young kid who was playing for Bristol City, but how he was to explode upon the scene in quite an unforgettable style.'

ANDY COLE
FACTS & FIGURES

To Newcastle United: March 1993 £1.75 million from
    Bristol City
From Newcastle United: January 1995 £7 million to
    Manchester United
Born: Nottingham 15 October 1971
Height: 5 ft 11 in.
Other senior clubs: Arsenal, Fulham, Blackburn Rovers
England international: 15 app, 1 goal
Newcastle United app & goals:
    Football League/Premier League: 70 app, 55 goals
    FA Cup: 4 app, 1 goal
    FL Cup: 7 app, 8 goals
    Europe: 3 app, 4 goals
    Total: 84 app, 68 goals
Strike-rate: League and Cup 81%

Activity at St. James' Park was feverish during the summer of 1993 as the Magpies prepared for life in the Premier League. Massive ground redevelopment was well under way and the club's refinancing from pauper to millionaire status was in full flow. David Kelly had made his exit while Gavin Peacock left too, returning to London because of family circumstances. Keegan planned to hand his young centre-forward an experienced partner as United began life once more at the top level. During July, the United boss spent £1.5 million on a former playing colleague for whom he held the highest respect, Peter Beardsley, and the former England, Liverpool and Everton star returned to Gallowgate to give Andy Cole the sort of playmaker young strikers dream about.

Newcastle's entry onto the Premier League stage also saw the introduction of a squad system to the Gallowgate dressing-room which meant that the No. 9 shirt was given even more significance. Now players were allocated a shirt – and a number – at the beginning of the season and more often than not they kept it for their entire Toon career. Whoever was now handed the No. 9 shirt had total ownership with their name emblazoned on the back. No one else could wear it while he was at the club and the No. 9 shirt at St. James' Park was even more treasured as only three players in the following decade and more took tenure: Cole, Ferdinand and Shearer.

Not surprisingly, perhaps, it took the Black'n'Whites time to adjust from Division One standards to the much higher level of the Premier League. It was a trip to Old Trafford during mid-August that gave United and Andy Cole a boost against the title holders. A strike from Cole earned the Geordies a point in characteristic style. A neat pass into the box by Niki Papavasiliou saw Cole dart clear of the back line and flick the ball deftly into the corner of the net.

Newcastle and Cole grew in confidence. They demolished poor Notts County in a two-legged League Cup tie, United's centre-forward grabbing a hat-trick in both games as Newcastle rattled 11 goals past the Magpies of Nottingham – one of Cole's home-town clubs. United toyed with the opposition and in a display of quick interchanges Cole clinically finished off delightful approach play.

Points were picked up in league action and by the time United defeated Liverpool at a wintry St. James' Park in November, the Magpies had found their feet, moving into fourth spot in the table. Cole had claimed an impressive 16 goals in 9 matches while over a 2-week period he almost reached double figures! Keegan's Entertainers, as they were affectionately branded, were about to make their mark – and Andy Cole was set to show he was the new star on screen in an era that now had the Premiership and Newcastle United beamed to a multi-million television audience.

Liverpool were out-played and out-manoeuvred as United won emphatically 3–0 with Cole striking a hat-trick inside 30 minutes of the opening half. He gave the Reds' giant defender Neil Ruddock an uncomfortable afternoon. All three goals were the result of stunning Magpie build-up and precise execution by United's centre-forward.

Each goal saw United play the ball neatly, quickly and effectively from midfield to the left, carving Liverpool open – a telling cross on each occasion finding Cole on the six-yard line. Andy did the rest. He pounced, firing the ball past Bruce Grobbelaar once, twice and three times. He was headline news. It was noted after his convincing performance against the Reds that Cole 'was top of Manchester United manager Alex Ferguson's shopping list'. That was laughed off, but was a significant piece of media gossip considering the dramatic events to unfold in the not too distant future.

Cole was now an ace predator. He had scored 21 goals in the season so far, and 33 in only 28 starts for the Magpies since his move north. A 100 per cent strike-rate was phenomenal. He had promptly become the new No. 9 hero and an overnight sensation. His rise from Arsenal reserve to the Premiership's hottest property was astonishing, Sir John Hall saying: 'Andy Cole is our new Jackie Milburn.'

It was not all rosy in the Geordies' camp though. There were moments of friction between player and manager as United's centre-forward attempted to come to terms with his rapid lifestyle transformation. Cole had to adjust to an unaccustomed way of living and at first found it sometimes difficult. The 21 year old had to cope with the newly found star status and that was not easy in the goldfish bowl of football-daft Tyneside.

Andy shunned the spotlight, finding life in Newcastle was a bit of a culture shock. He admitted later to being 'a little starstruck'. He was a quiet, even shy individual off the field and some said he was a bit of a loner, although he struck up close friendships with several people, including Geordie midfielder Lee Clark. Cole wanted a laid-back, private life but was never going to achieve that as United's No. 9 hero. He wrote in his autobiography: 'It was totally manic. I had never experienced anything like it before. It was like being beamed up to another planet after my life in London.' Life in the North-east revolved around football and more football. He added: 'Soon they hailed me their King, just like Jackie Milburn and Malcolm Macdonald.' But Cole didn't want the adulation or acclaim. He added: 'That's what I was forced to accept. Centre-forwards are the very core of Newcastle football culture.'

He also chose to live in the old mining town of Crook – a megastar in the middle of nowhere – and that was not a good move. In addition, Andy Cole was one of the first coloured players to really make an impression in the North-east. While racism wasn't widespread, it was a problem which, to Cole's credit, he did much to eliminate and bridge the racial gap – a process continued by the likes of Les Ferdinand and Tino Asprilla in future years to an extent that it is no longer a problem for any coloured player on Tyneside. Rob Lee recorded: 'I think he became a bit lonely and homesick.' Cole's difficulties were not all recognised by the club, but they soon rectified the situation.

These difficulties bubbled over into the action on the field too. Following a match against Southampton at The Dell in October 1993, Cole was involved in a bust-up with Keegan after his teammate and friend Lee Clark fell foul of the manager. Andy was left out of preparations for the following trip to London and went AWOL, missing the League Cup fixture with Wimbledon in the capital. A media frenzy followed. The press were even invited by Keegan to go and find his star centre-forward, as United's boss said that he had no idea where he was.

The rift was healed within a week though following a summit meeting in Jesmond. Cole moved from the backwaters of Crook into the heart of the city and continued on a much publicised path to enter the record books as United's all-time top goalscorer in a single season.

As Newcastle pushed to secure a European place Cole kept scoring, netting a hat-trick against Coventry City in a 4–0 victory. In midfield and attack, United were simply irresistible, so typical of United's play that season. Cole and Beardsley were backed by Rob Lee, Ruel Fox, Lee Clark and Scott Sellars. As a result, most teams couldn't cope with the onslaught. Coventry certainly didn't and Cole, although struggling with an injury, claimed another three goals to go past the 30-goal barrier for United in the season. There was a real chance that Andy could reach the long-standing record set by Hughie Gallacher and George Robledo of 39 goals over a campaign in the 13 fixtures that remained.

Cole was dynamite. His whippet-like pace was his main strength, being electric over 10 to 20 yards, able to turn in a flash and sprint away from a defender. Sharp in the box and especially strong on his right foot, he hit the ball true and hard, low into the corners more often than not. Andy had a short back-lift in shooting and could swivel in tight situations. At 5 ft 11 in. tall and with a lean physique, he wasn't a battler or aerial menace but he did harass and was quite able to hit the net with his head too. Cool and clinical in front of goal with great anticipation, Andy possessed self-belief, a vital attribute for any striker. Although inexperienced, Cole learnt quickly, improving his positional play and building up his stamina. Keegan said of his centre-forward: 'He was just phenomenal.' Albert Stubbins, a past No. 9 hero, was hugely impressed and said of the new kid on the block: 'He is a deadly finisher in the box. His speed of movement is exceptional. No one is quicker. He has the reflexes and quickness of thought that is needed to pounce on the split-second chance. And he is still learning.'

He was in some ways lucky to be in the right place at the right time. Cole joined United just as the Kevin Keegan bandwagon was set to roll, and the boss had a major influence on Cole's rise to prominence. So too did his partner up front, Peter Beardsley. Cole would be the first to recognise the contribution Beardsley made to his rocket to fame. Beardsley was terrific for Cole. They hit it off straight away. Beardsley's vision was on the same wavelength. Andy was to note: 'He was a gift from the gods,' and he later admitted that the Tynesider was 'the best striker I have operated alongside'. It was, as Keegan said 'the best partnership in the Premier League'.

Beardsley not only prompted and coached on the field, but the magical little Geordie scored plenty of goals too, 24 over the season in United's free-scoring line-up – one of the best pairings in the club's history. It earned Peter a recall to the international scene as well.

Cole was also in the England reckoning, being selected for the Under-21 side against Poland and Holland, as well as his country's B eleven to face the Republic of Ireland. Many wanted Cole to be even included in the full squad. There was a significant lobby to fast-track the United No. 9 to the very top and he reached a place on Graham Taylor's substitute's bench against San Marino. He was a certainty to win a full cap, but a change in manager saw the new England boss, Terry Venables, ignore the petition and Andy had to wait for a senior debut.

By the time Keegan's squad travelled to Anfield for an eagerly awaited return clash with Liverpool during April, United were on course to clinch a UEFA Cup slot. Andy Cole had amassed 38 goals and was verging on breaking the 40-goal barrier for the first time in the club's history. Newcastle rarely won at Anfield, but another milestone was reached against the Reds as United recorded a deserved 2–0 victory with Cole hitting a beauty, a lightning move that started with goalkeeper Pavel Srnicek. The Czech international threw the ball out to Scott Sellars who quickly fed Fox on the wing. A sprint and cross saw Cole collect the ball and dart into the box before driving past David James with a stinging low shot.

Andy was on target to set the record. For over 40 years, Hughie Gallacher's (1926–27) and George Robledo's (1951–52) totals of 39 goals stood unchallenged. United's No. 9 sensation was going to change all that. On a Wednesday evening, Aston Villa turned up to face a United eleven at the peak of their vibrant attacking game. Villa were thrashed 5–1 in front of the usual near-capacity crowd and just before half-time St. James' Park erupted as never before when Andy Cole broke clear to strike his 40th goal of the season – described in the press as 'a fairytale occasion for Cole'.

The record-breaking strike put the Black'n'Whites 3–1 ahead and raised the new roof of the remodelled St. James' Park. Sellars carved a hole in the Villa defence and Cole sprung away in chase of the midfielder's astute pass. Sprinting towards the Leazes End goal he drew Nigel Spink out to meet him, sending the Villa keeper one way with a dummy before turning the other way to strike a whizzing right-foot shot low into the corner of the net.

Cole was mobbed by all 11 members of his team – every colleague knowing the significance of that goal. Gallowgate detonated with an ovation lasting almost five minutes. The ear-splitting roar was deafening as cheering, applause and the now hugely popular 'Andy Cole' song echoed around the arena in a wave of appreciation.

The season closed with another victory, a 2–0 win against Arsenal with, aptly, Cole and Beardsley on the scoresheet. Newcastle ended in third place and Cole finished the campaign with 41 goals. For a player who had never played in the top flight before to then go out and tear it apart was quite an astonishing achievement. He had now taken his United tally to 53 goals in only 57 matches. Andy lifted the Adidas Golden Boot and earned the PFA Young Player of the Year award, honours richly deserved.

SALE OF THE CENTURY

Newcastle were out of the starting blocks like Olympic sprinters as the 1994–95 season began. Cole led the line where he left off with six goals in the first six matches, including a thunderbolt against Chelsea on Tyneside, running onto John Beresford's speculative forward punt, beating Chelsea defender Kjeldbjerg on the turn then lashing a tremendous shot from the edge of the box into the top corner with his 'wrong' left foot. Goalkeeper Kharine dived into thin air as the ball flew high into the net.

United looked serious challengers to Manchester United in the title race while they were tipped to also have a run in the two domestic trophies and the UEFA Cup.

As the Magpies travelled to Belgium to face Royal Antwerp they were top of the Premier League and looking for a trophy. Antwerp were to be brushed aside with consummate ease as the Magpies won 10–2 on aggregate. Robert Lee fired home a hat-trick in the first leg and Cole repeated the dose at Gallowgate. Keegan noted: 'We were so good it's frightening.'

Cole hit another goal against much tougher opposition in Athletic Bilbao in the UEFA Cup 2nd round as United took a 3–0 lead – a finely executed header following neat build-up play – also earning a penalty which Beardsley converted. But the Magpies gave away two late goals to their talented Spanish opponents and that proved fatal. From that game in October, United's season fell apart, dropping from top spot in the table to fifth as injuries – and an astonishing transfer – wrecked the best laid plans.

Cole had been suffering from a shin splint complaint for several weeks, an injury that had also affected him in the previous season. He had to drop out of the action and spend four weeks on the sidelines with what was called a stress fracture, although Cole properly described it as 'restricted blood flow, diagnosed as compartment syndrome'. He had surgery and missed five games. The injury was a niggling one that took time to fully clear up, as a result of which Andy played on while not fully fit. No doubt as a consequence his sharpness was temporarily lost and he went through the customary centre-forward drought, going nine games without a goal into the New Year of 1995.

By the time Cole was ready to return, moves were taking place 150 miles south that would rock St. James' Park and stun the football world. Rivals Manchester United had been mightily impressed with Andy Cole. Manager Alex Ferguson had witnessed first hand his meteoric rise to become one of the most feared strikers in the country. The Old Trafford boss wanted the young talent as his spearhead in attack alongside Cantona and Giggs. He wanted his pace, awareness and expert placement of shot in a red Manchester United shirt.

During January, Ferguson lodged what was a daring raid to secure the Magpies' centre-forward. He offered a staggering near £7 million package – at a time when the British record fee stood at £5 million following Chris Sutton's move to Blackburn to partner Alan Shearer.

Kevin Keegan was taken aback at first but the amount of money was huge and he was keen to obtain Ferguson's youthful starlet Keith Gillespie, a winger with lots to offer. The Toon's boss thought long and hard. He had already been considering a change in strategy in his team building and was eager to sign another striker to support Cole, having eyed QPR's formidable England centre-forward Les Ferdinand. Keegan confirmed in his autobiography *Kevin Keegan*: 'It presented me with a chance of a gamble which, if it came off, would make Newcastle an even more exciting side to watch.' Few were aware of Keegan's plans at the time, but eventually he would use the cash to replace Cole and purchase another raiding winger to complement Gillespie. Three players of quality for the price of one sounded very good business.

Keegan consulted his directors and Hall and Co. were as shocked as the Toon Army were soon to be. Current Chairman Freddy Shepherd remembered that it was a deal 'completely out of the blue'. Douglas Hall made the comment: 'It hit us like a bombshell at first just as it hit not only our fans but the rest of the country as well.' The board, though, backed their manager's view and sanctioned the transfer.

In the end Keegan and United dramatically agreed to the deal – reported as £6.25 million plus Keith Gillespie – a near £7 million record package. However, in reality the amount paid for Gillespie in the joint deal was way under United's valuation of the rising star. Keegan later wrote that 'in truth it was more like £8.5 million'. When the news hit the streets, Tyneside was in uproar – only matched by Keegan's own departure two years later. Headlines were nothing new to the Geordies; they had become accustomed to major upheavals and goings-on, but as Alan Oliver wrote in *The Pink*: 'Tyneside was in a deep state of shock on Tuesday, 10 January 1995 – that was the day it was revealed that Newcastle United were selling Andy Cole.' It was the sale of the century.

Cole held regal status in Newcastle. He had scored 68 goals in 84 fixtures in only 22 months on Tyneside. He was young, still improving and a certainty to wear his country's shirt. And United didn't need the money. 'How could Newcastle sell him?' was the cry – 'and to the Magpies' biggest rivals?' The decision appeared ludicrous.

United's centre-forward had not asked for a transfer and was equally as surprised when he received a phone call from his boss. At the time, he had no desire to move – he had finally become settled on Tyneside. Shepherd later confirmed: 'He didn't want to go,' adding 'and I know he was genuine in that.' Cole himself noted to reporters: 'I'm shocked because I didn't think Newcastle would sell me to an English club.' There had been some speculation that Cole wanted to leave the North-east, but he later admitted that 'nothing could have been further from the truth'.

His colleagues were bewildered as well. Peter Beardsley wrote in his book *My Life Story*: 'I heard about it when I reported for training on the Tuesday morning and at first I thought somebody was pulling my leg.' Rob Lee noted: 'I found out about it the same way our fans did, watching the lunchtime news on the telly.'

Keegan said at the time: 'I have taken a chance. I was shocked initially at the very thought of letting Andy go.' He added that the deal had 'put my reputation, and my neck, on the line', Keegan later saying 'I believed that it was the right deal at the right time for Newcastle United.' United's boss had to face the wrath of Newcastle's supporters and it took guts to directly stand up to a gathering of irate Geordies on the steps of St. James' Park as the deal was concluded.

Newcastle's fans were angry, but almost to a man backed Keegan's judgement, testimony to the rapport he held with the Toon Army. They had faith in their Messiah – and the faith was to be returned as Keegan eventually brought his congregation not one centre-forward hero to the fold, but two.

ANDY COLE No. 9 RATING	
Fan appeal – personality and presence	9
Strike-rate	8
Shooting – power and placement	8
Heading	7
Ball skills	8
Link-play – passing, assists, crossing, team-play	8
Pace	10
Commitment – work-rate, courage	8
Match-winner – power-play, big-match capability	8
Longevity with United	3
Trophy success, international and top football ranking	1
Total No. 9 rating	78

In the short term Keegan had now given himself a problem – who was going to fill Andy Cole's boots? Paul Kitson had been purchased from Derby County for £2.25 million in September 1994 as something of a utility forward. An Under-21 striker, the County Durham-born player usually played off a leader. He was a talented footballer, slightly built, nimble and athletic with battling qualities. He was able to shield the ball well, turn and hit the target, but up to then had not been guaranteed a place.

The only other real option for Keegan was to give Scot Alex Mathie an extended run in the centre-forward role. He had arrived from Greenock Morton in the summer of 1993 as a promising striker and up to then had mainly sat on the bench, although when he did deputise for Cole, he rarely let the side down. But the stocky, blond forward was soon to be sold, like Cole, although for considerably less – joining Ipswich Town a month later for £500,000. The manager handed the opportunity to Kitson – although not the No. 9 shirt. It was mothballed and destined for Keegan's new superstar.

Ironically the first fixture after the Cole sale was at Gallowgate against Manchester United, of all clubs – the end of an extraordinary week on Tyneside. With Cole and Gillespie barred from taking part, an electric atmosphere greeted the two teams – and the two protagonists of the day, Keegan and Ferguson. United's boss was given vociferous backing and it was Cole's stand-in Paul Kitson who took the headlines with an equalising goal in the 1–1 draw. Kitson worked his socks off and latched onto an Elliott ball into the box. He turned past Pallister before drilling a low shot through Schmeichel's legs from the corner of the six-yard box.

In the FA Cup Kitson also made the headlines, striking a fine hat-trick in a 3–0 victory at St. James' Park over Swansea City to send the Welshmen reeling. His first was a brilliant glancing header, then Kitson got on the end of a Hottiger cross to strike the second. His hat-trick goal was perfect execution, taking a lob forward into the box and chesting the ball down before hooking delicately over the goalkeeper.

Everyone knew though, including his manager, that Kitson was not the long-term answer and he didn't deserve murmurs of disapproval from sections of the crowd who were becoming impatient at the lack of a big-name signing. Kitson took it in his stride, *The Journal* noting that he 'gritted his teeth and got on with the job' as he was forced to play up front on his own. Although he was a grafter and scored a respectable 12 goals for United that season, Kitson would be at his best as support for an out and out centre-forward. But that was not to be, as he was to soon move on as bigger names moved in. With United drifting from a challenging position in the title race, Keegan knew only too well he had to land a big deal to replace Cole before supporters jumped to the conclusion that United had gone back to their old ways of selling their best players. With over £10 million to spend, he made a bid for Les Ferdinand, but was unable to persuade QPR to do business.

The Black'n'Whites boss was not to take no for an answer though. He was a long-standing admirer of the powerful Ferdinand and when the Rangers striker destroyed the Magpies in a 0–3 defeat, scoring twice, United's boss had him at the top of his wanted list, continuing to chase the Londoner for the rest of the 1994–95 season. He was one of the most prized assets in the Premier League and Newcastle were not alone in trying to tempt Les away from Loftus Road. Aston Villa and Everton wanted him too and there was speculation that Arsenal, Tottenham and Paris St Germain were also interested.

Newcastle United eventually got their man during the summer of 1995, the deal being concluded in the early hours at a Hertfordshire hotel. Keegan's silver tongue quickly persuaded Ferdinand that Newcastle was the place to be. He wrote in his autobiography *Sir Les*: 'They already had good players at Newcastle, but he said I was going to be just the first of a few major signings and the club was really going to have a go for the title. That was the sort of thing I wanted to hear.' Ferdinand even took advice from his predecessor, Andy Cole, and United's former No. 9 gave Tyneside a glowing report. It was the highlight of a close-season spending spree that turned United into the country's most talked-about club. Keegan spent £14 million on Warren Barton, Shaka Hislop, French pin-up star David Ginola – and, at last, Les Ferdinand.

Keegan smashed United's record fee twice in the space of a week, first paying £4 million for England full-back Barton, then £6 million for 28-year-old Ferdinand. The Londoner born of St Lucian parents was at the peak of his career, having smashed 100 goals for Rangers and Besiktas. At 5 ft 11 in. tall and with closely cropped hair, he was big, brave, forceful, equally as good in the air as on the floor and able to lead the line with genuine menace – a perfect fit for the United No. 9 shirt.

LES FERDINAND
FACTS & FIGURES

To Newcastle United: June 1995 £6 million from Queens
  Park Rangers
From Newcastle United: August 1997 £6 million to
  Tottenham Hotspur
Born: London 8 December 1966
Height: 5 ft 11 in.
Other senior clubs: Brentford, Besiktas, West Ham
  United, Leicester City, Bolton Wanderers
England international: 17 app, 5 goals
Newcastle United app & goals:
  Premier League: 68 app, 41 goals
  FA Cup: 5 app, 2 goals
  FL Cup: 6 app, 3 goals
  Europe: 4 app, 4 goals
  Others: 1 app, 0 goals
  Total: 84 app, 50 goals
Strike-rate: League and Cup 60% (overall 60%)

Newcastle United gave Ferdinand the bigger platform he needed and he was soon impressed with the surroundings of St. James' Park. He said that it was so different to what he was used to and remembered later: 'I just couldn't believe how many people there were outside just to see me. It brought home to me very quickly just how much football means to the people in Newcastle.'

Brought up street-wise in the tough Ladbroke Grove neighbourhood of Paddington, Ferdinand had left school without a decent career and moved from job to job before starting on the route to stardom. He cleaned cars, decorated houses and became a van driver for a period. He was a late developer on the football scene and thought his big chance had passed him by as he appeared in the rough and tumble of the local non-league circuit with Viking Sports, Southall and Hayes. Ferdinand did taste fame for a brief moment as Southall reached the FA Vase final in 1986 but no offers came his way from professional clubs until former Magpie boss, Jim Smith, gave Les an opportunity to join the QPR staff in March 1987.

It took Ferdinand a while to make an impression at Loftus Road and he looked to be going nowhere fast, being loaned out to Brentford and to far-off Turkey with Besiktas in season 1988–89. That proved to be the turning point in the big striker's career. He went from QPR novice to Turkish hero almost overnight – and the omen was that Besiktas play in black and white too! As Ferdinand matured and shook off his early laid-back and somewhat hot-headed nature, he knuckled down to making himself into a top player.

When he returned to Loftus Road the Londoner made an impact as a new boss took charge. Under Gerry Francis, Les flourished and started to hit the net as QPR's centre-forward. He was called into Graham Taylor's England squad and made his debut soon after against San Marino. Ferdinand was an established striker in the top flight often scoring spectacular goals after surging runs from deep into the very heart of the opposition. There was much rumour of a move to a bigger stage, especially after he totalled 26 goals in season 1994–95.

SIR LES LEADS THE CHARGE

The arrival of Les Ferdinand extinguished any lingering doubts over the departure of Andy Cole. All supporters in the country respected the big Cockney. From the first moment Les pulled on the black and white No. 9 shirt, he became another Geordie hero.

Ferdinand got off to a flying start as the 1995–96 campaign opened with a home fixture in the sun against Coventry City. An emphatic 3–0 victory was capped by a goal from the Toon's new No. 9 seven minutes from the end. United's striker broke free just over the halfway line, dashed wide towards the Gallowgate End and past the advancing City goalkeeper John Filan, then buried a 35-yard putt from an acute angle into the empty net. Sir Les, as he was to be nicknamed, had arrived. He later recalled: 'When I scored the place erupted. A day I'll never forget.' Ferdinand added: 'I can't remember having a better feeling on a football pitch.' Ferdinand had the Toon Army's approval. *The Journal*'s reporter noted that Les had 'showed enough to prove he will be an awesome presence up front'.

Keegan's new breed of Entertainers roared to the head of the Premiership and Ferdinand couldn't stop scoring. He netted 16 goals in his first 13 games in Magpie colours. Les noted: 'Everything went to plan and my confidence just soared. I was unstoppable.'

There was talk of silverware. Judges considered Keegan had built a side that could go all the way – and in a flamboyant, attacking style. Newcastle United had not lifted the title since 1927 – all of 69 years ago, but now there was a real opportunity to bring the trophy back to Tyneside. Sir Les led United's assault on the Premiership crown. Not since 1951 had the Magpies made a determined bid to land the league championship.

For much of the season Newcastle did everything right. They led the way at the top of the table with Ferdinand the axis of all United's dazzling approach play through midfield and from each wing. Against Bolton Wanderers, he struck two outstanding goals all about his vigour and pace. Paul Nunn in *The Journal* wrote: 'He scored the first with the sort of aerial power that Newcastle haven't seen since the days of Wyn Davies. His second was more like Supermac as he powered through the middle on a 40-yard run before striking his shot perfectly.'

During September and October Ferdinand bagged 12 goals in 8 consecutive matches. He was on course for a scoring record but at White Hart Lane against Spurs he just failed to log a new club record of netting in nine games in a row – with a glaring injury-time miss from only ten yards out.

Ferdinand was expertly served on the flanks by Keith Gillespie – fast repaying his manager's faith in his ability – and Frenchman David Ginola, two players at the top of their game. They displayed panache and punch in their different ways. Gillespie was direct, Ginola mesmerising and both rained in a torrent of dangerous crosses for Les to capitalise on. Peter Beardsley and Rob Lee prompted from midfield and Ferdinand had a field day with the best season of his career.

The Londoner was the focus of United's attack, one of the most fluent elevens going forward anywhere in recent years. He was a different player to the lithe and lissom Andy Cole. Ferdinand was well built and powerful, great in the air and with cutting pace for such a sturdy frame. He could hit the ball with force and was as courageous as they come, turning average crosses into good ones with his never-say-die attitude. He led United's attack with two wide men and a midfield quick to support, Les being largely left up front in isolation. But that did not bother him. While sometimes his first touch was not always the best and while, like all strikers, he occasionally failed to hit the net when he should have scored, Ferdinand's record was still to be first class for the Magpies: 50 goals in 2 seasons. Colleague Peter Beardsley described Les as simply 'the best in the business'.

Wimbledon suffered at the boot and head of Ferdinand. So did Everton. At St. James' Park against the Dons, the big striker struck a hat-trick as he reached the peak of his form. He led the line magnificently as United won 6–1, hitting the net after a stunning Ginola run and cross that invited Ferdinand to soar upwards and nod home. His second was a brave dive into a ruck from another telling cross, this time from Gillespie. And the young Northern Ireland winger was provider again as another centre was headed back by Lee for the Cockney to gobble up a close-in chance.

At Goodison Park as United won 3–1, Les forced his way through the Everton midfield and defence to hit the net with a fabulous goal to push his claims for an England place alongside Blackburn's Alan Shearer. Howey fed Ferdinand with the ball in the centre-circle and the United No. 9 shrugged off Watson's challenge, raced at Unsworth, then rammed a stinging 25-yard right-foot shot past Neville Southall into the bottom of the net. With much media pressure, England boss Terry Venables eventually gave Ferdinand an opportunity alongside Shearer. Although a regular in the national squad, a place in the side wasn't automatic and Ferdinand usually found himself on the bench. Many said the pair were too alike to play alongside each other, but they performed well together in their limited England outings – as was to be very shortly underlined in a black and white shirt.

Tyneside buzzed with anticipation of a title victory. Only one side could stop the Magpies: Manchester United – and Andy Cole. At Old Trafford, who else but Cole destroyed the Black'n'Whites – scoring in a 2–0 victory. That gave the Reds hope in clawing back a huge points deficit. However, the Magpies recovered from that Christmas setback to increase their lead at the top, but as the final quarter of the season arrived the immense pressure began to tell. And Ferdinand's goals dried up.

United's centre-forward wrote in his book, *Sir Les*: 'I know better than anybody else, that I should have scored more goals than I did. I know that I could, and should, have had another eight or ten goals.' Ferdinand went on: 'The chances didn't dry up – I just stopped taking them.' Rob Lee noted in his autobiography: 'It was no coincidence that we lost the title when Les went off the boil after Christmas.'

It was far from being Ferdinand's fault – he picked up a hip injury but continued nevertheless and other players' form dipped at the wrong time too. Les had scored 21 goals in his first 22 league and cup matches and then only 8 in his last 22, including a mere 3 during the vital title run-in – crucial statistics. It was the difference between champions and runners-up. No other player replaced Les in the goal stakes when he went through a barren patch. Colombian Tino Asprilla had been purchased by Keegan in another big deal, this time £7.5 million from Italian club Parma. A highly talented striker, he needed time to settle and adjust to the Premier League and couldn't complement Ferdinand at the decisive time.

Manchester United piled on the pressure as they mounted a comeback, winning 1–0 at St. James' Park in a terrific match the Magpies should have won, with Ferdinand twice being foiled by a brilliant Peter Schmeichel. As the title race came to boiling point, the Geordies critically dropped points in three crucial away fixtures: 3–4 against Liverpool in the Premiership's Match of the Decade, and at both Blackburn and Nottingham Forest. Ferdinand rattled the crossbar at the City Ground at a vital moment, then Forest levelled. United's No. 9 was to say: 'You could see the will drain out of the players after the Forest equaliser.'

United had lost out narrowly to the Manchester Reds. It was hard to take after leading the pack for so long. Keegan's cavalier and enterprising football was still much praised and so was Les Ferdinand. He totalled 29 goals and became as popular as any past No. 9 to wear the Magpie shirt. Ferdinand was a picture of style and elegance, communicated well and was light-hearted; he was the perfect ambassador. He was handsome too and coupled with David Ginola, had the Toon girls swooning. St. James' Park was at times more like a cat-walk than a football club. And like Cole before him, Les also did much to kill off any lingering racist elements on Tyneside. United could get no better than Les Ferdinand in the No. 9 shirt – or so everyone thought.

ENTER THE £15 MILLION GEORDIE

Only one player in the country was recognised as a better centre-forward than United's current No. 9, Les Ferdinand, and he was an exiled Geordie much admired by Kevin Keegan – Blackburn's Alan Shearer. The Tynesider had totalled an impressive tally of 30 goals or more in the previous 3 seasons. Such was Newcastle United's swelling financial wealth that when hints surfaced that Shearer was available, the Magpies went for glory. The cry to Keegan from Sir John, his son Douglas and Freddy Shepherd was, almost as one: 'Go for it!'

Shearer had become the most feared goalgetter in England and after a display of power and clinical finishing for his country in the Euro 96 tournament during the summer, was rated one of the best centre-forwards in the world. Newcastle were determined to lure another big star to Tyneside and further reinforce Keegan's formidable international squad. They lost out to sign Dennis Bergkamp and Roberto Baggio, were linked to Gabriel Batistuta, but had the edge in the chase for Shearer as the England leader was a Magpie supporter at heart and past Keegan disciple as a kid. Shearer also had a real passion for the No. 9 shirt – the black and white stripes meaning as much to him as any member of the Toon Army. United's camp realised that if Shearer landed back in Newcastle it would be a deal that would set the Tyne alight. Keegan said: 'We knew that if we didn't have a go we would regret it for the rest of our lives.'

Another battle royal was played out between Newcastle and Manchester United, this time for Shearer. Arsenal and Liverpool were also in the hunt, as were a number of foreign clubs, including Barcelona, Internazionale and Juventus. But with Alan not wishing to go abroad, the chase ended up a two-horse race. Newcastle needed to make sure he didn't end up at Old Trafford, for if that had materialised there would be no stopping the Reds, as Keegan confirmed: 'It would have finished the league as a contest.'

Alan later recalled that he was leaning towards Manchester United at first, but after he met Kevin Keegan, under cloak and dagger circumstances, was excited at the prospect of returning home and wearing the black and white shirt. That was the crucial factor which swayed it for the exiled Geordie.

The transfer was settled just as United's squad were set to fly to the

Far East on tour and much of the deal was concluded by mobile phone in a Heathrow hotel car park! Keegan opted out of the flight to Bangkok to close negotiations at a hush-hush gathering in Crewe, at the home of David Platt's mother-in-law! Keegan noted: 'The biggest deal in football history was wrapped up in an hour and a half.' Current Chairman Freddy Shepherd called it 'the best bit of business ever done'.

The fee was a new world record – at £15 million – although Alan himself noted that the all-in amount was actually more, at £15.6 million! It was £2 million more than the amount paid by AC Milan for Gianluigi Lentini and almost double the British record of £8.5 million for Stan Collymore. After signing for the Magpies, Shearer said: 'What appeals to me more than anything is wearing the No. 9 shirt for my home-town club.' He added: 'It was always my dream.'

He was whisked some 7,000 miles to meet his teammates in Singapore, in the middle of their exhibition tour. Back on Tyneside, Shearer fever hit the Toon. The city went berserk at the news that United had signed their favourite son. On his return, Shearer was unveiled to a vast media circus and massed ranks of the Toon Army at St. James' Park. Up to 20,000 had gathered to cheer him 'back hyem'. The scene was incredible, expertly stage-managed and beamed worldwide.

With Shearer now firmly installed as the club's new talisman Keegan had a dilemma. He always intended playing both Ferdinand and Shearer together in attack, but who would wear the No. 9 shirt? It had fitted Ferdinand perfectly, but Shearer longed to pull on what, for him, was the shirt of Geordie folklore. Shearer wrote in his book *My Story So Far*: 'I was going to wear the famous black and white shirt, what's more, it would have the No. 9 on the back.' And Shearer admitted: 'That was a very important detail for me. As a Newcastle fanatic, I knew what it meant to wear it. I wanted to follow in the proud tradition. It meant a lot to me to be able to join the long line of Newcastle centre-forwards who had worn the number before me.'

Kevin Keegan admitted in his autobiography that his biggest problem was 'persuading Les to give up his Number 9 shirt'. There was a bit of a tug of war. Ferdinand at first had no intentions of doing so, he was a touch angry too, but Keegan was persuasive. Les didn't like it, but understood the intense feeling that underpinned why Alan Shearer wanted to wear the shirt so much. So Shearer took over the No. 9 shirt, Ferdinand wearing No. 10, this after some debate over a bespoke No. 99 compromise!

Newcastle United, with Shearer and Ferdinand leading the line as a formidable twin spearhead, were ready to challenge Manchester United again for Premiership honours. They were installed as favourites for the title and after the returning Geordie made his first appearance at the unlikely venue of a packed Sincil Bank, home of Lincoln City, supporters did not have to wait long before the rivals met face to face.

In the traditional pre-season FA Charity Shield curtain-raiser at Wembley, the two Uniteds locked horns. It was soon clear Newcastle had some adjustments to make to accommodate both Shearer and Ferdinand up front. Alex Ferguson's men demolished the Geordies embarrassingly by 0–4. Yet in time the Magpies adapted to life with Shearer and soon inflicted revenge on the men from Old Trafford.

It took Keegan's expensive squad – worth in the order of £55 million – three weeks to settle. Alan Shearer rammed home his first goal on his Gallowgate debut against Wimbledon and remembered: 'It was very special. Wearing the No. 9 shirt at St. James' Park gave me a buzz and thrill.' Near the end, United were awarded a free-kick to the left of the Leazes End box. Only one man was going to hit this one. Shearer stepped up and sent a vicious curling shot over and around the wall into the right-hand corner of the net. It was a peach of a goal. Alan said: 'I always dreamed about scoring at St. James' Park.' He added: 'I fancied my chances and the ball flew into the net. I was ecstatic.'

It was in the last derby encounter to be played at Sunderland's Roker Park that Newcastle really got going. Les Ferdinand grabbed the winner in a 2–1 victory, heading in Ginola's corner with pace and precision. From that success on Wearside, United roared back to the top of the Premiership with Shearer and Ferdinand causing mayhem. Newcastle won six games out of six in Premier League action and the partnership plundered ten goals. Sir Les struck a purple patch hitting eight goals in six matches while Shearer found his touch too, striking six in seven games played and then recording a run, split by injury, of seven goals in seven consecutive appearances.

Many pundits reckoned the partnership would never work. Some said they were both target men. Others noted it was not a natural combination and both were used to being the main striker. But the sceptics were proved totally wrong. Kevin Keegan had no doubts that his £21 million strike-force would be a success. He said that 'it could be the most potent in the Premiership'. They needed time to blend together, but when they did it was dynamite. Rob Lee recorded that it was 'the best striking partnership I have seen anywhere, without any doubt'. In the season, Shearer and Ferdinand scored 49 goals – a formidable total considering both were out of action for lengthy periods.

As Manchester United took to the Gallowgate surface during October, Newcastle were ready to inflict a spot of revenge. Shearer and Ferdinand were awesome and gave the Reds a torrid 90 minutes as Keegan's cavalry charge destroyed Ferguson's machine and inflicted a 5–0 hammering, the Old Trafford club's worst reverse for years. Ferdinand wrote: 'There was a lot of fire welling up in everyone's stomachs.'

St. James' Park was a cauldron of noise as Newcastle put on a marvellous display in what was to become a television classic, dominant in midfield and simply irresistible in attack where Ginola and Beardsley combined with Shearer and Ferdinand with ostentatious precision. Shearer hammered a shot against the post early on, then Peacock headed in the opening goal and Ginola's magnificent cross-shot made it 2–0. Ferdinand leapt to power a perfect Shearer cross off the bar and past Schmeichel for a third – United's No. 9 taunting the travelling Reds support who had jeered him for choosing Gallowgate instead of Old Trafford – and Shearer inflicted more grief on Ferguson's men as he fired the ball into the Leazes net following marvellous Beardsley approach play. With Philippe Albert's exquisite fifth crowning the victory, Shearer described the triumph as 'probably the most complete performance I have been involved with'.

After that convincing statement of intent Newcastle United looked like heading for the championship. But injuries rocked Keegan's side – and in particular knocks to both front men. First Shearer was sidelined with a persistent groin problem and then his partner sustained a depressed fracture of the cheekbone, as well as other mishaps which kept him out of action. Had the dynamic duo not missed almost a dozen games each, Newcastle could have well secured Premiership silverware.

LES FERDINAND No. 9 RATING	
Fan appeal – personality and presence	9
Strike-rate	6
Shooting – power and placement	8
Heading	9
Ball skills	7
Link-play – passing, assists, crossing, team-play	8
Pace	8
Commitment – work-rate, courage	8
Match-winner – power-play, big-match capability	8
Longevity with United	2
Trophy success, international and top football ranking	2
Total No. 9 rating	75

Another blow was around the corner too – an even bigger one. In true Newcastle tradition, news broke during January that Kevin Keegan had quit Gallowgate after a disagreement over the direction of the club as United moved to plc status. Everyone in football – on Tyneside and beyond – was stunned. The players were equally shocked, although Les Ferdinand suspected something was wrong. He recorded: 'Keegan had been acting strangely, and the speculation made sense.' And Shearer, who had joined the Black'n'Whites in many respects because of Keegan's influence and presence, said: 'It was a traumatic time for everybody.' He added: 'I was devastated when he left.' Having only six months earlier spent £15 million on a new No. 9, Keegan had jumped ship. It was disappointing and perplexing to everyone.

Newcastle United's directors acted swiftly and positively. In came Kenny Dalglish, another icon of football and who had latterly guided Blackburn to the Premier League title with Shearer as his hit-man up front. Alan noted: 'He was one of the very few people capable of following Keegan.'

Dalglish certainly had the credentials both as a player and manager. But instead of building on his predecessor's talented squad the Scot started to dismantle it, player by player – including tearing apart the highly successful Shearer and Ferdinand combination.

The remainder of the 1996–97 season was something of an anti-climax compared to what had gone before. After slipping from the

279

head of the table, Dalglish gave the Black'n'Whites a boost to finish as runners-up for the second year in a row – and qualify for a crack at the new Champions League.

Alan Shearer top-scored with 28 goals and Ferdinand netted 21. Included in Shearer's haul was a spectacular late hat-trick against Leicester City at St. James' Park. United were 1–3 behind with only 14 minutes left and looked to be dead and buried. Then Shearer struck. He thumped home a ferocious free-kick from the edge of the box, then fired a cross-shot beyond Kasey Keller and in the 91st minute he grabbed a dramatic winner, tapping in a Lee cross following a brilliant passing move.

During the summer break speculation grew that the boss was prepared to offload Sir Les, now 30 years old, and re-figure his side for the coming season around Shearer. Dalglish considered that playing two big front men was a luxury, despite their formidable record together. Kenny had three international strikers to choose from: Shearer, Ferdinand and the enigmatic Asprilla. He made it clear he would not play them all, and even would only play one – that, undoubtedly, being Shearer.

As Newcastle prepared for the start of the 1997–98 programme a bid of £6 million for Ferdinand landed on Dalglish's desk from Tottenham Hotspur. That sort of money was too good to refuse for a player into his 30s. Like Cole before him, Ferdinand did not want to go; he was quite content on Tyneside and part of the best strike pairing in the business. He had no reason to go back to London, even to the club he favoured more than any. But if Dalglish was not going to play him, he was certainly not going to hang around on the substitutes' bench. Alan Shearer later noted that Les was the best player he played alongside. He said: 'We had one great year together and my only regret is that we did not have a lot longer.'

There was some debate and dispute over who actually arrived at the judgement to allow Ferdinand to head south; the manager or directors. Chairman Freddy Shepherd later confirmed: 'Kenny Dalglish had made the decision to sell Les. Spurs were paying £6 million for him and Kenny thought it was too good an offer to turn down.'

Sir Les departed with disappointment. He later said of the move: 'I was told it was for financial reasons. But I was under no illusions. Kenny Dalglish was the manager and I knew that if he had said his team, as it stood, would win the Championship, they would have kept me.' He continued: 'I would have loved to have stayed a lot longer.'

Les added: 'I had a terrific relationship with the Newcastle fans. I was only at Newcastle for two years; it really means a lot to be remembered so much after so short a time.'

The Toon Army were reluctant to see him go. Most thought United were crazy to break the partnership up. Ferdinand's popularity was huge – even six years later when Les turned out for Leicester City at Gallowgate the ovation he received was awe-inspiring. Only Hughie Gallacher, Jackie Milburn and Supermac have received such a welcome back. But the stage now was set for Alan Shearer – perhaps Newcastle United's greatest No. 9 hero of all.

No. 9 EXTRAS

COLE HUNT

Newcastle United and Bristol City were unable to complete the transfer of Andy Cole to Tyneside – until someone could find the centre-forward! No one could locate him and a frantic search took place, eventually tracking down the superstar to his local launderette doing a spot of washing! Cole said in his biography: 'I didn't need to think twice, not with Kevin Keegan as the man in charge at St. James' Park.' Keegan was Cole's hero as a kid.

SPONTANEOUS VERSE

It was halfway through the second half of the 7–1 thrashing of Leicester City on the last day of the 1992–93 season that Andy Cole's famous terrace song really came to life. In a break in play, a section of the crowd started to voice the song and spontaneously the No. 9 chant erupted around the whole stadium. Cole stood bemused as over 30,000 sang in harmony for several minutes:

> Andy Cole, Andy Cole
> He gets the ball and scores a goal,
> Andy, Andy Cole

NICKNAMES

Several nicknames were created by the Toon Army and local media and handed to Andy Cole during his short stay on Tyneside. He was dubbed The Predator, after a cult movie of the day, as well as Cole the Goal, but perhaps the most popular was King Cole.

STRIKE-RATE

Andy Cole's goal-ratio in a black and white shirt is, next to Hughie Gallacher, the best by any United player. He boasts an 81% strike-rate, marginally behind Wee Hughie on 82%. Cole's goalscoring peaked during November 1993 when he achieved a 114% strike-rate, while over seven consecutive months he averaged a goal a game.

COLE – AFTER TOON

Under Alex Ferguson's guidance Andy Cole progressed his game further in a red Manchester United shirt. Developing into an experienced all-round striker, he soon became the first man to net five goals in a single game in the Premier League, against Ipswich Town during March 1995. Andy was a huge hit at Old Trafford, scoring 122 goals for Manchester United and in the process lifting five Premiership titles, twice winning the FA Cup, as well as the coveted European Champions League trophy in 1999. He also won 15 England caps before moving to Blackburn Rovers in 2001 for an £8 million fee then rejoining Fulham during 2004.

TURKISH DELIGHT

Les Ferdinand showed that he had the potential to develop into a top striker during a loan period with Turkish club Besiktas. He made a huge impact netting 21 goals in 33 games in season 1988–89. Les was influential as Besikas lifted the Turkish cup, scoring the deciding goal in the second leg – a 40-yard run past three players before rounding Fenerbahce's German goalkeeper Schumacher and rolling the ball into the net.

SIR LES

The popular nickname of Sir Les stuck with him after a match for QPR against Luton Town in season 1990–91. Supporters in London reckoned he was so gentlemanly on and off the field that they gave him the affectionate title – a nickname United supporters latched onto immediately and developed into cult standing.

FAMILY FERDINAND

The Ferdinand family has made quite an impression on modern football. Apart from Les himself reaching the very top, his cousin is Rio Ferdinand, Manchester United's £30 million England defender, while also related is Anton Ferdinand, one of West Ham United's bright young stars.

EMERGENCY No. 9

With almost £29 million worth of striking talent in Shearer, Ferdinand and Asprilla out injured, United turned to midfield general Rob Lee for an important UEFA Cup meeting with Monaco during March 1997. The England international – while not pulling on the No. 9 shirt – effectively played up front on his own in the centre-forward role. As always, Lee gave 100 per cent, but United lost by a single goal.

PLAYER OF THE YEAR

Les Ferdinand's form with United as they so nearly lifted the Premiership crown in 1995–96 earned the No. 9 the PFA Player of the Year award, the first Magpie player to lift the prized trophy. Les came out top of the players' poll, just ahead of Alan Shearer, and received the award from Pele at the Grosvenor House Hotel in London. It wasn't all joy on the night though, as the centre-forward had his PFA winner's medal stolen during the evening.

SIR LES – AFTER TOON

Joining his boyhood favourites Tottenham Hotspur was the next best thing to staying at St. James' Park for Les Ferdinand. He remained at White Hart Lane for six seasons, but didn't reach the heights of his peak form at Gallowgate, claiming fewer than 50 goals. Often troubled by injury, Les moved across London to help West Ham United in January 2003 then on to Leicester City for the 2003–04 season. Following Leicester's relegation he signed for Bolton Wanderers in July 2004, extending his Premiership career at the age of 38.

ENGLAND'S STRIKE-FORCE

Glenn Hoddle selected Newcastle United's Alan Shearer and Les Ferdinand to form England's twin strike-force against Poland during October 1996 at Wembley – the first occasion a Magpie duo had done so. In an important World Cup qualifier, two goals from Shearer gave England a 2–1 victory in front of a 74,663 crowd.

FIRST-HAND VIEW

Peter Beardsley played alongside all three of United's centre-forward aristocrats and noted that 'Newcastle have fielded the greatest No. 9s ever to have played in the Premiership.'

Andy Cole:

'His first season was incredible. No one has had a better season for Newcastle United than Andy Cole – a one-off unbelievable season.'

Les Ferdinand:

'Another fantastic centre-forward – Les was a bit of Andy Cole and Alan Shearer rolled into one. He had a brilliant start in the Newcastle No. 9 shirt.'

Alan Shearer:

'Second to none and totally irreplaceable – the most consistent No. 9 there's been. A great leader with a fantastic character. Probably Newcastle United's best ever No. 9.'

KEV'S ARISTOCRATS

Kevin Keegan gave Newcastle United the Premiership's three greatest centre-forwards. At the close season of 2004, the competition's top goalscorers chart read:

1. Alan Shearer   243 goals
2. Andy Cole   163 goals
3. Les Ferdinand   148 goals

10. GEORDIE BOY
1997–2004

Alan Shearer

They were zany and fantastic days for the Toon Army. Newcastle's exuberant supporters had served at the court of King Cole and followed Sir Les into combat. Now the Geordie legions had God himself – Alan Shearer, one of their very own.

Like almost every other young boy living in and around Newcastle, Alan Shearer was brought up with black and white blood. Born and raised in Gosforth, the son of a Tyneside sheet-metal worker, his father, and the rest of the Shearer family, were big Newcastle United supporters.

At school he was no academic but loved sports and as young Geordie kids do, played football morning, noon and night, often pulling on his replica Toon shirt. The young Shearer was spotted early as having football ability and was selected for both the Newcastle and Northumberland Boys teams, also appearing for local youth clubs at Wallsend Boys Club and Cramlington Juniors.

He was aware of Newcastle United's No. 9 tradition as a kid. His father had been brought up on the legend of Jackie Milburn, then worshipped Len White, Wyn Davies and Malcolm Macdonald. Alan said: 'I knew it was extra special, something very special. When I was a kid, I always wanted to be a centre-forward. I wanted the buzz and thrill of scoring goals from an early age.'

Yet it wasn't the centre-forward shirt Shearer longed for at that time. During his teens, the '80s saw the No. 9 shirt – for the only time in the club's history – overshadowed by the No. 7 version which belonged to a certain Kevin Keegan. It was Keegan who became the young Shearer's hero, as he did for thousands of other Geordies at the time. Shearer noted in his autobiography: 'I used to spend hours a day dreaming about the time in the future when I would step out and emulate my idol. I was Keegan daft.'

Alan once ended up at one of Keegan's 'Blue Star Soccer Days' along with a few hundred other kids. He actually won a prize of a day out at United's training ground alongside Keegan and the players. The young Shearer also spent a few days trying to impress United's talent spotters, and even took his turn between the posts trying to stop goals rather than belt the ball into the net as he was to do at the highest level in the future.

He queued like thousands of other teenage Tyneside lads for almost six hours to see Kevin Keegan's first match for the Black'n'Whites against QPR in 1982 and the future England skipper was also a ballboy in Keegan's farewell match against Liverpool almost two years later – captured on film walking around the pitch as the celebrations were under way.

North-east talent spotter Jack Hixon, then working for Southampton, liked the look of the youngster. He watched him play for Newcastle Boys at Benfield Park in 1983 and started to build up a relationship with Shearer, which is still as strong over 20 years later. Alan also had the opportunity to impress at West Bromwich Albion, Manchester City and again at Newcastle – and was offered terms – but the influence of Hixon led the young Tynesider on a long journey south. Alan now started thinking about actually becoming a centre-forward and wearing that No. 9 shirt his father and others spoke legends of.

A teenage Shearer headed for Southampton, some 350 miles from Tyneside, to begin his professional career in September 1984. He signed on schoolboy terms becoming a trainee two years later. His progress at The Dell was swift and he had plenty of friendly Geordie voices around him, the Saints having been recently led by Lawrie McMenemy, while Dave Merrington was still on the coaching staff. There was also a healthy contingent of fellow North-easterners in the playing ranks at The Dell, including Steve Davis, Barry Wilson, Neil Maddison and Steve Baker, while Ian Branfoot was later appointed boss. Shearer was a confident young man, although not blessed with natural, silky talent like some; he worked hard and possessed great determination, coupled with a will to succeed.

His introduction to the senior game was dramatic, claiming headlines in the fashion that was to follow. Following brief substitute appearances against Chelsea and Oxford United, Alan lined up for his first full outing against Arsenal in April 1988 and rattled in a hat-trick, becoming the youngest debutant to do so in the top division. He was 17 years 240 days old.

Shearer was soon to take the No. 9 shirt at The Dell and has rarely worn any other number in club or international football since, Alan noting: 'It wouldn't be the same wearing another. It's No. 9 for me.' The man who was to dominate the goalscoring charts for the next decade and more had arrived. He became a regular in season 1990–91 and by the following campaign the exiled North-easterner had come of age and was well on the way to stardom.

The young Shearer soon made a big impression and was selected for the England Under-21 side in 1990, graduating from his country's youth set-up. He immediately made an impact in his country's shirt as well, scoring twice on his debut against Eire. In 11 appearances, he grabbed 13 goals – an Under-21 record for many years – helping the Young England side to victory in the Toulon International Tournament where Alan scored the winner in the final against France. He was the star of the Toulon festival and the name of Alan Shearer was noted as an England leader of the future.

Southampton had found a gem, but top clubs began to look at their emerging centre-forward. He netted 43 goals at club level with the Saints and judges could see that in a better side with quality players – as proved at Under-21 level – Shearer could be devastating. Twenty-one of those goals came as the rising star really established himself in the 1991–92 season.

Newcastle United and Kevin Keegan, by then manager at St. James' Park, were one of those clubs interested. As early as 1992, the Magpies made a bid to bring Alan back to Tyneside but as the club was still in the old Second Division, that move was always a hopeful try rather than a deal with real conviction. They were thwarted by Kenny Dalglish who was bankrolled at Blackburn by Jack Walker's millions. The future Magpie boss was willing to pay almost any price to claim

Shearer's signature on a contract. Manchester United were also interested and boss Alex Ferguson noted later that nobody at Old Trafford could understand why Shearer didn't join them. Rovers topped all bids during the summer and the 21-year-old Tynesider moved to Ewood Park for a £3.6 million fee, then a new British record.

In the traditional blue and white quarters of Blackburn, Alan proceeded to register 130 goals, almost a goal a game over 4 seasons, and was the key figure as Rovers lifted the Premier League title in 1995 – still the only club to have secured the crown other than Manchester United and Arsenal. Netting 37 goals in that season Shearer combined with Chris Sutton in attack, the pairing being dubbed the 'SAS' of the Premiership. But he still had his heart in his roots and at one point confessed during his stay at Ewood: 'I'd like to play for Newcastle United before I retire. The club is in my blood.' And when Shearer was on a return visit to Gosforth at the height of the Hall revolution the *Evening Chronicle*'s Alan Oliver wrote: 'Shearer was taken with the transformation of the Magpies like everyone else.' Oliver added that Shearer 'jumped into his car and headed for the ground and simply drove round and round the stadium. I accepted then that it was just a matter of time before Alan Shearer wore the black and white of his home town'.

With England, Shearer had graduated to the full line-up and was manager Terry Venables' choice at centre-forward for Euro 96, the biggest soccer fanfare in the country since the World Cup of 1966. It was in that tournament that Shearer stepped up to being an international striker – and rated as world-class.

He made his debut for England four years earlier against France in February 1992 as a 21 year old – and Alan scored in a 2–0 victory. He was actually voted man of the match at Wembley, having also set up the second goal for Gary Lineker. Shearer was now part of the England set-up and was destined to take over from Lineker as England's marksman. But it wasn't until Terry Venables took over from Graham Taylor that England's – and Shearer's – fortune changed on the international stage.

With only a modest goal record for England up to that balmy summer of 1996, Shearer suddenly burst into action wearing his nation's shirt. He was top scorer with five goals and was the country's champion. He scored vital goals against Switzerland and Scotland then grabbed two in the 4–1 demolition of Holland. Alan played well in both the quarter-final and semi-final against Spain and Germany as England almost reached the final. Perhaps they should have, as the popular 'Three Lions, Football's Coming Home' song echoed throughout the nation.

It was Baddiel and Skinner's monster hit that also vibrated around Tyneside and at St. James' Park when United splashed out that world-record fee immediately after Euro 96. The tune was the same but the words changed slightly and the Toon Army now proudly roared: 'Shearer's Coming Home.'

ALAN SHEARER
FACTS & FIGURES

To Newcastle United: July 1996 from Blackburn Rovers
  £15 million
Born: Newcastle upon Tyne 13 August 1970
Height: 6 ft
Other senior clubs: Southampton
England international: 63 app, 30 goals
Newcastle United app & goals:
  Premier League: 243 app, 131 goals
  FA Cup: 29 app, 19 goals
  FL Cup: 13 app, 6 goals
  Europe: 36 app, 17 goals
  Others: 1 app, 0 goals
  Total*: 322 app, 173 goals
Strike-rate: League and Cup 54% (overall 54%)

---

*To cs 2004

INJURY SETBACK

After Shearer's successful first season in the black and white No. 9 shirt, 1997–98 proved a frustrating one for all; for player, supporters and the club. As preparations for the new campaign began, Geordie fans were first rocked at the sale of Les Ferdinand, this soon after Dalglish had allowed David Ginola to join Spurs. Ferdinand was to team up with the French playmaker at White Hart Lane for a £6 million fee. It was the start of a ruinous break-up of Keegan's five years of successful team building – a move to be disastrous for Newcastle United.

But that was not the end of the bad news. Worse was to follow. Deciding to prepare for the new season with Alan Shearer as his spearhead, Dalglish saw his plans wrecked on the same weekend that Ferdinand joined Spurs; Shearer fractured his fibula, badly ruptured ligaments around his ankle and displaced a joint at Goodison Park in a pre-season exhibition Umbro Cup tournament. Against Chelsea, United's key man went down awkwardly in an innocuous stretch for the ball. There was no other player near him. Shearer's studs stuck in the turf and threw him forward, horribly twisting and breaking his lower leg. He was to be out of action for almost six months.

Newcastle were in a panic. After possessing the best two strikers in the country, they suddenly were without both of them. They did try to put a halt to the Ferdinand move but the transaction had gone too far. And in any event Ferdinand noted: 'Through pride and everything else I couldn't go back on it now.' Sometime afterwards Freddy Shepherd made the comment: 'Les's sale was a mistake. We lost a great player and a great partnership was broken up. It was a wasted partnership, for we only had it for one year.'

Newcastle struggled without Ferdinand and Shearer. Dalglish had already bolstered his attacking options, but his new men were a pale shadow of the previous season's awesome duo. Danish striker Jon Dahl Tomasson arrived on Tyneside from Dutch football, while Georgian Temuri Ketsbaia landed from AEK Athens. Neither, though, were out-and-out centre-forwards. The Scot had to find a stop-gap to cover what was going to be a lengthy period on the sidelines for Shearer. Dalglish turned to his former colleague at Anfield, Welsh international Ian Rush, now almost 36 years old and languishing in Leeds United's reserve side. And that was not the end to the ex-Anfield old-boys pact. United's boss also brought in the ageing John Barnes, he too being pushed up front on occasion.

Dalglish was also to soon pay £3.6 million for Swede Andreas Andersson, a young and promising striker with AC Milan. Rush and Andersson, though, were no Ferdinand and Shearer and despite the options Dalglish had, United struggled to find goals. After five years of being able to hit the net almost at will and averaging 94 goals a season, the Magpies scored a mere 58 in the coming months.

With this headache, the Black'n'Whites entered the all-important Champions League qualifying match with Croatia Zagreb fielding a patched-up line-up. Tino Asprilla was in the centre-forward role, the one player Dalglish still had who could produce a few fireworks in attack.

United won the tie with a dramatic late goal from Ketsbaia to send the Magpies into the new dream world of UEFA's glitzy Champions League.

The popular Asprilla was a character who could – if he was in the mood – fill the gap up front. The enigmatic Colombian also seemed to come alive in European action and against Barcelona at Gallowgate on the club's Champions League debut, Tino was simply magic – and in front of a worldwide audience of around 150 countries.

A play-anywhere forward, Asprilla operated essentially as the Magpies' centre-forward – in spite of his No. 11 squad number. Tino was quite sensational and Barcelona's big names had no answer to his tricky and explosive style. He made and scored the opening penalty then, as Keith Gillespie's brilliant wing-play created telling crosses, Asprilla rose like a gazelle to bullet two headers past goalkeeper Ruud Hesp.

United's Champions League opening jamboree was spectacular and the Magpies received much acclaim, but Newcastle's hopes of further progress in Europe were halted when Asprilla was injured in the Group match with Dynamo Kiev. The South American found a place alongside Alan Shearer in the treatment room and afterwards on the manager's hit-list – one of many to be shown the exit door by Dalglish.

The manager's attacking options now hinged on free transfer Ian Rush. Although Rush had been one of the country's greatest goal scorers of modern times, his best years were behind him. Newcastle supporters were to see little of the incisive diagonal runs, unselfish work-rate and precise finishing that had made Rush one of Europe's top strikers. He had topped almost 350 goals over a 16-year period with Liverpool (interspersed with a spell at Juventus) but the former Anfield goal-poacher hit the net only twice for the Black'n'Whites – although included was a precious strike at Goodison Park to take United past the 3rd round of the FA Cup. However, it was only a cameo glimpse of the real Rush.

Goals continued to be at a premium and as a result Newcastle struggled for the first time in the Premier League. They were desperate for a fit Alan Shearer. His recuperation was steady and signs of a return to action started to surface at Christmas. When Shearer was announced during January 1998 as one of the substitutes in the St. James' Park dugout for the contest with Bolton Wanderers, the Toon Army's hopes were raised. United were locked in a basement struggle and needed points. The script was already written: United's No. 9 came off the bench to a huge welcome and inspired United to a 2–1 victory. Shearer was back, and back to lead the Magpies to Wembley – and remarkably he even ended up top scorer, albeit with only seven goals.

FA CUP BREEDING

Raised with the tradition of United's FA Cup exploits, Alan Shearer knew how much the famous old trophy meant to Magpie supporters. He once said: 'The FA Cup means a lot. There's a real passion for the competition which you don't get elsewhere. It's a love affair.' Shearer captured the folklore bred into the region. He added: 'It's part and parcel of living up here. People might think I'm daft, but I'm not wrong. I'd rather win the Cup than the league.'

A Shearer-inspired Magpies entered the action against non-leaguers Stevenage Borough. Even though he wasn't yet fully fit, his presence and goalscoring nous were far too good for the Vauxhall Conference outfit. He scored three times in the somewhat unsavoury tie, the England skipper punishing the non-leaguers for ill-mannered gamesmanship where it matters – on the pitch.

Shearer was again the difference against Tranmere Rovers in the 5th round. He grabbed the winner with a stock header. Full-back Pistone made a strong run down the left and Alan was on the end of his fine cross. Barnsley stood between United and a semi-final place for the first time since Supermac's brace in 1974. With the FA Cup now creating its magic, United cruised through by a 3–1 scoreline.

The Magpies faced First Division strugglers Sheffield United in the semi-final at Old Trafford and they were firm favourites to reach Wembley. Back in 1974 it had been United's No. 9 Malcolm Macdonald who stole the show. More than 20 years later it was Alan Shearer's turn. It was the Geordie centre-forward's strike in the 59th minute that broke the deadlock, although Newcastle should have been comfortably in front by then. Shearer climbed to meet a John Barnes cross at the far post. He powered a header down towards the net only for goalkeeper Alan Kelly to block it well. Shearer was alert though – the first to pounce and get to the loose ball. He crashed it into the back of the net and the massed ranks of the Toon Army erupted.

After two successive championship races, the Toon Army was now ready to sample FA Cup fever at Wembley – however, just as in the Premiership chase, United also ended runners-up twice in back-to-back finals. United and Shearer faced Double winners Arsenal in front of the Twin Towers. The Tynesiders were underdogs and were expected to at least give the Gunners a test – fighting for the trophy all the way. But United's performance was reminiscent of the Black'n'Whites back in 1974 – a tame display against a dominant side. United lost 0–2 and Shearer was starved of service, although had his 65th-minute strike against the woodwork entered the net instead of rebounding to safety, it could have been different. Alan noted: 'I was right in line with my shot and was convinced it was going in. I couldn't for the life of me work out how it didn't.'

It was almost the same story 12 months later in 1999 as Shearer, again inspired by FA Cup traditions, led his home-town club back to Wembley. This time Manchester United were the dominant opposition and Newcastle lost again, by the same scoreline, and Shearer hardly got a kick. He described the defeat as 'a hammer blow'.

Lots had happened at St. James' Park between those Wembley appointments. The Magpies rarely stayed out of the headlines for long and following the club's poor display against Arsenal, boss Kenny Dalglish came under heavy criticism. Most considered the torrent of adverse comment was justified, United having slipped from stylish title challengers to mediocre fodder while Keegan's squad had all but been dismantled.

Dalglish acted to stem the discontent by taking out the cheque-book. One of his first signings during the summer of 1998 was to bring one of the much acclaimed French World Cup winners to Tyneside as a strike partner for Shearer. It wasn't rising stars Pires or Henry, nor Trezeguet. Instead Stephane Guivarc'h – a player who had a formidable goals record in domestic French action but little pedigree at international level. At £3.5 million, Guivarc'h flopped badly, managing a single goal against Liverpool before being sent on his way.

Dalglish did not last long as the 1998–99 season began, being replaced by another high-profile boss, Ruud Gullit. The former Dutch star started to remodel the squad. Out went Guivarc'h quickly – to Rangers – and in came support for Shearer in the considerable frame of Everton's captain, Duncan Ferguson, at £8 million. Gullit noted: 'When Les Ferdinand was at Newcastle, he did a specific job for Alan and that's why he scored so many goals. I brought Duncan to work in a similar way with him.'

As with Les Ferdinand, many reckoned the two big guys up front couldn't play together. But as with Ferdinand – and with both Mike Newell and Chris Sutton at Blackburn – Shearer formed a mouth-watering partnership with the Scot. The presence of Ferguson unshackled Shearer from being the lone target man. It gave Shearer more space, more chances would fall his way, and he could concentrate on his forte as a goal predator. The result – more goals. The only problem was keeping the big Scot fit and in the action.

Ferguson had been through a chequered career after making a name for himself with Dundee United and enjoying a dream move to Ibrox with Glasgow Rangers. Formidable in the air at 6 ft 4 in. tall and deceivingly skilful and quick for a big man, United coach Tommy Craig said of Ferguson: 'He is a battering ram who can play – a physically intimidating target man with a great first touch.' Ferguson was a fiery character and his quick temper had brought him into hot water with the Scottish Football Association, many considering Ferguson to be a marked man north of the border.

The new £23 million twin strike-force would be a formidable combination, although Shearer missed the Scot's first appearance against Wimbledon when Ferguson claimed two goals. His aggressive and passionate style gave United a fearsome front pairing, as Shearer was also not one to hold back. Ferguson was a belligerent character and scrapped for the ball too. Defenders were in for a torrid time. Stuart Pearce, then at St. James' Park on the final leg of his distinguished career, described the duo as 'the toughest physical challenge in British football'.

Ferguson, however, soon picked up a troublesome groin injury and was to miss most of the remainder of the programme – and then a persistent calf injury also kept him on the sidelines. Gullit and Shearer had to battle on without his menace in the air and delicate touch on the floor. In the end, Ferguson managed only 32 starts for the Geordies, hardly a satisfactory return for such an expensive purchase.

By now United were back on the scent of the FA Cup – and so was Alan Shearer. On course to get close to Jackie Milburn's all-time FA Cup goals record for the club, Shearer moved into overdrive and banged home a goal against Crystal Palace in the 3rd round. Then Alan did what he does best again in the 4th round, this time hitting the target against Bradford City.

He missed the tough deciding replay against his former club, Blackburn Rovers, and it was left to young 20-year-old French striker Louis Saha, on loan from Metz, to guide United through with a brilliant winner. Taking a defence-splitting 60-yard diagonal pass from German international Didi Hamann, Saha drilled a well-placed cross-shot into the net. Saha was to be released at the end of the season, a decision the Magpies regretted as he moved back to England with Fulham then on to Manchester United for almost £13 million as well as graduating into the French national side.

Newcastle's favourite son was back on the mark again in the quarter-final against Everton as the Black'n'Whites won convincingly 4–1. Shearer netted a beauty to round off a fine display – a piledriver from the edge of the box after delightful approach play by the distinctive bald-headed Ketsbaia.

United were back at Old Trafford for the semi-final – and the stage was set once more for Newcastle's No. 9, Alan Shearer. Tottenham Hotspur – with Les Ferdinand and David Ginola – faced the Magpies this time and a tense 90 minutes ended goalless. Extra time, though, brought goals and two for Alan Shearer on his way to taking his total for the season to 21.

It was Shearer's day again. He first converted a penalty in the 108th minute after Sol Campbell's hand ball – the most important and nerve-tingling spot-kick of his life. Then the Geordie idol struck a fabulous second nine minutes later. Silvio Maric laid the ball into Shearer's path 20 yards from goal. A first time swerving shot flew wide of keeper Walker and into the top corner of the net off the bar. Alan later described the goal: 'The ball came square to me on the edge of the box, I hit it on the run, and the ball curved away from the keeper high up into the net.' Brian Woolnough in *The Sun* described United's No. 9: 'This was Shearer, the stone cold killer, the man who may have cost millions but who also makes millions for his club.' The 26,000 United fans in Old Trafford's swaying North Stand were in Shearer heaven. The hero worship was at its peak – Toon fans even adorning the 65 ft Angel of the North landmark with a giant No. 9 replica shirt! Wembley beckoned again, but it was the Black'n'Whites who climbed the famous steps first and had to watch the trophy being presented to Roy Keane in the red shirt of Manchester United.

DOUBLE DUTCH

Alan Shearer had enjoyed an excellent relationship with both Kevin Keegan and Kenny Dalglish; however, the bond between star player and Ruud Gullit was not so healthy. As the 1999–2000 season unfolded, United's dressing-room spirit was anything but good.

Gullit ostracised long-serving midfielder Rob Lee and handed the captaincy to Shearer, although the way it was done almost forced Alan to reject it. There was conflict with other players too, for the

Dutchman, while being respected for what he had achieved in a sparkling career, did not appear to have man-management skills, being somewhat aloof from his team.

It was suspected that Gullit wasn't Shearer's number one fan and never fancied him as a top player – in perhaps the mould of some of his Dutch colleagues of the past. Indeed, sometime later Gullit was interviewed about his controversial period on Tyneside and his view of Shearer: 'I told him to his face he was the most overrated player I have seen.' Rob Lee recalled that 'the relationship between Alan and Ruud went downhill early on'. Stuart Pearce wrote in his autobiography *Psycho*: 'They didn't like each other and he [Gullit] tried to push Shearer into asking for a move.' The former England favourite added: 'There was no love lost between Alan and Ruud Gullit, as there was no love between a number of players and the manager.'

Gullit, it appeared, wanted to alter the team strategy and even offload the Geordie icon. He noted in an interview in the *News of the World*: 'If we were going to succeed as a team I knew we had to change the way Alan Shearer played, but he didn't want to change.'

All this internal strife came to a head during what many supporters still fervently consider is the most important clash of any season – a local Tyne versus Wear derby. Gullit chose to have both Shearer and Ferguson – £23 million worth of international striking talent – on the bench and instead fielded rookie Paul Robinson up front against the Black'n'Whites' sternest opponents.

Shearer later remarked: 'I'd never been dropped in my career before that match so to find myself on the bench for such an important game was a big shock.' And the way it was done – by simply pinning the team-sheet to the wall – added to the swirling storm that was about to whip through Gallowgate.

It didn't make any sense to have your best two players in the dugout. It was all double Dutch to many. Ruud was signing his own death warrant. It was as if the script had been pre-written; Sunderland won 1–2 in monsoon weather and condemnation followed from every quarter – from the boardroom, dressing-room and punter in the street. Gullit had chosen to take on United's biggest ever player – and a Geordie icon at that. There was only going to be one outcome – reminiscent of Duggie Livingstone's challenge to the aura around Jackie Milburn over 40 years before. The outcry was rapid and vitriolic from all quarters and the result was that Gullit was quickly on his way back to Holland.

During September 1999 in came an exiled local favourite and Newcastle United supporter at heart, Bobby Robson – former England player, successful Ipswich Town, Porto, Sporting Lisbon, PSV, Barcelona and national boss, the 66-year-old doyen of the managerial fraternity. He was respected by all and immediately set to work to repair a broken superteam.

Since Keegan's departure, United's stylish football had disappeared. Shearer had, on his arrival back in the summer of 1996, expected to be joining a side full of attacking quality. That only lasted for one season. He had to endure successive regimes that went off the rails. Now it was hoped new boss Bobby Robson would recapture the Entertainers' style and get the best out of Alan Shearer – still the country's top striker.

Robson had actually tried to sign Alan when at Barcelona and his influence immediately had an effect. First to be revitalised was Shearer. Alan was to say that there was 'a big possibility that I would have had to leave Newcastle United if Ruud Gullit had stayed'. Robson soon noted on his arrival: 'Alan was down when I took over – very down – just about on the point of leaving.' But the former England boss had a good chat to United's No. 9 and got him playing again. Rob Lee confirmed that 'Alan and Bobby got on very well from the word go'.

With Shearer, Ferguson and Rob Lee, as well as other outcasts Dabizas and Pistone, all back in the fold, Newcastle started to recapture their form. Robson was the difference. On his first game in charge at St. James' Park, the Magpies went nap against Sheffield Wednesday, winning 8–0 – with Shearer having a field day and scoring no fewer than five goals. His bagful equalled Andy Cole's Premiership record and is the best haul the striker has scored in a single fixture.

Shearer made a mockery of some who said he was way past his best, going on to record ten goals in four outings. He grabbed a first-half hat-trick against the Owls and did what Shearer does better than anyone: snap up the chances in and around the six-yard box. Ian Murtagh captured the Toon Army's feelings writing in *The Journal*: 'Here was a glorious throwback to the days of Kevin Keegan when this stadium rained goals and quaking opponents collapsed under the weight of Newcastle United's attacking rage.'

A fit Duncan Ferguson was also a boost for Robson. The Scot lined up with Shearer and established a flourishing partnership which brought 40 goals by the end of the season. Shearer claimed 30, his best return in a black and white shirt as United steered clear of any relegation threat. His influence that season was immense. Robson said: 'I do shudder to think where this club might have been without him.'

Ferguson played his part too as a twin striker and his effort to complement Shearer's double in a convincing 3–0 victory over Manchester United showed that, when fit and eager, Ferguson could be every bit as good as Ferdinand alongside United's England leader. The Scot lashed in a 20-yard volley past Mark Bosnich – but he was to be soon back in the treatment room.

The pair helped United climb to mid-table and on yet another FA Cup run resulting in the Toon's third visit to Wembley in successive seasons. Against Tottenham Hotspur in the 3rd round United faced a tough contest but following a 1–1 stalemate at White Hart Lane an invigorated Magpie eleven thrashed the Cockneys 6–1 on Tyneside. Alan Shearer was back amongst FA Cup glory, scoring twice in the final ten minutes to wrap up the convincing victory.

Alan had the FA Cup scent again as he netted in a 4–1 triumph over Sheffield United and then he was the talk of the Toon once more when he faced his old club Blackburn Rovers at Ewood Park. Newcastle's skipper was surprisingly given a hot reception by the Lancashire fans. That was a dangerous thing to do. Shearer struck two goals in Newcastle's fine 2–1 success; the first the result of a Ferguson headed flick, a dash clear and cool finish, the other a close-in conversion from a Domi run and cross.

In the quarter-final United faced giant-killers Tranmere Rovers and won through to another semi-final by a 3–2 margin. Shearer was one step from his third FA Cup final in a row – and was to be back at Wembley early as both semi-finals were staged at the soon to be demolished national stadium.

Wembley had been a happy hunting ground for the Black'n'Whites in the distant past but was now a graveyard and held a jinx over Newcastle United, just as the old Crystal Palace arena did to the Magpies' celebrated Edwardian side a century ago. Shearer was to say after another defeat in front of the marble domes, 1–2 to Chelsea, his fourth reverse there with the Magpies and sixth in club football: 'The sooner they knock this place down the better for Newcastle United.'

Not that United and Shearer played badly against Chelsea. Against the fashionable Londoners, the Toon deserved to win, but critically most of United's chances fell to others and not to the deadly boot of Shearer. He did create an equalising goal for Rob Lee after a typical wing surge and precision cross. He was probably United's best player, giving Chelsea's World Cup-winning defensive pairing of Desailly and Leboeuf an uncomfortable afternoon in the sun. But Shearer had lost out again in his ultimate goal of winning something with his hometown club.

Undeterred, the focus was again very much on a trophy as Newcastle entered the new millennium. Shearer was reignited and a proud skipper of the side at an enlarged St. James' Park now holding almost 52,000 every match day. And Shearer was even more determined now that the club was back on track under Robson's experienced guidance, although it would take a full season of rebuilding before the Geordies could say they had completed their renaissance.

Injury to their talisman was also to hamper the Magpies and Shearer was to return to the treatment room after feeling a twinge in a match with Middlesbrough. He played on but dropped out of contention with a tendonitis complaint during December 2000. Newcastle's centre-forward was sidelined for just about the rest of the season, although he made a brief comeback in February – only to quickly head back to see the surgeon.

United should have been able to rely on expensive new signing Carl Cort, but he too was injured soon after a £7 million move from Wimbledon. The leggy striker looked a good acquisition when he played, hitting goals, but unluckily he was crocked again on his return and eventually moved to Wolves for less than half the amount United splashed out and a meagre return of 8 goals in 28 appearances.

In stepped 18-year-old Shola Ameobi, a home-grown product raised on Tyneside although born in Nigeria. Ameobi was a talented striker, tall and with lots of skill, and was in many ways a raw Tino Asprilla. He showed audacious trickery, an eye for goal, and was soon in the England Under-21 reckoning. In the coming seasons, Ameobi was to establish himself as a Premiership striker.

Another bad injury to Shearer was a huge blow for both the team and for Alan personally. Although the Tynesider had achieved much in his career and scored so many goals, he remarkably had to do it in spite of a series of nasty injuries, some of which were career-threatening. At Ewood Park with Blackburn, he was out of action for eight months after cruciate ligament surgery, then suffered serious groin problems and that horrendous break at Goodison Park. Now it was another ominous injury that put the Shearer machine at risk, and there were to be more knocks to follow. All told, Newcastle's centre-forward has undergone more than a dozen operations in his career – yet has still kept going and still bagged the goals.

Shearer though is a man of great character. He had to be to recover from such mishaps. Kevin Keegan once said: 'You have to be brave to keep coming back from the type of serious injury he has suffered.' Shearer possesses single-minded determination to recover from each setback. And despite the injuries he never let up on the field. Once fit again he was quickly in the thick of the action, always willing to take the knocks in his rugged battles with centre-halves, while he would slide into a tackle without hesitation.

Shearer at this time decided to retire from international football, due in part to the catalogue of injuries. United's No. 9 proclaimed he would now concentrate on club football alone after 63 matches and 30 goals for his country. There were too many games and he needed a rest during the summer. At almost 30 years of age, his body simply could not cope with top-class action all year round. Alan's place in England's Hall of Fame is guaranteed. Appointed his country's skipper under Glenn Hoddle, only three players have scored more goals. He appeared in three European Championships and the 1998 World Cup finals in France.

TROPHY HUNT

Alan Shearer was given both a new partner and a new provider for the 2001–02 season; two signings that catapulted United back into the reckoning for, if not silverware, at least European qualification. With Ferguson having moved back to Goodison Park at a big loss after only 12 goals and Cort struggling to make an impact, Robson spent £6.5 million on Welsh international Craig Bellamy from Coventry City. Small, tigerish and fast, Bellamy proved to be the ideal partner.

Robson also splashed out another £9.5 million on lively French winger Laurent Robert to provide the ammunition for Shearer to feed on – just as Ginola and Gillespie had done for one short but productive season. Newcastle now had a potent front line again – capable of challenging Manchester United and Arsenal at the top of the Premiership.

Shearer returned to action a week into the new season, joining Bellamy and Robert for a double local feast against both Sunderland and Middlesbrough. When the crowd's favourite came off the bench at St. James' Park against the traditional Wear enemy, the reception was sensational. Out of action for over eight months apart from an odd comeback bid, he ran onto the pitch to a hero's welcome from over 50,000 and played out the final 15 minutes of a 1–1 draw. Then Shearer was back in the groove against Boro as a revitalised Magpie eleven won 4–1 – Alan twice bulging the net in familiar fashion after Robert's telling penetration.

Shearer and Bellamy were terrific and hit 42 goals as United chased for the title. By Christmas they topped the table following two stirring away victories at Arsenal and Leeds, Alan belting home some of his most notable strikes in a 27-goal haul. He scored his 100th Magpie goal against Ipswich Town during November 2001 and against Aston Villa in April the Gallowgate crowd were served up an unerring shot from a wide angle. Shearer recalled the goal from Rob Lee's diagonal ball: 'As it came to me, I met it on the volley and it flew straight into the far corner.'

Then a few days later United's skipper also fired home his 200th Premiership goal against Charlton Athletic. Gary Speed played Shearer clean through the middle and as Charlton keeper Dean Kiely came out, Alan whipped a right-foot shot with venom into the Gallowgate End net.

That was a special landmark. Shearer had been the first player to reach 100 goals in the Premiership. Now he was the first to hit 200. Described as the archetypal English centre-forward, no other British striker was better. Not blessed with the finesse of a Marco van Basten, or with terrific pace like Andy Cole, as Malcolm Macdonald said: 'Shearer has adapted his play brilliantly to take account of his limitations.' The Geordie worked hard to develop his all-round game to become the master No. 9. John Barnes wrote: 'Alan is not particularly quick but he usually reaches balls clipped over the top. He is not particularly tall but he scores frequently with his head. For someone who isn't particularly skilful, Alan can drop his shoulder and drill a 30-yard right-footer past a keeper.'

He works the channels like no other in the modern game and is one of the most intelligent players around. Alan's football brain is aware all the time, while most importantly, he knows where the goal is. Shearer has fabulous timing at striking the ball with either boot or head. Favouring his right, he can hit shots hard and true, or place them astutely into the corners. Dangerous close-in or from outside the box, his shooting can be awesome. In the air, he climbs and muscles his way to the ball, and invariably if he meets it the ball ends up in the net. An ace predator, a good delivery into the box always spells danger if Shearer is around. Bobby Robson noted: 'If you get the ball across goal he is going to be there to get an effort in on goal.' And valued colleague Rob Lee said: 'You can rely on him to put the ball in the back of the net, and if you had to put your house on any one player taking an opportunity in a game, this is the man.'

In later years Alan has played a lot with his back to goal for United where he acts as the traditional target man, holding the ball up and playing in others like Craig Bellamy. He copes with the ball played long, either flicking it on or taking it down under control, shielding it and then bringing teammates into the attack. And for years Shearer has proved he is the best crosser of the ball in a black and white shirt, able to screw it back with pace and precision, while many would also say he has been United's top centre-half too! At set-pieces he is consistently the player who clears at the near post.

Utterly resolute and mentally strong, managers Keegan and Dalglish admired him immensely. Keegan said: 'He is single-minded and focused.' His successor at St. James' Park, Kenny Dalglish, remarked: 'He has lots of qualities, on and off the pitch, and one of them is certainly his determination. That's possibly his biggest asset.' United and England colleague David Batty wrote in his autobiography that Alan had almost everything: 'Attitude, presence, confidence, influence, character and ability', although Batty did point out that his work-rate was not the best. The tigerish midfielder said: 'Alan used to stand in the middle while we ran around him.' Yet that was not unusual for goal-poachers. Another ex-Magpie England player, Chris Waddle, commented: 'He is almost the perfect centre-forward for the English game. He closes people down, he can hold the ball up, run with it, he's good in the air and he's dangerous inside or outside the box.'

Shearer plays the battling centre-forward's game better than anyone in modern times. Knowing all the tricks of his trade, he wins lots of free-kicks against defenders. He backs in and drops, he goes down on the half-turn. It can be infuriating for defenders. Not only that, Shearer is a fierce competitor and is not intimidated. Courageous, rugged and strong in the challenge, he possesses a combative streak, mixes it, takes knocks and gives them – but always plays the game fairly. He is simply a tough act. Shearer rarely loses his cool in the scrap either, having an exemplary record over 15 years as a regular, only twice being sent off and on both occasions, against Aston Villa and Charlton, he was harshly judged. Indeed, one decision at The Valley was reversed while the other is still to this day a travesty of justice imposed by referee Uriah Rennie.

Many eminent football names considered Shearer to be the perfect leader of men, an inspiration – an ideal skipper. He possesses a stable personality and is an outstanding ambassador for club and country – the genuine model professional in an era when many superstars have gone off the tracks. Back in 1996, on signing for Newcastle United, Henry Winter described Shearer in the *Daily Telegraph* as: 'Outwardly modest, yet inwardly driven; an uncomplaining warrior in a world of flying feet and elbows; a man committed to the team and his family; a manager's joy; the champion of the terraces. If any footballer is worth £15 million, Alan Shearer is.'

That record signing thrust Shearer into the limelight like never before. Yet he handled the media, his critics and plenty of 'Shearer Baiting' around the grounds with seemingly masterful ease and often he proved the doubters wrong or gave those who taunted him a taste of his goal power. Despite his sometimes straight face in front of the cameras, in the dressing-room or off-stage as David Batty noted: 'He is one of the biggest jokers in the pack.'

United's No. 9 hero handled the pressure and never looked like buckling under the colossal weight and expectation that has surrounded his every move and word on Tyneside. He came to terms with the celebrity status like few other icons in the region, even to the level of its unprecedented modern intensity. Shearer could never do the normal things; he would be swamped by well-wishers – even having to once arrange for a local department store to open after hours to allow the star to purchase furniture. But it worried him little. Deep down Shearer is a down-to-earth Geordie. As he once famously said: 'I'm just a sheet-metal worker's son from Gosforth.'

With Shearer in full flow, injury again wrecked the season for United – but this time not to their No. 9 spearhead. At a crucial stage in the title chase, Shearer lost Kieron Dyer's support from midfield, then with Bellamy picking up a serious knee injury in a 1–0 victory over Sunderland on Wearside, the cutting edge up front was lost. Yet again fate had robbed United of a consistent partnership in attack. After Ferguson and Cort, now Bellamy was out of action. In stepped the fit again Carl Cort to deputise in the final weeks of the season. United though were not the same threat without Bellamy buzzing around and feeding off the experienced shoulders of Shearer. However, the Magpies did claim fourth spot and a Champions League place as consolation, Shearer hitting the net with two goals at Ewood Park to secure the points.

Having missed United's last foray into Europe's showpiece due to injury and having only briefly tasted Champions League football at Blackburn, Shearer could now sample life on the biggest stage on offer. It was to be a very eventful tour of Europe this time round for the Magpies and United's No. 9 was in the thick of the action. With Bellamy back to form in what Shearer described as a 'sort of pace-power partnership' the Tynesiders, though, had a wretched start to their Group E campaign. They lost to Dynamo Kiev and Feyenoord, then lost again to Juventus in the Stadio Delle Alpi. The Geordies were unlucky when Shearer netted what was considered a 'good' goal in Turin but had his clinical header chalked off for offside.

No one in football gave the Magpies a hope of qualifying for the next stage, and few of even the most dedicated in the Toon Army did either. Yet amazingly Shearer led by example on the pitch to turn disaster into glory. Newcastle confounded all the critics by winning their last three games to qualify in dramatic record-breaking fashion at the De Kuip stadium, home of Feyenoord – a 3–2 triumph with an injury-time goal from Bellamy.

They had beaten Juventus and Kiev in return fixtures – thanks to goals from Griffin, Shearer and Bellamy – before that theatrical evening in Rotterdam sent the Magpies into the next mini-league of the glittering and money-spinning competition. Newcastle once more started disastrously – committing suicide within five minutes of the clash with Internazionale at Gallowgate. Bellamy reacted to stereotypical Italian pokes and kicks in the box, then so did Shearer who uncharacteristically lost his cool.

Bellamy saw the red card, while Shearer escaped on the night but was found guilty by a UEFA video trial and was banned for two games. He missed the trip to face Barcelona in the Nou Camp, but was back for the second of two meetings with Bayer Leverkusen, Shearer claiming a hat-trick as the Magpies destroyed the Germans at St. James' Park.

United's front two were back in tandem for the mouth-watering return with Inter at the awesome San Siro during March. Newcastle needed a victory and should have got one, with Shearer twice converting crosses, each time to put United ahead in front of a 53,459 crowd, including 10,000 Geordies. It would have been a tremendous victory but was not to be. Eventual finalists Inter pulled goals back to level at 1–1, then 2–2 and pinched a point.

Although the Tynesiders missed a place in the quarter-final, Shearer had a brilliant season logging another 25 goals, passing milestone after milestone on the way. He became Newcastle's top European goalscorer, overtaking Wyn Davies' total, then went past Hughie Gallacher's career effort for the Magpies. He now aimed for Jackie Milburn's top spot in the club's all-time goalscoring table. Then against Manchester City at St. James' Park during January 2003, Alan entered the record books by striking one of the quickest goals ever witnessed – after only ten seconds. Ex-United centre-half Steve Howey rolled the ball back from the kick-off to his keeper Carlo Nash. He took a poor first touch and Shearer was in like a flash. He charged the ball down, got a rebound and slid the ball into the empty net. It was timed at 10.4 seconds.

It was also opportune that Shearer set another landmark by notching his 300th league and cup goal at his former club, Blackburn Rovers, during the season, a confidently drilled penalty. Alan netted several corkers that year, including what he recognised as his best-ever goal against Everton a few weeks later, his 146th for the Black'n'Whites. It was also an important one in the chase for a Champions League place. In the 86th minute, United needed something special – and Shearer provided it. Laurent Robert swung a ball across field and Ameobi headed the ball down in front of the box. The ball sat up beautifully and Shearer struck a 76.5 mph volley from 22 yards that dipped wickedly and flew past Richard Wright in the Everton goal. Alan said: 'It was a case of head down, pull the trigger and let go. I just hit the ball as hard as I could.'

Few in the game have a bad word to say against Newcastle's standard-bearer. He is the best in the business and most say so. Blackburn Rovers boss and future Toon manager Graeme Souness noted as Alan approached 300 goals: 'I think he's up there with any centre-forward England have ever had; he's an absolute legend.'

With Shearer's goals and inspirational leadership Newcastle did have an outside chance of the Premier League in that 2002–03 season but as before, United's bid stuttered and fizzled out – mainly due to the loss of midfield anchor Gary Speed and yet another injury to Alan Shearer. Against Sunderland he fractured a bone in his ankle during a testy Tyne–Wear derby.

The Geordie ended the season battered, bruised and on crutches – his ankle in plaster. In many ways, it characterised the battle-scarred No. 9 idol and his never-say-die spirit for United's cause. Only two weeks before against Manchester United he broke a knuckle in his hand after a clash; a few days later against Aston Villa he ended the game blooded and with a giant head bandage – the legacy of four stitches in a wound; then in the next game, he limped off at the Stadium of Light with that foot injury.

Shearer is in many ways a throwback to yesteryear. He is a gutsy player who largely ignores the fancy tricks as well as the changing hairstyles and superstar trimmings of diamond earrings. Shearer is a warhorse of the old school with goals as his trademark. John Gibson wrote in *The Pink*: 'He is the epitome of what a No. 9 ought to be – strong, brave, powerful in the air, the shot of a sniper, and a true leader.'

ALAN SHEARER
No. 9 RATING

Fan appeal – personality and presence	10
Strike-rate	5
Shooting – power and placement	10
Heading	9
Ball-skills	7
Link-play – passing, assists, crossing, team-play	9
Pace	7
Commitment – work-rate, courage	9
Match-winner – power-play, big-match capability	9
Longevity with United	8
Trophy success, international and top football ranking	2
Total No. 9 rating	85

Shearer's reputation at that time was never as high. Even at 33 years old the goals kept coming as he played some of the best football of his career. As Chris Waddle noted: 'He matured with age.' Consistency – in spite of injury – has made him not only the best No. 9 of his generation but also one of the country's all-time greats. He has repeatedly hit the target season by season, averaging 20 goals each campaign in his Premiership career, a strike-rate of 64 per cent over 12 seasons. Statistics rarely lie.

A FINAL FLING

As a new season began Alan announced that he would retire at the top, at the end of the following 2004–05 season. The Toon captain wanted to go out in glory, winning a trophy for his club – one of the big reasons he joined the Magpies back in 1996. He was desperate to hold aloft some silverware for Newcastle United and noted: 'I don't care which one it is, as long as we get something before I go.' He had two campaigns, a final fling at lifting a trophy, his loyalty to his home-town club justly deserved.

Season 2003–04 did not start well, however. Craig Bellamy was again frustratingly sidelined with a knee injury and while Ameobi came into the line-up and performed well – improving his game all the time – the complementary bond of experience, pace and aggression that defenders hated with Bellamy and Shearer in harness was missing.

A Champions League qualifier defeat to Partizan Belgrade was a catastrophic blow and that setback took weeks to recover from. The club still had the UEFA Cup to go at, although they soon lost out to West Bromwich Albion in the League Cup, fielding a weakened squad line-up – minus the likes of Shearer and Speed as manager Bobby Robson rotated his squad and paid the penalty.

Nevertheless Shearer was, as the terrace song noted, the 'Same Old Shearer, Always Scoring'. He grabbed two goals at Leeds on the opening day of the Premier League programme and continued bulging the net en route to another 28 goals in the season. He possessed pride and class that stood out. Shay Given remarked in an interview for the *Sunday Times*: 'He's been phenomenal. He's the main man, our captain and our talisman.'

With Shearer in such good form, United gradually moved up the table and challenged for fourth place behind Arsenal, Manchester United and Chelsea, but were never likely to make a bid for the ultimate prize of the Premier League. Shearer's dreams of lifting the FA Cup for the Magpies also faded as Liverpool halted United's progress following a brilliant 3rd-round victory at the St Mary's Stadium in Southampton. His hopes of winning a trophy were diminishing rapidly, yet he was still scoring goals. After United defeated Fulham 3–2 in London when Shearer created one and scored twice, boss Bobby Robson commented: 'Alan Shearer gave an absolutely awesome performance. He was outstanding, his movement, his aerial power and the way he held the ball up all game.'

The UEFA Cup was all that was left. Newcastle had defeated NEC Breda and Basel and a hungry Craig Bellamy returned to play alongside Shearer to take care of Norwegian opposition Valerenga. The front pairing was too hot for the Real Mallorca defence as they netted five in the 7–1 aggregate triumph. Sir Bobby Robson's former club, PSV Eindhoven, stood between the Black'n'Whites and a semi-final place. A closely fought double header was played out which saw United squeeze through to meet French giants Olympique Marseille. Shearer was one step from the final.

The Magpies, however, needed their first-choice eleven on the pitch to have any real chance of lifting the trophy. And the unlucky hand of fate – in the shape of injury – rocked the Toon, and Shearer's bid to hold up silverware. Once again, at the crucial point of the season, four key players were ruled out. Firstly Kieron Dyer was sidelined; then Craig Bellamy, who had returned with gusto to renew a potent pairing with Shearer, netting seven goals, pulled a hamstring at Villa Park. England midfielder Jermaine Jenas joined the growing injury list and worse was to follow. Jonathan Woodgate, the king-pin of the defence, also pulled a muscle and was out for the rest of the season as well as the Euro 2004 Championship. The Magpies missed his vital influence at the back, not to mention Dyer's and Bellamy's piercing sprints in attack.

United now needed the erratic magic of Laurent Robert more than ever if they were to have any chance. Frustratingly though, the Frenchman did not appear to be in the mood. With a depleted side, the Magpies travelled to Provence all level following a 0–0 draw on Tyneside but in a hostile atmosphere of a near capacity 60,000 Velodrome stadium, Newcastle lost by two goals. Shearer's bid to land a trophy was over. He said: 'I'm very disappointed, but so is everyone. I've got another year to try and do it, so we'll have to wait and see.'

As an added blow United failed to qualify for the Champions League – taking a UEFA Cup place instead – following an end of season slump, although a year-long dismal away record proved their undoing. It had been a disappointing stop-start campaign with Shearer often starved of the service he thrives on – telling crosses into the box, Sir Bobby Robson once noting: 'It's flank play which gives Alan 30 or 40 per cent of his game.' He was still capable of scoring goals of 'Shear' brilliance on his own. Towards the end of the season in a mouth-watering clash with Chelsea at St. James' Park, he scored the winner with a stunning 25-yarder into the Gallowgate End net. Alan said: 'I had to take the ball into my feet and turn.' Then United's skipper hit it with his trusty right boot. The ball screamed into the top corner of the net. It was one of his best. Shearer confirmed: 'It's certainly up there in my top two or three.'

At the end of the 2003–04 season Shearer had totalled 173 goals for United, only 27 short of Jackie Milburn's all-time league and cup target. He also recorded a formidable total of 389 career goals in first-class football, and was heading to hit the magical 400 landmark. Very few centre-forwards in football's entire history have achieved that milestone at the top level. His place in English football's annals is assured alongside the likes of Dixie Dean, Tommy Lawton and Jimmy Greaves. The great Len Shackleton wrote just before he died in his updated and celebrated biography *Return of the Clown Prince*: 'At his peak, I felt that Shearer was as good as there has ever been.'

Life is rarely dull in the corridors of St. James' Park and as the 2004–05 season began a chain of events unfolded which culminated in the departure of Sir Bobby Robson after a miserable start to the new campaign. Newsflash followed newsflash: intense transfer activity that saw the arrival of Dutch centre-forward Patrick Kluivert amongst others, speculation surrounding Alan Shearer's future, as well as the record departure of Jonathan Woodgate to Real Madrid – and the near £25 million bid for Wayne Rooney – not to mention a conjunctivitis outbreak, a headlining Kieron Dyer bust-up and most importantly, a continuation of United's defensive frailty in Premiership action. This all resulted in Chairman Freddy Shepherd calling a halt to Robson's five-year reign at the end of August.

As is so often the case, history was to repeat itself four games into the season. Just as Ruud Gullit was to quickly depart after relegating Shearer to the bench for that Tyne–Wear derby in 1999, so too was Robson 'relieved of his duties' after leaving United's No. 9 out of the team for the visit to Villa Park.

It has frequently been touted that Alan Shearer would one day take the hot seat at Gallowgate. The sudden vacancy though was too soon for Shearer. After much speculation United's No. 9 noted: 'This is a huge club and a huge job and I do not think I am ready for it.' Alan added that he was 'too young' yet confirmed that he did 'want to be a manager one day. If it was at Newcastle in the future then that would be great'. But for now Shearer wanted to concentrate on his last season as a player and that bid for a trophy.

Newcastle looked elsewhere and eventually appointed Blackburn's Graeme Souness as boss with the hope that the ex-Liverpool and Scotland star would settle the camp and guide the Magpies – and their talismanic No. 9 – to silverware. A firm Shearer fan, he was even determined to attempt to persuade the former England leader to extend his playing career.

Now already a living legend on Tyneside, is Alan Shearer the pick of the whole line of distinguished centre-forwards who have worn the Shirt of Legends? That is difficult, even impossible to judge. Shearer's time occurred as football has developed into a fast, sophisticated and professional game, when media coverage has never been so intense. The limelight and glare of publicity is huge, at times overpowering. Hughie Gallacher never had that, neither did Jackie Milburn. Supermac experienced the spotlight, but nothing like to the extent that is now focused on modern football with its saturation television, radio and press coverage to a worldwide audience.

Newcastle United's No. 9 heroes have been, over time, a mix of players with different qualities. No two players have been the same. Some have been rip-roaring centre-forwards, some goal-poachers, others highly skilled individuals, some mean muscular types. They have been big and powerful as well as small and tricky. The finest to have pulled on the famous shirt are undoubtedly Gallacher, Milburn, Macdonald and Shearer, four top internationals. Look at their goal records – as Malcolm Macdonald himself once said: 'Put your goals on the table.' Gallacher recorded 143 for United and over 460 in his career. Milburn, all told, claimed 239 for the Magpies, Macdonald hit the net on 138 occasions wearing Toon colours, while Shearer is heading for a double century. All were different types of player, from very different eras. All contrasting breeds of men too; from Gallacher, the rough Scottish diamond, to Milburn's humble and gentlemanly nature. Of the four, only Jackie Milburn and Hughie Gallacher have achieved trophy success in black and white stripes so far. And that counts. Perhaps Shearer will join them in his last campaign wearing the captivating and mythical No. 9 shirt.

There are a few more games and goals to come from Alan Shearer yet. When this favourite Geordie Boy calls a day to the end of a truly marvellous career, the kudos and folklore of Newcastle United's No. 9 shirt will continue through generations to come as it has done for the last century. Maybe a bright and eager local youngster will take on the prized crown, capture the spirit and earn a name in history. Or maybe a headline multi-million signing from home or abroad will arrive on Tyneside and do the same. Whoever it is, supporters will continue the hero worship and expect much from the man wearing the Shirt of Legends. And the legend will live on.

No. 9 EXTRAS

KEEGAN ON SHEARER

The manager who spent the world-record fee to bring Shearer to Tyneside noted: 'He's a natural leader who conducts himself in a totally professional manner on and off the pitch. Alan has the respect of players at club and international levels and he's a fine role model for youngsters.'

GOAL SALUTE

Alan Shearer's famous right-arm-raised goal salute is one of the everlasting images of the first decade of Premiership football. From a teenager at The Dell, Alan has raced away in the same characteristic fashion and rarely has done anything different after hitting the net. There has been the odd variation now and again: at Blackburn – and occasionally with Newcastle – he went down on one knee, pointing to the crowd, while if the goal was a bit extra special, the celebration became a two-arm-raised address to the crowd.

SHEARER IN TUNE

During his time on Tyneside several songs have been composed with Alan Shearer the focus, both as supporter melodies and published discs, including 'Shearer's Back' (Busker), 'Hey Shearer, Ooh Ahh' (DJ Rob & DJ Spike) which includes the line 'Our super-striker wears the No. 9' and 'Shearer Shearer' (Dingo). Baddiel, Skinner and The Lightning Seeds' 'Three Lions' also had a Toon Army version, 'Shearer's Coming Home'. Other favourite supporter songs included 'Same Old Shearer, Always Scoring' and 'England, England's No 1 – England's No 1' as well as the Geordie drone of 'Shear—er, Shear—er, Shear—er'!

HIS MASTER'S VOICE

Alan Shearer on his home debut:

'I want to savour every second, because I know how special it's going to be.'

Alan Shearer on scoring for the first time in a black and white shirt:

'I had achieved something I had been dreaming about since I was a young kid.'

Alan Shearer on hitting the net:

'It's an unbelievable feeling for a Geordie, scoring in front of thousands of his own people.'

SCOTS TIME

Duncan Ferguson often fell foul of referees in Scotland before his move south. Worse followed when he was charged and found guilty of assaulting Paul McStay in an Old Firm match during April 1995. He was sentenced to three months in Glasgow's tough Barlinnie Prison. On release, he left his native country, joining Everton for a £4.3 million fee.

ENGLAND CALLS

Alan Shearer achieved a formidable record when his country called. He scored on his debut against France and captained the Under-21 and full sides, being appointed skipper of the senior eleven in August 1996. Only three other players have scored more goals for their country: Bobby Charlton (49), Gary Lineker (48) and Jimmy Greaves (44). Shearer is equal on 30 goals with Nat Lofthouse and Tom Finney.

HONOURS FEAST

Alan Shearer was awarded the OBE for his services to football in the Queen's Honours List in June 2001 while he also received the Freedom of Newcastle upon Tyne, an award that goes to a select few who have represented the city with distinction. Alan lifted the FWA Footballer of the Year award in 1994 and twice the PFA Player of the Year trophy, in 1995 and 1997.

PREMIERSHIP KING

Alan Shearer has been crowned the Premiership's undisputed king. He has scored most goals in a career, was the first to hit both 100 and 200 goals – the only man to reach the double century – as well as striking most goals in a season (34). He also shares (with Andy Cole) the scoring record in an individual Premier League fixture (5 goals). And as the Premier League announced their 10-Year Awards in 2003, Alan picked up accolades galore including the distinguished prize of the competition's Player of the Decade in addition to Top Goalscorer and the player who has made the most Outstanding Contribution. He also lifted the PFA's Player of the Decade award too.

ROBSON ON SHEARER

United's former manager Sir Bobby Robson said of his skipper:

'He leads the attack with courage and quality; he's a superb team player and an inspirational captain.'

'As a player he is up there with the very best – with the Lofthouses, Lawtons, Linekers and any other great striker you care to mention.'

GOAL KING

Alan Shearer's formidable international, league, cup and competitive match record is impressive:

Southampton	1987–1992	148 app, 38 goals	26% strike-rate
Blackburn Rovers	1992–1996	170 app, 130 goals	76% strike-rate
Newcastle United	1996–2004*	321 app, 173 goals	54% strike-rate
England (full)	1992–2000	63 app, 30 goals	48% strike-rate
England (B, u21, unofficial)		13 app,13 goals	100% strike-rate
Other competitive		10 app, 5 goals	50% strike-rate
Total*		725 app, 389 goals	54% strike-rate

*to cs 2004

SHEAR BRILLIANCE

Alan Shearer has scored many, many quite brilliant goals for Newcastle United and it's a difficult task to select his five best strikes in a black and white shirt. Alan picked his stunning volley against Everton as the best of the lot but left it to others to place the rest:

1 **v. Everton**: St. James' Park, December 2002, Premier League – an awesome dipping volley from outside the box.
2 **v. Chelsea**: St. James' Park, April 2004, Premier League – a turn and arrow-like shot from 25 yards.
3 **v. Tottenham Hotspur**: Old Trafford, April 1999, FA Cup – an unstoppable swerving drive into the top corner from the edge of the box.
4 **v. Aston Villa**: St. James' Park, November 2001, Premier League – a controlled, precision volley across Schmeichel and high into the net.
5 **v. Tottenham Hotspur**: St. James' Park, December 1996, Premier

League – a chase for the ball with three defenders, a chest down and volleyed finish into the top corner.

SHEAR CLASS

How the goals came for Newcastle United, all 173 of them:

Headers	41	24%
Shots close-in	26	15%
Shots 6 to 18 yards in the box	49	28%
Shots outside the box	16	9%
Free-kicks, direct	5	3%
Penalties	36	21%
Total*	173	

*to cs 2004

WHAT THEY SAY

Chairman, Freddy Shepherd:

'His leadership, his professionalism and his attitude are all magnificent.'

Jimmy Greaves:

'In the last ten years, Alan Shearer has been unquestionably the best – head and shoulders above everybody else.'

Pele:

'Everybody knows his talent. He is the kind of player I used to say I wanted in my team.'

APPENDIX

FACTS, FIGURES AND ODDITIES

The following analysis of Newcastle United's No. 9 stars does not necessarily include all players who have played in the centre-forward role over their career. Most of the statistics relate to those players who have normally operated in the No. 9 shirt over an extended period. Not generally considered in statistics are those men who have made occasional appearances as leader of the attack.

No. 9 RATING

While comparisons between players of different eras are difficult in the extreme, the No. 9 Rating included throughout this book attempts to score each of United's principal centre-forwards over the years. This analysis is a mix of factual statistical data and the author's personal impression from both watching as a spectator and through extensive research. A weighting score has also been included, e.g. players gain extra points for winning trophies with United, or becoming an international player, and conversely lose points if they have played a significant amount of their football out of the top division.

1 Jackie Milburn	86
2 Hughie Gallacher	85
2 Alan Shearer	85
4 Len White	83
5 Albert Stubbins	82
6 Malcolm Macdonald	81
7 Albert Shepherd	80
8 Andy Cole	78
9 Wyn Davies	76
10 Les Ferdinand	75
11 Chris Waddle	73
12 Neil Harris	72
12 Jack Allen	72
14 Bill Appleyard	71
14 Charlie Wayman	71
14 Billy Cairns	71
14 Jock Peddie	71
18 Vic Keeble	70
19 Jack Smith	69
20 Barrie Thomas	68
21 Mick Quinn	66
22 Ron McGarry	65

No. 9 TIMEFRAME

United's prominent centre-forwards over the years, league and cup matches, strike-rate and honours with the Magpies:

Willie Thompson				
1892–97	5 yrs	100 app 49 gls	49%	
Jock Peddie				
1897–1902	5 yrs	136 app 78 gls	57%	Scot trial, Div2 prom
Bob McColl				
1901–04	3 yrs	67 app 20 gls	30%	Scotland
Bill Appleyard				
1903–08	5 yrs	145 app 87 gls	60%	Eng res, LChw, FACf
Albert Shepherd				
1908–14	6 yrs	123 app 92 gls	75%	England, LChw, FACw
Billy Hibbert				
1911–20	9 yrs	155 app 49 gls	32%	Eng trial

Neil Harris
1920–25   5½ yrs   194 app 101 gls   52%   Scotland, FACw
Hughie Gallacher
1925–30   5 yrs   174 app 143 gls   82%   Scotland, LChw
Jack Allen
1931–34   3½ yrs   90 app 41 gls   46%   FACw
Jack Smith
1934–38   3½ yrs   112 app 73 gls   65%
Billy Cairns
1933–44   10 yrs   90 app 53 gls   59%
Albert Stubbins
1936–46   9½ yrs   30 app 6 gls   20%   England war*
Charlie Wayman
1941–47   6 yrs   53 app 36 gls   68%
Jackie Milburn
1943–57   14 yrs   397 app 200 gls   50%   England, FACw,
                                             Div2 prom
Vic Keeble
1952–57   5½ yrs   120 app 67 gls   56%   FACw
Len White
1953–62   9 yrs   269 app 153 gls   57%   FACw
Barrie Thomas
1962–64   2½ yrs   78 app 50 gls   64%
Ron McGarry
1962–67   4 yrs   132 app 46 gls   35%   Div2ch
Wyn Davies
1966–71   5 yrs   216 app 53 gls   25%   Wales, ICFCw
Malcolm Macdonald
1971–76   5 yrs   228 app 121 gls   53%   England, FACf, FLCf
Micky Burns
1974–78   4 yrs   180 app 48 gls   27%   FLCf
Peter Withe
1978–80   2 yrs   83 app 27 gls   33%
Imre Varadi
1981–83   2 yrs   90 app 42 gls   47%
Chris Waddle
1980–85   5 yrs   191 app 52 gls   27%   England, Div2 prom
Paul Goddard
1986–88   2 yrs   70 app 23 gls   33%

Mirandinha
1987–90   2 yrs‡   63 app 23 gls   37%
Mick Quinn
1989–92   3½ yrs   133 app 63 gls   47%
David Kelly
1991–93   2 yrs   79 app 38 gls   48%   Eire, Div1ch
Andy Cole
1993–95   2 yrs   84 app 68 gls   81%   Div1ch
Les Ferdinand
1995–97   2 yrs   83 app 50 gls   60%   England
Alan Shearer (to cs 2004)
1996–2004   8 yrs   321 app 173 gls   54%   England, FACf

Footnotes:

*Albert Stubbins scored a further 231 goals in 188 appearances during wartime with an overall strike-rate of 109%.

‡Mirandinha spent a year on loan back at Palmeiras before permanent deal completed in 1990.

MOST APPEARANCES
In a Newcastle United career, league and cup matches, all positions:

1 Jimmy Lawrence   496 app
2 Frank Hudspeth   472 app
3 Frank Clark   457 app
4 Bill McCracken   432 app
5 Alf McMichael   431 app
6 David Craig   412 app
7 Bobby Mitchell   408 app
8 Jackie Milburn   397 app
9 Robert Lee   380 app
10 Wilf Low   367 app
10 Tom McDonald   367 app

As a regular centre-forward:

1 Jackie Milburn   397 app
2 Alan Shearer   321 app (to cs 2004)
3 Len White   269 app
4 Malcolm Macdonald   228 app
5 Wyn Davies   216 app

Most appearances per competition as a centre-forward:
League app – 353, Jackie Milburn
FA Cup app – 44, Jackie Milburn
FL Cup app – 18, Malcolm Macdonald
European app – 36, Alan Shearer (to cs 2004)
Wartime app – 188, Albert Stubbins

MOST GOALS

In a Newcastle United career, league and cup matches, all positions:

1 Jackie Milburn	200 goals	
2 Alan Shearer	173 goals (to cs 2004)	
3 Len White	153 goals	
4 Hughie Gallacher	143 goals	
5 Malcolm Macdonald	121 goals	
6 Peter Beardsley	119 goals	
7 Tom McDonald	113 goals	
7 Bobby Mitchell	113 goals	
9 Neil Harris	101 goals	
10 Bryan Robson	97 goals	

As centre-forward, league and cup matches:

1 Jackie Milburn	200 goals
2 Alan Shearer	173 goals (to cs 2004)
3 Len White	153 goals
4 Hughie Gallacher	143 goals
5 Malcolm Macdonald	121 goals

Most goals per competition as a centre-forward:
League goals – 177, Jackie Milburn
FA Cup goals – 23, Jackie Milburn
FL Cup goals – 12, Malcolm Macdonald
European goals – 17, Alan Shearer (to cs 2004)
Wartime goals – 231, Albert Stubbins

No. 9 STRIKE-RATE

As a regular centre-forward over an extended period, league and cup matches:

1 Hughie Gallacher	82%
2 Andy Cole	81%
3 Albert Shepherd	75%

4 Jack Smith   65%
5 Barrie Thomas   64%

AVERAGE GOALS PER SEASON
As a regular centre-forward over an extended period, league and cup matches:
1 Hughie Gallacher   29
2 Malcolm Macdonald   24
3 Alan Shearer   22 (to cs 2004)
4 Jackie Milburn   18
4 Neil Harris   18
Also, including wartime football:
Albert Stubbins   30

TOP SCORER
Most occasions as United's top goalscorer, league and cup matches:
Alan Shearer   8 (to cs 2004)
Hughie Gallacher   5

30 GOALS AND OVER PER SEASON
League and cup matches as a regular centre-forward:
41 goals, Andy Cole 1993–94
39 goals, Hughie Gallacher 1926–27
34 goals, Hughie Gallacher 1929–30
34 goals, Mick Quinn 1989–90
34 goals, Charlie Wayman 1946–47
33 goals, Albert Shepherd 1910–11
31 goals, Albert Shepherd 1909–10
30 goals, Alan Shearer 1999–2000

Wartime football:
43 goals, Albert Stubbins 1943–44
43 goals, Albert Stubbins 1944–45
42 goals, Albert Stubbins 1942–43
40 goals, Albert Stubbins 1945–46

SCORING DEBUTS
Operating as a centre-forward for United in league and cup matches:
4 goals: Mick Quinn v. Leeds United Aug 1989
2 goals: Hughie Gallacher v. Everton Dec 1925

2 goals: George Stobbart v. Coventry City Sept 1946
2 goals: Duncan Ferguson v. Wimbledon Nov 1998
1 goal by: L. Ferdinand, J. Smith, T. Hall, T. Blyth, J. Campbell,
 A. Frost, J. Logan, G. Mole, T. Mordue, A. Shepherd, R. Williams,
 S. Guivarc'h.
Note: While Jackie Milburn scored two goals on his first-class debut in January 1946 against Barnsley (FA Cup), he did not wear the No. 9 shirt. Bob McColl did likewise.

No. 9 HAT-TRICKS
League and cup matches as a regular centre-forward:
14   Hughie Gallacher
9   Jackie Milburn
8   Albert Shepherd
8   Len White

Wartime football:
29   Albert Stubbins

MOST GOALS IN A MATCH
League and cup matches as a regular centre-forward:
5 goals: by Alan Shearer v. Sheffield Wednesday September 1999
4 goals: by A. Shepherd (5 times), H. Gallacher (3 times), W. Cairns
 (2 times), C. Wayman (2 times), M. Quinn, V. Keeble, R. Smellie,
 L. White, J. Smith.

Wartime football:
5 goals: by Albert Stubbins (5 times), W. Cairns.

RECORD TRANSFERS
United have constantly broken the bank to bring a famous No. 9 to St. James' Park.
All are club records:

Alan Shearer	£15 million, July 1996 from Blackburn Rovers (world record)
Les Ferdinand	£6 million, June 1995 from QPR
Andy Cole	£1.75 million, March 1993 from Bristol City
Mirandinha	£575,000, August 1987 from Palmeiras
Paul Goddard	£415,000, November 1986 from West Ham United

Peter Withe	£200,000, August 1978 from Nottingham Forest
Malcolm Macdonald	£180,000, May 1971 from Luton Town
Wyn Davies	£80,000, October 1966 from Bolton Wanderers
Barrie Thomas	£45,000, January 1962 from Scunthorpe United
George Lowrie	£18,500, March 1948 from Coventry City
Hughie Gallacher	£6,500, December 1925 from Airdrie
Neil Harris	£3,300, May 1920 from Partick Thistle
Billy Hibbert	£1,950, October 1911 from Bury (UK record)

GEORDIE No. 9s

Centre-forwards born on the banks of the Tyne to appear in league and cup football for United:

Jack Allen	b. Newburn
Billy Cairns	b. Newcastle
Paul Cannell	b. Heaton
Bill Curry	b. Walker
Andy Donaldson	b. Benwell
Chris Guthrie	b. Dilston
Tom Hall	b. Newburn
George Hope	b. Haltwhistle
Arthur Horsfield	b. Newcastle
Joe McClarence	b. Wallsend
Jack Peart	b. South Shields
Tom Phillipson	b. Ryton
George Pyke	b. Gateshead
Dave Robinson	b. Walkergate
Alan Shearer	b. Gosforth
John Soulsby	b. Gateshead
Albert Stubbins	b. Wallsend
Frank Thompson	b. Birtley
Chris Waddle	b. Heworth
John Watson	b. South Shields

SHORT SERVICE

Mick Harford returned to Newcastle United in March 1982 en route for Birmingham City for only the matter of minutes, or as long as it took to sign transfer forms, all to enable United to receive funds owed from debt stricken Bristol City. In his first spell at St. James' Park, Harford only stayed for eight months after joining the staff from Lincoln City.

Ken Leek cost a substantial £25,000 fee in May 1961 but left six months later in November for Birmingham City.

Stephane Guivarc'h arrived on Tyneside from the French World Cup-winning side for a £3.54 million fee in June 1998 but remained on Tyneside only five months before joining Rangers.

LONG SERVICE

13 years 308 days by Jackie Milburn, 1943–57
11 years 173 days by Billy Cairns, 1933–44

FROM THE WING

Both Len White and Jackie Milburn, two of the club's biggest No. 9 heroes, began on the right-wing for the Magpies – but made a name for themselves as centre-forward, both winning the FA Cup for United and scoring over 150 goals.

YOUNGEST AND OLDEST

Youngest:
17 years 86 days, Tony Lormor, January 1988 v. Tottenham Hotspur

Oldest:
36 years 80 days, Ian Rush, January 1998 v. Sheffield Wednesday
Note: In wartime football, Ernie Taylor made his debut in the No. 9 shirt at the age of 17 years 17 days. He later developed into a celebrated midfield player.

SMALLEST AND TALLEST

Shortest centre-forwards:
5 ft 5 in. Joe Ford
5 ft 5 in. Hughie Gallacher
5 ft 6 in. Charlie Wayman

Wartime football:
5 ft 4 in. Ernie Taylor

Tallest centre-forwards:
6 ft 4 in. George Reilly
6 ft 4 in. Duncan Ferguson
6 ft 4 in. Carl Cort

No. 9 SKIPPERS
On a regular basis:
Hughie Gallacher, 1926–28
Alan Shearer, 1999–2004 (to cs 2004)

No. 9 NICKNAMES
Cockles – Bill Appleyard
King Cole – Andy Cole
The Mighty Wyn – Wyn Davies
Sir Les – Les Ferdinand
Hughie – Joe Ford
Wee Hughie – Hughie Gallacher
Sarge – Paul Goddard
Hurricane Hutch – Duncan Hutchison
Camel – Vic Keeble
Ned – David Kelly
Supermac – Malcolm Macdonald
Cassius – Ron McGarry
Wor Jackie – Jackie Milburn
Tucker – Tom Mordue
The Mighty Quinn – Mick Quinn
Rambo – George Reilly
The Silent Assassin – Albert Stubbins
Waddler – Chris Waddle
Monte – Jon Wilkinson

DERBY HEROES
3 goals: by Alex Tait v. Sunderland, December 1956
Tait is the only United centre-forward to hit a hat-trick in a Tyne v. Wear clash.

Tom Hall scored on his debut against Sunderland in September 1913, just after joining United from Roker Park.

INJURED No. 9s
Bob Blanthorne broke a leg on his debut against Bradford City in September 1908 and didn't play for United again.

Ray Clarke sustained a serious knee injury and was forced to retire from the game in 1981.

John Duncan was injured in a clash and a knee problem halted his football career in 1953.

324

Joe Ford fractured his leg on his debut against Grimsby Town in January 1932 and didn't play again.

Willie Scott broke his leg just before the Second World War and afterwards didn't play a senior game for United.

Albert Shepherd clashed with the Blackburn Rovers' goalkeeper in 1911, an injury that forced him to miss that year's FA Cup final and one that wrecked his career.

George Lowrie was injured soon after his record purchase to St. James' Park in 1948 and appeared on only 12 occasions.

Billy Scott picked up a bad knee injury in season 1923–24 that forced his retirement after two years of attempted recovery.

HONOURABLE No. 9s

Honoured as a Newcastle United player:

OBE: Alan Shearer

Freedom of Newcastle on Tyne: Jackie Milburn, Alan Shearer

PFA/FWA Footballer of the Year: Alan Shearer 1995, 1997, Les Ferdinand 1996

PFA Young Player of the Year: Andy Cole 1994

Premier League Player of the Decade: Alan Shearer 2003

INTERNATIONAL No. 9s

Regular centre-forwards capped as a Newcastle United player:

England – A. Shearer, L. Ferdinand, A. Shepherd, J. Milburn, A. Stubbins, C. Waddle, M. Macdonald

Scotland – N. Harris, H. Gallacher, R. McColl

Wales – W. Davies, G. Lowrie, R. Williams, K. Leek

Republic of Ireland – D. Kelly

France – S. Guivarc'h

Note: George Robledo gained the majority of his 21 caps for Chile as a centre-forward, although he was not the Magpie's regular No. 9.

MOST CAPPED No. 9s

Capped as a Newcastle United player:

35 caps, Alan Shearer for England (total 63 caps)

14 caps, Malcolm Macdonald for England (total 14 caps)

13 caps, Jackie Milburn for England (total 13 caps)

13 caps, Hughie Gallacher for Scotland (total 20 caps)

Most full international goals as a Newcastle United player:
19 goals, Alan Shearer for England
18 goals, Hughie Gallacher for Scotland
10 goals, Jackie Milburn for England

No. 9 ODDITIES

Over more than a century of football there have been many one-off or unusual appearances in the centre-forward role.

- **Steve Watson** actually signed for Newcastle United as a play-anywhere kid but developed into a popular right-back. However, against Liverpool in an important League Cup tie at Anfield during 1995 he operated as a lone centre-forward after Les Ferdinand was led from the field injured. Watson scored a brilliant solo goal in the 77th minute to win the match for United.
- **Bob Stokoe** made his debut at centre-forward on Christmas Day 1950 against Middlesbrough, scoring in a 1–2 defeat at Ayresome Park. Normally a wing-half, and later a regular centre-half for the Magpies, Stokoe again deputised in the leader's role three years later against Burnley.
- **Tommy Cassidy** appeared on four occasions in the No. 9 shirt during season 1973–74. The Irish midfielder stood in for Malcolm Macdonald and John Tudor and was remarkably effective, scoring against Ipswich Town and as the press noted was 'always prepared to go at defences'.
- **John McGrath** was a notable stopper centre-half, but one who could play a bit too. He took on the centre-forward shirt against Charlton and Rotherham in 1963 with both McGarry and Thomas out injured. Big John scored against the South Yorkshire team.
- **Bill Thompson**, like McGrath, was a tough defender and he also moved up front for several games during season 1965–66 when United were desperate for a target in attack. He also managed to find the net and while he gave his all, it was noted that he 'looked just what he was, a converted centre-half'.
- **Dave Robinson** totalled 10 games for United between 1988 and 1992, but never a full match, all his outings coming from the substitutes' bench.
- **Ollie Burton** had played in various positions for United: full-back, centre-half and in midfield. He took on the No. 9 role against Sunderland in March 1966 and made an impact, helping United to

a rewarding 2–0 derby victory. The Welshman battled for 90 minutes and at one point clashed with Sunderland skipper Charlie Hurley, the Wearside stopper having to be carried from the field with a knee injury.

- **Andy Thorn** was manager Jim Smith's choice for the last five games of the 1988–89 season as centre-forward. The defender stood in for the out of favour Mirandinha but the Black'n'Whites struggled, failing to win a game.

- **John Duncan** was purchased as a reserve defender during November 1950 and was given an odd outing in the right-back position. But he was later converted to centre-forward and scored twice against Aston Villa in December 1951 before a bad knee injury halted his progress.

- **Steve Howey** began his career as an out-and-out striker, a bright young centre-forward who was eager to impress. He made over 30 appearances for the Magpies as a centre-forward before being switched to centre-half in 1991. He was so successful that he earned four caps for England.

- **Kenny Mitchell**, like Howey, was a youthful forward at Gallowgate. He also saw action as a centre-forward for United before moving to the last line of defence and becoming a useful utility player at centre-half or full-back.

- **Jackie Rutherford** is one of United's greatest ever players, winning honours galore during the years prior to the First World War. More recognised as an outside-right, the Tynesider made appearances early in his career at centre-forward against Wolves and scored twice – and soon after grabbed another two goals against Nottingham Forest. He then switched to the wing and played over 300 games for United and won 11 England caps.

- **Ernie Taylor** became a wonderful midfielder during '50s soccer, but he appeared once for United at centre-forward – in wartime football against Huddersfield Town in September 1942. He was only a few days over 17 years of age, the youngest No. 9 on record. And at 5 ft 4 in. he is also the smallest.

- **Malcolm Scott** spent most of his United career as a reserve defender, but against Leeds United during season 1959–60 he moved up front and scored twice in a 3–2 victory. He went on to play in the No. 9 shirt on another two occasions that campaign.

- **Jimmy Loughlin** was a talented reserve striker to both Neil Harris and Hughie Gallacher. In a rare outing at centre-forward – his very first match in the role – he fired home a hat-trick against Leicester City during September 1925.

- **Roy Bentley** became a noted No. 9 for both Chelsea and England after he left Tyneside, but before that move south he mainly operated at inside-forward for United. However in season 1946–47 Roy took over the centre-forward shirt for a brief spell of four matches. He showed he could operate as a striker by scoring a hat-trick against Bradford Park Avenue.

- **Frank Houghton** was a versatile player and during season 1949–50 was handed the No. 9 shirt for a few matches with both Milburn and Robledo out of action. The Irishman did well, scoring three goals in a five-game run.

- **Donald Howe** guested for United in wartime football and the respected Bolton Wanderers inside-forward scored no fewer than five goals in the No. 9 shirt against York City in October 1939 as United won 9–2. It was Howe's one and only appearance for United.

- **Eddie Carr** was another notable wartime guest. The locally born Arsenal striker's first game at centre-forward for United resulted in a hat-trick against Leeds United in 1942. His next ended with another three goals, against York City.

- **Billy Foulkes**, normally an inside-forward, appeared for the first time at centre-forward against Cardiff City in season 1952–53 and scored twice as a stand-in for the missing Milburn and Robledo.

- **Curtis Booth** was tried at centre-forward in a Northern Victory League derby match with Sunderland in January 1919. United won 4–3 at St. James' Park and Booth struck two goals into the Wearsiders' net.

- **Tom McBain** played only once at centre-forward for United, in April 1932 against Portsmouth at Fratton Park. United lost heavily, 0–6.

- **Alex Gardner** is more noted as an accomplished midfielder, but switching to centre-forward in place of Jock Peddie in season 1899–1900 he was a success, netting in both games, against Stoke and Sunderland.

- **Colin Veitch** was another of United's Edwardian Greats. He was a truly versatile master, playing almost in every role for the Magpies including centre-forward. Included was an outing in the FA Cup final against Everton in 1906.

- **Finlay Speedie** was a utility expert too. The Scottish international took the centre-forward shirt in season 1906–07 and scored in his first two games against Stoke and Derby County.

- **George Jobey** scored on his first appearance in the centre-forward position against Liverpool in season 1907–08. He later deputised for Albert Shepherd in the leader's role in the biggest game of the season, the 1911 FA Cup final – playing in the replay too.
- **Willie Cowan** was a highly skilled inside-forward who deputised for Neil Harris during season 1924–25. He scored a hat-trick at centre-forward against Aston Villa. The following season, he grabbed two goals in another switch against Bolton Wanderers.
- **Jackie Cape** was more at home hogging the touch-line but during 1932 against Southport in an important FA Cup tie, he took over Jack Allen's role at centre-forward and scored twice in the 9–0 victory.
- **Jimmy Richardson** developed into a marvellous England inside-forward with United. He was also useful in the centre-forward position when needed. Against Aston Villa in season 1932–33 he deputised for Jack Allen and struck two goals.
- **Robert Lee** once operated as a lone striker, in the centre-forward role, against Monaco during 1996 as a result of strikers Ferdinand, Shearer and Asprilla all being sidelined.

BRIEF ENCOUNTERS

Many other players have appeared in an odd game, achieved a short run or played out of position for Newcastle United at centre-forward, while several players who only had a brief encounter with United at centre-forward later made a big impact elsewhere in the leader's role. They include:

Harry Hardinge (Sheffield United and England), Tom Phillipson (Wolves), Roy Bentley (Chelsea and England), Jack Wilson (Manchester United), Mick Harford (Luton, Chelsea and England), Jack Peart (Notts County and Football League).

BIBLIOGRAPHY

Books

Adamson, Richard, *Bogotá Bandit. The Outlaw Life of Charlie Mitten.* Mainstream, 1996.

Appleton, Arthur, *Hotbed of Soccer.* R. Hart-Davis, 1960.

Barnes, John, *John Barnes. The Autobiography.* Headline, 1999.

Batty, David, *David Batty. The Autobiography.* Headline, 2001.

Beardsley, Peter, *Peter Beardsley, My Life Story.* Collins Willow, 1996.

Beardsley, Peter and Andy Cairns, *Beardsley. An Autobiography.* Stanley Paul, 1988.

Beardsley, Peter and Tony Hardisty, *Proud To Be a Geordie.* Knight Fletcher, 1986.

Beasant, Dave and Dave Smith, *Tales of the Unexpected. The Dave Beasant Story.* Mainstream, 1989.

Bell, Stan. *Born To Soccer.* Bells Books.

Bentley, Roy, *Going for Goal.* Museum Press, 1955.

Channon, Mick, *Man on the Run. An Autobiography.* Arthur Barker, 1986.

Charlton, Jack and Peter Byrne, *Jack Charlton. The Autobiography.* Partridge, 1996.

Clark, Frank and Nick Kehoe, *Kicking With Both Feet.* Headline, 1999.

Cole, Andy and Peter Fitton, *Andy Cole. The Autobiography.* Manchester United Books, 1999.

Crowe, Charlie, *A Crowe Amongst The Magpies.* Tups Books, 1998.

Crowe, Charlie and Mike Kirkup, *Charlie Crowe's Newcastle United Scrapbook.* The People's History, 2001.

Dalglish, Kenny and Henry Winter, *Dalglish. My Autobiography.* Hodder & Stoughton, 1996.

Eastham, George, *Determined to Win.* Stanley Paul, 1964.

BIBLIOGRAPHY

Farmer, David and Peter Stead, *Ivor Allchurch MBE*. C. Davies, 1998.

Ferdinand, Les, *Sir Les. The Autobiography of Les Ferdinand*. Headline, 1997.

Gibson, John, *Newcastle United. A Pictorial History*. Archive, 1988.
The Newcastle United Story. Arthur Barker, 1985.
The Newcastle United Story. Pelham, 1969.
The Newcastle United Story No. 2. Pelham, 1970.
The Newcastle United Story No. 3. Pelham, 1972.
United . . . Behind the Headlines. Newcastle Evening Chronicle, 1996.
Wor Jackie. The Jackie Milburn Story. Sportsprint J. Donald. 1990.

Ginola, David and Amy Lawrence, *Ginola. From St Tropez to St. James*. Headline, 1996.

Ginola, David and Neil Silver, *David Ginola Le Magnifique*. Collins Willow, 2000.

Gowling, Alan, *Football Inside Out*. Souvenir Press, 1977.

Gullit, Ruud, *Ruud Gullit. My Autobiography*. Century, 1998.

Hannen, Mark, *Geordie Passion*. Publishing Corporation, 1994.

Hendrie, John, *Don't Call Me Happy: John Hendrie. The Autobiography*. Middlesbrough FC, 1997.

Inglis, Simon, *League Football and the Men Who Made It*. Collins Willow, 1988.

Joannou, Paul, *The Black'n'White Alphabet*. Polar, 1996.
The Hughie Gallacher Story. Breedon Books, 1989.
United: The First 100 Years & More – Millennium Edition. Polar, 2000.

Joannou, Paul, Steve Corke and Bill Swann, *The Essential History of Newcastle United*. WHSmith, 2003.
Newcastle United: A Complete Record. Breedon Books, 1990.

Keegan, Kevin, *Kevin Keegan. My Autobiography*. Little Brown, 1997.

Keegan, Kevin and Mike Langley, *Against The World*. Book Club Associates, 1979.

Keegan, Kevin and John Roberts, *Kevin Keegan*. Arthur Barker, 1977.

King, Ray, *Hands, Feet & Balls. Life Behind the Iron Curtain*. Rex, 1998.

Kirkup, Mike, *Jackie Milburn: In Black and White*. Stanley Paul, 1990.

Lee, Rob and Carl Liddle, *Come In Number 37. Rob Lee. The Autobiography*. Collins Willow, 2000.

Macdonald, Malcolm, *Malcolm Macdonald. An Autobiography*. Arthur Barker, 1983.
Win! Pelham Books, 1977.

Macdonald, Malcolm and Colin Malam, *Supermac. My Autobiography*. Highdown, 2003.

Macdonald, Malcolm and Brian Woolnough, *Never Afraid To Miss*. Cassell, 1980.

Milburn, Jackie, *Golden Goals: Jackie Milburn*. Soccer Book Club, 1957. *Jackie Milburn's Newcastle United Scrapbook*. Souvenir Press, 1981.

Milburn, Jack junior, *Jackie Milburn. A Man of Two Halves*. Mainstream, 2003.

Moncur, Bob and John Gibson, *United We Stand*. Pelham, 1971.

Moynihan, John, *Kevin Keegan. Black & White*. Collins Willow, 1993.

Oliver, Alan, *Geordie Messiah. The Keegan Years*. Mainstream, 1997.

Peacock, Gavin and Alan Comfort, *Never Walk Alone*. Hodder & Stoughton, 1994.

Pearce, Stuart and Bob Harris, *Psycho. Stuart Pearce. The Autobiography*. Headline, 2000.

Quinn, Mick and Oliver Harvey, *Who Ate All The Pies?* Virgin, 2003.

Robson, Bobby, *Time on the Grass*. Arthur Barker, 1982.

Robson, Bobby and Bob Harris, *Bobby Robson. An Englishman Abroad*. Pan, 1998.

Robson, Bryan, *The Sporting Worlds of Bryan 'Pop' Robson*. Oriel, 1970.

Rush, Ian and Ken Gorman, *Ian Rush. An Autobiography*. Ebury, 1996.

Shackleton, Len, *Len Shackleton. Clown Prince of Soccer*. N. Kaye, 1955. *Len Shackleton. Return of the Clown Prince*. GHKN, 2000.

Shearer, Alan and Dave Harrison, *Shearer. My Story So Far*. Hodder & Stoughton, 1998.

Simpson, Ronnie, *Sure it's a Grand Old Team to Play For*. Souvenir Press, 1967.

Smith, Jim and Mark Dawson, *Bald Eagle. The Jim Smith Story*. Mainstream, 1990.

Stein, Mel, *Chris Waddle. The Authorised Biography*. Cockerel, 1988. *Gazza – the Authorised Biography of Paul Gascoigne*. Bantam, 1996. *Haway The Lad – the Authorised Biography of Paul Gascoigne*. Partridge, 1994.

Tomas, Jason, *The Goal Machine. Portrait of a Football Superstar* (Alan Shearer). Mainstream, 1997.

Tully, Paul, *The All Time Greats*. Newcastle Evening Chronicle.

Tyne & Wear Museums Service, *Football Under The Skin*. Tyne & Wear Museums Service, 1988.

Various club histories nationwide and yearbooks.

BIBLIOGRAPHY

NEWSPAPERS, PERIODICALS

Gallacher, Hughie, 'Ups and Downs of My Football Life'. *Sunday Post*, 1931.

'Hughie Gallacher Tells All'. *Weekly Chronicle*, 1950.

Veitch, Colin, 'My Life Story'. *Sunday Sun*, 1931.

Various newspapers, notably Tyneside's *The Journal*, *Evening Chronicle* and *The Pink*.

Newcastle United official match-day magazines, programmes and handbooks, various seasons and matches.

The *Black'n'White* and *Scene@St.James* club magazines.

VIDEOS, DVDs & TAPES

Chris Waddle. The French Way. Pickwick, 1993.

The Magnificent No. 9s. River City, 1991.

Newcastle United. The Official History. Granada, 2003.

The R.S. McColl Story. Demus/BBC Radio Scotland, 2002.

Shearer's Century. Newcastle United/Tyne Tees Television, 2001.

Supermac: The Malcolm Macdonald Story. Polygram, 1992.

A Tribute to Jackie Milburn. Tyne Tees Television, 1989.

Newcastle United official season videos and DVDs, various seasons.